Tax Appeals

Law and Practice at the FTT

5th Edition

Keith Gordon

© 2022 Claritax Books Ltd

All rights reserved. No part of this publication may be reproduced or distributed in any form or by any means, or stored in a database or retrieval system, without the prior written permission of the publishers.

Official material is reproduced under the terms of the Open Government Licence (see www.nationalarchives.gov.uk/doc/open-government-licence).

Disclaimer

This publication is sold with the understanding that neither the publishers nor the author, with regard to this publication, are engaged in providing legal or professional services.

The material contained in this publication does not constitute tax advice and readers are advised that they should always obtain such professional advice before acting, or refraining from acting, on any information contained in this book. Readers are also advised that UK tax law is subject to frequent and unpredictable change.

Every effort has been taken to compile the contents of this book accurately and carefully. However, neither the publishers nor the author can accept any responsibility or liability to any person, whether a purchaser of this book or not, in respect of anything done or omitted to be done by any such person in reliance, partly or wholly, on any part or on the whole of the contents of this book.

Claritax Books is a trading name of Claritax Books Ltd.

Company number 07658388
VAT number 114 9371 20

Law date

The text is based on the tax law as at 3 January 2022.

The first three editions of this work were entitled *Tax Chamber Hearings*.

1st edition September 2011
This 5th edition February 2022

WORLD LAND TRUST™
www.carbonbalancedprint.com
CBP2250

The carbon emissions of the paper used to produce this book have been offset via the World Land Trust's Carbon Balanced Paper scheme.

This product is made of material from well-managed, FSC®-certified forests and other controlled sources.

Tax Appeals

Law and Practice at the FTT

5th Edition

Keith Gordon

Published by:

Claritax Books Ltd
6 Grosvenor Park Road
Chester, CH1 1QQ

www.claritaxbooks.com

ISBN: 978-1-912386-60-4

Main titles from Claritax Books

General tax annuals

- Capital Gains Tax
- Income Tax
- Inheritance Tax
- National Insurance Contributions
- Stamp Duty Land Tax
- Value Added Tax

Specialist tax annuals

- Advising British Expats
- A-Z of Plant & Machinery
- Capital Allowances
- Financial Planning with Trusts
- Pension Tax Guide
- Property Investment

Other specialist titles

- Construction Industry Scheme
- Discovery Assessments
- Disguised Remuneration
- Employee Share Schemes
- Employee-Ownership Trusts
- Employment Status
- Enterprise Investment Scheme
- Furnished Holiday Lettings
- Living and Working Abroad
- Main Residence Relief
- Personal Representatives
- Research and Development
- Residence: The Definition in Practice
- Schedule 36 notices
- Tax Appeals
- Tax Losses
- Taxation of Partnerships
- Taxpayer Safeguards and the Rule of Law

See www.claritaxbooks.com for details of all our titles.

About the author

Keith M Gordon MA (Oxon), FCA, CTA (Fellow), Barrister practises from Temple Tax Chambers in London. He previously worked as a chartered accountant and chartered tax adviser. His practice covers all areas of tax, and also related areas including partnership disputes and professional negligence. He regularly appears in the Tax Chamber and the higher Courts.

Keith lectures and writes extensively and won the "tax writer of the year" category in the 2013 LexisNexis Taxation awards, having been a runner-up in 2006 and 2012. In 2009, Keith won the "CTA of the year" category and in 2019 he won the award for "outstanding contribution to tax".

Keith's recent cases include *Albatel* (at the FTT) and *Ritchie* (at the Upper Tribunal). He was also junior Counsel for the taxpayer in *Jones v Garnett (the "Arctic Systems" case)* in the Court of Appeal and the House of Lords.

In loving memory of my grandparents:
Sydney and Sallie Gordon, Bernard and Zelda Summers

Preface to the fifth edition

I am delighted to have had the opportunity to prepare a fifth edition of this book. The support and constructive comments received in relation to the first four editions have been most encouraging and I hope that this edition continues to satisfy the needs of tribunal users. In the meantime, I am always happy to receive any pointers as to matters that should be addressed in future editions.

The tribunal is designed to be an accessible forum in which (primarily) disputes between taxpayers and HMRC are resolved. In particular, taxpayers should usually be able to present their case without fear of having to pay HMRC's costs should they prove to be unsuccessful. Another aspect of this accessibility is the fact that decisions of the First-tier are not binding in other cases: this means that a taxpayer is not necessarily disadvantaged by running an argument that was previously dismissed in another case.

However, it should be said that these lofty principles are to some extent less apparent in practice, as highlighted in a recent report by the Institute for Fiscal Studies (*The tax tribunals: the next 10 years*). In particular, when HMRC are unhappy with a decision of the FTT, they can "up the ante" by seeking to take the case on appeal to the Upper Tribunal (where an unsuccessful taxpayer is less likely to be protected from a claim for HMRC's costs). Furthermore, many arguments that a taxpayer might wish to run are currently outside the tribunal's jurisdiction, meaning that the tribunal is compelled to strike out the case.

Most importantly, the tribunal is governed by a set of procedural rules. As much as those rules are intended to ensure that the more straightforward cases are dealt with in a relatively informal fashion, it would be a mistake for parties to treat compliance with those rules as an optional luxury. The tribunal will expect parties to comply, unless there is good reason for non-compliance. Unexplained and repeated non-compliance is likely to lead to cases being struck out. If a taxpayer instructs a professional adviser to conduct the case, then the tribunal will expect the professional adviser to have sufficient knowledge to do so in accordance with the rules.

Such compliance is not difficult. It just needs the attitude that, when litigating a case in the tribunal, parties (or their advisers) need to recognise that progressing the case in accordance with the rules and the tribunal's directions need to be given sufficient priority. This book is intended to guide users (whether first-time or regular litigators) through the process.

In the three years since the last edition, the case law on the tribunal's procedure rules has continued to evolve, with such developments being fully reflected in the text. However, the most significant impact on the tribunal's workings in the period has undoubtedly been the Coronavirus pandemic. After what was in effect an initial suspension of operations as the tribunal came to terms with lockdowns, the tribunal swiftly adapted to online hearings for most cases which, fortuitously, was something being trialled at a time when Covid-19 was probably no more than an unnamed virus in a far-off laboratory. The tribunal's processes have been aided by a series of new procedural rules and practice directions, as well as a flexible approach being displayed by the tribunal's judiciary, staff and other users.

Even though many of the formal measures are intended to be temporary, to be removed when the health emergency is more or less over, there are likely to be many permanent legacies from the pandemic, most particularly the increased use of online hearings for case management and similar procedural hearings.

Furthermore, as at the time of writing, it seems clear that a return to "normal", or even "a new normal", is not yet imminent. Accordingly, the text reflects the rules as they are in place now, with an indication as to what might change in the future.

This edition also contains a new section which discusses situations where the tribunal proceedings are considered to be an abuse of process.

I have also taken the opportunity to cut down the appendix which described the transitional rules applicable for cases transferred into the tribunal from predecessor tribunals as at 1 April 2009, on the assumption that such cases will be either non-existent or subject to such exceptional circumstances that any generic guidance will be of very limited value.

As before, this publication would not have been possible without the support and efforts of Ray Chidell at Claritax Books. Similarly, full credit must be given to the unfailing support of my wife, Deborah, and our daughter, Sarah, to whom I remain ever-grateful.

Keith M Gordon
Lincoln's Inn, February 2022

Abbreviations

2007 Act	The Tribunals, Courts and Enforcement Act 2007
AAC	Administrative Appeals Chamber
ADR	Alternative dispute resolution
CAA 2001	Capital Allowances Act 2001
CGT	Capital gains tax
Ch.	Chapter
ChD	Chancery Division
CPR	Civil procedure rules
DBR	Director of Border Revenue
DOTAS	Disclosure of tax avoidance schemes
EAT	Employment Appeal Tribunal
EWCA	England and Wales Court of Appeal
EWHC	England and Wales High Court
FA	Finance Act
FTT	First-tier Tribunal
HMRC	HM Revenue and Customs
IHT	Inheritance tax
IHTA 1984	Inheritance Tax Act 1984
ITA 2007	Income Tax Act 2007
ITEPA 2003	Income Tax (Earnings and Pensions) Act 2003
ITTOIA 2005	Income Tax (Trading and Other Income) Act 2005
LLP	Limited liability partnership
LSS	Litigation and settlement strategy
oao	On the application of
para.	Paragraph
POTAS	Promoters of tax avoidance schemes
Pt.	Part
RSTPA	Revenue Scotland and Tax Powers Act
s.	Section
Sch.	Schedule
SI	Statutory instrument
Sp C	Special Commissioners
t/a	Trading as
TC	Tax Chamber
TCC	Tax and Chancery Chamber
TCEA 2007	Tribunals Courts and Enforcement Act 2007
TCGA 1992	Taxation of Chargeable Gains Act 1992
TIOPA 2010	Taxation (International and Other Provisions) Act 2010
TMA 1970	Taxes Management Act 1970
UKEAT	United Kingdom Employment Appeals Tribunal
UKFTT	United Kingdom First-Tier Tribunal
UKHL	United Kingdom House of Lords

UKSC	United Kingdom Supreme Court
UKUT	United Kingdom Upper Tribunal
UT	Upper Tribunal
VATA 1994	Value Added Tax Act 1994
WRA	Welsh Revenue Authority

Table of contents

Main titles from Claritax Books iv
About the author v
Preface to the fifth edition ix
Abbreviations xii
Ten top tips 1

1. **Overview of the book** 3

2. **Preliminary matters and internal reviews**
   - 2.1 The matters that can be argued in the Tax Chamber 5
   - 2.2 Alternatives to bringing a case to the tribunal 17
   - 2.3 Bringing a case to the tribunal and internal review 21
   - 2.4 Considerations for late appeals 30
   - 2.5 Abuse of process 40

3. **The Tribunal Procedure Rules**
   - 3.1 Introduction to rules 45
   - 3.2 Rule 1 – Citation, application and interpretation 46
   - 3.3 Rule 2 – Overriding objective and parties' obligation to co-operate with the Tribunal 49
   - 3.4 Rule 3 – Alternative dispute resolution and arbitration 57

4. **General powers and provisions under the rules**
   - 4.1 Rule 4 – Delegation to staff 59
   - 4.2 Rule 5 – Case management powers 60
   - 4.3 Rule 5A – Coronavirus temporary rule (decisions without a hearing) 87
   - 4.4 Rule 6 – Procedure for applying for and giving directions 88
   - 4.5 Rule 7 – Failure to comply with rules etc. 91
   - 4.6 Rule 8 – Striking out a party's case 94
   - 4.7 Rule 9 – Substitution and addition of parties 115
   - 4.8 Rule 10 – Orders for costs 120
   - 4.9 Rule 11 – Representatives 162
   - 4.10 Rule 12 – Calculating time 166

	4.11	Rule 13 – Sending and delivery of documents 167
	4.12	Rule 14 – Use of documents and information 169
	4.13	Rule 15 – Evidence and submissions 171
	4.14	Rule 16 – Summoning or citation of witnesses and orders to answer questions or produce documents 187
	4.15	Rule 17 – Withdrawal 199
	4.16	Rule 18 – Lead cases 205

5. Procedures before a hearing

	5.1	Introduction 211
	5.2	Rule 19 – Proceedings without notice to a respondent 212
	5.3	Rule 20 – Starting appeal proceedings 215
	5.4	Rule 21 – Starting proceedings by originating application or reference 219
	5.5	Rule 22 – Hardship applications 222
	5.6	Rule 23 – Allocation of cases to categories 224
	5.7	Rule 24 – Basic cases 234
	5.8	Rule 25 – Respondent's statement of case 236
	5.9	Rule 26 – Further steps in a Default Paper case 243
	5.10	Rule 27 – Further steps in a Standard or Complex case 246
	5.11	Rule 28 – Transfer of Complex cases to the Upper Tribunal 251

6. The directions stage

	6.1	Introduction 257
	6.2	When directions are given 257
	6.3	Directions hearings 257
	6.4	Variability of directions 257
	6.5	Typical directions 258
	6.6	Other case management hearings 264

7. Procedures at a hearing

	7.1	Rule 29 – Determination with or without a hearing ... 266
	7.2	Rule 30 – Entitlement to attend a hearing 268
	7.3	Rule 31 – Notice of hearings 269
	7.4	Rule 32 – Public and private hearings 270

	7.5	Rule 32A – Coronavirus temporary rule (recording of remote hearings).................280
	7.6	Rule 33 – Hearings in a party's absence......................282

8. At the hearing – practical considerations
- 8.1 Introduction..................285
- 8.2 The tribunal regulates its own procedures.....................285
- 8.3 The lines of argument..................287
- 8.4 The people in the tribunal room..................288
- 8.5 Formalities during the hearing..................290
- 8.6 Standard of proof..................295
- 8.7 Burden of proof..................296
- 8.8 Who speaks when?..................300
- 8.9 Reference to earlier cases..................310
- 8.10 Decisions..................310

9. Procedures after a hearing
- 9.1 Rule 34 – Consent orders..................314
- 9.2 Rule 35 – Notice of decisions and reasons..................315
- 9.3 Rule 36 – Interpretation..................320
- 9.4 Rule 37 – Clerical mistakes and accidental slips or omissions..................324
- 9.5 Rule 38 – Setting aside a decision which disposes of proceedings..................325
- 9.6 Rule 39 – Application for permission to appeal..................332
- 9.7 Rule 40 – Tribunal's consideration of application for permission to appeal..................350
- 9.8 Rule 41 – Review of a decision..................353
- 9.9 Rule 42 – Power to treat an application as a different type of application..................356

10. The Scottish tax tribunal
- 10.1 Introduction..................358
- 10.2 The tribunal's rules..................358

Appendix 1 – Allocation of HMRC decisions to the Chambers of the First-tier Tribunal..................389
Appendix 2 – Allocation of Tax Chamber cases to the different categories..................391
Appendix 3 – Constitution of tribunals in particular cases..................394

Appendix 4 – Specimen statement of agreed facts and issues 396
Appendix 5 – Specimen witness statement.. 398
Appendix 6 – Specimen skeleton argument... 400
Appendix 7 – Useful websites... 402
Appendix 8 – Transitional rules... 403
Appendix 9 – Statutory instruments.. 404

Glossary.. 407
Table of primary legislation 411
Table of statutory instruments 419
Index of First-tier Tribunal rules... 421
Index of Upper Tribunal rules 423
Index of cases... 425
General index... 441

Ten top tips

The tribunal will strive to reach a just result. However, sometimes misunderstandings can arise, which can lead to an adverse outcome for your case.

The following ten tips are proposed with a view to reducing or avoiding the risk of such misunderstandings:

1. Treat all correspondence from the tribunal or relating to the tribunal proceedings as a matter of priority. Of course, the tribunal will often set a time limit which allows for some flexibility. But it is important that all incoming communications are reviewed promptly so that time limits are not unwittingly overlooked. Ensure that any e-mail or postal address used for tribunal proceedings is regularly monitored. See **3.3.4**.

2. If a time limit is looking unlikely to be met, seek a realistic extension at the earliest opportunity. Do not leave it till the last minute (unless of course it is a last-minute problem).

3. Before making any application, you should generally run a draft past the other side before approaching the tribunal. The only real exception is if there is no time. But for the reasons already explained, that should itself be exceptional. See **4.4.2**.

4. In communications with the tribunal, ensure that the other side is copied in. Use "cc" rather than "bcc" so that the tribunal can immediately see that a copy has been sent to the other side.

5. During the litigation process, there will be considerable correspondence between the parties. This should not be copied to the tribunal – send correspondence to the tribunal only when the tribunal has requested it or if the tribunal is being asked to make a decision.

6. When the tribunal first allocates the case to a category, (see **5.6**) check whether it has been allocated to the Complex case category. If so, consider whether or not you wish to remain within the costs regime. If not, ensure that you opt out in good time (generally within 28 days).

7. Although rare, the tribunal will sometimes reallocate a case to a different category at a later stage in proceedings. Check tribunal correspondence carefully and, if there has been a recategorisation to the Complex case category, then take the steps in the previous paragraph.

8. If HMRC withdraw from a case, do not let them persuade you to withdraw your appeal from the tribunal. The correct way forward is for a consent order from the tribunal formally concluding the case in your favour. See **9.1.3**.

9. Do not learn litigation conduct from HMRC. Some things they do very well; others they do simply because they can get away with it.

10. Do not make rash assumptions about the conduct of a case. In *Hansard v HMRC* [2018] UKFTT 292 (TC), the taxpayer's adviser explained his non-attendance at a hearing thus: in the light of communications from HMRC, he had assumed that the hearing would be cancelled to allow discussions to take place between the parties. In the absence of any contact with the tribunal, such an assumption was described by the tribunal as "wholly unwarranted and a rash course of action".

1.　Overview of the book

This book guides the reader through the various stages of taking a case to the Tax Chamber. It covers:

- preliminary matters and internal reviews (**Chapter 2**):
    - the matters that can be argued in the Tax Chamber; and
    - the process of notifying the dispute to the Tax Chamber;
- an introduction to the Tribunal Procedure Rules (**Chapter 3**);
- the principles underlying the tribunal's procedures (**Chapter 4**);
- the procedural rules for the stages prior to the hearing (**Chapter 5**);
- typical directions before a hearing (**Chapter 6**);
- the hearing itself – the rules (**Chapter 7**);
- the hearing – practical considerations (**Chapter 8**);
- the procedural stages to be followed once a decision is given (**Chapter 9**).

In **Chapters 3**, **4**, **5**, **7** and **9**, the text is generally headed by the relevant Tribunal Procedure Rule with commentary to follow.

Chapter 10 sets out the rules applying in the Scottish tax tribunal (which has jurisdiction over specific Scottish taxes).

The appendices cover:

- the allocation of HMRC decisions to the various Chambers of the FTT (**Appendix 1**);
- the allocation of cases to the different categories (**Appendix 2**);
- the constitution of tribunals for particular cases (**Appendix 3**);
- specimen documents (**Appendices 4 to 6**);
- useful websites **(Appendix 7)**; and

- the transitional rules applicable for cases transferred into the tribunal from predecessor tribunals as at 1 April 2009 (**Appendix 8**).

It should be noted that the Tax Chamber has responsibilities to hear tax-related appeals against decisions of the National Crime Agency, the Director of Border Revenue, (since 29 November 2010) the Independent Parliamentary Standards Authority relating to MPs' expenses and (since 21 December 2017) the Welsh Revenue Authority. However, given that the vast majority of the Tax Chamber's work will involve disputes between HMRC and taxpayers, payers of National Insurance Contributions and either payers or recipients of statutory payments such as Statutory Sick Pay, the text will assume that the reader will be referring to it in the context of such disputes. For simplicity, the term "taxpayer" will be used in all such cases.

Law: SI 2010/2655, art. 7

2. Preliminary matters and internal reviews

2.1 The matters that can be argued in the Tax Chamber

2.1.1 Appealable decisions

When one talks about proceedings in the Tax Chamber, most people will think of appeals. Such appeals will often be against assessments to tax or amendments made to closure notices resulting in an increase of tax. However, appeals can also be made against refusals by HMRC to postpone tax that has been assessed and is already subject to an appeal, penalty assessments, refusals to suspend a penalty, information requests, PAYE codes or, for example, a wide range of other decisions that can be made by HMRC as listed in VATA 1994, s. 83. For these purposes, National Insurance Contributions are treated as if they were a tax.

These types of decision, all known as appealable decisions, can all be referred to the Tax Chamber. Although often recommended, it is not necessary for a matter to have been through the internal review procedure (see **2.3.1** below) before it is notified to the tribunal.

2.1.2 Other matters that can be referred to the Tax Chamber

The Tax Chamber may also hear other types of dispute between HMRC and taxpayers. These include (but are not restricted to):

- refusals by HMRC to allow an appeal to be made out of time;
- hardship applications (which are often a precursor to appeals against assessments for VAT and other indirect taxes if the tax in dispute is not paid upfront);
- requests by taxpayers for HMRC to issue a closure notice (partial or final) in respect of a self-assessment enquiry (applicable to income tax and CGT, corporation tax, stamp duty, annual tax on enveloped dwellings and (for disposals before 6 April 2019) non-resident CGT);
- referrals of questions to the tribunal during the course of an enquiry; and
- disputes concerning the apportionment of amounts for the purposes of capital allowances.

These other matters are not subject to the internal review procedures and require an application to be made directly to the tribunal in accordance with the relevant statute.

Similarly, where HMRC seek prior approval from a tribunal of a prospective information notice or inspection, direct application to the tribunal should be made by them.

Law: TMA 1970, s. 28ZA, 28A(4), 49; VAT 1994, s. 84(3B)(b); FA 1998, Sch. 18, para. 31A, 33(1); FA 2003, Sch. 10, para. 19(2), 24(1); FA 2008, Sch. 36, para. 3, 5, 13

2.1.3 Matters that cannot be referred to the Tax Chamber

Some decisions by HMRC, however, may not be taken to the Tax Chamber. These will generally be those cases where HMRC have been given statutory discretion (for example, to allow group relief claims to be made beyond the normal statutory time limits) or, simply, where the statute has declined to confer on taxpayers the right of appeal (for example, in relation to the issue of accelerated payment notices). In such cases, an adverse decision from HMRC can generally be challenged only by way of judicial review.

Judicial review is beyond the scope of this book. However, it is worth emphasising that such proceedings should almost invariably be commenced in the High Court (in Scotland, in the Court of Session), even though it can sometimes be possible for proceedings to be subsequently transferred to the Upper Tribunal.

More importantly, there are very strict time limits and pre-claim procedures that apply for judicial review proceedings. In cases where such proceedings are contemplated, the reader is strongly advised to obtain legal advice at a very early stage, generally within one month of any adverse decision being made.

When appeals can be made against exercises of HMRC discretion, it should be noted, however, that there are instances where the statute specifically provides that questions involving the exercise of discretion by HMRC can be referred to the tribunal (for example, the refusal to suspend a penalty). Another example is a decision to withdraw gross payment status under the construction industry scheme, where the statute provides the tribunal not only the normal appellate powers, but also the right to review judicially the decision-making process (see *Whitter*). Those exceptional cases come within the scope of the appealable decisions above. See also **8.6.1**.

See also **2.1.4** for a discussion of when judicial review style arguments might be deployed in the tribunal.

Case: *HMRC v JP Whitter (Water Well Engineers) Ltd* [2015] UKUT 392 (TCC)

Social security matters

Since 1999, HMRC have had an increasing role dealing with social security payments. On the whole, appeals against social security decisions should be made to the Social Entitlement Chamber of the First-tier Tribunal, for which a separate set of procedure rules applies (SI 2008/2685).

Tax Credits cases are considered to be social security for such purposes (although any residual employer penalty cases are reserved to the Tax Chamber). However, disputes concerning liability for and entitlement to statutory payments (such as statutory maternity pay and statutory sick pay) are within the remit of the Tax Chamber.

The allocation of cases to the various chambers is dealt with by statutory instrument, the *First-tier Tribunal and Upper Tribunal (Chambers) Order* 2010. See **Appendix 1**.

Law: SI 2010/2655

2.1.4 Public law arguments in the Tax Chamber

Although not directly connected with the establishment of the Tax Chamber, one debate that has surfaced during its lifetime is the entitlement of the Tax Chamber to hear appeals on grounds of an alleged breach of public law by HMRC. The difficulty is that matters of public law are ordinarily justiciable by way of judicial review and judicial review is the sole preserve of the higher courts

Legitimate expectation challenges

This debate was initially concerned with a particular branch of public law challenge, being whether there has been a breach of a taxpayer's "legitimate expectation". Typically this arises in cases where a taxpayer is arguing that HMRC should be bound by a promise made by them, perhaps in extra-statutory guidance (or alternatively in a clearance letter), from which HMRC are appearing to resile.

Initial challenges to the traditional view (Oxfam and subsequent cases)

Although the traditional view was always that such matters could not be pursued in the tribunal – on the basis that, unlike the High Court (or Court of Session in Scotland), the tribunal does not have jurisdiction to hear public law arguments – a less restrictive view started to be adopted following the comments by Sales J in the *Oxfam* case. The tribunal started to accept jurisdiction to hear such cases in the context of VAT matters (*CGI* and *Hanover*) but then rejected jurisdiction in another VAT case (*Magdalene*). *Magdalene* was proposing to appeal against the decision to the Upper Tribunal, but that appeal was subsequently withdrawn.

In the context of direct tax, the point arose in two cases concerning PAYE. In *Clark*, the matter was deferred until the tribunal had heard full legal argument; however, in a follow-up case involving different taxpayers (*Prince*), the tribunal considered that the tribunal was permitted to hear public law arguments only in VAT cases.

Cases: *Oxfam v HMRC* [2009] EWHC 3078 (Ch); *CGI Group (Europe) Ltd v HMRC* [2010] UKFTT 224 (TC); *Hanover Company Services Ltd v HMRC* [2010] UKFTT 256 (TC); *Clark v HMRC* [2011] UKFTT 302 (TC); *The Master and Fellows of St Mary Magdalene College in the University of Cambridge v HMRC* [2011] UKFTT 680 (TC); *Prince and Others v HMRC* [2012] UKFTT 157 (TC)

The reassertion of the traditional view (Noor)

Subsequent to those decisions, the Upper Tribunal revisited the question in the context of VAT in the case of *Noor*. As the Upper Tribunal made clear, that case was heard without representation by the taxpayer. However, being a decision of the Upper Tribunal, it was binding on the First-tier. In *Noor*, the Upper Tribunal expressed doubts as to the correctness of the comments in *Oxfam* and concluded that, absent any express legislation conferring judicial-review style powers onto the First-tier, taxpayers are not entitled to make any challenge in the First-tier on the basis of a taxpayer's legitimate expectation. This restricted approach also seemed to have been adopted by the Court of Appeal in *BT*.

However, it is noteworthy that the Upper Tribunal (albeit without full argument on the point) appeared to have no hesitation in allowing a taxpayer's appeal solely on the ground of a breach of an earlier promise by HMRC in *Spring Salmon*. Similarly, in *Bishop*, the tribunal did make it clear that a taxpayer could appeal against the unlawful exercise by HMRC of a discretion when making an assessment – that was distinct from an argument that HMRC had simply acted unfairly.

Those two cases were initially no more than outliers as the tribunal generally adopted the more restrictive approach as set out in *Noor*.

Cases: *HMRC v Noor* [2013] UKUT 71 (TCC); *LH Bishop Electric Company Ltd v HMRC* [2013] UKFTT 522 (TC); *Trustees of the BT Pension Scheme v HMRC* [2015] EWCA Civ 713; *Spring Salmon and Seafood Ltd v HMRC* [2016] UKUT 313 (TCC)

Further erosion of the traditional view (Beadle)

However, the introduction of accelerated payment notices (APNs) in 2014 has led to the matter being considered afresh.

APNs cannot be the subject of appeal and any direct challenge against them must therefore be by way of judicial review. However, non-compliance with an APN leads to a penalty assessment, which may be the subject of an appeal to the tribunal. The question that emerges is whether a collateral challenge can be made to an APN in the course of an appeal against a penalty. In other words, can a tribunal hearing a penalty appeal consider questions about the validity of the underlying APN?

In *Beadle*, the Court of Appeal stated the principle thus:

> "Where a public body brings enforcement action against a person in a court or tribunal (including a court or tribunal whose only jurisdiction is statutory) the promotion of the rule of law and fairness means, in general, that person may defend themselves by challenging the validity of the enforcement decision or some antecedent decision on public law grounds, save where the scope for challenging alleged unlawful conduct has been circumscribed by the relevant statutory scheme, which excludes such a challenge. The question accordingly is whether the statutory scheme in question excludes the ability to raise a public law defence in civil (or criminal) proceedings

that are dependent on the validity of an underlying administrative act."

Thus, the ordinary position is that collateral challenges can in fact be made against non-appealable notices if brought in the course of a subsequent appeal against a penalty issued for non-compliance with the notice. This was indeed the previously accepted position for non-appealable information notices issued under TMA 1970 (see *Essex*, *Taylor* and *Kempton*). However, the Court of Appeal then proceeded to say that the nature of the APN scheme implicitly precluded such collateral challenges.

What takes APNs outside the norm was not made clear. However, a slightly more nuanced approach was taken in the subsequent case of *Sheiling*, which also considered an appeal against a penalty issued for non-compliance with an APN. The taxpayer challenged the penalty on the basis that it had a reasonable excuse for non-compliance because it believed the APN to be flawed on a procedural basis. Rather than follow the conclusion of *Beadle* unthinkingly, the Upper Tribunal considered that a taxpayer's belief in a procedural flaw in an APN was something that could be considered as part of a reasonable excuse defence. (The Upper Tribunal had considered that Mr Beadle's challenge was on the basis of a substantive rather than a procedural flaw and this distinction therefore permitted the Upper Tribunal to adopt a different approach.) Although the *Sheiling* case proceeded to the Court of Appeal, the jurisdiction point was not examined any further. (The author suspects that HMRC were not willing to risk that the apparent exception identified by the Court of Appeal in *Beadle*, which had already suffered some damage at the hands of the Upper Tribunal, might be questioned any further.)

A similar approach has been taken by the Upper Tribunal in cases that concern challenges to penalties for non-submission of a tax return (for example, *Rogers*). In those cases, the Upper Tribunal has allowed taxpayers to challenge the validity of the original notice requiring the submission of a tax return by a particular date (such notice not being appealable) in the course of an appeal against a penalty for non-compliance.

Cases: *Essex v Inland Revenue Commissioners* (1980) 53 TC 719; *R v Inland Revenue ex p Taylor (No. 2)* [1990] BTC 281; *Kempton v Special Commissioners* [1992] BTC 553; *Beadle v HMRC* [2020] EWCA Civ 562; *Sheiling Properties Ltd v HMRC* [2020] UKUT 175 (TCC)

2.1 The matters that can be argued in the Tax Chamber

Is the Beadle approach limited to certain categories of case?

The APN and tax return cases represent the type of case where there have effectively been two decisions by HMRC: the non-appealable decision and the subsequent appealable penalty for non-compliance. Therefore, although *Beadle* confirms that there is no blanket ban on tribunals considering public law arguments, it does not directly address the question as to whether appealable decisions themselves can be challenged on public law points.

Nevertheless, the case has reignited the debate. For example, in *KSM*, the Upper Tribunal considered that the approach given in *Beadle* meant that (absent any clear statutory pointers) the tribunal is not precluded from hearing public law arguments in any type of appeal.

Cases: *Beadle v HMRC* [2020] EWCA Civ 562; *KSM Henryk Zeman SP Zoo v HMRC* [2021] UKUT 182 (TCC)

No special rule for legitimate expectation cases

It will also be seen that the issue has expanded from the original range of legitimate expectation cases to any cases where a taxpayer wishes to bring any public law argument to support an appeal. The position was neatly summarised by the Upper Tribunal in *Birkett*. Furthermore, that confirms that public law arguments can be deployed, if at all, only as part of a challenge against an appealable decision or as part of another matter that is before the tribunal. The tribunal does not have jurisdiction to hear standalone cases based upon a breach of legitimate expectations.

Furthermore, the *Harrison* case, which considered both *Beadle* and *KSM*, made the following points:

- HMRC's view that the tribunals can never consider public law arguments or that there is a strong presumption against such arguments being considered in the tribunals "overstates matters"; and
- "Ultimately, the task in each case is to construe the right of appeal conferred by the statute or secondary legislation."

Cases: *R & J Birkett t/a The Orchards Residential Home v HMRC* [2017] UKUT 89 (TCC); *Beadle v HMRC* [2020] EWCA Civ 562; *KSM Henryk Zeman SP Zoo v HMRC* [2021] UKUT 182 (TCC); *Harrison's Executors v HMRC* [2021] UKUT 273 (TCC)

Ch. 2 – Preliminary matters and internal reviews

Some judicial review cases must be made in the higher courts

It is worth emphasising that no court or tribunal has suggested that the First-tier has the jurisdiction to hear a judicial review. Accordingly, there will be many instances where a taxpayer will be obliged to challenge a non-appealable decision in the High Court (or Court of Session). See the examples below.

Example 1

Howard considers that he has disposed of shares in a personal trading company in accordance with HMRC's published guidance. Given that the other conditions for business asset disposal relief are met, he duly claims the relief on the disposal.

HMRC decide that they do not wish to apply their own guidance in Howard's case and assess him as being liable to CGT at the higher rates.

Traditionally, Howard would have had the option either:

- to appeal against the assessment on the conventional basis that the company was indeed a personal trading company – that appeal being heard in the tribunal;
- to seek judicial review of HMRC's failure to apply their own guidance – the judicial review claim being heard in the High Court or the Court of Session; or
- to commence both actions – with one probably being stayed pending resolution of the other.

If the tribunal were to be entitled to hear arguments based upon legitimate expectation, however, Howard would then have the option to raise such arguments as part of his appeal in the tribunal. (Whilst doubts remain as to the scope of the First-tier's jurisdiction, it would be wise to make a protective claim for judicial review. In such a circumstance, the debate will then turn to which set of proceedings should be heard first. See **2.1.3**.)

Example 2

Mitchell has received a taxpayer notice under FA 2008, Sch. 36 requesting certain documentation. The notice has been pre-approved by the tribunal and so Mitchell is unable to appeal against the notice to the tribunal under para. 29.

Mitchell feels particularly aggrieved because he considers that the information notice was issued in breach of a promise made to him by HMRC and he wishes to commence a challenge based upon a breach of his legitimate expectation.

Because the tribunal has no jurisdiction to hear any challenge to the information notice, it would not be able to hear arguments on the possible breach of Mitchell's legitimate expectation. Such a challenge may be mounted only by way of judicial review.

On the other hand, Mitchell could take the risk and refuse to comply with the notice and instead raise the public law arguments in the course of an appeal against the inevitable penalty that will follow.

The current state of the law

However, if there is a decision with a statutory right of appeal to the tribunal, the *KSM* decision suggests that the validity of the decision (from a public law perspective) can be challenged in the course of any such appeal.

It should be noted that HMRC are unlikely to be content with the position as set out in *KSM*. However, as they won the case on other grounds they are unlikely to have the opportunity to raise the point until another case emerges.

In the case of some appealable decisions, the grounds of appeal are tightly circumscribed by the statute itself. For example, appeals against third-party information notices under FA 2008, Sch. 36 may be made only on the ground of onerousness. Does this mean that the taxpayer may not make a public law challenge in such cases but could do so in those where the appeal rights are more general in nature?

In the author's view, any statutory restriction of the grounds of appeal will not preclude a public law challenge as well. The reason for this is that the public law challenge attacks the appealable decision itself (but not its substance). In essence, to take the example of an assessment, a taxpayer will be saying that the breach of public law (if upheld) renders the original assessment a nullity. Indeed, by saying that it was an unlawful assessment, the tribunal is effectively saying that there is no decision at all within the tribunal's jurisdiction.

It might be thought that this leads to an anomaly in that the tribunal is disavowing any jurisdiction and therefore leaves the taxpayer high and dry. However, as accepted in *Jacques*, a tribunal always has jurisdiction to consider its own jurisdiction. Furthermore, in *Odhams*, the High Court made it clear that a tribunal cannot assume jurisdiction simply with the consent of the parties. In the event of a finding that the decision is a nullity, the tribunal is doing more than setting it aside: the decision is quashed as if it had never been made.

Although not expressed in these terms, many challenges to discovery assessments have implicitly accepted this approach. Whilst there are some challenges to discovery assessments that have to be made by way of appeal to the tribunal, more fundamental questions, such as whether a discovery has been made, have been considered by the tribunal (and its statutory predecessors) for over 100 years without demur.

Law: FA 2008, Sch. 36, para. 29, 30
Cases: *Odhams Leisure Group Ltd v HMCE* [1992] BVC 11; *BW Jacques v HMRC* (2005) Sp C 513; *KSM Henryk Zeman SP Zoo v HMRC* [2021] UKUT 182 (TCC)

Precautions that should be taken given the uncertainty

The ultimate resolution of this debate is unclear and might not be known, if at all, for many years. Indeed, the whole advantage of having judicial review style appeals in the First-tier is to save a taxpayer the expense of pursuing a judicial review. However, in order for the debate to be resolved, it is likely (in the absence of any clarifying legislation) that a taxpayer will have to be prepared to argue the point at least as far as the Court of Appeal (or, in Scotland, to the Court of Session).

Accordingly, to avoid any risk of a case being struck out for want of jurisdiction or for being too late to mount a judicial review, a taxpayer wishing to make a public law challenge in the meantime should consider commencing separate judicial review proceedings (either instead of, or together with, an appeal to the FTT). See also **2.1.3**.

2.1.5 Arguments on proportionality

Another area where the tribunal started to assert its jurisdiction is in the context of penalties. Statute generally determines non-compliance penalties (for example, late payments and late returns) as fixed amounts although in certain cases HMRC have the discretion to mitigate them.

In *Preferred Refrigeration*, the tribunal on its own initiative considered whether in the context of a surcharge for the late payment of VAT (where HMRC did not have the express discretion to reduce the penalty) it ought to reduce the penalty on grounds of its being disproportionate (described as "going beyond what is necessary to achieve a legitimate aim of the State").

This approach was endorsed by the Upper Tribunal in *Total Technology* (although the Upper Tribunal considered that the penalties charged were not disproportionate in that case).

In *Bosher*, however, the same constitution of the Upper Tribunal considered that the scope of the tribunal to consider arguments on proportionality was limited to VAT surcharge cases where statute did not confer any right on HMRC or the taxpayer to issue more modest penalties. *Bosher* concerned penalties for late filing of returns under the Construction Industry Scheme. As such penalties are subject to the possibility of mitigation under TMA 1970, s. 102 (and failure to mitigate properly can be challenged by way of judicial review), human rights law had not been breached, even though the costs of mounting a judicial review challenge were likely to be prohibitively expensive.

On the other hand, it should be noted that in *Le Bistingo* the First-tier had a few weeks earlier concluded that in a case "which does not involve significant sums of money .... [judicial review] is not in practice an option, and therefore not an effective remedy".

Law: TMA 1970, s. 102
Cases: *Preferred Refrigeration Ltd v HMRC* [2011] UKFTT 466 (TC); *HMRC v Total Technology (Engineering) Ltd* [2012] UKUT 418 (TCC); *HMRC v Bosher* [2013] UKUT 579 (TCC); *Le Bistingo Ltd v HMRC* [2013] UKFTT 524 (TC)

2.1.6 Parallel proceedings

The current reluctance of the First-tier to accept jurisdiction for cases which turn on public law matters will mean that there is often a need for taxpayers to commence an appeal in the First-tier at the same time as commencing judicial review proceedings. Care must be taken to ensure that the different time limits which govern different types of proceedings are all observed.

When there are two sets of proceedings, the question that then logically follows is which set should proceed first. This has been considered (with different outcomes) in the context of residence cases where taxpayers were relying on HMRC's former IR20 guidance. In all such cases, it was accepted that the taxpayer needed only to succeed in one of the sets of proceedings in order to be ultimately successful.

In *Davies*, the Supreme Court confirmed that it was appropriate for the judicial review claim to be heard first and for the tribunal proceedings to be stayed in the meantime. Although traditionally viewed as an expensive source of justice, judicial review claims can nevertheless be simpler and cheaper than long, evidence-heavy appeals in the tribunal, which are typical of residence cases. (Of course, one major difference between those two strands of the case is that costs are usually payable to the winner of a judicial review whereas, in the tribunal, the usual position is that each side bears its own costs. See rule 10.)

It should be noted, however, that in *Hankinson*, a case with broadly similar facts to *Davies*, the High Court acceded to HMRC's request that the disputed facts relevant to a judicial review could be determined by the FTT in the course of a substantive appeal against an assessment. A similar result was achieved in *Daniel* when the taxpayer had wanted to pursue the judicial review ahead of the substantive appeal.

In *HT*, the tribunal noted that there were only limited degrees of overlap between the appeal and the judicial review proceedings. Furthermore, the judicial review was at a very early stage (with permission still to be granted on some grounds) and to wait for that could cause the taxpayers some prejudice. For these reasons, the tribunal refused HMRC's request for a stay in favour of the judicial review.

Ultimately, all cases should be considered on their own merits. In *Hankinson*, it was not necessarily argued by the taxpayer that the judicial review should be heard first (i.e. ahead of the appeal). However, this was the main issue in *Daniel* and *Davies*.

Another option that should be considered is combining judicial review proceedings and the appeal by transferring both sets of provisions to the Upper Tribunal. See also the example at **5.11.3** below.

Cases: *R (oao Davies and another) v HMRC* [2011] UKSC 47; *R (oao Hankinson) v HMRC* [2009] EWHC 1774 (Admin); *Daniel v HMRC* [2012] EWCA Civ 1741; *HT & Co (Drinks) Ltd v HMRC* [2015] UKFTT 664 (TC)

2.2 Alternatives to bringing a case to the tribunal

2.2.1 Alternative dispute resolution

One increasingly common way of resolving disputes between taxpayers and HMRC is "alternative dispute resolution", often referred to as ADR. ADR permits a more consensual settlement to be reached between a taxpayer and HMRC.

It is often favoured by HMRC as the costs of preparing a case for ADR are considerably cheaper than the costs of preparing a case for a tribunal. Taxpayers should find ADR attractive for similar reasons.

Another advantage of ADR is that the use of an intermediary (often, but not always, an HMRC officer acting independently) permits parties to ascertain the other side's concerns. For example, the author was involved in a case concerning a taxpayer who was claiming to have been working full-time abroad for the duration of a tax year. Throughout the previous correspondence, HMRC's residence team expressed their concern that the evidence to date did not satisfy HMRC's view that the taxpayer was in fact working full-time abroad, without elaborating further. In the course of the ADR, it became apparent that HMRC's main concern was the surprise that the taxpayer would have spent so much time away from his wife and young children in the second half of the tax year, in stark contrast with the time they had spent together in the previous six months. With this knowledge, the taxpayer quickly produced evidence of the wife and children's regular travel to visit the taxpayer during this period – previously, their journeys had not been thought to be in issue and therefore their travel documents were not produced originally – and the case concluded soon afterwards.

ADR takes different forms – usually a form of shuttle diplomacy in a single day, although sometimes it can take place over an extended period of time.

There will be many occasions where ADR will not be successful in that the parties will not be in a position to reach full agreement on the matters in dispute. However, the attractiveness of ADR is that neither party is obliged to reach any settlement at the end of the process. Unlike Tribunal proceedings, where the parties effectively leave it for the tribunal to determine the final position (meaning that both parties could come out dissatisfied), the terms of any ADR settlement are not binding on the parties until agreed by them. Subject to constraints imposed on HMRC by their litigation and settlement strategy (see **2.2.2** below), it will often be possible for ADR to give rise to some form of compromise, where the parties each concede on a number of issues in order to reach a negotiated solution. Another potential advantage of ADR is that it can narrow the number of areas of dispute, allowing any remaining tribunal process to be far more streamlined than might otherwise be the case.

Another potential advantage of ADR is that it allows positions to be debated without prejudicing a party from adopting a different position should the ADR not prove to be successful and should the case therefore require resolution by the tribunal. Indeed, even if the ADR is unsuccessful, it is often a useful exercise as it allows a taxpayer to get an opportunity to understand HMRC's views of a particular matter and where the taxpayer's own case is more likely to be challenged at any subsequent tribunal proceedings.

Furthermore, it is widely acknowledged (particularly by the judiciary) that ADR proceedings are "without prejudice" so that what one party says to the other in the course of the ADR may not be used by the other party outside the ADR setting. However, HMRC are frequently asserting that, as public servants, they are not permitted to ignore facts that have been brought to their attention and, therefore, this widely recognised attraction of ADR is not available to taxpayers when in dispute with HMRC. HMRC's attempts to erode a fundamental principle of ADR have attracted criticism although, as yet, the matter has not been considered by a judge. In the meantime, the author's view is that the taxpayer should resist any attempt by HMRC to water down the general principle that ADR proceedings are without prejudice.

When to use ADR

It is often best to commence ADR proceedings before HMRC have even made an appealable decision. However, this is not a fixed requirement. Under the tribunal rules (see rule 3 below), it is even possible for a case that is already before the tribunal to be stayed (or, in Scotland, sisted) so as to permit the parties to ascertain whether they might be able to reach any settlement.

As noted in *Ecko*, the tribunal should encourage the parties to pursue any form of settlement but it cannot compel them to do so.

Case: *Ecko Ltd t/a Subway v HMRC* [2019] UKFTT 715 (TC)

Applying for ADR

If a taxpayer wishes to pursue ADR in a particular case, an application should be made using HMRC's online form.

Guidance: https://www.gov.uk/guidance/tax-disputes-alternative-dispute-resolution-adr

2.2.2 Litigation and settlement strategy

In some ways, the concept of ADR is contrary to the stance adopted by HMRC in its litigation and settlement strategy ("LSS") where HMRC have publicly stated that they will not settle cases by "splitting the difference": if they have advice that theirs is a strong case, they will not generally settle for less than 100% of the tax they believe to be due. In practice, deals can still be done, although it is usually necessary to show that the ultimate result can be reconciled with a possible outcome from the litigation (even if the justification for the outcome is not particularly logical). See the examples below.

Example 1

Bryony has a dispute concerning the deductibility of two expenses from her trading profits: one concerns a cost of £20,000, the other a cost of £40,000.

Strictly, the LSS will not permit HMRC officers to "do deals". However, anecdotal advice suggests that Bryony might be able to settle her dispute by agreeing with HMRC to a disallowance of only £20,000 or £40,000. It won't be possible to settle with a disallowance of, say, £30,000.

Example 2

Charlie has claimed to be neither resident nor ordinarily resident over three successive tax years. HMRC take a different view and have assessed him as resident in each year, giving rise to tax liabilities of £20,000, £60,000 and £40,000.

Suppose that both Charlie and HMRC have independently received advice suggesting that their overall chances of success in any subsequent litigation are about 50%. Even though it is most likely that Charlie is either resident in all three years or non-resident in all three years, HMRC officers acting under the LSS might nevertheless be able to accept a settlement based upon Charlie being resident in years 1 and 3 but not resident in year 2.

Example 3

White has sold 100 shares and claimed entrepreneurs' relief. HMRC dispute his entitlement to the relief. It is suggested by White's accountant that a compromise might be reached if the relief can be granted in relation to 50 shares but the claim abandoned on the other 50 shares.

Some HMRC officers will consider such an approach to be contrary to the spirit of the LSS and refuse to adopt it. Others might be more flexible. Ultimately, it will be down to the attitude of the officer and the willingness of the officer to reach an amicable settlement. Officers are likely to be more willing to adopt such an approach if there can be identified some factual basis for treating some shares differently from others (perhaps they are of a different class or acquired on a different date), even if that factual difference does not necessarily justify the different treatment.

Failure to embark upon ADR is stated under the 2007 Act as not being grounds to affect the overall outcome of the dispute between the parties. However, as seen in *Garritt-Critchley*, one party's unreasonable refusal to attempt ADR (or even the rigid adherence to the LSS rather than reaching an overall settlement that reflects the perceived likelihood of success) could amount to unreasonable conduct within the meaning of rule 10, allowing costs orders to be made.

Law: TCEA 2007, s. 24(1)(b)
Case: *Garritt-Critchley v Ronnan* [2014] EWHC 1774 (Ch)
Guidance: https://www.gov.uk/government/publications/litigation-and-settlement-strategy-lss

2.3 Bringing a case to the tribunal and internal review

The method of bringing a case to the tribunal will depend on the type of case and, initially, whether or not the case concerns an appealable decision.

Prior to the introduction of the tribunal system in 2009, it was generally HMRC who controlled the timing of cases coming to the tribunal's attention. Although taxpayers had the right to notify the matter to the tribunal unilaterally, very few were aware of this right and, therefore, the right was rarely exercised.

Under the current rules, it is generally the taxpayer who notifies the case to the tribunal. However, HMRC can, to an extent, control the timing by offering a taxpayer an internal review, as this will eventually bring the matter to a head, leading the taxpayer to accept HMRC's position (or being deemed to accept HMRC's position) or being required to notify the case to the tribunal. However, unlike the position before 2009, it is not possible for HMRC to delay bringing the matter to the tribunal.

2.3.1 *Responding to an appealable decision*

Once an appealable decision is made, the taxpayer should respond within 30 days of the decision date (or, in the case of information notices, 30 days from the date of receipt). Taxpayers are strongly advised to do so even if they think that the matter will be resolved in another way (for example, by way of judicial review or by reference to the Adjudicator).

Direct and indirect tax cases

The process differs slightly for each of the taxes so care should be taken to ensure that the correct procedure is followed.

Direct tax cases

In direct tax cases, in general, the taxpayer should make any appeal against the assessment by writing to the decision-making officer within the 30 days stating disagreement with the decision and giving the grounds for such disagreement. As confirmed in *Thuishyanthan*, failure to notify HMRC first of any appeal will mean that the tribunal has no jurisdiction to hear the case and would lead to the tribunal being required to strike out any appeal made directly to it.

Even if an appeal is made, the tax charged by the assessment is ordinarily payable 30 days after the assessment is made. However, in virtually all cases, the taxpayer also has the right (and usually exercises it) to defer the need to pay the tax at that stage. A so-called "postponement" application should therefore generally be made to HMRC at the same time as any appeal. (It will be noted that a postponement application will not reduce the impact of any interest charge should the tax turn out to be payable.)

The taxpayer then has the right to notify the tribunal of the case at any time after an appeal has been made, except at certain stages during the internal review process if applicable (see below). In practice, however, the tribunal is rarely notified of the appeal at this stage. Instead, it is usual for the parties to carry on negotiating before the appeal is subject to any internal review or notified to the tribunal.

Law: TMA 1970, s. 49A(2), 49H (and similar provisions elsewhere)
Case: *Thuishyanthan v HMRC* [2016] UKFTT 186 (TC)

Indirect tax cases

In indirect tax cases, the taxpayer has two alternative responses to an appealable decision. The taxpayer should either accept the offer of an internal review (which is an essential part of the appealable decision) or, alternatively, notify the case directly to the tribunal. In either case, the taxpayer should respond within 30 days of the appealable decision.

Law: VATA 1994, s. 83A, 83C, 83G (and similar provisions elsewhere)

2.3.2 Internal reviews

As with ADR, the ostensible purpose of the internal review process is to allow some cases to be settled without the need for the tribunal to be involved.

Although available in virtually all cases, their main benefit is in fact-based cases which are not technically complicated, for example cases involving penalties where a reviewing officer might be able to see matters from a more independent viewpoint than his or her colleague.

In the more technical cases, internal reviews are less likely to give rise to a different outcome – partly because both the original officer making the decision and any officer in the course of the internal review are likely to obtain advice from the same technical experts within HMRC and to adhere to HMRC's view of the law. Nevertheless, except where time is of the essence, the author generally recommends that an internal review should be considered. He offers two reasons:

- first, should the review be successful, it will prove considerably cheaper than pursuing the appeal directly to the tribunal; and
- secondly, the process forces the parties to set out their views in a single document each: this facilitates the shepherding of the respective arguments should the matter then proceed to the tribunal. Indeed, the author often prefers to get involved in any appeal at the internal review stage so as to elicit early clarification of HMRC's position on certain issues.

It should always be noted, however, that internal reviews are not necessarily a one-way street for taxpayers. For example, an internal reviewer can decide to increase the amount being charged by HMRC if it is considered that the original officer has understated the correct amount to charge. Although a tribunal can similarly increase the amount charged, despite it being a taxpayer's appeal, that rarely happens.

During the conduct of an internal review, the taxpayer may not notify the matter to the tribunal.

Law: TMA 1970, s. 49D; VATA 1994, s. 83G (and similar provisions elsewhere)

Where internal review is not always available

There are a few situations where internal review is not permitted. These are those situations where there is what HMRC call a "jeopardy amendment", effectively an interim assessment made in the middle of an enquiry where there is a perceived loss of tax. Although an appeal may be made against such amendments, all appeal rights (for example, internal review and tribunal adjudication) are suspended until such time as the enquiry finally comes to an end.

Law: TMA 1970, s. 31(2); FA 1998, Sch. 18, para. 30(5); FA 2003, Sch. 10, para. 35(3); FA 2013, Sch. 33, para. 35(2)

Direct and indirect tax cases

Again, the process differs slightly for each of the taxes so care should be taken to ensure that the correct procedure is followed.

Direct tax cases

In direct tax cases the taxpayer may, at any time after an appeal has been made, request an internal review. HMRC would then be obliged to carry out such a review.

Alternatively, HMRC may unilaterally offer the taxpayer an internal review. If HMRC do so, the taxpayer must respond within 30 days, either by accepting the offer or by notifying the case to the tribunal. Failure to do either will mean that HMRC's view becomes final.

Some letters issued by HMRC, purporting to be an offer of internal review, do not actually constitute an offer. As a result, it might be possible to argue that the 30 day time limit that runs from the date of an offer is not in fact triggered. This argument could be particularly useful if a taxpayer is late in responding to such an offer from HMRC. This is because the legislation does not expressly allow a taxpayer to make a late acceptance; in such situations, the taxpayer must notify the matter to the tribunal and seek the tribunal's permission to have the late appeal admitted.

An offer by HMRC of an internal review should be accompanied by a statement of HMRC's view of the matter. This should permit the taxpayer to have a single document which sets out the factual and legal bases for HMRC's position. The document should therefore act as a starting point in any future discussions.

In cases where HMRC do not offer an internal review, the process may be triggered by the taxpayer. This can be done as early as the initial lodging of the appeal against HMRC's decision. Alternatively, it can be done at a later stage (provided that the matter has not already been notified to the tribunal). A request by a taxpayer for an internal review is not complicated. It can be as simple as saying "The taxpayer requests an internal review of the decision."

HMRC are meant to respond to any such request by preparing the single document which sets out the factual and legal bases for their position, allowing it to act as a starting point in any future discussions. This document ought to be prepared within 30 days of HMRC receiving the request for an internal review. However the statute does allow HMRC "such longer period as is reasonable". In cases where HMRC have spent too long in responding, the taxpayer can always short-circuit the process and unilaterally notify the appeal to the tribunal.

Law: TMA 1970, s. 49B, 49C, 49D (and similar provisions elsewhere)

Indirect tax cases

As noted at **2.3.1**, an offer of internal review is meant to be inherent in a notice of appealable decision. If the taxpayer wishes to proceed with the internal review, then the taxpayer should accept the offer within 30 days of the decision date.

Some indirect tax cases may be taken to the tribunal by third parties (i.e. persons other than the taxpayer). For example, as VAT is often borne by the ultimate consumer rather than the person supplying the goods or services, it might be the consumer who has the financial interest in determining the correct VAT treatment. Where such third parties have not already notified a dispute to the tribunal, they may instead pursue the internal review process by making a request to HMRC within 30 days of that person becoming aware of the decision.

The 30-day period may be extended by HMRC. Such an extension must be made during the 30-day period itself and notified to the taxpayer (in cases where it is the taxpayer who will accept the offer of internal review) or the third party (in those cases where the third party has the right to take the matter to the tribunal).

The taxpayer (or third party) may alternatively accept an offer of (or request) an internal review outside the relevant 30-day time limit. However, HMRC are obliged to undertake the internal review in such circumstances only if they are satisfied that the taxpayer, or the third party:

- had a reasonable excuse for not accepting the offer or requiring the review within the time allowed; and
- made the request without unreasonable delay after the excuse had ceased to apply.

Rather anomalously, if HMRC refuse to undertake an internal review in such circumstances, a taxpayer previously had the automatic right to notify the appeal to the tribunal, provided that the tribunal was notified of the appeal within 30 days of HMRC's refusal. This interpretation was confirmed in *Scanwell*. The legislation was amended, however, with effect for review requests made on or after 1 June 2014 so as to require a taxpayer in that situation to obtain permission from the tribunal.

Law: VATA 1994, s. 83A(1), 83B, 83C(1), 83D, 83E, 83G(4); SI 2014/1264
Case: *Scanwell Freight Services Ltd v HMRC* [2014] UKFTT 106 (TC)

All cases – conduct of internal reviews

A taxpayer is not obliged to engage in the internal review process beyond merely accepting any offer of internal review or (in the case of some direct tax cases) requesting an internal review. However, the benefits of the internal review process are more usually obtained when the taxpayer responds to the document setting out HMRC's view of the matter.

From the author's perspective, this is often an ideal time to get Counsel involved as the document prepared as part of the internal review process will usually amount to the first draft of any subsequent skeleton argument that would be deployed at the tribunal.

In practice, the internal review is supposed to be carried out by an officer independent from the original officer dealing with the case. In one case, the author was aware that the internal review was to be carried out by an officer in the same room as the original officer. Even though it was asserted by HMRC that the two operated independently of each other, HMRC were persuaded that it would be better if an officer located elsewhere carried out the internal review so as to give the perception of independence.

The normal period for internal review is 45 days, starting from HMRC's receipt of the taxpayer's acceptance or request for the internal review. However, the parties can agree to vary this period (either to extend it or to shorten it). Indeed, it is not uncommon for periods to be repeatedly extended, provided that both parties agree to the extension.

If HMRC fail to complete the internal review in time, then the original decision is treated as the conclusion of the internal review, but HMRC are required to notify this fact to the taxpayer (or third party). In practice, the taxpayer (or third party) will usually (but is not obliged to) consent to a retrospective extension of the internal review period.

Law: TMA 1970, s. 49E; VATA 1994, s. 83F (and similar provisions elsewhere)

All cases – incomplete internal reviews

There are cases in which the internal review appears to be little more than a "rubber stamp" of the prior decision. Furthermore, in some cases, it is not clear whether a taxpayer's representations have been even considered. In *Bloomsbury*, the tribunal recognised that the nature and extent of the review should be "as appear appropriate to HMRC in the circumstances". However, where matters have been overlooked or representations have not been taken into account, the tribunal held that the review might not be complete and, therefore, the time limits for notifying the case to the tribunal (see below) will not be triggered.

A taxpayer adopting this approach will risk missing a time limit for notifying the appeal to the tribunal. However, a tribunal is very likely to allow a late appeal if a serious and timely attempt to clarify matters with HMRC is made. In any event, if the internal review was incomplete, there should be no need for the tribunal's discretion as the time limits will not have started to run.

Case: *Bloomsbury Verlag GmbH v HMRC* [2015] UKFTT 660 (TC)

All cases – after an internal review

If an internal review has been carried out, then once again the taxpayer will have 30 days (from the date of the review) to notify the case to the tribunal (assuming, of course, that the taxpayer remains dissatisfied with the outcome). Otherwise, the conclusions of the review will be treated as agreed.

If the 30-day period has passed, an appeal may still be notified to the tribunal. However, in such circumstances, the appeal will not be admitted unless the tribunal gives permission. The factors that govern the tribunal's consideration of whether or not to admit such late appeals are discussed at **2.4.4**. Strictly, HMRC have no right to overlook a taxpayer's delay. However, in practice, if HMRC do not object to the late notification to the tribunal, the tribunal is unlikely to refuse to admit the late appeal.

In those cases where HMRC have failed to complete the internal review process within the statutory 45 days (or the time period agreed by the parties), the 30-day time period does not start to run until the day after HMRC finally notify the taxpayers of the conclusions of the review.

Law: TMA 1970, s. 49G, 49H; VATA 1994, s. 83G (and similar provisions elsewhere)

The subject matter of any subsequent appeal

In *Half Penny*, the tribunal concluded that the outcome of an internal review displaces the original decision. Therefore, it is the outcome of the internal review decision which becomes the subject matter of any subsequent appeal in the tribunal.

This approach was followed very soon afterwards in *Archer*. In that case, there was an appeal against a refusal to consider special circumstances in relation to a penalty. Although the matter had been considered by the original decision-maker, the internal reviewer did not properly consider special circumstances and, therefore, to this extent the decision was flawed, enabling the matter to be revisited by the tribunal itself.

However, this view is not universally accepted and will require determination by the Upper Tribunal in due course.

Cases: *Half Penny Accountants Ltd v HMRC* [2016] UKFTT 45 (TC); *Archer v HMRC* [2016] UKFTT 141 (TC)

2.3.3 When to bring other cases to the tribunal

When dealing with other types of case, there are no such rigid time limits.

This includes those cases where a taxpayer has failed to notify an appeal to HMRC in time and HMRC have refused to admit the appeal. Accordingly, the internal review processes discussed at **2.3.2** cannot be invoked. In such cases, the taxpayer has the right to apply to the tribunal itself for a direction that the appeal nevertheless be admitted by HMRC. Although there is axiomatically no time limit for the application to the tribunal, it will be advisable for the taxpayer to act promptly in any such case. The considerations to be applied by the tribunal in such cases are summarised at **2.4.4**.

In cases where a referral is being made to the tribunal in the course of an enquiry, the referral should be made jointly by the taxpayer and HMRC.

Law: TMA 1970, s. 28ZA(2), 42(3); FA 1998, Sch. 18, para. 31A(2); CAA 2001, s. 204(3); FA 2003, Sch. 10, para. 19(2)

2.3.4 How to bring cases to the tribunal

When HMRC seek prior approval from a tribunal of a prospective information notice or inspection, the procedures are considered at **5.2** below.

The procedures for taxpayers to bring a case (an appeal or an application for a closure notice) to the tribunal are considered at **5.3** and **5.4** (below).

2.3.5 "Litigation friends"

There may be circumstances in which a taxpayer is mentally incapacitated (either in the proper sense of the phrase or simply by being a minor) and precluded from commencing legal proceedings or giving instructions to a professional adviser.

It has been held in judicial review proceedings that the tribunal rules are sufficiently broadly drafted so as to permit a friend or relative to act as the agent of the taxpayer so as to liaise with the tribunal or, where appropriate, to give instructions to a professional representative.

Case: *R (oao C) v. FTT Procedure Committee, the Lord Chancellor* [2016] EWHC 707 (Admin), as applied by the EAT in *Jhuti v Royal Mail Group* UKEAT/0061/17/RN

2.3.6 Undischarged bankrupts and companies in administration

Conversely, taxpayers are precluded from pursuing a case if they are insolvent. A taxpayer's rights to litigate a case in such circumstances are transferred to the taxpayer's trustee in bankruptcy or administrator who takes over full ownership of the case, including the right not to pursue it. In some cases, the taxpayer might be re-assigned the litigation rights, but this is a matter for the trustee in bankruptcy or administrator in any particular case.

2.4 Considerations for late appeals

2.4.1 Right to appeal late

The discussion in **2.3.1** above makes clear that taxpayers should generally do the following within 30 days:

- give a written appeal against the appealable decision to HMRC; or
- (in indirect tax cases) either accept the offer of an internal review or notify the appeal direct to the tribunal.

In income tax, CGT, corporation tax, stamp duty, stamp duty land tax, stamp duty reserve tax, inheritance tax and annual tax on enveloped dwellings cases (as well as non-resident CGT cases for disposals before 6 April 2019), however, HMRC have the express permission to accept appeals against their assessments, determinations and amendments more than 30 days after such a decision is made.

Law: TMA 1970, s. 49(2); FA 1999, Sch. 17, para. 11A(2); FA 2003, Sch. 10, para. 44(2); IHTA 1984, s. 223(2); SI 1986/1711, reg. 9(2); FA 2013, Sch. 33, para. 37(2)

2.4.2 Exercise of discretion by HMRC

Although HMRC have a general discretion to accept appeals made late in such cases, they are obliged to accept late notices of appeal in cases where:

- the taxpayer has given written notice requesting the appeal to be accepted;
- HMRC are satisfied that there was a reasonable excuse for not giving the notice before the relevant time limit; and
- HMRC are satisfied that the request was made without unreasonable delay after the reasonable excuse ceased.

In *Dudley*, a case dealing with a wholly different situation but turning on a similar test, HMRC tried to argue that "reasonable excuse" was limited to exceptional circumstances. The tribunal disagreed with that argument and held that the phrase should be given its normal meaning. This approach was emphatically confirmed by the Upper Tribunal in *O'Flaherty*:

> "There is no requirement that the circumstances must be exceptional."

The different arguments were reconciled in *World of Enterprise*. There, the tribunal emphasised that the statutory words "reasonable excuse" were to be given their plain and ordinary meaning without unnecessary embellishment. However, the tribunal considered that circumstances giving rise to a claim of reasonable excuse should be "exceptional in the sense that such excuse would be unlikely to be ordinary". Although some tribunal decisions continue to employ an "exceptional reasons" test, the author considers that to represent the wrong approach. In the context of penalty appeals, the Upper Tribunal in *Perrin* has emphatically rejected any idea that the words "reasonable excuse" should have any additional gloss of events being unforeseen or unavoidable.

Law: TMA 1970, s. 49(3); FA 1999, Sch. 17, para. 11A(3); FA 2003, Sch. 10, para. 44(3); IHTA 1984, s. 223(3); SI 1986/1711, reg. 9(3)

Cases: *N A Dudley Electrical Contractors Ltd* [2011] UKFTT 260 (TC); *World of Enterprise Ltd v HMRC* [2011] UKFTT 719 (TC); *O'Flaherty v HMRC* [2013] UKUT 161 (TCC); *Perrin v HMRC* [2018] UKUT 156 (TCC)

2.4.3 Reference to the tribunal

Strictly, there is no formal procedure for asking the tribunal to require HMRC to accept an appeal made late. A letter would suffice explaining the dates on which the appealable decision and the attempted appeal were made and the date on which HMRC refused to accept the appeal.

However, it is always helpful for taxpayers to provide a brief outline of the arguments it would wish to make to assist the tribunal with the handling of the case. See "Allocation of cases to categories" at **5.6** below.

In *Ashraf*, the tribunal considered that the taxpayer must first ask HMRC to consent to a late appeal, but that such a request need not be in writing. The tribunal was willing to allow an oral request at the hearing itself to satisfy this requirement.

It was made clear in *Sood* that once HMRC have themselves admitted a late appeal then they cannot later undo that decision by requiring the tribunal to adjudicate whether or not the late appeal should be admitted: the tribunal's jurisdiction on this question exists only if a request has been made of HMRC which HMRC have then refused.

Cases: *Ashraf v HMRC* [2016] UKFTT 453 (TC); *Sood v HMRC* [2019] UKFTT 368 (TC)

2.4.4 Exercise of discretion by the tribunal

It was held in *Browallia* and *Cook* that the tribunal's discretion is not limited to ascertaining whether or not there was a reasonable excuse for the lateness of the appeal. Instead, the tribunal should consider the overall fairness to the respective parties and the risk of injustice being caused by the right of appeal being denied or, conversely, the late appeal being admitted.

Cases: *R (on the application of Browallia Cal Limited) v General Commissioners of Income Tax for the City of London* [2003] EWHC 2779 (Admin); *R (on the application of Cook) v General Commissioners* [2007] EWHC 167 (Admin)

Factors to consider

Over the years, a number of different cases have set out lists of factors that should be considered by a tribunal when deciding whether or

2.4 Considerations for late appeals

not to admit an appeal out of time. There can be some danger in applying many of those cases. Most importantly, a lot of those cases pre-date the key *BPP* case where the Supreme Court emphasised the importance of compliance with time limits.

Other reasons for exercising caution in relation to those earlier cases is that many apply a provision in the Civil Procedure Rules notwithstanding the following facts: that the CPR is not directly applicable in the tribunal, the rule was not actually designed with late appeals in mind (but for the slightly different matter of relief from sanctions when a time limit had been missed) and that the CPR rule had in fact been replaced.

In *Worldpay*, the tribunal derived from *BPP* that the CPR can be a guide for the tribunal. However, it is the author's view that this slightly misrepresents what the Supreme Court held. The Supreme Court noted that the case law on missed time limits was likely to be informative – it did not say that the CPR should be followed where there was no analogous provision in the tribunal's rules.

Another danger of relying on old cases is that it can disguise the fact that cases turn on their own individual merits and whilst certain questions should always be asked, it is not a case of working through a checklist. A tribunal must consider the merits of each case on its own facts.

It should also be remembered that these cases are ultimately decided by the judge in question considering the case before him or her. In such situations, it must be accepted that different judges could reach different conclusions, with neither conclusion being legally "wrong".

In *Buckinghamshire*, the tribunal distilled the effect of the previous case law and said that the tribunal should consider the following:

- the purpose of the time limit;
- the length of the delay;
- whether or not there is a good explanation for the delay;
- the consequences for the respective parties of granting an extension; and
- the consequences for the respective parties of refusing an extension.

Very shortly afterwards, in *Martland*, the Upper Tribunal had its own attempt at refining the principles.

In particular, it made it clear that the exercise of the First-tier's discretion did not directly engage the overriding objective in rule 2, although it acknowledged that the principle embodied in rule 2 is broad and applies just as much in the exercise of judicial discretion as it does to more routine procedural matters.

It continued by laying down a three-stage test:

- First, the First-tier should establish the length of the delay.
- Secondly, the reason or reasons for the default should be established.
- Thirdly, the tribunal should evaluate all the circumstances of the case.

Although very short delays (usually amounting to a breach being neither serious nor significant) would usually mean little time would need to be spent on the second and third stages, the Upper Tribunal emphasised that those two stages should still be considered.

Evaluating all the circumstances of the case should involve a balancing exercise which will essentially assess the merits of the reason(s) for the delay and the respective prejudice to the parties that would be caused by the granting or refusal of permission. This balancing exercise should also take into account the particular importance of the need for litigation to be conducted efficiently, at a proportionate cost, and for statutory time limits to be respected. In both *Katib* and *BMW*, the Upper Tribunal considered that the First-tier had erred in not giving this latter factor sufficient weight.

In the course of the process, the First-tier can have regard to any obvious strength or weakness of the taxpayer's case (this is part of the prejudice). However, the Upper Tribunal emphasised that this should not descend into a detailed analysis of the underlying merits of the appeal. As the tribunal noted in *Duncombe*:

> "This is not so that it can carry out a detailed evaluation of the case, but so that it can form a general impression of its strength or weakness to weigh in the balance. To that limited extent, an applicant should be afforded the opportunity to persuade the FTT that the merits of the appeal are on the face of it

overwhelmingly in his/her favour and the respondents the corresponding opportunity to point out the weakness of the applicant's case. In considering this point, the FTT should be very wary of taking into account evidence which is in dispute and should not do so unless there are exceptional circumstances."

In *De Silva*, applying the *Martland* criteria, the Upper Tribunal gave the following additional guidance:

"Any obvious strength or weakness in the Appellant's case can be taken into account, but without descending into a detailed analysis of the underlying merits of the appeal. In considering this point, evidence which is in dispute should not generally be taken into account and, we should add, evidence which is untested should not be assumed to be true."

In *Martland*, the Upper Tribunal has adopted the approach that permits the overall impression of the merits of the case to be factored into the balance, even in those cases when the merits are neither very strong nor very weak (which will represent the vast majority of cases). In this process, the tribunal should only rarely take into account evidence that is in dispute. However, care might need to be taken with the final sentence of the extract from *De Silva* above. It does not mean that untested evidence should be dismissed out of hand: instead, the tribunal should, when forming its overall impression of the case, recognise that untested evidence might not be accepted were the case to proceed to full trial.

In *Martland*, the Upper Tribunal identified two factors that would rarely carry any weight in the balancing exercise:

- shortage of funds (and any consequent inability to instruct a professional adviser); and
- being a litigant in person.

Indeed, in *Moss*, the tribunal referred to Court of Appeal authority to say that "shortage of funds does not provide a good reason for delay".

Similarly, in *Katib*, the Upper Tribunal remarked that incompetence by a taxpayer's professional advisers is unlikely to be persuasive. In this regard, the First-tier in *Duncombe* noted that there is no difference between a litigant whose representative failed to submit an appeal on time and a litigant whose representative failed to advise about the time limit.

In *Websons*, the Upper Tribunal was dealing with a case where (had the appeal been admitted late) it would simply have been stayed behind a lead case. The tribunal considered that that issue did not diminish the need to conduct litigation efficiently and therefore did not represent a trump card that ousted a proper consideration of the *Martland* criteria.

Cases: *HMRC v BPP Holdings Ltd* [2017] UKSC 55; *Worldpay (UK) Ltd v HMRC* [2019] UKFTT 235 (TC); *Martland v HMRC* [2018] UKUT 178 (TCC); *Buckinghamshire Bingo Ltd v HMRC* [2018] UKFTT 257 (TC); *Katib v HMRC* [2019] UKUT 189 (TCC); *Moss v HMRC* [2019] UKFTT 686 (TC); *HMRC v Websons (8) Ltd* [2020] UKUT 154 (TCC); *Duncombe v HMRC* [2020] UKFTT 248 (TC); *HMRC v BMW Shipping Agents Ltd* [2021] UKUT 91 (TCC); *De Silva v HMRC* [2021] UKUT 275 (TCC)

Examples in practice

It is important to remember that each case is decided on its own merits. For example, in *Snapcrest*, the tribunal held that a delay of seven days "was neither serious nor significant". However, it was emphasised that that description was not universally apt but in the context of a statutory appeal period of 30 days. The tribunal noted that the delay had arisen because the taxpayer had mistakenly assumed that HMRC would engage in further discussion in the light of new material and extend the appeal deadline accordingly. Whilst the taxpayer had acted reasonably (albeit mistakenly), other taxpayers aware of the facts of the case would probably be taking a risk by consciously adopting a similar approach. Instead, a taxpayer in a similar position ought to make "its appeal on time whilst simultaneously pursuing its investigations".

Booth saw permission being given despite a 30-month delay caused by the taxpayer's clear failure to understand the tax system, because the tribunal recognised that it was very likely that HMRC's estimates of the taxpayer's income were overstated.

Furthermore, in *Ashfield*, the tribunal allowed a late appeal after four years. In that case, the delay was caused by the timely notice of appeal being blocked by the tribunal's firewall. Although electronic communications to the tribunal are automatically acknowledged (and the sender in this case would not have received such an acknowledgement), the tribunal noted that a first-time user would not have known to expect such an acknowledgement and, therefore, its absence should not have caused any unnecessary concern. The tribunal also noted that there was a significant sum of money at stake and only limited evidence of any prejudice to HMRC in having to revisit the case.

A different outcome was reached by the Upper Tribunal in *Turek*. Having summarised the key issues, the tribunal noted:

> "If the delay were shorter, the reasons for that delay better or the merits of Mr Turek's appeal obviously strong we might well have considered that the balance lay in favour of granting permission for a late appeal given the significant cost that Mr Turek would suffer if he lost the Vehicle. However, faced with a long delay which is effectively unexplained and no obviously strong merits, we have reached the clear conclusion that we should not grant such permission."

In *Adair*, there was a group of taxpayers with practically identical cases who belatedly wished to appeal and be added to another group of taxpayers with similar cases. It was accepted by the tribunal that, because of the similarity between the cases, little prejudice (in the sense of significant extra work) would be caused to HMRC by the addition of the new group of potential appellants. What potentially reinforced their case was that the appellants had been attempting to resolve the matter informally with HMRC, without commencing an appeal. Although this might have been a helpful factor in many cases, the late appeals were refused by the tribunal because of what it considered to be unreasonable delays in dealing with HMRC. However, in *Cummine*, another case with very similar issues and decided at the same time as *Adair* and by the same judge, the taxpayer had a good reason for most of the period of delay. That tipped the balance in his favour.

In *Sunrise*, the tribunal noted in particular that the taxpayer had been led by HMRC to assume that it would receive a repayment if similar litigation involving another taxpayer had been won by the taxpayer. Accordingly, to use the tribunal's own words "there was no need for Sunrise to appeal". It was only when, after the other taxpayer had won its case and HMRC then announced a further reason to withhold repayment, did the need for a formal notification of the appeal to the tribunal become necessary. Although not determinative, this did amount to a good reason for the delay.

Cases: *Booth v HMRC* [2018] UKFTT 694 (TC); *Border Revenue v Turek* [2020] UKUT 167 (TCC); *Ashfield v HMRC* [2020] UKFTT 110 (TC); *Snapcrest v HMRC* [2020] UKFTT 320 (TC); *Adair v HMRC* [2021] UKFTT 66 (TC); *Cummine v HMRC* [2021] UKFTT 67 (TC); *Sunrise Medical Ltd v HMRC* [2021] UKFTT 316 (TC)

Late appeals in academic cases

The case of *Workstation* concerned VAT default surcharges where the amount of the surcharge (effectively, a penalty) arising as a result of particular default is dependent on the number of previous defaults in a prescribed period. The tribunal concluded that, on an appeal against a particular surcharge, it was not technically possibly to appeal against any assertion that the previous occasions were in fact defaults, even though the point was entirely relevant to the amount payable (or indeed whether or not any surcharge was payable at all).

As the tribunal concluded, this could lead to pointless appeals in respect of earlier defaults, particularly given HMRC's administrative practice of not pursuing default surcharges in certain low-value cases (even though they still count towards the number of defaults in the event of a later default). The tribunal expressed the likelihood, however, that a late appeal might be admitted in such circumstances.

It is thought that a similar approach ought to be taken in cases where the earlier appeal is not strictly academic (in that HMRC do seek to impose a surcharge) but where the taxpayer for commercial reasons chooses not to appeal against it on cost grounds.

Case: *Workstation Farnham Ltd v HMRC* [2015] UKFTT 37 (TC)

2.4.5 Late appeals versus late notifications to the tribunal

It will be seen at **2.3.2** that there is a similar 30-day time limit for taxpayers who have received the conclusions from an internal review by HMRC. If the taxpayer wishes to continue to challenge the HMRC position (as it stands following the internal review), the taxpayer is obliged to notify the tribunal of the case within 30 days of the conclusion of the internal review.

Similarly, taxpayers who are offered an internal review are given a 30-day period (from the date of the offer) to respond: in that period, they should either accept the offer or notify the tribunal of the case. If neither is done within the 30-day period, then HMRC's view becomes final.

Section 118(2) permits HMRC to receive acceptances of such offers outside the 30-day time limit if the taxpayer has a reasonable excuse for the delay (and the taxpayer acted promptly once the reasonable excuse ceased). Any such refusal by HMRC can itself be referred to the tribunal. However, if the taxpayer does not respond to the offer within the 30-day period and, outside the 30-day period, notifies the tribunal of case, the case can proceed only if the tribunal gives permission. This request for permission must be included in the application form for the tribunal (see **5.3.2**).

The principles applied by the tribunal are (and should be) the same as those that are applied in cases where a taxpayer makes an appeal to HMRC outside the 30-day timeframe (see **2.4.4**). However, as a matter of strict law, the process is different in that it is based upon different statutory provisions.

Earlier cases suggested that the balancing exercise ought to be carried out in accordance with the overriding objective (see rule 2 and **3.3** below) to deal with a case fairly and justly. However, this approach was partly due to a previous wording of rule 20(4). As explained in *Aston Markland*, however, neither such application involves the tribunal exercising any power under the Rules or the interpretation of any rule or practice direction. For this reason, as a matter of strict law, it is not technically necessary for the tribunal to consider the overriding objective. Nevertheless, in practice, this will be of little consequence because the balancing exercise undertaken by the tribunal will endeavour to determine whether or not fairness and justice should lead to the late appeal or prevent the late notification from being admitted.

The key difference between the two types of application is that, unlike late appeals, HMRC do not have the discretion to allow cases to proceed to the tribunal when notification is late: that is solely the preserve of the tribunal. However, the lack of any opposition from HMRC should generally tip the balance in the taxpayer's favour, though as a matter of strict law HMRC's accommodation in such cases should not be determinative of the issue.

In *Shahzad*, the tribunal considered that a ten-day delay in notifying the dispute to the tribunal should be forgiven because the period included the Christmas break and the genuine confusion that the taxpayer exhibited about his tax liabilities.

Law: TMA 1970, s. 118; VATA 1994, s. 83E(2); SI 2009/273, rule 20(4)
Cases: *Shahzad v HMRC* [2011] UKFTT 397 (TC); *Aston Markland v HMRC* [2011] UKFTT 559 (TC)

2.5 Abuse of process

2.5.1 Overview

Although not expressly covered by the tribunal rules, there is a set of principles which seeks to ensure that the tribunal process is not abused by either party.

In *Spring Capital*, the First-tier referred to the *Badaloo* case and suggested that the Upper Tribunal had said that cases that amounted to an abuse of process could be struck out under rule 8(3)(c) (no prospect of success). In the author's respectful view, this approach seems a little circular even if the end destination is obviously correct. Furthermore, reference to the *Badaloo* decision itself shows that the Upper Tribunal's comments were restricted to the features of that particular case which had been challenged as abusive in nature.

As has since been confirmed by the Court of Appeal in *Shiner*, cases that amount to an abuse of process can be properly struck out in accordance with the tribunal's inherent powers of case management without reference to rule 8. However, as the court held, rule 8(3)(c) is drafted sufficiently widely to permit strike-outs under that rule as well when a case amounts to an abuse of process.

It should also be remembered that the term "abuse of process" is a broad term. Within its remit are:

- situations where a party to litigation is advancing a case in the wrong forum (for example, attempting to run a judicial review in the tribunal – see **2.1.3**); and

- situations where there is no express statutory prohibition on the party advancing a particular case in the tribunal but the party's arguments infringe some common law principle.

Cases: *Badaloo t/a Church Hill Finance v The Financial Conduct Authority* [2017] UKUT 158 (TCC); *Spring Capital Ltd v HMRC* [2017] UKFTT 465 (TC); *Shiner v HMRC* [2018] EWCA Civ 31

2.5.2 Res judicata or issue estoppel

One general prohibition is the trying of the same issue more than once. It is often said that this is not applicable to tax cases because there is no issue with the same parties arguing the same point on more than one occasion. However, care has to be taken when applying this principle.

For example, there is nothing intrinsically wrong with a taxpayer and HMRC arguing about the same point in relation to different tax years. Ultimately, they will be separate appeals in relation to two different appealable decisions: one in relation to one tax year and one in relation to another tax year. Accordingly, the tribunal will have full jurisdiction to hear what is ultimately a repeat set of arguments concerning what is ultimately the same set of facts (albeit occurring on a different set of dates).

The principles were set out by the tribunal in the case of *Gulliver* which made it clear that HMRC (and, by extension, taxpayers) were not even bound by previous decisions that might have been made in relation to the facts in the context of an earlier tax year.

Where the principle will clearly apply is where a particular appeal has been settled by the parties (whether by the tribunal or by an agreement under TMA 1970, s. 54 (or equivalent elsewhere)). In that case, the matter will have been concluded and it is not open for the tribunal to reconsider the matter. For example, in *The Open University*, the OU sought to review the VAT treatment of its services made to the BBC over a 16-year period (1978 to 1994). However, back in 1982, the former VAT and Duties Tribunal had considered the matter in relation to one quarter (that ending September 1981), dismissing the OU's appeal. It later became clear that the tribunal had erred in that earlier decision and this led to the questions being reconsidered afresh. However, the September 1981 quarter could not be part of that reconsideration as the VAT treatment in that quarter was *res judicata*.

Law: TMA 1970, s. 54

Cases: *The Open University v HMRC* [2013] UKFTT 326 (TC); *Gulliver v HMRC* [2017] UKFTT 222 (TC)

2.5.3 Other abuses of process

An abuse of process arises where a party's conduct is consistent with the rules but is nevertheless considered to be inappropriate. An example would be where a taxpayer seeks a direction requiring HMRC to issue a closure notice immediately after such an application has been rejected, at least where there has been no material change in the facts in the meantime. Another example would be if HMRC sought the tribunal's approval to issue a Schedule 36 notice immediately after having had such an application rejected as inappropriate.

The general guidance given to tribunals is to consider the matter holistically. The leading case is the House of Lords' decision in *Johnson* which advocated:

> "a broad, merits-based judgment which takes account of the public and private interests involved and also takes account of all the facts of the case, focusing attention on the crucial question whether, in all the circumstances, a party is misusing or abusing the process of the court by seeking to raise before it the issue which could have been raised before."

The Upper Tribunal took such an approach in *Gardner-Shaw*, where HMRC tried to re-argue an issue in one set of cases which had been stayed behind a lead case where HMRC had previously lost the point. That approach was described as "to play fast and loose with the test case procedure".

The principles, as applicable in the First-tier, have been identified by the tribunal in its decision in *Spring Capital*. More recently, the Court of Appeal considered those principles from a wider perspective (i.e. not just tax litigation) in *Kishore*, even though it was in fact a tax case.

In *Kishore*, the taxpayer had been denied a credit for input tax on the basis that the transactions were fraudulent and that Mr Kishore either knew or should have known of that fact. In the course of his appeal, Mr Kishore failed to comply with tribunal directions, leading to the striking out of his appeal. Subsequently, HMRC issued penalty assessments which Mr Kishore again sought to challenge, raising arguments that had been pertinent to the earlier (now struck-out) appeal. HMRC sought to preclude Mr Kishore from raising these arguments, contending that it was an abuse of process to run arguments that should and could have been advanced in earlier proceedings. They also made the point that it is more abusive to re-run arguments in situations where the earlier proceedings had been struck out (as was the case here).

However, the court noted that this was not a case of a taxpayer bringing a duplicate claim (being the typical situation where a court might consider abuse to arise); rather, "in substance he is defending himself, challenging penalties which HMRC have sought to impose on him".

Furthermore, the court indicated a reluctance to prevent a taxpayer from defending himself against a tax penalty, which is a punitive measure attracting greater protection from the courts. It did say that the matter was likely to be more balanced in a case where both the earlier case and the later case concerned tax penalties and the earlier case had been struck out. However, the court made it clear that this was only a factor to be taken into account and not determinative of the matter.

The court also considered that the broad merits-based approach was more likely to consider re-litigation of a point abusive in cases "where a Tribunal had already decided a point [rather than where] the previous proceedings had never been the subject of a decision but had instead been struck out".

Finally, the court noted the fact that when the earlier proceedings were struck out Mr Kishore had not been advised of the penalty assessments. This was held by the court to be a relevant factor (in favour of the taxpayer) when applying the broad merits-based approach.

Cases: *Johnson v Gore Wood & Co* [2002] 2 AC 1; *Spring Capital Ltd v HMRC* [2017] UKFTT 465 (TC); *Gardner-Shaw v HMRC* [2018] UKUT 419 (TCC); *HMRC v Kishore* [2021] EWCA Civ 1565

2.5.4 Remitted hearings

On the other hand, there are occasions when an appeal proceeds to the Upper Tribunal and perhaps the higher courts. At the end of the appellate process, the appellate court then sends ("remits") the case back to the First-tier for a further hearing.

Sometimes, the remittal is on narrow terms, for example to determine a particular set of facts with new evidence. However, sometimes the matter is remitted to the First-tier for a completely new hearing. In this latter scenario, the original hearing is set aside and therefore the principle of *res judicata* cannot be invoked.

This was the situation in *Ulster* where HMRC sought to use the fresh hearing as an opportunity to introduce a new argument. The taxpayer argued that this amounted to an abuse of process. Although that argument might have succeeded in some instances, the tribunal considered it was not appropriate on the facts of that particular case and therefore HMRC were permitted to start all over again.

Case: *Ulster Metal Refiners Ltd v HMRC* [2019] UKFTT 385 (TC)

3. The Tribunal Procedure Rules

3.1 Introduction to rules

3.1.1 Overview

The *Tribunals, Courts and Enforcement Act* 2007 requires the publication of rules to govern the procedure of cases before the tribunal. The stated purposes of such rules include ensuring that:

- justice is done;
- the tribunal system is accessible and fair; and
- proceedings are handled quickly and efficiently.

In practice, there are different sets of rules for each of the tribunal's Chambers, reflecting the different nature of the hearings in each. This book focuses solely on the rules applicable in the Tax Chamber, published as the *Tribunal Procedure (First-tier Tribunal) (Tax Chamber) Rules* 2009, referred to in this book as "the Rules".

Law: TCEA 2007, s. 22; SI 2009/273

3.1.2 The parts of the Tax Chamber Rules

The Rules are divided into four parts:

- The first deals with introductory matters and is analysed in this chapter.
- The second considers the tribunal's general powers and is considered in **Chapter 4**.
- The third part deals with the rules that focus on procedures that take place before a case is heard at the tribunal and at the hearing itself. Those procedures are considered in **Chapters 5 and 7** respectively.
- Part 4 is looked at in **Chapter 9**. It deals with procedures that take place after a hearing.

Chapters 6 and **8** deal with matters for which there are no specific rules: **Chapter 6** considers the directions that are usually given, particularly in Standard and Complex cases, to ensure that the parties are prepared for the tribunal hearing. **Chapter 8** looks at procedures at the hearing itself.

Strictly, rules 34 and 35 form part of Part 3 of the Rules. However, as they deal with the determination of the case, they are considered in **Chapter 9** as if they were part of Part 4.

3.2 Rule 1 – Citation, application and interpretation

1(1) These Rules may be cited as the Tribunal Procedure (First-tier Tribunal) (Tax Chamber) Rules 2009 and come into force on 1st April 2009.

1(2) These Rules apply to proceedings before the Tax Chamber of the First-tier Tribunal.

1(3) In these Rules–

"the 2007 Act" means the Tribunals, Courts and Enforcement Act 2007;

"appellant" means–

(a) the person who starts proceedings (whether by bringing or notifying an appeal, by making an originating application, by a reference, or otherwise);

(b) in proceedings started jointly by more than one person, such persons acting jointly or each such person, as the context requires;

(c) a person substituted as an appellant under rule 9 (substitution and addition of parties);

"Basic case" means a case allocated to the Basic category under rule 23 (allocation of cases to categories);

"CAA case" means an application under section 563 of the Capital Allowances Act 2001;

"Complex case" means a case allocated to the Complex category under rule 23 (allocation of cases to categories);

"Compliance Officer" means the Compliance Officer for IPSA;

"Default Paper case" means a case allocated to the Default Paper category under rule 23 (allocation of cases to categories);

"devolved Welsh case" means an appeal, referral or application under—

(a) a Measure or Act of the National Assembly for Wales; or

(b) an instrument made under a Measure or Act of the National Assembly for Wales;

"document" means anything in which information is recorded in any form, and an obligation under these Rules to provide or allow access to a document or a copy of a document for any purpose means, unless the Tribunal directs otherwise, an obligation to provide or allow access to such document or copy in a legible form or in a form which can be readily made into a legible form;

"financial restrictions civil penalty case" means an appeal under paragraph 26(3) or 28(1) of Schedule 7 to the Counter-Terrorism Act 2008;

"hearing" means an oral hearing and includes a hearing conducted in whole or in part by video link, telephone or other means of instantaneous two-way electronic communication;

"HMRC" means Her Majesty's Revenue and Customs but also includes–

(a) the Serious Organised Crime Agency when carrying out functions under section 317 of the Proceeds of Crime Act 2002; and

(b) the Director of Border Revenue when carrying out functions under section 7 of the Borders, Citizenship and Immigration Act 2009;

"IPSA" means the Independent Parliamentary Standards Authority;

"MP expenses case" means an appeal under the Parliamentary Standards Act 2009;

"party" means a person who is (or was at the time that the Tribunal disposed of the proceedings) an appellant or respondent in proceedings before the Tribunal;

"practice direction" means a direction given under section 23 of the 2007 Act;

"respondent" means–

(a) in a case other than an MP expenses case or a devolved Welsh case–

   (i) HMRC, where HMRC is not an appellant;

   (ii) in proceedings brought by HMRC alone, a person against whom the proceedings are brought or to whom the proceedings relate;

(b) in a[n] MP expenses case, the Compliance Officer;

(ba) in a devolved Welsh case—

   (i) WRA, where WRA is not an appellant;

   (ii) in proceedings brought by WRA alone, a person against whom the proceedings are brought or to whom the proceedings relate; and

(c) in any case, a person substituted or added as a respondent under rule 9 (substitution and addition of parties);

"Standard case" means a case allocated to the Standard category under rule 23 (allocation of cases to categories);

"Tribunal" means the First-tier Tribunal[;]

"WRA" means the Welsh Revenue Authority.

3.2.1 Overview

It is considered that most of these definitions are self-explanatory and they are not discussed further.

A practice direction is effectively a standardised direction (i.e. a procedural decision given by the tribunal usually telling one party to do something by a particular date) which governs all cases unless expressly disapplied in a particular case. Depending on their scope, they will need to be approved by the Lord Chancellor and/or the judge who is in overall charge of the tribunals (the Senior President of Tribunals).

Law: TCEA 2007, s. 23

Practice statements

Because of the procedural difficulties involved in getting a practice direction issued, the Tax Chamber has started to issue practice statements which do much the same thing. These are statements informally issued by the Chamber President setting out the normal course of events in particular situations. However, as they do not quite have the status of a practice direction, it will be necessary for the tribunal to issue a specific direction in each individual case if they are to be given effect.

Examples

Examples of practice directions and practice statements applying to the Tax Chamber include:

- rules determining the initial allocation of cases to the various categories (see rule 23 and **Appendix 2**); and
- guidance concerning the composition of tribunals for cases within particular categories (see **Appendix 3**).

See also rule 4.

3.3 Rule 2 – Overriding objective and parties' obligation to co-operate with the Tribunal

2(1)   The overriding objective of these Rules is to enable the Tribunal to deal with cases fairly and justly.

2(2)   Dealing with a case fairly and justly includes–

(a) dealing with the case in ways which are proportionate to the importance of the case, the complexity of the

> issues, the anticipated costs and the resources of the parties;
>
> (b) avoiding unnecessary formality and seeking flexibility in the proceedings;
>
> (c) ensuring, so far as practicable, that the parties are able to participate fully in the proceedings;
>
> (d) using any special expertise of the Tribunal effectively; and
>
> (e) avoiding delay, so far as compatible with proper consideration of the issues.
>
> 2(3) The Tribunal must seek to give effect to the overriding objective when it–
>
> (a) exercises any power under these Rules; or
>
> (b) interprets any rule or practice direction.
>
> 2(4) Parties must–
>
> (a) help the Tribunal to further the overriding objective; and
>
> (b) co-operate with the Tribunal generally.

3.3.1 Overview

This rule lies at the heart of all of the tribunal's procedures. The rule, often referred to simply as "the overriding objective", will usually be explicitly cited whenever the tribunal is asked to exercise its discretion (for example, to decide whether or not late evidence should be admitted). The rule will be implicitly considered whenever the tribunal decides how a particular hearing should be conducted or when deciding any other procedural matter.

Although rule 2(2) gives a list of ways in which the overriding objective should be achieved, this list is not exhaustive. In *General Healthcare*, the tribunal held that parties should regularly review time estimates given for a hearing and promptly notify the tribunal if estimates appear to be either too long or too short so that the tribunal's list of hearing dates can be adjusted.

Case: *General Healthcare Group Ltd v HMRC* [2014] UKFTT 1087 (TC)

3.3 Rule 2 – Overriding objective and parties' obligation to co-operate with the Tribunal

Change of approach

The Court of Appeal's landmark decision in *BPP* led to (or at least endorsed) a significant shift by the tribunal towards a far stricter approach to compliance with the procedure rules and directions. This change is best summarised by the tribunal's decision in *European*:

> "An overly-indulgent attitude to compliance with rules, practice statements and directions has been firmly consigned to the past. The landscape of case management has been coloured by recent judicial authority, but it is important in my view not to allow the big picture, which remains the interests of fairness and justice, to become obscured. Due regard must in all cases be had to the need for Tribunal rules and directions to be complied with, with special significance attaching to that factor in considering relief from sanctions, but that is only one factor, albeit an important one, in the overall assessment of fairness and justice in all the circumstances of the case. This case is one of an in-time application for an extension of time, with good reasons for the delay inherent in such an extension, and where the balance of prejudice clearly favours granting the application. It is accordingly, in my judgment, in the interests of fairness and justice to allow HMRC's application."

Although the Supreme Court's subsequent decision made it clear that it was not necessarily endorsing everything said in the Court of Appeal, the approach in *European* appears to be fully in accordance with the court's final decision.

The decision in *Browne* took a similar view when it considered that a taxpayer's late application for permission to appeal should be rejected, even though the delay had been the fault of the taxpayer's representative.

Cases: *BPP Holdings Ltd v HMRC* [2016] EWCA Civ 121; *HMRC v BPP Holdings Ltd* [2017] UKSC 55; *European Food Brokers Ltd v HMRC* [2017] UKFTT 196 (TC); *Browne v HMRC* [2017] UKFTT 867 (TC)

3.3.2 When the overriding objective is not invoked

Strictly, however, the overriding objective is invoked only when the tribunal is exercising a power under the Rules. As noted in *Aleena*, it does not give the tribunal power to do anything not within the scope of the rules.

Thus, for example, a taxpayer's application for HMRC to admit a late appeal (see **2.4.4** above) is a matter that the tribunal should consider without regard to the overriding objective. (Of course, the procedures taken by the tribunal in the course of any such application should themselves be governed by the overriding objective.)

Similarly, in *Aston Markland*, the tribunal considered that applications under rule 20(4) for the tribunal to admit a case where late notification had been made to the tribunal (see **2.4.5** above and **5.3.3** below) should likewise be considered without regard to the overriding objective. This is because the power to admit a case late comes from statute and not from the Rules themselves.

Cases: *Aston Markland v HMRC* [2011] UKFTT 559 (TC); *Aleena Electronics Ltd v HMRC* [2011] UKFTT 608 (TC).

3.3.3   Fairly and justly

The key expression in the overriding objective is "fairly and justly", certain aspects of which are expanded upon in rule 2(2). It should be stated that dealing with a case fairly and justly does not necessarily mean the tribunal reaching the correct answer. As noted by Lord Bingham in *O'Brien*, "justice requires not only that the right answer be given but also that it be achieved by a trial process which is fair to all parties".

For example, in *Xentric*, it was considered that evidence which might be relevant to the proceedings (and would therefore help the tribunal reach the *correct* answer) should be excluded because its admission so late in the proceedings would cause unfairness to another party. See, further, rule 15 discussed at **4.13.4** below. Similarly, in *Stockler*, where after a long drawn-out litigation during which the taxpayer was initially represented by Counsel, the tribunal refused to allow the taxpayer to introduce a new ground of appeal (based upon a human rights argument) very late on in the proceedings.

In *Hill*, the Upper Tribunal endorsed the view that the First-tier is permitted to take a more active (inquisitorial) stance than is usual and use its own specialist knowledge, particularly where a party is not represented. But (in the case of a strike-out application by HMRC) the tribunal should not try "to devise ingenious arguments simply in order to keep an appeal alive".

3.3 Rule 2 – Overriding objective and parties' obligation to co-operate with the Tribunal

The overriding objective was also discussed in *Feltham*. The tribunal noted that "flexibility is needed to achieve fairness and justice", commenting that this was particularly true in cases allocated to the Basic and Standard categories (see **5.6** below).

In *Carlton*, the taxpayer asked the tribunal to admit a substituted notice of appeal (under rule 5(3)(c)). However, under the overriding duty, the tribunal considered that the application should be revised as an application to treat the document as a fresh (albeit late) notice of appeal (under rule 20).

On very different facts, in *Ritchie*, the Upper Tribunal noted that fairness does not necessarily require formality.

In *Chartwell*, the Court of Appeal noted that the potential impact of delay on other court users is also a relevant factor when considering where the interests of justice lie. The tribunal has certainly taken this into account when applying rule 2 (see, for example, *Gold Nuts*).

Cases: *O'Brien v Chief Constable of South Wales Police* [2005] 2 AC 534 [2005]; *Xentric Limited v HMRC* [2010] UKFTT 249 (TC); *Feltham v HMRC* [2011] UKFTT 612 (TC); *Stockler v HMRC* [2012] UKFTT 404 (TC); *Chartwell Estate Agents v Fergies Properties* [2014] EWCA Civ 506; *Carlton Clubs Ltd v HMRC* [2016] UKFTT 562 (TC); *Gold Nuts Ltd v HMRC* [2017] UKFTT 354 (TC); *HMRC v Hill* [2018] UKUT 45 (TCC); *HMRC v Ritchie* [2019] UKUT 71 (TCC)

Range of arguments

For example, if a party turned up at the tribunal with a new argument for which the other party were unprepared, the tribunal might adjourn proceedings to permit the other party to prepare a response. In particular, the tribunal considered that, particularly in Basic and Standard cases, taxpayers should not ordinarily be limited to arguments raised in their grounds of appeal (and, by extension, it is suggested that HMRC should not be limited to arguments in their statement of case).

Furthermore, the tribunal in *Feltham* acknowledged that the tribunal should, where appropriate, raise issues that have not been identified by the parties to ensure that the taxpayer is taxed in accordance with the law.

Ultimately, what the tribunal should do in any particular case depends on what would be fair and just in the circumstances.

Sometimes, this might require more time to be given to allow a party to respond to a new argument; sometimes, the new argument should not be admitted.

In an employment case (*Woodhouse*), the Employment Appeal Tribunal considered the approach to be taken when one party seeks to introduce a new argument. It held that a consideration of all the relevant factors should be undertaken. However, when considering the prospective new argument's prospects of success, it would not be appropriate for that to be judged by reference to the evidence already before the tribunal, as that would have been prepared without the new argument in mind.

In *BAV*, the tribunal noted that advising the other side of a new legal argument (which required no factual evidence) a month before the hearing should ordinarily be sufficient notice (at least when served on a party that was legally represented). If, however, that was insufficient notice then it would be open for the other party to seek an adjournment.

Conversely, in *Worldpay*, the tribunal suggested that "it is normally going too far to raise something new in a skeleton argument as that is almost certainly too late to give fair warning".

Ritchie considered the right of a tribunal to introduce new arguments. Although that is indeed an option, the Upper Tribunal considered that the First-tier had erred in its approach in that particular case.

In *Outram*, HMRC attempted to introduce a new argument in the course of its skeleton argument, just a few weeks ahead of the hearing. The new argument was held to be just about arguable, so the tribunal then proceeded to consider whether it was appropriate for the late amendment to HMRC's case to be permitted. However, the reasons for the delay were weak and, if the point were admitted, the parties would need to spend the last couple of weeks before the hearing rushing around to find evidence to address the point. The tribunal accordingly directed that the new argument could not be pursued.

Cases: *Feltham v HMRC* [2011] UKFTT 612 (TC); *Woodhouse v Hampshire Hospitals NHS Trust* (2012) UKEAT/0132/12/DM; *HMRC v Ritchie* [2019] UKUT 71 (TCC); *BAV-TMW-Globaler-Immobilien-Spezialfonds v HMRC* [2019] UKFTT 233 (TC); *Worldpay (UK) Ltd v HMRC* [2019] UKFTT 235 (TC); *Outram v HMRC* [2021] UKFTT 29 (TC)

Using any special expertise of the tribunal effectively

The FTT is considered to be an "expert tribunal" in that it deals with a specific range of issues for which its judges and members are assumed to have some experience. In this way, it contrasts with the general courts which will have a wide range of issues to deal with. It should not be assumed, however, that a judge at any particular hearing will necessarily be an expert in the precise subject matter relevant to the case.

Nevertheless, when judges and members have professional experience in the field and when particular issues regularly crop up in different hearings, an element of expertise will build up which should facilitate the better handling of cases by the tribunal. However, it is clear that the tribunal should make clear when this expertise is applied. In *Rennie Smith*, the tribunal noted:

> "In every case where the Tribunal deploys their own expertise it is essential [for the Tribunal] to articulate exactly what that expertise or knowledge might be in order to give both parties an opportunity to address any issues that might arise therefrom."

Case: *Rennie Smith & Co v HMRC* [2013] UKFTT 638 (TC)

3.3.4 Duty on parties (rule 2(4))

Paragraph (4) imposes an obligation on the parties to help the tribunal to further this overriding objective and to co-operate with the tribunal generally. It is suggested that a party's breach of this obligation could cause the tribunal to award costs under rule 10.

In *MHA*, a social security case, the Upper Tribunal held that the parties' duty included "ensuring as far as possible that their case is ready by the time of the hearing".

It was held in *Scofield* that this duty overrode a party's attempts to obtain a partisan advantage in any particular case.

In *BPP*, the Supreme Court confirmed that, notwithstanding the more informal nature of tribunal proceedings, any order, direction or practice direction issued by the tribunal should be "complied with in like manner to a court's".

The subsequent decision of *Rashidi* emphasises that litigants should not adopt too casual an attitude towards tribunal proceedings. In that case, the taxpayer did not monitor the e-mail address he had given to HMRC and the tribunal for correspondence purposes. Not only did this lead to the case being decided against him in his absence but it was also the main reason for the tribunal's refusal to set aside that decision under rule 38.

In *European*, the tribunal noted that time limits should generally be complied with but equally recognised that this is not always possible. It distinguished between those cases where an extension to a time limit was being sought prospectively and those where a time limit had already been missed. In the latter case, the specific considerations previously endorsed in *Data Select* continue to be pertinent. They are:

- What is the purpose of the time limit?
- How long was the delay?
- Is there a good explanation for the delay?
- What will be the consequences for the parties of an extension?
- What will be the consequences for the parties of a refusal to extend time?

In *Jafari*, the tribunal criticised HMRC's representative for not bringing to the tribunal's attention case law which undermined HMRC's case:

> "It is one thing for HMRC to take a principled stance that certain decisions of the Courts and Tribunals contain errors of law and to argue accordingly (but frankly) in affected cases. But it is quite another thing to gloss over decisions which HMRC knows but dislikes and to proceed as if they do not exist. Doing so obscures the true position and risks the Tribunal coming to a legally insupportable conclusion."

By not acting with the necessary candour:

> "HMRC failed to meet its obligation to help the Tribunal to further the overriding objective of dealing with cases fairly and justly under Rule 2(4)(a)."

Cases: *MHA v Secretary of State for Work and Pensions* [2009] UKUT 211 (AAC); *Data Select Ltd v HMRC* [2012] UKUT 187 (TCC); *Scofield v HMRC* [2012] UKFTT 673 (TC); *Rashidi v HMRC* [2016] UKFTT 357 (TC); *HMRC v BPP Holdings Ltd* [2017] UKSC 55; *European Food Brokers Ltd v HMRC* [2017] UKFTT 196 (TC); *Jafari v HMRC* [2019] UKFTT 692 (TC)

3.3.5 The breadth of the tribunal's discretion

Despite the best endeavours of the tribunal and the parties, it will not be uncommon for unexpected difficulties to arise during the litigation process.

Often these will be capable of resolution by the parties themselves (perhaps by agreeing a short extension before a witness statement is produced or, even, agreeing to accelerate the production of the document so as to allow the other side an opportunity to consider it). In such cases, the tribunal will usually (but not necessarily always) endorse the parties' agreed position. However, there will often be occasions when the tribunal has to take a more active role.

In all situations, the parties and the tribunal should strive to further the overriding objective.

The case of *Mungavin* illustrates how the First-tier was required to deal with a case which had been unfortunately delayed due to the serious illness of the taxpayers' barrister. On the taxpayers' appeal, the Upper Tribunal upheld the First-tier's approach, making the point that any challenge would have succeeded only if it could have been shown that the First-tier's approach was "unfair".

Case: *Mungavin v HMRC* [2020] UKUT 11 (TCC)

3.4 Rule 3 – Alternative dispute resolution and arbitration

> 3(1) The Tribunal should seek, where appropriate–
>
>   (a) to bring to the attention of the parties the availability of any appropriate alternative procedure for the resolution of the dispute; and

> (b) if the parties wish and provided that it is compatible with the overriding objective, to facilitate the use of the procedure.
>
> 3(2) Part 1 of the Arbitration Act 1996 does not apply to proceedings before the Tribunal.

3.4.1 Overview

Although not traditionally associated with tax disputes, mediation and other methods of resolving disputes that are applied elsewhere in the civil courts should be considered as alternative ways of having a case considered.

One form of dispute resolution, alternative dispute resolution (ADR), is now widely available in the context of tax disputes. ADR is an option that should be considered before HMRC even reach an appealable decision. However, it can be available at later stages and, as rule 3 makes clear, even when the litigation process is fully underway. See **2.2.1** above. At one stage, HMRC started to refuse to consider ADR once litigation has started. However, they have since backtracked from that and formally recognised that it is never too late for parties to seek to resolve a case amicably.

In *Garritt-Critchley*, the High Court considered that in a fact-sensitive case, a party's refusal to consider mediation amounted to unreasonable conduct and led to that party being ordered to pay costs on the indemnity basis (see **4.8.9** below).

Case: *Garritt-Critchley v Ronnan* [2014] EWHC 1774 (Ch)

4. General powers and provisions under the rules

4.1 Rule 4 – Delegation to staff

4(1) Staff appointed under section 40(1) of the 2007 Act (tribunal staff and services) or section 2(1) of the Courts Act 2003 (court officers, staff and services) may, if authorised by the Senior President of Tribunals under paragraph 3(3) of Schedule 5 to the 2007 Act, carry out functions of a judicial nature permitted or required to be done by the Tribunal.

4(2) [Revoked from 21 July 2020].

4(3) Within 14 days after the date that the Tribunal sends notice of a decision made by a member of staff under paragraph (1) to a party, that party may make a written application to the Tribunal requiring that decision to be considered afresh by a judge.

4.1.1 Overview

This rule deals with cases where a practice direction has been granted allowing administrative staff of the tribunal to carry out certain functions of a quasi-judicial nature. This ensures that the tribunal can operate more efficiently without judges being required to deal with every decision-making process.

4.1.2 Practice direction 10 March 2009

Under a practice statement made by the Senior President of Tribunals on 10 March 2009, the functions that may be so delegated are those under:

- rule 5 (case management directions);
- rule 23 (allocation of cases to categories); and
- rule 32 (whether hearings should be in private or in public).

The practice statement limits the delegation to individuals duly authorised for the purpose by the President of the Tax Chamber.

Guidance: https://tinyurl.com/ksfw95ju (Delegation of functions to staff in relation to the FTT and the Finance and Tax Chamber of the Upper Tribunal)

4.1.3 Judicial oversight

Because it is essential that the use of any such delegation is subject to judicial oversight, parties can require that any such decision by a staff member be reconsidered by a judge. Such a request should be made in writing within 14 days of the date on which the tribunal sends to the party the notice of the original decision by the member of staff.

The rule provides that, on an application under paragraph (3), the decision by the judge should be made "afresh". This means that the judge effectively remakes the decision; it amounts to more than merely considering the reasonableness of the original decision.

4.1.4 When is a document "sent" (rule 4(3))?

For a case concerning the effect of a time limit when a document is sent to the wrong address, see the discussion of the *Rana* case in the context of rule 5(3)(a) (see **4.2.4**).

Case: *Rana v London Borough of Ealing* [2018] EWCA Civ 2074

4.2 Rule 5 – Case management powers

5(1) Subject to the provisions of the 2007 Act and any other enactment, the Tribunal may regulate its own procedure.

5(2) The Tribunal may give a direction in relation to the conduct or disposal of proceedings at any time, including a direction amending, suspending or setting aside an earlier direction.

5(3) In particular, and without restricting the general powers in paragraphs (1) and (2), the Tribunal may by direction–

(a) extend or shorten the time for complying with any rule, practice direction or direction, unless such extension or shortening would conflict with a provision of another enactment setting down a time limit;

(b) consolidate or hear together two or more sets of proceedings or parts of proceedings raising common issues, or treat a case as a lead case (whether in accordance with rule 18 (lead cases) or otherwise);

(c) permit or require a party to amend a document;

(d) permit or require a party or another person to provide documents, information or submissions to the Tribunal or a party;

(e) deal with an issue in the proceedings as a preliminary issue;

(f) hold a hearing to consider any matter, including a case management hearing;

(g) decide the form of any hearing;

(h) adjourn or postpone a hearing;

(i) require a party to produce a bundle for a hearing;

(j) stay (or, in Scotland, sist) proceedings;

(k) transfer proceedings to another tribunal if that other tribunal has jurisdiction in relation to the proceedings and, because of a change of circumstances since the proceedings were started–

   (i) the Tribunal no longer has jurisdiction in relation to the proceedings; or

   (ii) the Tribunal considers that the other tribunal is a more appropriate forum for the determination of the case;

(l) suspend the effect of its own decision pending the determination by the Tribunal or the Upper Tribunal, as the case may be, of an application for permission to appeal, a review or an appeal.

4.2.1 Overview

This rule (particularly when allied with rule 2) lies at the heart of the flexibility of proceedings in the tribunal.

The tribunal's ability to regulate its own procedure is confirmed by rule 5(1).

Rule 5(2) and (3) illustrate the range of directions that the tribunal may make in relation to a case.

Delegation to staff

Under paragraph 2 of a practice direction given by the Senior President of Tribunals, a duly authorised member of the tribunal's staff may carry out any of the tribunal's duties under this rule. See also rule 4 and **4.1.2** and **4.1.3** above.

Guidance: https://tinyurl.com/ksfw95ju (Delegation of functions to staff in relation to the FTT and the Finance and Tax Chamber of the Upper Tribunal)

4.2.2 Regulation of procedure (rule 5(1))

In *Foulser*, the tribunal considered the extent of any inherent jurisdiction it had to make case management directions in circumstances not expressly provided for within the Rules. It concluded, albeit provisionally, that rule 5 is worded widely, so that in an appropriate case, the tribunal could make directions as fairness and justice demand in circumstances other than those provided for elsewhere in the Rules.

That case concerned an application for a striking out of HMRC's case (see rule 8 below) in circumstances where it was considered that for HMRC to continue with the proceedings would have been inherently unfair. The tribunal distinguished between cases of unfairness generally and those where the unfairness arises within the proceedings themselves. The latter can be dealt with by the tribunal but the former (in which category the case fell) can be dealt with only by way of judicial review.

However, it was held in *Eclipse* that the tribunal cannot use the flexibility of the provisions in rules 2 and 5 so as to make a direction which conflicts with a specific rule elsewhere. In *Eclipse*, the FTT had directed that HMRC share the taxpayer's costs in preparing bundles for a hearing. As the case was not one where the tribunal had power to make costs orders in the absence of litigation misconduct (see rule 10(1)(a),(b), discussed at **4.8.3**, **4.8.4** and **4.8.5**), the Upper Tribunal considered that the FTT had exceeded its jurisdiction.

Cases: *Foulser v HMRC* [2011] UKFTT 642 (TC); *Eclipse Film Partners No. 35 LLP v HMRC* [2016] UKSC 24

4.2.3 Freedom to make directions (rule 5(2))

Rule 5(2) is important because it makes clear that directions by the tribunal can be amended, suspended or set aside by the tribunal itself; consequently, parties are not necessarily obliged to make appeals against such decisions to the Upper Tribunal. However, care needs to be taken to understand when an appeal is appropriate and when it is appropriate to make a fresh application in the tribunal itself.

This is because a direction by the tribunal will have been made on the basis of how the tribunal considers the case is best handled. If facts subsequently change, it is only right that the tribunal should have the opportunity to revisit the issue if a party considers that to be appropriate. Indeed, in such a case, it would not necessarily be appropriate for the Upper Tribunal to consider the issue because the Upper Tribunal's role would be limited to ascertaining whether or not the Tax Chamber's original decision was wrong in law, and not whether or not the decision remains appropriate in view of the subsequent change in circumstances.

In *Serco*, a similar provision was held to say that, if a party is unhappy with a direction given by the tribunal, in most cases an appeal should be made. It would be permissible to return to the original tribunal only if there has been a material change of circumstances since the original direction was made or it was based on a misstatement (of law or fact). Although there may be other occasions when an appeal is not necessary, such occasions were described as "rare ... [and] ... out of the ordinary".

In *Tibbles*, the Court of Appeal gave the following additional pointers:

- the discretion to vary directions should normally be limited to cases where there has been a material change of circumstances, or where the facts (on which the original directions were based) were misstated; but
- where the facts or arguments were (or ought to have been) known at the time of the original order then it is unlikely that the order can be revisited.

In *Gardner-Shaw*, the tribunal referred to *Tibbles* and noted that the test was "something out of the ordinary" and not "exceptional".

Although the taxpayers successfully appealed against the decision to the Upper Tribunal, this statement of principle was not disputed.

See also rule 6(5) below which concerns a party's entitlement to apply for a direction to be amended, suspended or set aside.

Cases: *Tibbles v SIG plc* [2012] EWCA Civ 518; *Serco Ltd v Wells* (2016) UKEAT/0330/15/RN; *Gardner-Shaw UK Ltd v HMRC* [2018] UKFTT 432 (TC)

Further application of the principles

For example, in *Grace*, the Tax Chamber was asked to allow the taxpayer to adduce further evidence beyond that permitted by an earlier direction. HMRC had resisted that application on the basis that the taxpayer should have instead appealed against the original decision to the Upper Tribunal. The judge held (in an oral decision) that this was the type of procedural decision that should not be appealed against but simply resubmitted to the tribunal.

However, it would not be appropriate to ask the tribunal to reconsider a matter where the decision (albeit procedural) is inherently a final decision (such as a decision as to whether or not a party is entitled to its costs) or where the circumstances are such that nothing has changed since the earlier decision was made. In such a case, the party objecting to the decision must appeal against it and point to an error of law made by the FTT.

Case: *Grace v HMRC* [2011] UKFTT 36 (TC)

The views of the parties

In *Pinewood*, the tribunal noted that it was entitled to make case management decisions contrary to the wishes of both parties if the overriding objective determined such a course of action.

Case: *Pinewood Studios Ltd v HMRC* [2012] UKFTT 370 (TC)

4.2.4 Examples of directions

Rule 5(3) provides a list of directions that can be made by the tribunal. The list is not exhaustive. For example, in *Elbrook*, the tribunal considered whether or not to carry out a site visit so as to gain a greater understanding of the facts of the case. It was considered that, even if that would allow the tribunal to derive some assistance, it would not be a productive use of the tribunal's time. A site visit did, however, take place in *London Luton*.

In *Foulser*, the tribunal considered that, although the provisions of rule 5(3) were drafted in a permissive way, the tribunal, if justice and fairness dictated, could equally restrict the way in which a party presented its case. Thus, rule 5(3)(d) could be used as a basis for the tribunal to prevent a party from relying upon documents obtained unlawfully or to prevent a party making submissions which would amount to a collateral attack on a previous final judgment.

See also rule 15(1)(f) which entitles the tribunal to give a direction so far as the timing of witness evidence. When read with rules 5(3)(a) and 7(2)(b), it can be seen that evidence will not necessarily be excluded if it is served late.

Cases: *Foulser v HMRC* [2011] UKFTT 642 (TC); *Elbrook (Cash and Carry) Ltd v HMRC* [2017] UKFTT 143 (TC); *London Luton Hotel BPRA Property Fund LLP* [2019] UKFTT 212 (TC)

Revising time limits in other rules or directions (rule 5(3)(a))

Rule 5(3)(a) makes clear that time limits are inherently flexible: they can be shortened or extended (subject to ensuring that this does not conflict with any statute or statutory instrument).

This does not mean that parties should ignore time limits. However, if a time limit is likely to be missed, the tribunal will be permitted to extend it if fairness (i.e. the overriding objective) so dictates. In the same way, the tribunal can allow for a party to file a document (say) after the passing of a time limit previously laid down if it would be in the interests of fairness and justice to do so.

In *European*, the tribunal noted that time limits should generally be complied with but equally recognised that this is not always possible. It distinguished between those cases where an extension to a time limit was being sought prospectively and those where a time limit had already been missed. (See also **3.3.4**.)

In *Copthorn*, the tribunal prospectively suspended the time limit for a party seeking permission to appeal because the case involved a number of different issues. Whilst some of these issues were still in the process of being resolved, it made sense for the costs of commencing appeal proceedings to be avoided as an appeal might prove to be unnecessary.

In *RP Baker*, the tribunal had to consider whether an application for costs (under rule 10) should be admitted in case where one of the documents required to be included in the application was provided three days late. The tribunal expressly adopted the principles that are applied when considering whether an appeal out of time should be admitted. See **2.4.4**.

Since the *Baker* case, however, the Upper Tribunal's decision in *Martland* has become the leading authority when considering whether an appeal out of time should be admitted. The *Martland* criteria (see **2.4.4**) were explicitly followed in *Kersner* where the taxpayer was seeking an extension of the period for opting out of the costs regime.

However, in *Tucker*, the tribunal accepted that a slightly modified version of the *Martland* approach should be followed in cases where a party is seeking relief from a sanction (i.e. the party is asking the tribunal for permission to do something, having previously failed to comply with a rule or tribunal direction). In such cases, the tribunal held that the tribunal should not seek an overall impression of the merits of the party's case, except in those extreme cases where the prospects were either obviously very good or very poor.

In *BMW*, the Upper Tribunal made clear that a factor that must be given particular prominence is the importance for litigation to be conducted efficiently and at proportionate cost and for time limits be respected.

Cases: *Copthorn Holdings Ltd v HMRC* [2013] UKFTT 190 (TC); *RP Baker (Oxford) Ltd v HMRC* [2014] UKFTT 420 (TC); *European Food Brokers Ltd v HMRC* [2017] UKFTT 196 (TC); *Martland v HMRC* [2018] UKUT 178 (TCC); *Kersner v HMRC* [2019] UKFTT 221 (TCC); *Tucker v HMRC* [2019] UKFTT 569 (TC); *HMRC v BMW Shipping Agents Ltd* [2021] UKUT 91 (TCC)

When the rules provide for something to be done within a certain period after a document is sent to the parties

A number of rules provide that something should be done within a specified period after a document is "sent by the Tribunal". In *Rana*, the Court of Appeal held that the date that a document is sent to the parties can include a date on which the tribunal (through its own carelessness) sends the document to the wrong address.

The obvious unfairness of such a decision should, however, be mitigated (as the court considered should have happened in *Rana*) by the tribunal exercising its discretion to extend time (under what in the tribunal is rule 5(3)(a)).

Case: *Rana v London Borough of Ealing* [2018] EWCA Civ 2074

Consolidating cases etc (rule 5(3)(b))

Cases will often be consolidated where they deal with the same issues involving the same taxpayer (for example, an appeal against an assessment in respect of different accounting periods or tax years where the notification is made to the tribunal on different occasions).

Another direction is for cases to be heard together. This will occur if the tribunal considers it appropriate for the arguments to be heard by the same tribunal at the same time, but the cases nevertheless retain their separate identity.

The difference was explained in *Rapid Brickwork*:

> "But joining is not consolidation. Consolidation requires the two appeals to be treated as a single appeal. Once consolidated the appeal is known by a single case reference [w]hereas these two appeals have retained their distinct numbers on directions, on letters to and from the tribunal, and in the Tribunal's computer records."

For example, in *Fanfield* and *Thexton Training*, the two companies' appeals were heard together as they permitted the tribunal to see the range of factual scenarios that could exist. Although the appeals were allowed in both cases, having the cases heard together did not necessarily lead to that result.

In *Rapid Brickwork*, the relevance of the question was in the context of an opt-out of the costs regime (see rule 10). Had the two appeals been consolidated then the earlier opt-out of one appeal would have governed the later appeal which might have been (but in that case had not been) consolidated with it.

In *Maharani*, the High Court listed the following factors as relevant when considering whether two cases should be consolidated:
- the degree of overlap of relevant evidence;
- the commonality of witnesses;
- the degree of difficulty in segregating different parts of the evidence in relation to separate appeals;
- the risk in separate appeals of the evidence and cross-examination in the second appeal being influenced by that in the first;
- the risk of evidence of witnesses in one case being believed, but in respect of the same evidential matters not being believed in the other case;
- the inconvenience of witnesses in being required to give evidence on two separate occasions in relation to essentially the same subject matter;
- whether delay will be occasioned by the appeals being consolidated; and
- the risk of prejudice (if the appeals are heard either separately or together).

In *Manhattan*, the tribunal emphasised that the list was not meant to be exhaustive. Having considered it appropriate to expedite the hearing for one part of the case, it duly added a further consideration, being whether consolidation would make expedition of the case difficult.

In *First Talk*, the tribunal directed that two related companies' appeals should be joined and heard together. The reasoning was that there was considerable evidence common to both companies' appeals and "there would be a very substantial saving of time if this evidence only had to be heard once at a joined hearing". However, the tribunal went further and held that joining the cases would be in the interests of justice: first, it would avoid putting both parties to unnecessary expense; secondly, it would avoid the risk of conflicting decisions being reached on the same facts by different tribunals.

In *Acornwood*, however, the tribunal noted that "although, at first sight, the gathering together of several similar cases so that they can be heard together seems to be an economical course, in practice it creates real difficulties and leads to delay". As a warning for the future, it suggested that, with hindsight, it might "have been better not to link the appeals with the references, to identify fewer lead cases or to focus, in the references, on one tax year". (The references were by members of Acornwood LLP under TMA, s. 28ZA in the course of enquiries into their personal tax returns where there was overlap with the LLP's appeals.)

See also rule 18, which provides for special procedures in cases where a lead case is selected under that rule. Lead cases can also be selected under rule 5(3)(b), in which case the provisions of rule 18 will not apply.

Cases: *Maharani Restaurant v HMCE* [1999] STC 295; *Fanfield Ltd v HMRC, Thexton Training Ltd v HMRC* [2011] UKFTT 42 (TC); *First Talk Mobile Ltd v HMRC, First Talk Ltd v HMRC* [2011] UKFTT 423 (TC); *Acornwood LLP v HMRC* [2014] UKFTT 416 (TC); *Rapid Brickwork Ltd v HMRC* [2017] UKFTT 194 (TC); *Manhattan Systems Ltd v HMRC* [2017] UKFTT 862 (TC)

Amending documents (rule 5(3)(c))

The overriding objective encourages flexibility of proceedings. Accordingly, it is the author's view that the parties should generally try to adapt if the case evolves during the litigation process. For example, as evidence comes to light, the other party might drop part of its case. Alternatively, as case law evolves elsewhere, arguments might need to be revised.

In most cases, it should be appropriate for the revised case to be communicated in good time to the other side so as to allow that party to prepare properly for the hearing. Indeed, as confirmed in *Ritchie*, it is technically possible for the tribunal to introduce a new argument at the hearing itself.

On the other hand, there will be cases in which justice is best served by the formal amendment of one or more of the documents before the tribunal. Typically, such documents will be the taxpayer's grounds of appeal or HMRC's statement of case. The purpose of such amendments would be to make it clear that a particular argument is being added or dropped.

Ultimately, it is for the tribunal to decide what formality is necessary on a case-by-case basis. However, in *Rogers*, the Upper Tribunal endorsed "a degree of informality ... in the context of a default paper case involving modest penalties", suggesting that a more formal approach (but not necessarily stipulating how formal) would be appropriate in a more complicated case. Nevertheless, the tribunal made the point that the words used when setting out the arguments being advanced "should be sufficient to identify the precise point that is made so that the other party can respond to it as necessary and the FTT can determine it". In that case, the Upper Tribunal distinguished between an argument that a penalty assessment was invalid and an argument that the preceding notice triggering an obligation to file a tax return (which had not been complied with and which gave rise to the subsequent penalty) was invalid.

In *Award*, it was suggested that a party cannot be compelled to amend a statement of case. Logically, the same could be said concerning a taxpayer's notice of appeal and parties' skeleton arguments. However, the author wonders whether the assumption in *Award* is in fact incorrect. The *Award* case concerned a situation where HMRC's statement of case was unclear. Having initially sought an amendment of the statement of case, the taxpayer changed the application so as to require HMRC to produce a document clarifying certain points (sometimes referred to as "further and better particulars"). In that case, it was clearly unnecessary to amend the original document.

Although the following cases concern formal applications for the amendment of documents, the author's view is that the principles apply with equal force to any attempt by a party to adapt its case during the course of the litigation process.

In *Mander*, the tribunal held that, in order to give rise to a fair trial, the usual rule would be for "all grounds of appeal which have at least some merit" to be considered. The only usual exception to this rule would be in cases where the point has arisen "too late to give the other party time to respond".

Another exception could arise if the point was being taken so late that it deprived the other party of the opportunity to take remedial action. In *Mander*, HMRC were concerned that they would now be too late to issue a revised notice to replace the one that, according to the taxpayer's late point, had been invalidly issued.

In *Rosen*, the tribunal adopted the principle that the tribunal should "allow an amendment which will enable the real dispute between the parties to be adjudicated". In another decision issued on the same day (*Kishore*), the tribunal refused an application by HMRC to introduce a new issue at the hearing itself, because it would inevitably require an adjournment (and, therefore, a delay) so as to permit new evidence to be gathered.

As was made clear in *North Weald*, the approach to be taken by the tribunal is similar to the balancing exercise undertaken when a party seeks to appeal to the tribunal out of time. See **2.4.4**. The point was echoed in *Mehrban*, which commented on the similarity of the approach adopted by the tribunal in the context of rule 5(3)(c) with the later case law on late appeals as consolidated in the case of *Martland*.

Similarly, in *McEnroe*, the tribunal adopted the *Martland* approach, but only after first considering whether the proposed new ground had any real prospect of success.

Nevertheless, in *Microring*, the tribunal declined to adopt the three-part approach in *Martland* and instead considered merely whether permitting the proposed amendment would be in accordance with the overriding objective.

Furthermore, in *Whittalls*, the Upper Tribunal emphasised that different criteria would apply to admission of new grounds in the course of further appeals to the Upper Tribunal (or the higher courts).

In *Scott*, the tribunal considered that a new ground of appeal should not be allowed to be added if it was considered that it would be bound to fail. However, a new ground should be permitted (assuming it was not raised too late, etc.) if it was at least arguable (even if the judge was not persuaded as to its merits).

In *Brown*, it was held that "amend" did not permit a party to revoke a document altogether. Furthermore, as confirmed by the Upper Tribunal in *GLL*, the meaning of "documents" is limited to those formal documents before the tribunal, such as a statement of case and skeleton argument. The term did not cover other routine correspondence that might be had with the tribunal during the course of the proceedings.

Cases: *John Mander Pension Trustees Ltd v HMRC* [2012] UKFTT 686 (TC); *Kishore v HMRC* [2013] UKFTT 465 (TC); *Rosen v HMRC* [2013] UKFTT 466 (TC); *North Weald Golf Club v HMRC* [2014] UKFTT 130 (TC); *Scott v HMRC* [2016] UKFTT 171 (TC); *N Brown Group plc v HMRC* [2016] UKFTT 445 (TC); *Award Drinks Ltd (in liquidation) v HMRC* [2017] UKFTT 509 (TC); *Martland v HMRC* [2018] UKUT 178 (TCC); *GLL BVK Internazionaler Immobilien Spezialfonds v HMRC* [2019] UKUT 17 (TCC); *Microring Ltd v HMRC* [2019] UKFTT 456 (TC); *HMRC v Ritchie* [2019] UKUT 71 (TCC); *Whittalls Wines Ltd v HMRC* [2019] UKUT 260 (TCC); *Mehrban v HMRC* [2019] UKFTT 603 (TC); *HMRC v Rogers* [2019] UKUT 406 (TCC); *McEnroe v HMRC* [2021] UKFTT 94 (TC)

Requiring the provision of a document (rule 5(3)(d))

There are times when a party requires a document which is held by another party (not necessarily a party to the actual case). If the document is needed for the adjudication of the dispute, the tribunal may direct that the person holding the document makes it available to the tribunal or to one (or all) of the parties.

In the author's experience, the tribunal is generally unwilling to make such an order against one of the parties until after the parties have set out which documents they intend to rely on (see **5.10.2** below) and also provided their witness statements (see **6.5.1** below). Nevertheless, the author has certainly seen HMRC making requests at earlier stages in the litigation, only for the tribunal to declare such requests to be premature. Of course, each application should be considered on its own merits.

The author has also seen cases of HMRC requesting a document in the hope that it will contain something useful to assist its case or even something on which it could build a case. That would amount to a "fishing expedition" and should be resisted. See also **4.14.2**.

In *Push*, the tribunal said that the application in that case was not a typical application under rule 5(3)(d) but instead an application for co-operation from the European Commission for materials that might shed light on the meaning of certain provisions of European law. Accordingly, the approach to be taken was to consider whether those documents were "essential in order to dispel all doubts which [the tribunal] may have as regards the validity of the EU act concerned".

See also the discussion on rule 16 below.

Cases: *Igen Distribution Ltd (in liquidation) v HMRC* [2020] UKFTT 328 (TC); *Push Energy Ltd v HMRC* [2021] UKFTT 97 (TC)

The form of any hearing (rule 5(3)(g))

In *Cresswell*, the tribunal considered it inappropriate to relocate a hearing to Cardiff for the convenience of the taxpayer's preferred advocate. The author considers that the decision was probably right but an unusual one and should not be seen as a precedent; a taxpayer's preferred location (if reasonable) will usually be accommodated if proper notice is given early in the process.

Less controversially, it is suggested, was the tribunal's consequential decision which refused to allow the preferred advocate to participate in a two-day hearing via a telephone. The tribunal accepted that there might be cases where such an arrangement was appropriate, but thought that they would be rare.

Indeed, a telephone hearing took place in at least one of the *Spring Capital* cases.

Since those cases, video hearings started to be trialled by the tribunal and very soon afterwards became the temporary norm. Had the *Cresswell* application been considered three years later and had the option of a video hearing been put forward, it is possible (but by no means certain) that the tribunal would have granted the request. In particular, the objections to a very long telephone hearing would have been less compelling. However, the views of the other party and the nature of any witness evidence would also been factors that the tribunal would have to take into account.

Cases: *Cresswell v HMRC* [2017] UKFTT 481 (TC); *Spring Capital Ltd v HMRC* [2018] UKFTT 250 (TC)

Adjourning a hearing (rule 5(3)(h))

In *MHA*, a social security case, the Upper Tribunal held that, when considering whether or not an adjournment should be granted, "the starting point is the reason for the application". In that case, the reason was for additional evidence to be adduced. Therefore, the tribunal was required to consider how useful the additional evidence would be, bearing in mind:

- the evidence already before the tribunal;
- the evidence likely to be obtained if the proceedings were adjourned;
- how long the adjournment would need to be; and
- whether the tribunal could use its expertise to compensate for the lack of additional evidence.

The Upper Tribunal continued by stating that adjournments should not be granted if they are merely a tactical manoeuvre designed to put off the day when, in a tax case, tax would need to be paid.

The Upper Tribunal also considered the potential impact of the adjournment sought on the tribunal system, but commented that the system as a whole is unlikely to be of great significance in most cases and it would be an exceptional case in which an adjournment would be refused solely on account of the needs of the system as a whole. The author suggests that this might be more of an issue if a lead case had been selected and a great number of cases were dependent on its outcome. An adjournment in the lead case to accommodate a new but relatively minor matter might well be considered inappropriate. Conversely, if the new matter affected a large number of the cases that were dependent on the lead case, that fact might itself tip the balance in favour of an adjournment.

In *Wright*, it was noted that an adjournment on medical grounds would normally be given. However, where there was a risk that medical grounds would lead to an indefinite adjournment, the public interest in the finality of litigation would at some point prevail. In another case, *Westminster*, the Upper Tribunal noted that the First-tier was "initially inclined to conclude in favour of an adjournment [but it was] the nature of the medical evidence and the uncertainty as to when, if at all, [the individual] would be able to participate that ultimately tipped the balance in the other direction".

In *Mattu*, a case which started in the Upper Tribunal, the Upper Tribunal refused to grant an adjournment on the basis of an unsubstantiated self-diagnosis and self-admission into a hospital. The tribunal noted that, were the case to proceed in the taxpayer's absence, HMRC would withdraw an allegation of dishonesty (which implicitly would have merited the taxpayer's presence). Furthermore, the tribunal made it clear that the case was primarily one of law rather than fact and that it would take a flexible approach to the timing of proceedings so as to allow the taxpayer to give evidence.

Cases: *MHA v Secretary of State for Work and Pensions* [2009] UKUT 211 (AAC); *Wright (No. 2) v HMRC* [2013] UKUT 481 (TCC); *Westminster Trading Ltd v HMRC* [2017] UKUT 23 (TCC); *HMRC v Mattu* [2021] UKUT 245 (TCC)

Staying (or, in Scotland, sisting) proceedings (rule 5(3)(j))

One principle of justice is the avoidance or minimisation of a delay before a matter is considered by a tribunal. Indeed, in *DEFRA v Downs*, Sullivan LJ considered a stay to be the exception rather than the rule: reasons supporting a stay would be "normally some form of irremediable harm if no stay is granted". However, there will conversely be cases in which the interests of justice point towards matters being put on hold. For example, it would not be an appropriate use of the tribunal's or the parties' resources for a case to be heard if the matter might subsequently prove to be academic.

This might be (as in *Davies*) because the taxpayer has commenced parallel proceedings in another court or tribunal which, if successful, would obviate the need for the tribunal hearing. Alternatively, the matter might involve a question of law that is already the subject of another appeal in relation to another taxpayer: in such a case, it would often make sense for the tribunal and the parties to see how that other case progresses before deciding the matter in hand.

Thus, in *Teletape*, the tribunal, following the Court of Session in *RBS Deutschland*, said that a stay would be appropriate if a tribunal or Court "considered that a decision in another Court would be of material assistance in resolving the issues before [it] and that it was expedient to do so". The tribunal also acknowledged that cases can sometimes be stayed for years on this basis. However, if a long stay is proposed, the applicant would need to show that the outcome in the other case is likely to render unnecessary a hearing in the stayed case. The tribunal also noted that the key question is the administration of justice and not merely the various parties' views on whether or not any delay is prejudicial to their case.

In *Ticketmaster*, the Upper Tribunal noted that "the dual considerations of material assistance and expediency, identified in *RBS*, are simply a rewrapping of the overriding objective". Accordingly, it considered that a tribunal should give due weight to the questions of material expediency and expediency, "but, ultimately, the tribunal must ensure that the case is dealt with fairly and justly". *Ticketmaster* was not a case in the Tax Chamber. However, in *Barclays*, the tribunal had no hesitation in adopting the *Ticketmaster* approach. The author considers the tribunal to have been entirely correct in taking that view.

The earlier *RBS* approach was followed in *Pinewood* where, despite a clear difference in facts, the tribunal considered that another appeal on the same question of law which was being heard in the Upper Tribunal could mean that it was appropriate for the case to be stayed. Similarly, in *Gandalf*, the tribunal held:

> "Different factual scenarios are not in themselves a reason to refuse the stay. [The tribunal] must consider the questions of interpretation referred [to the other court] and the likelihood [that the court] ... would uncover issues of legal principle which will materially assist in the resolution of the issues in the appeals before the Tribunal."

Nevertheless, in *Waverton*, it was recognised that there is still a difference between cases involving merely similar legal issues and those where there are also factual distinctions between the two cases.

As noted in *Degorce*, "the question is not whether the determination of another court might provide assistance, but whether it will provide assistance". In refusing an application for a stay, the tribunal was also conscious of the benefits in not delaying the hearing of oral evidence from witnesses.

In *Gardner-Shaw*, the considered that the net effect of *DEFRA* was no different from that in *RBS*. The tribunal went on to consider the balancing exercise, noting that a continued stay could have had a detrimental effect on the taxpayers' continued ability to trade.

In *Global*, the tribunal considered that criminal proceedings elsewhere should take precedence over the appeal in the tribunal as there was a risk of prejudice in the criminal proceedings in respect of findings of fact that the tribunal might make. A different conclusion, however, was reached in *Aabsolute Bond*.

Similarly, in *Dong*, a stay was requested pending the resolution of criminal proceedings. The tribunal did not consider that the existence of those proceedings was determinative, given that the criminal court and/or the tribunal could take measures to prevent the criminal proceedings being prejudiced. However, because the two sets of proceedings were otherwise likely to be heard at the same time, a provisional stay was directed so as to ensure that the parties could properly prepare for both.

In *Badzyan*, the tribunal accepted that a stay was appropriate to allow a related appeal to progress. But HMRC's request that the stay be indefinite was rejected. It directed a six-month stay so as to allow the situation to be reviewed.

In *Peries*, the tribunal considered that parallel proceedings in the High Court were not sufficient to give rise to a stay in the tribunal. The distinction was that, in theory at least, the High Court proceedings would not make the tribunal appeal academic.

The tribunal also considered in *Peries* that the shortage of funds was not in itself a reason to stay proceedings in the tribunal as parties are not required to instruct lawyers. It is arguable that this might depend on the circumstances of the particular case, especially if a taxpayer's impecuniosity is reasonably likely to be short-lived. However, a tribunal will always ensure that unrepresented taxpayers are given a fair hearing, so there would have to be a good reason to show why a stay is appropriate in other cases.

In *Dollar*, the tribunal was faced with a number of unattractive options. It was unwilling to stand down witnesses who were ready to give evidence at a full appeal hearing taking place a week after the application hearing and it was also unwilling to duck the stay application and leave it for the tribunal due to hear the full appeal. On the other hand, there was one aspect of the appeal which was already due to be heard by the Upper Tribunal (following a transfer under rule 28), and the First-tier was not willing to risk a duplication of effort if the matter were to be decided by the First-tier in the meantime. Balancing these concerns, the FTT directed that the hearing proceed as originally planned, with all evidence heard at that

Ch. 4 – General powers and provisions under the rules

time, but stayed all matters of law relating to the issue that will be considered by the Upper Tribunal in that other case.

Cases: *Global Active Holdings (in the appeal of Global Active Technologies (dissolved) v HMRC)* (2006) VDT 19715; *HMRC v RBS Deutschland Holdings GmbH* [2006] CSIH 10; *DEFRA v Downs* [2009] EWCA Civ 257; *Peries v HMRC* [2011] UKFTT 674 (TC); *R(oao Davies and another) v HMRC* [2011] UKSC 47; *Daryanani and Others t/a Teletape v HMRC* [2012] UKFTT 319 (TC); *Pinewood Studios Ltd v HMRC* [2012] UKFTT 370 (TC); *Gandalf IT Ltd v HMRC* [2012] UKFTT 573 (TC); *Aabsolute Bond Ltd v HMRC* [2012] UKFTT 603 (TC); *Gui Hui Dong v NCA* [2016] UKFTT 116 (TC); *Degorce v HMRC* [2016] UKFTT 429 (TC); *Badzyan v HMRC* [2017] UKFTT 439 (TC); *Waverton Property LLP v HMRC* [2017] UKFTT 853 (TC); *Gardner-Shaw UK Ltd v HMRC* [2018] UKFTT 313 (TC); *Ticketmaster UK Ltd v The Information Commissioner* [2021] UKFTT 83 (GRC); *Barclays Services Ltd v HMRC* [2021] UKFTT 151 (TC); *Dollar Financial UK Ltd v HMRC* [2021] UKFTT 218 (TC)

4.2.5 Other case management decisions

Expediting a hearing

Occasionally, it is considered that a case is particularly urgent and needs to be determined sooner than when it would otherwise be heard. In *Manhattan*, the tribunal considered that a party seeking to expedite a hearing had to prove the "objective urgency" of the matter, for which there is a high threshold. The other party's view is rarely of importance, except to the extent that the expedition of the hearing would cause it some real prejudice. Nevertheless, this did not preclude that other party from making any representations in response to the application.

In the *Manhattan* case itself, the tribunal noted that the case involved HMRC compulsorily deregistering a taxpayer from VAT, which could lead to a real likelihood of serious irreversible damage. Consequently, the tribunal considered that, in such cases, HMRC should be prepared to make the appeal ready for a hearing with reasonable expedition and that the tribunal should issue case management directions on such a basis.

In *Impact*, the tribunal acknowledged that it may be possible to justify expedition on grounds other than a real likelihood of serious irreversible damage. That case, however, concerned the potential collapse of a business where the tribunal accepted that oral evidence of a director was acceptable (subject to being challenged under cross-examination): documentary and/or expert evidence were not essential.

Cases: *Manhattan Systems Ltd v HMRC* [2017] UKFTT 862 (TC); *Impact Contracting Solutions Ltd v HMRC* [2019] UKFTT 646 (TC)

4.2.6 Preliminary matters

Although one might imagine that a tribunal would wish to deal with all issues in one go, there are sometimes cases where a different approach is appropriate.

For example, the determination of one discrete issue might determine the entire dispute between the parties. In such a case, it might prove unnecessary for the parties and the tribunal to consider the entirety of the dispute as it might be resolved far more simply.

This approach was considered by the Special Commissioner in *Hankinson* (the first of many hearings involving that taxpayer). Mr Hankinson faced a discovery assessment which was raised on the basis that he had negligently assessed himself to have been non-resident in the 1998-99 tax year. Mr Hankinson wanted the question of negligence to be resolved as a preliminary matter so as to obviate the need for a detailed resolution of his actual residence status. The Special Commissioner held that "the purpose of a preliminary hearing can only be to decide issues that will dispose of the case or at least substantially reduce the area of dispute".

In that case, it was considered that the two separate questions that required resolution (the taxpayer's residence status and his alleged negligence in considering himself to be non-resident) involved a substantial overlap of facts and evidence. For this reason, the Special Commissioner declined to treat the question of negligence as a preliminary matter. However, as subsequent case law makes clear (*Milligan*, *Arunvill*), a preliminary hearing can be considered appropriate in some discovery cases.

In *Kishore*, the tribunal refused an application by HMRC to have a matter treated at a preliminary hearing. One of the reasons given was the fact that the matter would require evidence and such matters are best left for final hearings.

In *Wrottesley*, the Upper Tribunal referred to a list of criteria to be considered before deciding whether to order the determination of a preliminary issue. These are:

- The matter should be approached on the basis that the power to deal with matters separately at a preliminary hearing should be exercised with caution and used sparingly.

- The power should be exercised only where there is a "succinct, knockout point" which will dispose of the case or an aspect of the case. In this context an aspect of the case would normally mean a separate issue rather than a point which is a step in the analysis in arriving at a conclusion on a single issue. In addition, if there is a risk that determination of the preliminary issue may prove to be irrelevant then the point is unlikely to be a "knockout" one.

- An aspect of the requirement that the point must be a succinct one is that it must be capable of being decided after a relatively short hearing (as compared to the rest of the case) and without significant delay. This is unlikely if (a) the issue cannot be entirely divorced from the evidence and submissions relevant to the rest of the case, or (b) if a substantial body of evidence will require to be considered. This point explains why preliminary questions will usually be points of law. The tribunal should be particularly cautious on matters of mixed fact and law.

- Regard should be had to whether there is any risk that determination of the preliminary issue could hinder the tribunal in arriving at a just result at a subsequent hearing of the remainder of the case. This is clearly more likely if the issues overlap in some way.

- Account should be taken of any potential for overall delay, making allowance for the possibility of a separate appeal on the preliminary issue.

- The possibility that determination of the preliminary issue may result in there being no need for a further hearing should be considered.

- Consideration should be given to whether determination of the preliminary issue would significantly cut down the cost and time required for pre-trial preparation or for the trial itself, or whether it could in fact increase costs overall.
- The tribunal should at all times have in mind the overall objective of the tribunal rules, namely, to enable the tribunal to deal with cases fairly and justly.

As for the first of these criteria, it was noted in *Coast Telecom* that caution should operate as a tie-breaker rather than a criterion in its own right.

It is noteworthy that, in *Mehrban*, the tribunal was dealing with a discovery assessment in a back-duty case involving a small general store. The tribunal disposed of the appeal by concluding that the discovery assessments were invalid and the tribunal therefore did not need to embark upon the many other grounds of appeal raised by the taxpayer. Although the tribunal was conscious that the validity of the discovery assessments was likely to be the subject of further appeals, the tribunal noted that "much time, energy and expense could have been saved if the 'discovery issue' had been dealt with as a preliminary issue".

The author has seen cases (where the preliminary issue would not have disposed of the whole appeal) where a matter has been dealt with as a preliminary issue but with any subsequent appeal being deferred until after resolution of the rest of the appeal. This approach reduces the risk of the substantive appeal being delayed for an inordinately long period pending the final resolution of the preliminary issue.

Cases: *Hankinson v HMRC* (2008) Sp C 649; *Kishore v HMRC* [2013] UKFTT 465 (TC); *Rt Hon Baron Wrottesley v HMRC* [2015] UKUT 637 (TCC); *Milligan v HMRC* [2017] UKFTT 552 (TC); *Arunvill Global Equity Trading Ltd v HMRC* [2018] UKFTT 378 (TC); *Coast Telecom Ltd v HMRC* [2019] UKFTT 596 (TC); *Mehrban v HMRC* [2021] UKFTT 53 (TC)

Decisions in principle

Related to this is the concept of decisions in principle.

Very often, the tribunal will be faced with two different types of dispute – a legal question and a practical question which is dependent on the outcome of the legal question. For example, there might be issues concerning the correct amount of the assessment but the parties might also disagree as to whether the assessment was validly issued in the first place. Alternatively, the tribunal might be faced with an appeal against an information notice where the taxpayer is challenging both the validity of the notice itself as well as the request for the individual pieces of information specified on the notice.

In many cases, it is pragmatic for all questions to be dealt with at the same time. In others, however, it will be sufficient for the tribunal to reach a decision "in principle" which will cover the legal issues.

The tribunal will usually do so when it is confident that the parties will be able to resolve any consequential matters between themselves (for example, agreed adjustments to the assessments). In such cases, the tribunal will announce that the parties have the right to return to the tribunal if those other matters still require resolution. However, it is usually the case that such a return visit will prove unnecessary.

The *Murray Group* case is an example, however, where the parties were unable to reach an agreement, following a decision on the principles. Furthermore, it was a case where HMRC (who lost in the First-tier) were seeking to appeal against the decision, whilst there were still matters to be resolved in the First-tier. That meant a dispute as to which of the outstanding matters should be heard first: HMRC's appeal in the Upper Tribunal or the remaining matters in the First-tier (so that the taxpayer's appeal could be fully concluded in the First-tier and the Upper Tribunal could then be seised of the whole case).

There is no single right answer in such cases: each depends on the circumstances of the particular case. In *Murray Group*, the tribunal favoured HMRC's preferred approach of proceeding with the appeal in the Upper Tribunal and staying the proceedings in the First-tier.

In *Vaccine Research*, a different question arose. A decision in principle was given which was then upheld in the Upper Tribunal. The parties could not then reach a conclusion on the remaining issues and the matter went back to the First-tier. The taxpayer wanted to introduce new arguments that were consequential on the earlier proceedings and which had not already been resolved. Applying a holistic approach of fairness, the First-tier said that these new arguments could be raised.

Cases: *HMRC v Murray Group Holdings Ltd* (2013) FTC/15/2013; *The Vaccine Research Limited Partnership v HMRC* [2018] UKFTT 597 (TC)

4.2.7 Choosing a particular judge

DDR concerned a case in which, at a preliminary stage in the proceedings, one judge had refused to admit new evidence into a case, but – at a subsequent hearing – another judge considered that new evidence could be adduced by HMRC. The taxpayer applied to the tribunal to have that later direction set aside and requested that the first judge hear the application. The application was, in the end, heard by a third judge who ruled that the tribunal was "independent" and parties cannot choose which "judge or member … hears their case or any interim application made in respect of it". The tribunal referred to the *Tribunals, Courts and Enforcement Act* 2007, noting that the choice of judge is a matter of the discretion of the President of Tribunals, although this is something that may be delegated to the respective Chamber President.

It was further suggested that the procedure in rule 5(2) cannot be used by a party in order to choose any particular judge. The tribunal reached this conclusion because the allocation of a particular judge does not relate to the "conduct or disposal of proceedings" and the tribunal considered that the scope of the rule implies that it is limited to "the conduct of proceedings *by the parties*".

Although the author recognises that the allocation of judge is a matter for the President of Tribunals, he is not persuaded that such matters cannot be the subject of a direction under rule 5 (in which the tribunal effectively imposes a direction on itself). Indeed, the author was involved with one case in the Tax Chamber which turned on a specific and specialist point of employment law. It was noted that the list of people entitled to sit as judges in the Tax Chambers includes Employment Tribunal judges and it was considered that the interest of justice would dictate that the case be heard by a judge with the relevant expertise.

An application was therefore made to for the case to be heard by such a judge (albeit not for any specific individual). Although the application eventually succeeded given the exceptional nature of the case, it was stated that the request should not have been made by application but merely by letter to the President of the Chamber. It is not clear to the author why this should be the case and why the ordinary application process is inappropriate, especially given the differing view taken by the other party in the case (HMRC). However, should the issue ever arise again, the author's experience should be noted.

Law: TCEA 2007, s. 4(1)(e), Sch. 4, para. 14

Case: *DDR Distributions Ltd v HMRC* [2012] UKFTT 443 (TC)

4.2.8 Challenging a judge for bias

It is extremely unlikely that a judge would be biased in favour of one party. Occasionally, however, cases arise in which, although there is no actual bias, there is nevertheless the risk of bias.

When a challenge should be made

In such cases, the risk should be highlighted to the tribunal at the earliest opportunity so that the individual member (or members) of the tribunal can have the chance to recuse themselves from the proceedings. In such cases, it is alternatively possible for parties to waive concerns of bias provided that it is properly brought to their attention and they have the opportunity to make a reasoned decision whether or not to proceed with the case.

This is what happened in *Bhardwaj* and therefore, despite perceived bias having arisen, the claimant was unable to use this as the basis of her subsequent appeal, because the original tribunal had given her (and she declined) the opportunity to have a fresh hearing.

Case: *Bhardwaj v FDA & Others* (2012) UKEAT/0157/11/ZT

An incorrect assertion of bias

In *Watson*, the taxpayer's accountant was described as having "a significant misconception as to the status of the Tribunals". This was because he described HMRC as the judge's "ultimate paymaster". The decision notice therefore made a point of explaining that the tribunals are part of an entirely separate government department, the Ministry of Justice, and HMRC has no influence (whether financial or otherwise) on the result of any appeal.

In the author's view, the accountant's letter was expressing a slightly different concern. Although the Ministry of Justice and its judges are separate from HMRC and do not operate under HMRC control, the author infers that the accountant was merely noting the fact that the Ministry of Justice is funded from the Exchequer in the same way as other government departments and this funding is therefore (indirectly) dependent on HMRC being able to collect tax. In the author's view, this indirect tension is probably inevitable. However, the author has no reason to believe that this at all influences the way that any judge deals with a case and is happy that the cases are decided on their individual merits.

Another rejection of the suggestion of bias arose in *Couldwell* when the judge distinguished between a robust rejection of an argument put forward on behalf of a taxpayer and "views ... in such extreme and unbalanced terms as to throw doubt on [the judge's] ability to try the issue with an objective judicial mind".

A similar position was taken by the Upper Tribunal in *Butt*.

Cases: *Watson t/a Kirkwood Coaches v HMRC* [2013] UKFTT 553 (TC); *Couldwell Concrete Flooring Ltd v HMRC (No. 2)* [2017] UKFTT 85 (TC); *Butt v HMRC* [2017] UKUT 325 (TCC)

Connection between judges and parties

A risk of bias can exist if there is a connection between the judge and one of the parties. Alternatively, a risk arises if the judge has made comments which can give the impression of prejudging the issue before the tribunal. For example, in *Oni* (an employment case), the judge made comments about the employee's conduct of the case: those comments would have been relevant had a costs application been made. However, at that stage, no such application had been made and the comments were directed at the strength of the employee's claim itself. It was held on appeal that the subsequent (perhaps inevitable) costs application should have been heard by a differently constituted tribunal so as to avoid the risk of the matter appearing to have been prejudged.

As noted in the subsequent case of *Hussain*, this does not preclude a judge providing early warning of the risk of a possible costs claim from the other side. The test in all such cases is that pertaining to allegations of judicial bias, being whether the tribunal's prior conduct "would cause the informed and impartial observer to consider that there was a possibility of bias".

A similar issue arose in *Sheth*. Dr Sheth successfully appealed to the Upper Tribunal against a decision of the FTT to refuse him permission to bring a late appeal. In the course of its deliberations, the FTT had expressed views concerning the strength of Dr Sheth's case. Doing so was wholly appropriate given the exercise that the FTT was undertaking (see **2.4.4** and **2.4.5**). However, given that the case was proceeding to a full hearing, the Upper Tribunal considered it appropriate for the full case to be heard by a judge who had not yet formed even any preliminary views on the strength of Dr Sheth's case.

One of the strengths of the Tax Chamber is that most of its judges are tax specialists, some of whom are only part-time judges and with a full-time professional practice at the Bar or as a solicitor. It will often be the case, therefore, that an individual will serve as a judge on one occasion and subsequently appear as an advocate. In general, this should cause no difficulties. However, the employment case of *Bhardwaj* demonstrates that any member with whom the individual sat in a judicial capacity should not appear as a member in a subsequent case in which the individual subsequently appears as an advocate.

It is possible that this issue has not arisen in the Tax Chamber because of careful steps taken by the tribunals service to avoid such difficulties. Nevertheless, the point is mentioned for the purposes of completeness.

Cases: *Oni v NHS Leicester City* (2012) UKEAT/0144/12/LA; *Bhardwaj v FDA & Others* (2012) UKEAT/0157/11/ZT; *Hussain v Nottingham Healthcare NHS Trust* (2016) UKEAT/0080/16/DM; *Sheth v HMRC* [2021] UKUT 164 (TCC)

4.2.9 Applying for directions

See rule 6 which considers the procedure for parties to apply for such directions.

4.3 Rule 5A – Coronavirus temporary rule (decisions without a hearing)

5A(1) Notwithstanding anything in rule 24(2) (basic cases), rule 26(7) (further steps in a default paper case) and rule 29 (determination with or without a hearing), the Tribunal may make a decision which disposes of proceedings without a hearing if the Tribunal considers that the conditions in paragraph (2) are satisfied.

5A(2) The conditions are that–

(a) the matter is urgent;

(b) it is not reasonably practicable for there to be a hearing (including a hearing where the proceedings would be conducted wholly or partly as video proceedings or audio proceedings); and

(c) it is in the interests of justice to do so.

5A(3) This rule does not prejudice any power of the Tribunal to make a decision which disposes of proceedings without a hearing otherwise than under this rule.

4.3.1 Overview

This rule is the first of three temporary provisions introduced following the onset of the Covid-19 pandemic. It took effect on 10 April 2020 and is due to expire on 24 March 2022.

However, a minister can accelerate the expiry date or (for up to six months at a time) defer the expiry date.

The rule provides a temporary relaxation of the usual position that requires a hearing before any decision is made for the disposal of proceedings.

Law: *Coronavirus Act* 2020, s. 89(1), 90; SI 2020/416, r. 1(2)

4.3.2 Removal of need for a hearing (rule 5A(1))

The rule initially makes reference to the provisions in rule 24(2) (see **5.7**), rule 26(7) (see **5.9.4**) and rule 29 (see **7.1.1**). For each of the various categories of case (see **5.6.3**), other than the default paper category, those rules each provide the general position that a hearing must take place before any decision is made that disposes of the proceedings (or a part of the proceedings).

The rule continues to provide that the need for a hearing can, however, be suspended if certain conditions are satisfied.

4.3.3 When a hearing may be dispensed with (rule 5A(2))

Three conditions need to be satisfied if the need for a hearing is to be dispensed with. They are that:

- the matter is urgent;
- it is not reasonably practicable for there to be a hearing (including a hearing where the proceedings would be conducted wholly or partly as video proceedings or audio proceedings); and
- it is in the interests of justice to do so.

These are exacting conditions for truly exceptional cases. The author is unaware of the power having been exercised in the Tax Chamber since its introduction.

4.3.4 Other cases when a hearing is unnecessary (rule 5A(3))

Finally, the rule ensures that this temporary measure does not affect other provisions that also permit the tribunal to make a decision which disposes of proceedings without a hearing. For example:

- strike-outs for breach of an unless order (**4.6.2**);
- the determination of default paper cases (**5.9.4**); and
- when the parties and the tribunal agree that a hearing is not necessary (**7.1.3**).

4.4 Rule 6 – Procedure for applying for and giving directions

6(1) The Tribunal may give a direction on the application of one or more of the parties or on its own initiative.

6(2) An application for a direction may be made–

(a) by sending or delivering a written application to the Tribunal; or

(b) orally during the course of a hearing.

4.4 Rule 6 – Procedure for applying for and giving directions

> 6(3) An application for a direction must include the reasons for making that application.
>
> 6(4) Unless the Tribunal considers that there is good reason not to do so, the Tribunal must send written notice of any direction to every party and to any other person affected by the direction.
>
> 6(5) If a party or other person sent notice of the direction under paragraph (4) wishes to challenge a direction which the Tribunal has given, they may do so by applying for another direction which amends, suspends or sets aside the first direction.

4.4.1 Overview

This rule makes it clear that the tribunal may unilaterally make a direction. It will often do so as a matter of course to lay down a timetable so as to get a case ready for the eventual hearing. The tribunal may also issue directions unilaterally if it is unsure whether or not a case is proceeding and wishes to prompt a response from one or other of the parties.

Alternatively, any party may apply to the tribunal for a direction to be made. This will often be done if the party wishes the case to be handled in a particular way (or, for example, if it wishes the tribunal to extend the time for compliance with an earlier direction).

4.4.2 Applying for directions (rule 6(2), (3))

Ordinarily, a party making an application will do so in writing sent or delivered to the tribunal. There is no standard form – a letter will suffice, so will an e-mail.

However, the need for a direction (or an application for a direction) will not always be apparent until one is actually at a hearing. Therefore, an application for a direction may also be made orally at a hearing.

Need for reasons

Even if an application is made orally, it is necessary for reasons to be given for it. In other words, the application should be along the following lines: "I am asking the tribunal to direct X because Y".

Seeking prior agreement

Although parties may unilaterally write to the tribunal to seek a direction, it is generally appropriate for a party first to ascertain whether or not the proposed course of action is agreed by the other parties. This should obviate the need for the tribunal to seek the views of the other parties and/or to propose a course of action subject to the receipt of any objections.

Although the practice until now in the Tax Chamber has been to accommodate unilateral applications, the author believes that parties should adopt a more collaborative approach in accordance with the Upper Tribunal's guidance in *Dorset*, wherever reasonably practicable. Accordingly, parties should generally seek the other's view before contacting the tribunal and, where agreement is reached, this should be made clear to the tribunal. Although not required to do so, the tribunal will generally respect the parties' agreed position.

In *BPP*, the Court of Appeal's view was that HMRC ought to try to reach agreement with the taxpayer in cases where HMRC were likely to miss a time limit. The tribunal is very likely to adopt this approach. Furthermore, in *Huitson*, the Upper Tribunal described HMRC's failure to send the taxpayer copies of correspondence with the tribunal as failing to co-operate with the tribunal and therefore a breach of the overriding objective

Although the Supreme Court in *BPP* did not refer to this part of the Court of Appeal's judgment, the author sees no reason to suggest that it is wrong in law.

Cases: *Dorset Healthcare NHS Foundation Trust v MH* [2009] UKUT 4 (AAC); *BPP Holdings Ltd v HMRC* [2016] EWCA Civ 121; *HMRC v BPP Holdings Ltd* [2017] UKSC 55; *Huitson v HMRC* [2017] UKUT 715 (TCC)

4.4.3 Dealing with applications for directions

If an application for a direction is made orally, the tribunal will usually explain there and then how it will wish to deal with it.

If an application is made in writing, however, it will not always be appropriate for the matter to be dealt with at a hearing. Very often, the tribunal (either a judge or a member of the tribunal staff) will take a view as to the appropriate approach and will make a direction without a hearing.

Examples will include applications for the postponement of a previously-arranged hearing, requests for the extensions of time limits for the preparation and submission of documents and applications for the re-categorisation of a case.

4.4.4 Notice of directions (rule 6(4), (5))

As a general rule, the tribunal should then send written notice of any direction to each of the parties and also to any other person affected by the direction. There is no such requirement, however, if the tribunal considers that there is good reason not to give such notice.

Any person who is sent such a notice and wishes to challenge a direction given by the tribunal may do so by applying for another direction which amends, suspends or sets aside the first direction.

Rule 6(5) was considered in *DDR*. The tribunal expressed concern that directions could, if the rule were interpreted literally, be the subject of endless litigation and inferred that there should be some restriction on the use of the provision. Noting the similarity with the provisions in rule 38, it was considered that applications under rule 6(5) should be made only "in limited circumstances, and in particular where circumstances have changed, [there was an] obvious error of law in [the] direction, [a] procedural irregularity in relation to the hearing at which [the] direction [was] made, [or] a party did not appear and was not represented at the directions hearing". *DDR* was endorsed by the Upper Tribunal in *Clear*.

See also **4.2.3** above.

Cases: *DDR Distributions Ltd v HMRC* [2012] UKFTT 443 (TC); *Clear plc (in liquidation) v HMRC* (2014) PTA/88/2011

4.5 Rule 7 – Failure to comply with rules etc.

> 7(1) An irregularity resulting from a failure to comply with any requirement in these Rules, a practice direction or a direction does not of itself render void the proceedings or any step taken in the proceedings.
>
> 7(2) If a party has failed to comply with a requirement in these Rules, a practice direction or a direction, the Tribunal may take such action as it considers just, which may include–
>
> (a) waiving the requirement;

> (b) requiring the failure to be remedied;
> (c) exercising its power under rule 8 (striking out a party's case);
> (d) restricting a party's participation in proceedings; or
> (e) exercising its power under paragraph (3).
>
> 7(3) The Tribunal may refer to the Upper Tribunal, and ask the Upper Tribunal to exercise its power under section 25 of the 2007 Act (Upper Tribunal to have powers of High Court or Court of Session) in relation to, any failure by a person to comply with a requirement imposed by the Tribunal–
>
> > (a) to attend at any place for the purpose of giving evidence;
> > (b) otherwise to make themselves available to give evidence;
> > (c) to swear an oath in connection with the giving of evidence;
> > (d) to give evidence as a witness;
> > (e) to produce a document; or
> > (f) to facilitate the inspection of a document or any other thing (including any premises).

4.5.1 Overview

This rule further emphasises the flexibility of tribunal proceedings, subject to the caveat that rules and directions should not be routinely ignored.

4.5.2 Tribunal's failure to comply (rule 7(1))

Wherever the tribunal fails to observe any requirement in the Procedure Rules, a practice direction or any other direction, there is an argument that this could give rise to a procedural irregularity that renders void either the proceedings or some step taken in the proceedings.

Rule 7(1) provides that any such irregularity does not have such an effect. In other words, the lawfulness of any subsequent decision by the tribunal cannot be brought into question merely because a procedural irregularity has occurred.

The rule does not, however, allow the tribunal to waive any formality set out in statute. Therefore, for example, a direct tax appeal may be notified to the tribunal only if the taxpayer has first made an appeal to HMRC (see **2.3.1**). If that condition is not met, the tribunal has no power to waive it.

Law: TMA 1970, s. 49A(2), 49H (and similar provisions elsewhere)

4.5.3   A party's failure to comply (rule 7(2))

If a party has failed to comply with any requirement in the Procedure Rules, a practice direction or any other direction (but, again, not any statutory requirement), the tribunal may take any such action as it considers just, including:

- waiving the requirement;
- requiring the failure to be remedied;
- exercising its power to strike out a party's case (under rule 8);
- restricting a party's participation in the proceedings; or
- in cases involving failures to provide information, exercising its power to refer the matter to the Upper Tribunal under rule 7(3).

The overriding restriction on the tribunal's action in the event of any such compliance failure is that the tribunal must act justly. Thus parties should not expect the tribunal to overlook a breach automatically: it will need to be shown that justice requires the breach to be overlooked.

As noted by the tribunal in *Eclipse (No. 2)*, "it is a truism that directions made by the tribunal are meant to be complied with". This was subsequently the clear message from the Supreme Court in *BPP*.

In *Moreton*, the tribunal considered HMRC's failure to deal with a particular issue in their statement of case (see rule 25) and applied rule 7(2)(d) so as to prevent HMRC from cross-examining the taxpayer's expert witness on a particular aspect of the appeal.

Cases: *Eclipse Film Partners No. 35 LLP v HMRC* (No. 2) [2010] UKFTT 448 (FT); *Moreton Alarm Services (MAS) Ltd v HMRC* [2016] UKFTT 192 (TC); *HMRC v BPP Holdings Ltd* [2017] UKSC 55

4.5.4 Failures to provide information (rule 7(3))

Rule 7(3) provides some balance to parties where another party has shown reluctance to provide certain information despite being so required by the tribunal.

The FTT has no powers of its own to compel a person to comply. However, the Upper Tribunal does under s. 25 of the 2007 Act. To ensure that the FTT's requirements cannot be routinely ignored, rule 7(3) entitles the tribunal to refer any of the following matters to the Upper Tribunal in relation to a breach of a requirement by the tribunal:

- a failure to attend at any place for the purpose of giving evidence;
- any other failure to make oneself available to give evidence;
- a failure to swear an oath in connection with the giving of evidence;
- a failure to give evidence as a witness;
- a failure to produce a document; or
- in order to facilitate the inspection of a document or any other thing (for example, premises).

This rule corresponds with rule 16 where such requirements can be imposed by the tribunal.

Upper Tribunal's powers

Under s. 25, the Upper Tribunal has the same powers, rights, privileges and authority as the High Court (in England and Wales and in Northern Ireland) and as the Court of Session (in Scotland). These courts have inherent jurisdiction to fine or even imprison individuals for non-compliance with orders.

Law: TCEA 2007, s. 25

4.6 Rule 8 – Striking out a party's case

> 8(1) The proceedings, or the appropriate part of them, will automatically be struck out if the appellant has failed to comply with a direction that stated that failure by a party

4.6 Rule 8 – Striking out a party's case

to comply with the direction would lead to the striking out of the proceedings or that part of them.

8(2) The Tribunal must strike out the whole or a part of the proceedings if the Tribunal–

(a) does not have jurisdiction in relation to the proceedings or that part of them; and

(b) does not exercise its power under rule 5(3)(k)(i) (transfer to another court or tribunal) in relation to the proceedings or that part of them.

8(3) The Tribunal may strike out the whole or a part of the proceedings if–

(a) the appellant has failed to comply with a direction which stated that failure by the appellant to comply with the direction could lead to the striking out of the proceedings or part of them;

(b) the appellant has failed to co-operate with the Tribunal to such an extent that the Tribunal cannot deal with the proceedings fairly and justly; or

(c) the Tribunal considers there is no reasonable prospect of the appellant's case, or part of it, succeeding.

8(4) The Tribunal may not strike out the whole or a part of the proceedings under paragraphs (2) or (3)(b) or (c) without first giving the appellant an opportunity to make representations in relation to the proposed striking out.

8(5) If the proceedings, or part of them, have been struck out under paragraphs (1) or (3)(a), the appellant may apply for the proceedings, or part of them, to be reinstated.

8(6) An application under paragraph (5) must be made in writing and received by the Tribunal within 28 days after the date that the Tribunal sent notification of the striking out to the appellant.

8(7) This rule applies to a respondent as it applies to an appellant except that–

95

> (a) a reference to the striking out of the proceedings must be read as a reference to the barring of the respondent from taking further part in the proceedings; and
>
> (b) a reference to an application for the reinstatement of proceedings which have been struck out must be read as a reference to an application for the lifting of the bar on the respondent taking further part in the proceedings.
>
> 8(8) If a respondent has been barred from taking further part in proceedings under this rule and that bar has not been lifted, the Tribunal need not consider any response or other submissions made by that respondent, and may summarily determine any or all issues against that respondent.

4.6.1 Overview

Rule 8 provides further reminders that failures to comply with tribunal directions can have serious consequences. However, its scope is wider and it in fact deals with a range of situations in which the tribunal can strike out the whole or part of proceedings.

A strike out means that any argument in respect of the proceedings (or part of them) is simply ignored as if it did not exist. The case of *Foulser* considered the extent to which a tribunal could strike out a case other than in accordance with rule 8. The tribunal considered that such a direction could be given under rule 5 if fairness and justice dictate. (See **4.2.2** above.)

In *BPP*, the Supreme Court recognised that a strike-out could lead to a potential windfall for the other party. However, that factor should not be taken into account "save in exceptional circumstances" as otherwise it would "undermine the utility of the sanction". Nevertheless, the court recognised that it ought not to be used in cases where it would be "impermissibly harsh".

Cases: *Foulser v HMRC* [2011] UKFTT 642 (TC); *HMRC v BPP Holdings Ltd* [2017] UKSC 55

Distinction between appellants and respondents

The rule operates differently so far as appellants and respondents are concerned. Generally, the rule is worded in respect of appellants but (albeit in a tempered way) is extended so as to apply to respondents. See rule 8(7), (8).

4.6.2 Breach of "unless orders" (rule 8(1))

Rule 8(1) deals with a type of direction that is often known as an "unless order". Such a direction provides, quite explicitly, that an appellant's case (or part of the case) will be struck out unless the appellant complies with the direction. For example:

> "Unless X provides information Y to the tribunal and to HMRC by 5pm on date Z, X's case will be automatically struck out."

As made clear in *Bussau*, there is a distinction between such a direction and one which says that, on failure to comply with the direction, a party's case "may be struck out". In relation to the latter type of direction, see rule 8(3)(a) and **4.6.4** below.

Case: *Bussau v HMRC* [2020] UKFTT 38 (TC)

When unless orders should be granted

Generally, unless orders should be used when a party has been repeatedly lax in complying with tribunal directions so that any continued failures do not further prejudice the other party's preparation of the case. As stated in *Staysure*, there should generally have been a "knowing failure to comply with directions".

In *Marcan Shipping*, the Court of Appeal held that an unless order ought not be made without a judge carefully considering whether or not it would be appropriate to impose such a sanction in the circumstances. In so doing, an unless order was described as "one of the most powerful weapons in the court's case management armoury and should not be deployed unless its consequences can be justified".

Although *Marcan* was decided in relation to a different set of procedure rules, it is suggested that its principles are equally applicable to the Tax Chamber. Accordingly, as noted in *Khan*, an unless order is "an order of last resort".

In one unreported case in which the author was involved, HMRC had argued for the imposition of an unless order in anticipation of a possible breach of a direction by the taxpayer. The judge (correctly, it is suggested) refused to grant an unless order in those circumstances: HMRC's application was precipitous. This reflects the approach outlined in *Marcan*. Given the severity of the strike out sanction, HMRC's application should have waited until at least one failure to comply had occurred. And even then it is suggested that a lesser sanction would have been more appropriate.

Cases: *Marcan Shipping (London) Ltd v Kefalas* [2007] EWCA Civ 463; *Staysure v HMRC* [2019] UKFTT 524 (TC); *Khan v HMRC* [2019] UKFTT 751 (TC)

Automatic effect of unless orders

If an unless order has been given by the tribunal, the strike out takes place automatically. In other words, it requires no further action by the tribunal to take effect.

Marcan stressed that even though a strike out is deemed to have had automatic effect, a party can effectively seek its reinstatement retrospectively by applying for an extension of the period in which to comply (under rule 5(3)(a)). This is in addition to (but in practice would often be exercised in conjunction with) the right to seek a reinstatement under rule 8(5). In *Foneshops*, it was not suggested that the tribunal had ceased to have jurisdiction regarding the appeal following the case being automatically struck out. And this was similarly the underlying assumption in *Blackburn*.

In *Second Mezzanine*, the tribunal considered that an unless order could have effect even if compliance with the order was an impossibility.

Cases: *Marcan Shipping (London) Ltd v Kefalas* [2007] EWCA Civ 463; *Foneshops Ltd v HMRC* [2013] UKFTT 675 (TC); *Blackburn Bros Cattle Company Ltd v HMRC* [2014] UKFTT 47 (TC); *Second Mezzanine Film Fund LLP v HMRC* [2019] UKFTT 283 (TC)

Reinstatement of cases struck out

Rule 8(5) permits certain cases that have been struck out to be reinstated. See **4.6.7** below.

In addition, as happened in *Nowroozi*, the tribunal may retrospectively extend a time limit so as to convert non-compliance into compliance with a direction (rule 5(3)(a)).

Case: *Nowroozi v HMRC* [2019] UKFTT 533 (TC)

Challenging unless orders

In certain cases, however, it may be possible to challenge the order itself. As the EAT held in *Mace*, an unless order "must identify with clarity what is required for compliance". Without such certainty as to what has to be done (and whether it has been done as required), the order will not be enforceable.

A similar theme emerges from another EAT decision, *Ijomah*, which emphasised that "particular care and attention needs to be given, both when making, and interpreting, such an Order".

Where there is any ambiguity, it should be construed so far as possible to eliminate or minimise the potential effect of depriving a party of a claim or defence which is properly pleaded and perfectly capable of being fairly litigated.

Cases: *Mace v Ponders End International* (2014) UKEAT/491/13/LA; *Ijomah v Nottinghamshire Healthcare NHS Foundation Trust* (2020) UKEAT/289/19/RN

4.6.3　Mandatory strike outs (rule 8(2))

The tribunal is obliged to strike out the whole or part of any proceedings in respect of which it does not have jurisdiction. Thus, for example, if a taxpayer has appealed to the tribunal against an information notice and the information notice has already been pre-approved by the tribunal (so that the taxpayer has no right of appeal), the tribunal must strike out the taxpayer's appeal.

As shown in *Woodstream*, it is not sufficient for the tribunal to consider that the question of the tribunal's jurisdiction is "arguable". If the tribunal's jurisdiction is in question, the tribunal must fully grapple with that issue and reach a definitive decision.

Indeed, as confirmed in *Dollar*, a strike-out under rule 8(2)(a) does not require any application by either party "and if not raised by the parties must be raised [by the tribunal on its own motion]".

In *Westminster*, this power was used to strike out a case where the taxpayer had effectively notified the tribunal of an appeal (several years late) when in fact the tribunal had already dealt with the appeal (and dismissed it) on an earlier occasion.

In *Wimpole*, the tribunal struck out a case for lack of jurisdiction in a case where the taxpayer company had been struck off the Register of Companies. The tribunal considered that it had no jurisdiction in a case where the appellant had ceased to exist. It is suggested that such a statement ought to be modified so as to allow situations where a cause of action is transferred from the appellant to another person or persons.

In a Scottish case (*Fife*), the tribunal struck out an appeal which had been made prematurely (during a period in which the appealable decision was still in the course of a review).

In some cases, the tribunal might have had jurisdiction to hear a matter but (due to a change in circumstances or a change in the law) no longer has such jurisdiction. Under rule 5(3)(k)(i), the tribunal may transfer the proceedings to another tribunal (assuming that the transferee tribunal does have jurisdiction). In such circumstances, the mandatory strike out will not apply if the proceedings have been so transferred.

Law: FA 2008, Sch. 36, para. 29(3)

Cases: *Westminster College of Computing Ltd v HMRC* [2014] UKFTT 132 (TC); *Wimpole Interiors Ltd v HMRC* [2014] UKFTT 424 (TC); *HMRC v Woodstream Europe Ltd* [2018] UKUT 398 (TCC); *Fife Resources Solutions LLP v Revenue Scotland* [2018] FTSTC 1; *Dollar Financial UK Ltd v HMRC* [2021] UKFTT 253 (TC)

4.6.4 Discretionary strike outs (rule 8(3))

Rule 8(3) provides for three other circumstances in which the tribunal may strike out the whole or part of the proceedings. In each case, the tribunal has to consider the overriding objective (rule 2) when exercising this power. As noted in *Hill*, these are relevant only if the tribunal has jurisdiction over the appeal.

Case: *HMRC v Hill* [2018] UKUT 45 (TCC)

Where failure compliance follows warning of strike out (rule 8(3)(a))

The first circumstance is where a direction is given which falls slightly short of being an unless order. Rule 8(3)(a) provides that a strike out may occur if the direction which has not been complied with "stated that failure … to comply … could lead to the striking out of the proceedings or part of them". It is suggested that this rule cannot be used, therefore, to justify the striking out of proceedings when the written direction did not contain such an express warning, even if a judge had given an oral indication to the party in default that a further failure would be frowned upon.

But see also rule 8(3)(b).

In *Khan*, the tribunal identified a number of principles concerning the granting of an unless order under rule 8(3)(a):

- as unless orders are an order of last resort, if a party intentionally or deliberately flouts an unless order, the party can expect no mercy;
- a decision to strike out a case will depend on the particular facts and circumstances before the tribunal;
- litigation must be conducted efficiently and at a proportionate cost, which requires time limits to be followed;
- a party cannot hide behind the defaults of his or her representative, although striking out should be used to punish misconduct by a representative only if that sanction is proportionate in the light of the circumstances of the case; and
- a relevant consideration is whether the obligations have since been complied with and that there is no evidence of deliberate non-compliance.

Case: *Khan v HMRC* [2019] UKFTT 751 (TC)

Where failures preclude proceedings being dealt with fairly and justly (rule 8(3)(b))

The second circumstance is given by rule 8(3)(b). It applies if a party's failures to co-operate with the tribunal are to such an extent that the tribunal cannot deal with the proceedings fairly and justly.

In *PGPH*, this was described as "high hurdle" although it should be noted that that decision was shaped to some extent by the Upper Tribunal's decision in *BPP* which has since been reversed by the Court of Appeal and the Supreme Court.

An example (but only one such example) of this would be repeated failures to provide evidence or a statement of case so that a delay to the substantive hearing would be inevitable, and where such a delay would put the other party at a significant disadvantage, perhaps because of the terminal illness of a key witness.

It will be seen that a strike out would be available to the tribunal in such circumstances even if no prior warning had been expressly given concerning the continued failure to co-operate. Indeed, in the most exceptional of cases, it would be possible to invoke this rule where there had been such serious failures by a party even if no subsequent attempts are made to get that party to co-operate.

In *O'Brien*, the tribunal noted that no warning was necessary but gave the parties the opportunity to make representations. That was a case where the facts could have justified a striking out on the basis of rule 8(3)(b), but where an unless order was given and the case was decided on the basis of rule 8(1).

In *First Class*, the tribunal identified two situations in which a strike out would be appropriate under rule 8(3)(b), noting that there could be further such situations:

- The first was where a party "has already been so prejudiced by [the other party's] conduct in a matter which cannot be remedied and that therefore the proceedings cannot be fair and just".
- The second situation was where there has been a course of conduct which, whilst not sufficient to prevent the appeal from being dealt with fairly and justly, amounts to a course of conduct which, if it had continued, would mean that the appeal could not be dealt with fairly and justly.

The tribunal considered that that particular case potentially fell within the latter category, highlighting "mismanagement of this appeal and late compliance with directions". Particular instances included the appellant's letters not being replied to promptly, failures to make disclosures that they had agreed to make, ignoring the clear terms of a tribunal direction and serving a defence on an application at the last minute. In short, HMRC were held not to have "shown courtesy to the appellant nor respect the orders of the Tribunal". The tribunal accepted that with a change of personnel within HMRC and additional reassurances, this poor conduct was less likely to continue. Otherwise, the tribunal said it would be likely to have granted the taxpayer's application for HMRC to be disbarred from future participation in the appeal.

In *McKee*, the tribunal considered that the taxpayer's refusal to respond to "repeated requests and indeed Directions for production of witness statements and any supporting documentation" would have justified a strike-out under rule 8(3)(b). (Because of prior warnings, the strike out was in fact given under rule 8(3)(a).) Although the tribunal recognised some of the difficulties being experienced by the taxpayer, these were not sufficient to excuse the failings.

In *Nutro*, the taxpayer's repeated misstatements in relation to procedural matters were held to go "to the core of cooperation with the Tribunal" and led to the striking out of its case under rule 8(3)(b).

In *JSM*, there was clear evidence to suggest that a witness's evidence was fabricated. It is implicit in the decision that this would have been sufficient to justify a striking out under this rule. However, HMRC's very long delay in raising the point militated against the tribunal taking that course of action (leaving the credibility of the witness to be challenged through cross-examination instead).

A catalogue of five failures to comply with three different sets of directions over a period of five months and an apparent indifference to a strike-out application led the tribunal in *XG* to strike out the company's appeal under rule 8(3)(b).

In *Chidzoy*, an employment case, the Employment Tribunal exercised the equivalent provision to strike out a claimant's case after she had breached a warning from the tribunal not to discuss the case with anyone else in the course of a break while she was still giving evidence (see **8.8.3** below). The tribunal took the following circumstances into account before exercising its powers to strike out the case:

- that the claimant had heard the warning six times due to earlier adjournments in the course of her evidence;
- that it was not considered appropriate to strike out only the part of the claimant's case relating to the known topic of the unauthorised conversation;

- that there had been a complete loss of trust in the claimant (given, in addition, that the claimant knew of the respondent's concerns about the unauthorised conversation but did not alert the tribunal to the issue and that there was inconsistent evidence emanating from the claimant and her solicitor in relation to the conversation); and
- that it was not considered proportionate to direct that the case be heard by a differently-constituted tribunal.

The tribunal in *Chidzoy* also summarised the approach to take and the factors to take into account when considering a strike-out in cases due to unreasonable conduct:

- there must first be a conclusion that proceedings have been conducted unreasonably by a party or on the party's behalf;
- whether a fair hearing still take place;
- if not, what remedy is considered appropriate and whether there is a lesser but more proportionate remedy; and
- even if a strike-out is appropriate, what the consequences are of such a decision (for example, if the hearing is only a preliminary hearing, it might still be appropriate to permit the party to participate at a later stage).

In *Vimaleswaran*, the tribunal was faced with compliance failures and dishonest statements by the taxpayer's representative. The tribunal considered that the taxpayer should not be protected by the fact that the compliance failures were not his but those of his representative. On the other hand, in the absence of clear knowledge by the taxpayer of the representative's dishonesty, the tribunal made its decision on whether to strike out the appeal without taking into account those dishonest statements. The tribunal also disregarded the history of non-compliance prior to the appeal process starting.

In *Galldris*, the tribunal deprecated considerable delays by HMRC in producing a statement of case for which there was no satisfactory explanation. Nevertheless, albeit "somewhat reluctantly", it held that "it cannot be concluded that such non-compliance prevents the

4.6   Rule 8 – Striking out a party's case

Tribunal from dealing with the proceedings fairly and justly". Accordingly, it declined to debar HMRC from the proceedings.

Cases: *O'Brien v HMRC* [2012] UKFTT 581 (TC); *First Class Communications Ltd v HMRC* [2013] FTT 90 (TC); *McKee v HMRC* [2014] UKFTT 806 (TC); *Nutro UK Ltd v HMRC* [2014] UKFTT 971 (TC); *PGPH Ltd v HMRC* [2016] UKFTT 46 (TC); *JSM Construction Ltd v HMRC* [2016] UKFTT 163 (TC); *BPP Holdings Ltd v HMRC* [2016] EWCA Civ 121; *HMRC v BPP Holdings Ltd* [2017] UKSC 55; *XG Concept Ltd v HMRC* [2017] UKFTT 92 (TC); *Chidzoy v BBC* (2018) UKEAT/0097/17/BA; *Vimaleswaran v HMRC* [2019] UKFTT 222 (TC); *Galldris LLP v HMRC* [2021] UKFTT 331 (TC)

Where no reasonable prospect of success

Rule 8(3)(c) provides for the third circumstance in which the tribunal may strike out the whole or part of the proceedings. This is where the tribunal considers that there is no reasonable prospect of the party's case or part of it succeeding.

This test is subtly different from that applicable in the Civil Procedure Rules ("CPR") which refer to "no *real prospect* of succeeding on the claim ... or successfully defending the claim". In the context of the CPR, in *Three Rivers*, the test was held to exclude cases where the prospect of success was merely fanciful.

If a party were to request a strike out under this rule, it would have the burden of proving that any claims as to prospects of success were unreasonable. In *Enviroengineering*, the tribunal held that there was no reasonable prospect of the company's case succeeding where its claims to correct its returns for bad debt relief (being the subject of the appeal) were several years late.

In *Colaingrove*, the former VAT and Duties Tribunal expressed reservations about striking out a case if it was only going to lead to a further dispute. In that case, the issue was whether a withholding of a repayment of VAT constituted an appealable decision: if it did not then any appeal ought to be struck out, but the tribunal recognised that any subsequent appealable decision (i.e. a formal refusal to repay) would simply lead to a further appeal. Thus, HMRC's application for a strike out was refused. The approach was followed in *Sub One* in respect of an appeal against a letter that suggested that VAT was payable, but which HMRC argued fell short of amounting to an assessment.

In *Sutton*, in a decision where the tribunal struck out a taxpayer's case as having no reasonable prospects of succeeding, the taxpayer was gently warned of the risk of a costs order (see rule 10(1)(b)) in a case where the taxpayer's husband had lost an appeal on precisely the same point and on materially identical facts at the First-tier and permission to appeal against the decision was refused both by the First-tier and, subsequently, by the Upper Tribunal.

It was confirmed in *Fairford* that HMRC can rely on this rule even in cases where HMRC have the burden of proof, although in that case HMRC could not overcome the hurdle set out in the rule.

In *The First De Sales*, the Upper Tribunal confirmed the following principles deriving from the CPR (hence the references to "court" and "claimant"):

- The court must consider whether the claimant has a "realistic" as opposed to a "fanciful" prospect of success. A "realistic" claim is one that carries some degree of conviction.

- In reaching its conclusion the court must not conduct a "mini-trial". This does not mean that the court must take at face value and without analysis everything that a claimant says in his statements before the court. In some cases it may be clear that there is no real substance in factual assertions made, particularly if contradicted by contemporaneous documents. However, in reaching its conclusion the court must take into account not only the evidence actually placed before it on the application for summary judgment, but also the evidence that can reasonably be expected to be available at trial.

- Although a case may turn out at trial not to be really complicated, it does not follow that it should be decided without the fuller investigation into the facts at trial than is possible or permissible on summary judgment. Thus the court should hesitate about making a final decision without a trial, even where there is no obvious conflict of fact at the time of the application, where reasonable grounds exist for believing that a fuller investigation into the facts of the case would add to or alter the evidence available to a trial judge and so affect the outcome of the case.

- On the other hand, it is not uncommon for an application to give rise to a short point of law or construction and, if the court is satisfied that it has before it all the evidence necessary for the proper determination of the question and that the parties have had an adequate opportunity to address it in argument, it should grasp the nettle and decide it. The reason is quite simple: if the respondent's case is bad in law, he will in truth have no real prospect of succeeding on his claim or successfully defending the claim against him, as the case may be. Similarly, if the applicant's case is bad in law, the sooner that is determined, the better. If it is possible to show by evidence that although material in the form of documents or oral evidence that would put the documents in another light is not currently before the court, such material is likely to exist and can be expected to be available at trial, it would be wrong to give summary judgment because there would be a real, as opposed to a fanciful, prospect of success. However, it is not enough simply to argue that the case should be allowed to go to trial because something may turn up which would have a bearing on the question of construction.

See also the discussion on abuse of process at **2.5** above.

Law: *Civil Procedure Rules*, rule 24.2(a) (see https://www.justice.gov.uk/courts/procedure-rules/civil/rules)

Cases: *Three Rivers DC v Bank of England* [2001] UKHL 16; *Colaingrove Ltd v HMCE* (2001) VDT 16,981; *Sub One Ltd (t/a Subway) v HMRC* [2009] UKFTT 385 (TC); *Enviroengineering Ltd v HMRC* [2011] UKFTT 366 (TC); *Sutton v HMRC* [2014] UKFTT 44 (TC); *Fairford Group Limited plc (in liquidation) v HMRC* [2014] UKFTT 319 (TC); *The First De Sales Limited Partnership v HMRC* [2018] UKUT 396 (TCC)

When an oral hearing should be given

In *SRN*, the Upper Tribunal noted that the draconian effect of a strike-out meant that there should be a presumption in favour of any strike-out application being decided after an oral hearing, rather than being determined only on the papers.

Case: *SRN Horizons Ltd v HMRC* [2017] UKUT 246 (TCC)

4.6.5 Approaches to strike-out applications

A strike-out application effectively denies a party its opportunity to argue its case. As noted by the Upper Tribunal in *Sharma*, this could have human rights repercussions as it could be seen as denying the party its right to a fair trial. However, the tribunal concluded that "by exercising the strike out jurisdiction in an appropriate way, the Tribunal is discharging rather than overriding its obligation to provide a fair and public hearing". Accordingly, the tribunal concluded that the "power must be exercised with care".

In *Igen*, the tribunal also made clear the care to be exercised before applying a strike-out, suggesting that a tribunal should first consider "whether there is any other procedural tool which could be used – justly, fairly and proportionately – to allow [the] case to be managed fairly and justly". It also suggested that a party's prior history of non-compliance can be an important factor to be considered when carrying out this exercise.

In *van de Wiele*, the Upper Tribunal made it clear that a strike-out application should not turn into a mini-trial. If the party "has a case which has a real, and not simply a fanciful, prospect of success on a particular issue, an order should not be made". However, just because an application for a strike out raises a difficult issue, it does not mean that that cannot be addressed at a strike out hearing.

The warning in *Garland* should always be heeded. In particular, a strike-out application will often mean an additional hearing. In many cases (particularly default paper cases and basic cases), it would be a better use of tribunal resources for no application to be made at all and the arguments deployed at the full hearing.

In *Hill*, HMRC were warned that they ought to consider the range of tribunal decisions which have a bearing on the application (including those unfavourable to them) and not to present simply a single decision which would seem to support them.

Cases: *Sharma v Financial Services Authority* [2010] UKUT 25 (FS); *Michel van de Wiele NV v Pensions Regulator* [2011] UKUT B3 (FS); *Garland v HMRC* [2016] UKFTT 573 (TC); *Hill v HMRC* [2017] UKFTT 277 (TC); *Igen Distribution Ltd (in liquidation) v HMRC* [2020] UKFTT 328 (TC)

4.6.6 Requirement to allow party to make representations (rule 8(4))

A decision to strike out proceedings or part of them should not come out of the blue. This is because rule 8(4) provides that, whenever it is proposed to strike out the whole or a part of the proceedings, the party should first be given an opportunity to make representations in relation to the proposed striking out.

Rule 8(4) applies in respect of:

- mandatory strike outs under rule 8(2);
- discretionary strike outs either:
    - for lack of co-operation under rule 8(3)(b) or
    - where there is no reasonable prospect of success under rule 8(3)(c).

Those representations might be in writing or made orally at a hearing, as the tribunal may decide.

When prior representations not needed

By implication, there is no obligation on the tribunal to seek representations in cases of breaches of unless orders (rule 8(1)) or in those cases where the party breaches an order which states that failure to comply could lead to a striking out (rule 8(3)(a)). It is suggested that it would be inappropriate for representations to be sought in the former case, given that the strike out is an automatic consequence of the party's failure. In the latter case, whilst representations need not be sought by the tribunal, it does not mean that a tribunal is precluded from seeking them.

In any event, in both of those types of case, the direction itself would normally have followed an opportunity for representations. However, this should also be considered in light of the provisions of rule 8(5).

4.6.7 Reinstatement application (rule 8(5), (6))

Given that proceedings can be struck out (either automatically or by the tribunal at its discretion) without the party being required to make representations, the right to a fair trial will sometimes dictate that the party should have the opportunity to apply for the proceedings or part of them to be reinstated.

In *BPP University*, the tribunal considered that in those cases where there had already been a hearing which led to the striking out, a reinstatement application would be appropriate only if there had been a change of factual circumstances since the relevant decision was made. This decision was subsequently endorsed by the Upper Tribunal (*BPP Holdings*).

Cases: BPP University College of Professional Studies Ltd v HMRC (No. 2) [2014] UKFTT 917 (TC); HMRC v BPP Holdings Ltd [2014] UKUT 496 (TCC)

When reinstatement applications may be made

The rule itself applies solely to those cases where representations need not be sought by the tribunal prior to the striking out (i.e. breaches of unless orders and failures to comply with orders containing a warning of a possible strike out).

However, in *Jumbogate*, it was confirmed that rule 5(2) (which permits directions to be set aside and amended) can be invoked in other cases. Of course, if the tribunal had received representations which were not accepted then an appeal to the Upper Tribunal might be appropriate instead. However, in the absence of any error of law, such an appeal ought not to succeed and the party's only hope would be for a second bite of the cherry by applying to the tribunal for reconsideration.

In *Reno*, the tribunal was faced with a case that had been struck out and where the application to reinstate the case had itself been struck out. The tribunal accepted that it had jurisdiction to reinstate the reinstatement application.

Cases: Jumbogate Ltd v HMRC [2015] UKFTT 64 (TC); Reno v HMRC [2019]] UKFT 184 (TC)

Test to be applied

In *Nowroozi*, the tribunal followed the approach set down in *Martland* as discussed at **2.4.4**. That approach is broadly consistent with earlier cases concerning reinstatement applications. Although it is considered that applications should generally follow the *Martland* three-stage approach, earlier case law might provide some additional guidance.

4.6 Rule 8 – Striking out a party's case

In *Jumbogate*, the key principle was stated to be the overriding objective (see rule 2). A party making such an application would therefore need to demonstrate why fairness and justice mean that reinstatement is appropriate, notwithstanding the circumstances that led to the strike out in the first place. It was confirmed in *Trans-Int* that the tribunal had to consider the overriding objective when determining whether or not to reinstate a case.

In *Synergy*, the Upper Tribunal held that this fairness test should be considered by reference to the facts at the time any reinstatement application is being considered, not when the original strike out took place.

In *Trans-Int*, a case concerning a breach of an unless order, the tribunal wondered whether the notice of the hearing that had led to the unless order (which had been sent to the company's former advisers) had ever been forwarded to the company. Given this doubt, the tribunal held that the major consideration should be whether or not the appeal (if reinstated) would have a reasonable possibility of success: it was clearly stated that this test was less stringent than whether the appeal was likely to succeed.

In one case with which the author had become involved, HMRC themselves (actually, prompted by their Counsel) withdrew their objections to the reinstatement of an appeal as soon as it became apparent that the taxpayers had not seen the original order warning of the possible striking out of the case.

In *Globalised*, the tribunal noted the lack of specific guidance in the rules as to the criteria to be applied in reinstatement applications. However, it considered that the provisions in rule 38 (set aside applications) were analogous and sought to apply the rule 38 provisions as if they also governed rule 8. The author considers that although circumstances listed in rule 38 might identify some suitable cases for a reinstatement, the tribunal's approach was wrong in law and a tribunal should not consider itself bound by the provisions that govern set aside applications.

Indeed, in *Jumbogate*, the tribunal suggested that the following factors should be considered when exercising its discretion as to whether a case should be reinstated:

- whether the appeal is arguable and has a reasonable prospect of success;
- the reasons for the strike out;
- whether there has been any material change (in circumstances) since the strike out;
- whether the other party would be prejudiced if the strike out were set aside;
- the prejudice to the applicant if the strike out were not set aside; and
- the parties' conduct.

In *Chappell*, the Upper Tribunal expressly stated that the strength of the applicant's case should generally be disregarded in the balancing exercise, at least in cases involving a breach of an unless order. The *Trans-Int* case (discussed above) would appear to be one exception to this general rule.

In *Viking*, the taxpayer had had its appeal struck out following its failure to comply with a direction concerning the provision of a list of documents, which had been backed up with an unless order. The fact that that failure had still not been remedied was a significant factor pointing against the reinstatement of the case. As the tribunal noted:

> "Where proceedings have been struck out on the ground that an appellant has failed to comply with a direction and consequential unless order then it seems to me that any application for reinstatement should not be granted unless the appellant has complied or provided a compelling explanation for the failure to comply."

The author endorses this view. It means that a difficult choice might have to be made in a case where the (now late) compliance would be particularly onerous (or expensive) and, therefore, it might be tempting not to undertake the exercise unless it was known that the appeal had been reinstated. The author would be tempted to encourage compliance nevertheless (even if it is going to lead to wasted costs, such being the price for the earlier failings). However, each case will turn on its own merits and therefore there cannot be any universal approach.

BMW noted that the seriousness of a party's earlier failures (which led to the strike-out) are no bar to the subsequent reinstatement.

In *Foneshops*, the tribunal considered that a taxpayer prioritising family over money issues was not a basis for excusing a breach of a direction given by the tribunal which was subject to an unless order.

Cases: *Synergy Child Services Ltd v Ofsted* [2009] UKUT 125 (AAC); *Trans-Int SRL v HMRC* [2011] UKFTT 326 (TC); *Globalised Corporation Ltd v HMRC* [2012] UKFTT 556 (TC); *Foneshops Ltd v HMRC* [2013] UKFTT 675 (TC); *Jumbogate Ltd v HMRC* [2015] UKFTT 64 (TC); *Martland v HMRC* [2018] UKUT 178 (TCC); *Nowroozi v HMRC* [2019] UKFTT 533 (TC); *Chappell v Pension Regulator* [2019] UKUT 209 (TCC); *Viking Enterprises Ltd v HMRC* [2020] UKFTT 306 (TC); *HMRC v BMW Shipping Agents Ltd* [2021] UKUT 91 (TCC).

Time limit

A reinstatement application should be made in writing so that it is received by the tribunal within 28 days after the notification of the strike out is sent out by the tribunal.

4.6.8 Distinction between appellants and respondents (rule 8(7), (8))

Rule 8 is subject to what might initially be perceived as a fundamental unfairness. The consequences of a strike out apply in their full force only to appellants. In the overwhelming majority of cases in the Tax Chamber, the appellants will be taxpayers challenging HMRC decisions.

So far as respondents (who will usually be HMRC) are concerned, the strike out rules continue to apply. However, rather than, as is the case with an appellant, having their case (or part of it) dismissed, the consequence for respondents is less severe: a respondent is merely barred from taking further part in the proceedings. Similarly, a reinstatement application by the respondent will mean an application merely to be allowed again to take part in the proceedings.

Thus, in the typical case where a taxpayer needs to disprove an assessment:

- a strike out against the appellant would amount to the taxpayer losing the case; whereas

- a strike out against the respondents would amount to HMRC being barred from further participation in the case, but the taxpayer would still need to disprove the assessment (albeit unopposed).

Nevertheless, rule 8(8) does permit the tribunal to ignore any response or submission from a respondent that has been barred from taking further part in proceedings and the tribunal may, in such cases, determine any or all of the issues against that respondent. Indeed, in *van de Wiele*, the Upper Tribunal suggested that, even though barring a respondent appears to fall short of striking out their case altogether, "the reality is that once the Tribunal has decided that the respondent can take no further part in the proceedings relating to an issue or argument, then the issue or argument is dead". However, it appears that these comments should be read in the context of that case, where the disbar was caused because of a finding that the particular issue or argument had no reasonable prospect of success. Where a respondent has been disbarred for other reasons, it is suggested that this should not automatically lead to a finding in favour of an appellant.

In *Whitehill*, the tribunal (without any representations being made to it) had to consider a case where HMRC were disbarred from participation in the case without having even served a statement of case. In those circumstances, the tribunal considered that the ordinary course of events should be that the taxpayer's appeal is summarily allowed by comparing the situation to ordinary litigation where a defence is not filed. On the facts of that case, the tribunal could have reached the same decision without such analysis since the case concerned a penalty and was one where HMRC had the burden of proof. Nevertheless, the tribunal's analysis has allowed an indication of the likely outcome in cases where taxpayers would ordinarily have the burden of proof.

In *Bailey*, a similar view was taken in a case where HMRC had failed to tell the tribunal whether or not it wished to contest the case.

See rule 9 below for a situation in which there can be a respondent other than HMRC.

Cases: *Michel van de Wiele NV v Pensions Regulator* [2011] UKUT B3 (FS); *Whitehill Pelham Ltd v HMRC* [2017] UKFTT 781 (TC); *Bailey v HMRC* [2019] UKFTT 94 (TC)

The BPP case

It should be noted that the tribunal usually shows a reluctance to disbar HMRC from future participation in proceedings, preferring instead to let a full trial proceed. In *BPP*, however, HMRC tried to argue that they should not be precluded from participating in a case as a result of their public duty to protect the Exchequer. However, the Supreme Court considered that such an approach would "set a dangerous precedent".

In the subsequent hearing of the appeal (*BPP University*), therefore, the case was decided in the absence of HMRC. The tribunal was then obliged to consider how the rules operated in such circumstances.

The tribunal held that, as well as being obliged to prevent HMRC from making further representations, it had the right (but not the obligation) to ignore any submissions or representations made by HMRC prior to the direction disbarring them.

Cases: *HMRC v BPP Holdings Ltd* [2017] UKSC 55; *BPP University College of Professional Studies Ltd v HMRC* [2018] UKFTT 454 (TC)

4.7 Rule 9 – Substitution and addition of parties

9(1) The Tribunal may give a direction substituting a party if–

(a) the wrong person has been named as a party; or

(b) the substitution has become necessary because of a change in circumstances since the start of proceedings.

9(2) The Tribunal may give a direction adding a person to the proceedings as a respondent.

9(3) A person who is not a party to proceedings may make an application to be added as a party under this rule.

9(4) If the Tribunal refuses an application under paragraph (3) it must consider whether to permit the person who made the application to provide submissions or evidence to the Tribunal.

9(5) If the Tribunal gives a direction under paragraph (1) or (2) it may give such consequential directions as it considers appropriate.

4.7.1 Overview

Rule 9 provides the framework for getting parties substituted or added to proceedings.

4.7.2 Substitution of parties (rule 9(1))

A party can be substituted if the wrong person has been named as a party. This allows corrections to be made. In *McFadzean*, the Upper Tribunal said that the question of wrongness may be considered either at the time that the case is notified to the tribunal or when a substitution application is made.

This case arose in the context of an appeal against a scheme sanction charge under the pensions code. Although originally imposed on Mr McFadzean, the pension scheme administrator, it had been believed that a company had since been appointed scheme administrator in his place. As a result, it was the company that notified the appeal to the tribunal. However, when it transpired that the appointment was ineffective, the tribunal sought to substitute Mr McFadzean as the appellant under rule 9(1)(a). This was later upheld by the Upper Tribunal.

A more likely scenario is where there has been a change in circumstances since the start of proceedings. In such a situation, it may be necessary for the tribunal to effect a substitution of a party, in which case the tribunal may do so. For example, if an individual dies, any litigation will vest in the individual's personal representatives.

In *New Miles*, the tribunal held that it could also be used in cases where a right to reclaim VAT had been assigned to another person, so that the assignee could be substituted for the original appellant. However, *Skywell* shows that a substitution will not be effected if the assignment is void. In *Skywell*, the assignment was considered void for "champerty" (the unlawful transfer of litigation rights if not part of an otherwise commercial transaction).

The rule was also used in *MCashback* to permit an individual partner to pursue an appeal against a closure notice issued to a partnership in circumstances where the partnership itself did not wish to challenge the closure notice.

Cases: *New Miles Ltd v HMRC (on the application of Hilton-Foster)* [2012] UKFTT 33 (TC); *Skywell (UK) Ltd v HMRC* [2012] UKFTT 611 (TC); *MCashback Software 6 LLP v HMRC* [2013] UKFTT 679 (TC); *McFadzean v HMRC* [2019] UKUT 349 (TCC)

4.7.3 Addition of parties (rule 9(2))

Alternatively, the tribunal might consider it appropriate to add a party to proceedings. As noted in *Pierhead*, this will most likely be appropriate only in cases where the additional party has a close financial interest in the outcome of the case: for example, if the case concerns the deemed disposal proceeds for a chargeable asset received by a party to the proceedings, it might also be appropriate for the purchaser to be added as a party as the deemed disposal proceeds would equal the purchaser's deemed purchase price.

This was the outcome in *Bradonbay* where the determination of the appellant's VAT repayment claim could have led to HMRC seeking to recover the same VAT previously repaid to a third party (as an input tax credit). The tribunal concluded that the risk of conflicting decisions arising from separate proceedings involving the two taxpayers should be avoided if possible.

A person so added will be treated as another respondent.

Such an application was considered by the Upper Tribunal in the *HSBC* case. However, the issues there concerned the differently worded rules applicable in the Upper Tribunal. Therefore, besides an underlying theme that such applications should not be routinely granted, the decision is of little direct relevance to applications being made in the First-tier.

Cases: *Bradonbay Ltd v HMRC* [2015] UKFTT 229 (TC); *Pierhead Drinks Ltd v HMRC* [2019] UKUT 7 (TCC); *HSBC Electronic Data Processing (Guangdong) Ltd v HMRC* [2021] UKUT 58 (TCC)

4.7.4 Application to be added (rule 9(3))

Rule 9(3) provides that a person who is not a party to proceedings may apply to the tribunal to be added as a party. In *Space Maker*, the tribunal held that, except where substitution of a party under rule 9(1) applies, a party may not be added as an appellant. Therefore, if an application to be added as a party is allowed, the party will be added as a respondent (as per rule 9(2)).

Case: *Space Maker Storage 2 Ltd (in liquidation) v HMRC* [2014] UKFTT 296 (TC)

4.7.5 Alternative direction (rule 9(4))

In many cases, however, it will not be appropriate for a person to be added to the party despite the financial interest of the other party. In such cases, the tribunal should refuse to add the person as a respondent. However, the tribunal must consider whether or not it should permit the other person to give evidence or to make submissions to the tribunal.

This would enable the other person to have the right to be heard as if that person were a party, but without giving the person all the rights available to (and responsibilities on) parties (for example the right to pay, or the risk of being ordered to pay, costs).

Without formally making a decision in this regard, in *MCashback* the tribunal considered that this might have been an option in the event that there is an appeal being taken by a partnership, but an individual partner wishes to make different arguments from the rest of the firm.

Case: *MCashback Software 6 LLP v HMRC* [2013] UKFTT 679 (TC)

4.7.6 Considerations for the tribunal

The tribunal's powers under rule 9(1) and (2) are all discretionary and, therefore, the tribunal must consider each case on the basis of the overriding objective. In *McFadzean*, the following issues arose in the course of the taxpayer's appeal to the Upper Tribunal:

- When the First-tier made the original decision, it arguably had the effect of "adding" Mr McFadzean to the proceedings as an appellant, rather than substituting him. However, this was a consequence of the fact that various appeals (involving the original appellant) had previously been

4.7 Rule 9 – Substitution and addition of parties

consolidated and that only one of those appeals required the substitution of Mr McFadzean as an appellant. The Upper Tribunal considered that the First-tier's decision to substitute Mr McFadzean as a sole appellant should be understood in the context of the single appeal to which that related (and any consequential administrative matters – which might involve the de-consolidation of the appeals – could be left until afterwards).

- A substitution as a party in the proceedings could amount to the substitute party losing the right of an internal review. The Upper Tribunal considered that to be irrelevant but refused to rule out the possibility that this could ever be a relevant consideration in the exercise of the tribunal's discretion.

- Unlike the rules in the civil courts, a substitution under rule 9(1) does not require the substitute's consent. However, this reinforces the view that the tribunal should consider carefully any objections put forward by the proposed new appellant.

Case: *McFadzean v HMRC* [2019] UKUT 349 (TCC)

4.7.7 Consequences and consequential directions

In *Warren*, it was noted that a substitute party effectively stands in the shoes of the substituted party. Therefore, in a complex case, the substitute party could become subject to (or excluded from) the costs-shifting rules depending on whether the previous party had opted out of those rules (see rule 10(1)(c) below).

Rule 9(5), however, permits the tribunal to make any consequential directions that are considered appropriate if a person has been substituted or added as a party under rule 9(1), (2). In *Warren*, it was held that this provision might give the substitute a fresh opportunity to consider the question of costs-shifting.

Case: *Warren v HMRC* [2017] UKFTT 521 (TC)

4.8 Rule 10 – Orders for costs

10(1) The Tribunal may only make an order in respect of costs (or, in Scotland, expenses)–

    (a) under section 29(4) of the 2007 Act (wasted costs) and costs incurred in applying for such costs;

    (b) if the Tribunal considers that a party or their representative has acted unreasonably in bringing, defending or conducting the proceedings;

    (c) if–

        (i) the proceedings have been allocated as a Complex case under rule 23 (allocation of cases to categories); and

        (ii) the taxpayer (or, where more than one party is a taxpayer, one of them) has not sent or delivered a written request to the Tribunal, within 28 days of receiving notice that the case had been allocated as a Complex case, that the proceedings be excluded from potential liability for costs or expenses under this sub-paragraph; or

    (d) in a MP expenses case, if–

        (i) the case has been allocated as a Complex case under rule 23 (allocation of cases to categories); and

        (ii) the appellant has not sent or delivered a written request to the Tribunal, within 28 days of receiving notice that the case had been allocated as a Complex case, that the proceedings be excluded from potential liability for costs or expenses under this sub-paragraph.

10(2) The Tribunal may make an order under paragraph (1) on an application or of its own initiative.

10(3) A person making an application for an order under paragraph (1) must–

    (a) send or deliver a written application to the Tribunal and to the person against whom it is proposed that the order be made; and

(b) send or deliver with the application a schedule of the costs or expenses claimed in sufficient detail to allow the Tribunal to undertake a summary assessment of such costs or expenses if it decides to do so.

10(4) An application for an order under paragraph (1) may be made at any time during the proceedings but may not be made later than 28 days after the date on which the Tribunal sends–

(a) a decision notice recording the decision which finally disposes of all issues in the proceedings; or

(b) notice under rule 17(2) of its receipt of a withdrawal which ends the proceedings.

10(5) The Tribunal may not make an order under paragraph (1) against a person (the "paying person") without first–

(a) giving that person an opportunity to make representations; and

(b) if the paying person is an individual, considering that person's financial means.

10(6) The amount of costs (or, in Scotland, expenses) to be paid under an order under paragraph (1) may be ascertained by–

(a) summary assessment by the Tribunal;

(b) agreement of a specified sum by the paying person and the person entitled to receive the costs or expenses (the "receiving person"); or

(c) assessment of the whole or a specified part of the costs or expenses, including the costs or expenses of the assessment incurred by the receiving person, if not agreed.

10(7) Following an order for assessment under paragraph (6)(c) the paying person or the receiving person may apply–

(a) in England and Wales, to a county court, the High Court or the Costs Office of the Supreme Court [now known as the Senior Courts Costs Office] (as specified in the order) for a detailed assessment of the costs on the standard basis or, if specified in the order, on the

> indemnity basis; and the Civil Procedure Rules 1998 shall apply, with necessary modifications, to that application and assessment as if the proceedings in the tribunal had been proceedings in a court to which the Civil Procedure Rules 1998 apply;
>
> (b) in Scotland, to the Auditor of the Sheriff Court or the Court of Session (as specified in the order) for the taxation of the expenses according to the fees payable in that court; or
>
> (c) in Northern Ireland, to the Taxing Office of the High Court of Northern Ireland for taxation on the standard basis or, if specified in the order, on the indemnity basis.
>
> 10(7A) Upon making an order for the assessment of costs, the Tribunal may order an amount to be paid on account before the costs or expenses are assessed.
>
> 10(8) In this rule "taxpayer" means a party who is liable to pay, or has paid, the tax, duty, levy or penalty to which the proceedings relate or part of such tax, duty, levy or penalty, or whose liability to do so is in issue in the proceedings[.]

4.8.1 Overview

Rule 10 marks one of the differences between the Tax Chamber and the other chambers of the First-tier. It concerns the payment of costs and the tribunal's powers to make an order concerning costs.

There are essentially three scenarios in which such an order may be made:

- wasted costs;
- unreasonable conduct; and
- Complex cases.

These are considered in further detail below.

In *Golden*, the tribunal held that awards may be made against third parties (e.g. directors of corporate appellants) in cases in the first and third categories (i.e. not cases relying on unreasonable conduct).

The tribunal does not have any power to make costs orders in other situations. This led to an anomalous position in relation to cases involving wasted costs in that the tribunal had the power to make a wasted costs order, but a party could not ordinarily claim the costs of applying for such an order. This was rectified by an amendment to the rules with effect from 1 April 2013. Rule 10(1)(a) now specifically permits the tribunal to make orders in relation to costs incurred by a party in applying for wasted costs.

However, one issue that arises on occasions is the costs of preparation of the bundles of documents that are needed for a tribunal hearing. Although common sense might dictate that these costs be shared by the parties, the Court of Appeal confirmed in *Eclipse* that such an arrangement cannot be the subject of a direction by the tribunal, except in cases allocated to the Complex category.

This was later confirmed by the Supreme Court although the Court suggested that a restitution-based claim in the High Court might have entitled the taxpayer to recover a share of the costs from HMRC.

Cases: *Eclipse Film Partners No. 35 LLP v HMRC* [2014] EWCA Civ 184; *Golden Harvest Wholesale Ltd v HMRC* [2020] UKFTT 369 (TC)

Application in Scotland

In Scotland, references to "costs" should be read as "expenses".

Procedure

The tribunal can make a costs order of its own initiative – in that a party need not apply for one. However, a party may, alternatively, make an application for such an order (rule 10(2)). The latter is the most common (if not the invariable) practice.

One leading text book on legal costs ("*Cook on Costs*") in an earlier edition had suggested, however, that the application should almost always be made by the aggrieved party so as to avoid the tribunal being put in the "difficult and embarrassing" position as both prosecutor and adjudicator. The comments in *Cook on Costs* were strictly directed to wasted costs orders. However, given the differences between the cost rules in the civil courts and those in the tribunal, it is considered that the same approach should apply for all cost matters in the tribunal.

Indeed, in *Oni*, the Employment Appeal Tribunal criticised an Employment Tribunal for making comments about one party's conduct (which would have been relevant to a costs application) ahead of any costs application actually being made.

In *Jackson Grundy*, the Upper Tribunal considered that certain comments by the First-tier could have been seen as pre-judging any subsequent costs application, although those comments were "rescued" by the fact that the First-tier recognised that it could not make any decision about costs pending any application by one of the parties. However, the Upper Tribunal did subsequently criticise the costs award that was later given by the First-tier on the basis that the First-tier (differently constituted) had seemingly relied upon the previous criticism of HMRC's behaviour without making fresh findings of facts in response to the costs application.

See also **4.8.11** below.

Cases: *Oni v NHS Leicester City* (2012) UKEAT/0144/12/LA; *HMRC v Jackson Grundy Ltd* [2017] UKUT 180 (TCC)
Guidance: *Cook on Costs* 2012, LexisNexis 2011, para. 32.17

4.8.2 Scope of costs orders

Conduct before the case is notified to the tribunal

As noted in *Oats*, costs orders cannot be given in respect of conduct arising prior to the case coming within the tribunal's jurisdiction. It is suggested, however, that the *continuation* of previous unreasonable conduct, for example, can give rise to a costs order.

This was emphasised by the Court of Appeal in *Distinctive*. The focus is on the parties' conduct after the case is notified to the tribunal. However, with emphasis added, "there *may* be circumstances in which behaviour before the appeal is brought is relevant to the tribunal's assessment of the reasonableness of the conduct post-commencement".

Cases: *Oats Services Ltd v HMRC* [2011] UKFTT 455 (TC); *Distinctive Care Ltd v HMRC* [2019] EWCA Civ 1010

Costs arising before the case is notified to the tribunal

It was, however, held in *Wilson* that *costs* incurred *before* the case is notified to the tribunal may nevertheless be the subject of a costs order provided that the *conduct* complained of takes place *after* the notification of the appeal to the tribunal and the costs claimed can be shown to be "incidental" to the tribunal proceedings. In *RA Drinks*, the tribunal specifically suggested that the costs of preparing a notice of appeal should be capable of inclusion.

In *Distinctive*, the Court of Appeal confirmed this position, adopting the approach that one considers the cost of obtaining "materials ultimately proving of use and service in the action". The court was not prepared to define this any more clearly, preferring to leave this for a judge (often a costs judge) to determine on a case-by-case basis. However, the court refused to rule out the possibility of a claim for the costs of the internal review process (subject to those costs being ultimately of use for the subsequent appeal). Although that was in the context of rule 10(1)(b), in *Roger Preston*, the tribunal saw no reason to apply the same approach in cases covered by rule 10(1)(c).

In addition, in *Distinctive*, the Court of Appeal emphasised two further points concerning the recoverability of costs:

- First, it was not dependent on whether the taxpayer sought an internal review or notified the appeal direct to the tribunal.
- Secondly, it did not turn on the subjective intention of the party when incurring the costs.

Cases: *G Wilson (Glaziers) Ltd v HMRC* [2012] UKFTT 387 (TC); *RA Drinks Ltd v HMRC* [2014] UKFTT 304 (TC); *Distinctive Care Ltd v HMRC* [2019] EWCA Civ 1010; *Roger Preston Group Ltd v HMRC* [2021] UKFTT 132 (TC)

Costs are awarded only exceptionally

It should be realised, however, that costs orders are the exception even in the Tax Chamber. As a general rule, each side will bear its own costs (if any) irrespective of which side eventually wins the case.

However, the "exceptionality" relates to the fact that it should be exceptional for the conditions for a costs order to be met. In cases where those conditions are satisfied, a tribunal should not resist making a costs order simply on the grounds that such orders represent an exception.

Furthermore, within the relatively rare context of a complex case (where the opt-out has not been exercised), costs orders should be considered to be the norm.

4.8.3 Wasted costs (rule 10(1)(a))

Wasted costs are considered by the 2007 Act. They are any costs incurred by a party either:

- as a result of any improper, unreasonable or negligent act or omission on the part of any legal or other representative (or any employee of such a representative) or
- which, in the light of any such conduct occurring after the costs were incurred, it is considered by the tribunal to be unreasonable for the party to be expected to pay.

A representative is any person exercising a right of audience or the right to conduct proceedings in the tribunal on behalf of a party.

In *Catanã*, the Upper Tribunal explained the purpose of a wasted costs order:

> "to require a representative – usually but not always a solicitor or barrister – either to pay the costs of his client's opponent, or to forgo costs which might otherwise be recoverable, because of his own inadequate conduct. It is a means of sheltering the client from the consequences of his representative's failings."

Section 29 provides that the tribunal may disallow such costs or order the representative to meet them.

Example 1

Suppose Andy's representatives are being slow in providing information requested by the tribunal. Eventually, HMRC make an application for, and obtain, an unless order (see **4.6.2** above) requiring compliance within 30 days.

Subsequently, Andy's representatives fail to comply with the unless order due to negligence. They then apply to the tribunal for the case to be reinstated. They charge Andy £800 to deal with the reinstatement application.

Under section 29(5), the fees of £800 would come within the first heading of wasted costs, being costs incurred as a result of any

> improper, unreasonable or negligent conduct on the part of a representative.
>
> It is arguable that the tribunal could order Andy's representatives to pay those fees back to Andy. However, the rules are not entirely clear and it is suggested that such a matter ought to be dealt with between Andy and his representatives outside the tribunal structure (via a contractual dispute).
>
> Nevertheless, supposing the case is one where Andy eventually wins and, because of the nature of the case, Andy is entitled to receive his costs from HMRC, the tribunal can disallow the £800 as wasted costs.

> **Example 2**
>
> Continuing with the facts in the previous example, suppose HMRC had incurred costs of £1,000 when obtaining the unless order.
>
> The tribunal might consider the £1,000 costs incurred by HMRC when obtaining the unless order to come within the second heading – if, in the light of Andy's advisers' subsequent failings, it is considered that it would be unreasonable for them to have to pay them. If so, HMRC may seek an order from the tribunal directing that they be paid the £1,000 by Andy or his representatives.

In *Catanã*, the Upper Tribunal confirmed that a wasted costs order can be made even if the representative has acted in accordance with a client's instructions.

Law: TCEA 2007, s. 29(4), (5), (6)
Case: *Catanã v HMRC* [2012] UKUT 172 (TCC)

4.8.4 When a wasted costs order should be made

The Court of Appeal in *Ridehalgh* (in relation to a materially identical provision in the *Senior Courts Act* 1981) confirmed that a wasted costs order should be made only if a three-stage test is satisfied:

- there has to be the improper, unreasonable or negligent conduct by the representative;
- that conduct has to have caused the applicant to incur unnecessary expenditure; and

- the tribunal has to be satisfied that it would be just to order the representative to compensate the applicant for some or all of those costs.

Law: *Senior Courts Act* 1981, s. 51(6); *Civil Procedure Rules,* rule 48.7
Case: *Ridehalgh v Horsefield* [1994] Ch 205

Improper conduct

In *Ridehalgh*, "improper conduct" was held to cover any conduct which would ordinarily justify serious professional sanction (such as disbarment, striking off, suspension from practice or some other serious professional penalty). However, the court stated that the term was not limited to such behaviour and covered any "conduct which would be regarded as improper according to the consensus of professional (including judicial) opinion ... whether or not it violates the letter of a professional code".

Case: *Ridehalgh v Horsefield* [1994] Ch 205

Unreasonable conduct

In *Ridehalgh*, the phrase unreasonable conduct was held to describe aptly "conduct which is vexatious, designed to harass the other side rather than advance the resolution of the case [whether or not] the product of excessive zeal and not improper motive". The court held that conduct cannot be judged purely on the basis of hindsight: "the acid test is whether the conduct permits of a reasonable explanation"; an approach that might be regarded as optimistic, if based on a practitioner's judgment, would not be unreasonable.

However, in *Hills* it was considered inappropriate to follow the *Ridehalgh* approach. *Hills* also suggested that opting out of the costs regime for complex cases, having previously stated that that would not occur, could be held to be unreasonable conduct.

In *Ping*, the tribunal considered that one party unreasonably withholding key evidence or information could lead to a wasted costs order against an adviser. The tribunal had in mind the situation where the party belatedly provides the evidence or information that persuades the other party to abandon the case at a much later stage (and after more costs would have been incurred) than would have been the case had the evidence or information been put forward in a more timely manner.

In *Altion*, a representative was found to have acted unreasonably by failing to take adequate checks as to the identity of his clients. This decision was based on the particular facts of the case and should not open the door to HMRC and the tribunal seeking to verify every representative's client identity checks. The case concerned applications for the restoration of goods that were confiscated for non-payment of duties. The concern was raised (and upheld by the tribunal) that the proceedings had been commenced by an alleged representative without the consent or even the knowledge of the persons against whom the confiscation orders had been made.

In *Environmental*, the tribunal held that a representative's failure to attend a hearing it knew about (and then to request a postponement when contacted by the tribunal staff) amounted to wholly unreasonable conduct, warranting a wasted costs order.

In *Lenity*, the tribunal considered that the mere fact that a party had to be encouraged to comply with an order by way of an "unless order" (see **4.6.2**) did not amount to unreasonable conduct so as to merit a costs order. However, including documents on a list of documents (see rule 27) and then refusing to disclose them was considered to be unreasonable.

Cases: *Ridehalgh v Horsefield* [1994] Ch 205; *Ping Kong Lam v HMRC* [2014] UKFTT 79 (TC); *Home Office v Altion Ltd* [2014] UKFTT 574 (TC); *Environmental Practical Solutions Ltd v HMRC* [2014] UKFTT 1118 (TC); *Hills v HMRC* [2016] UKUT 266 (TCC); *Lenity v HMRC* [2021] UKFTT 272 (TC)

Negligent conduct

In *Ridehalgh*, the court based its definition on the standard required for an ordinary claim in negligence (though noting that some of the technical aspects for such a claim would not be relevant). In particular, it held that an applicant would have to show "advice, acts or omissions in the course of [a representative's] professional work which no member of the profession who was reasonably well-informed and competent would have given or done or omitted to do ... an error ... such as no reasonably well-informed and competent member of that profession could have made".

Case: *Ridehalgh v Horsefield* [1994] Ch 205

4.8.5 Unreasonable conduct (rule 10(1)(b))

The most likely costs order in the Tax Chamber is where a party (or the party's representative) has acted unreasonably in bringing, defending or conducting the proceedings. In *HJ*, the Upper Tribunal held that "unreasonable" should be given the same meaning as it is given in wasted costs cases (see the discussion on *Ridehalgh* above). It should be noted that this was not the position of the First-tier in *Wammee* which, comparing the wording of the various provisions in s. 29 of the 2007 Act, concluded that "the fact that a party or representative acts *negligently* does not, without more, mean that he or she has acted 'unreasonably' ".

In any event, unreasonable conduct is generally accepted to include situations where a party's case was hopeless and the party (or representative) should have known that. However, a hopeless case on its own will not justify a costs award and, as per *Ad Hoc*, will certainly not justify costs on the indemnity basis. As concluded in *Maryan*, the rule focuses on the unreasonableness in "defending ... the proceedings". Therefore, HMRC are given some leeway so that they can consider the merits of their case. If they do not withdraw from the proceedings within a reasonable period, however, they then risk being subject to a costs order.

In *Hare Wines*, the tribunal confirmed that references in the case law to resisting a case which was "obviously meritorious" should be interpreted as saying that it would be unreasonable if one were to challenge a case which "clearly would succeed".

If one side's case is hopeless then one possible course of action would be for the other side to seek a strike out under rule 8(3)(c). However, in *Ad Hoc*, the tribunal confirmed that a decision not to make such an application does not weaken the party's subsequent costs application. Indeed, strike-out applications should be made with care (see **4.6.5** above).

Law: TCEA 2007, s. 29(2)

Cases: *Ridehalgh v Horsefield* [1994] Ch 205; *HJ v London Borough of Brent (SEN)* [2011] UKUT 191 (AAC); *Maryan t/a Hazeldene Catering v HMRC* [2012] UKFTT 215 (TC); *Ad Hoc Property Management Ltd v HMRC* [2019] UKFTT 315 (TC); *Hare Wines Ltd v HMRC* [2019] UKFTT 556 (TC); *Wammee Holdings Ltd v HMRC* [2020] UKFTT 240 (TC)

When the case is weak

In *Infocom*, the tribunal awarded HMRC their costs for resisting the taxpayer's application for the reinstatement of a case after it had previously been struck out on the basis that, given the taxpayer's long record of prior failings without any good excuse, the reinstatement application was bound to fail. Although it is quite possible that those previous failings might also have represented unreasonable conduct, the application before the tribunal referred only to the costs of the reinstatement application and, therefore, any earlier misconduct was not in itself relevant for the costs application (except so far as to show the inevitable outcome of the reinstatement application).

In *Wood Green*, the tribunal also said that there would be a strong argument that the defence (by HMRC) of proceedings was unreasonable if HMRC had failed to consider properly the applicability of relevant legal authority and the relevant facts had been brought to HMRC's attention in good time. In that case, the tribunal declined to give a costs award because there were other live issues in the case which needed to be resolved by the tribunal.

Cases: *Wood Green Animal Shelters v HMRC* [2013] UKFTT 566 (TC); *Infocom IT (UK) Ltd v HMRC* [2016] UKFTT 319 (TC)

Generally poor conduct

Unreasonable conduct will also include situations where the case was not itself hopeless or very weak, but the party has been either particularly lax in complying with requests for information or is otherwise generally disruptive.

General guidance on what constitutes unreasonable conduct

In *Distinctive*, the Upper Tribunal endorsed eight principles and added a ninth of its own:

(1) the threshold implied by the words "acted unreasonably" is lower than the threshold of acting "wholly unreasonably" which had previously applied in relation to proceedings before the Special Commissioners;

(2) it is possible for a single piece of conduct to amount to acting unreasonably;

(3) actions include omissions;

(4) a failure to undertake a rigorous review of the subject matter of the appeal when proceedings are commenced can amount to unreasonable conduct;

(5) there is no single way of acting reasonably, there may well be a range of reasonable conduct;

(6) the focus should be on the standard of handling the case (which the tribunal understood to refer to the proceedings before the FTT rather than to the wider dispute between the parties) rather than the quality of the original decision;

(7) the fact that an argument fails before the FTT does not necessarily mean that the party running that argument was acting unreasonably in doing so; to reach that threshold, the party must generally persist in an argument in the face of an unbeatable argument to the contrary;

(8) the power to award costs under Rule 10 should not become a "backdoor method of costs shifting".

(9) questions of reasonableness should be assessed by reference to the facts and circumstances at the time or times of the acts (or omissions) in question, and not with the benefit of hindsight.

In *Marshall*, the Upper Tribunal endorsed the view that a tribunal can review the adequacy of HMRC's own internal functions when reviewing what is or is not reasonable conduct.

Cases: *Marshall & Co v HMRC* [2016] UKUT 116 (TCC); *Distinctive Care Ltd v HMRC* [2018] UKUT 155 (TCC)

When a party abandons its case or drops an issue

In situations where HMRC abandon their case before the tribunal has determined the matter, it is tempting to think that this evidences that HMRC's decision to proceed with the case in the first place was unreasonable (and, clearly, the same could be said of taxpayers who withdraw their appeal at a late stage). In *Tarafdar*, the Upper Tribunal said that the correct approach was to consider the following three questions:

(1) What was the reason for the withdrawal of that party from the appeal?

(2) Having regard to that reason, could that party have withdrawn at an earlier stage in the proceedings?

(3) Was it unreasonable for that party not to have withdrawn at an earlier stage?

In *Haworth*, the tribunal accepted that the same approach should apply if a particular aspect of a case was dropped part way through proceedings.

In *Waller*, it was considered that HMRC withdrawing their assessments soon after the case was notified to the tribunal (which came after a long, albeit flawed, investigation) was sufficiently prompt as not to amount to the unreasonable defending of proceedings. For an example of a later withdrawal where a costs order was given, see *Atkins*.

In *Zanaco*, the tribunal declined to make a costs order despite a 19-month interval between the notification of the case to the tribunal and HMRC's withdrawal of the assessment. However, that was a case where HMRC's reasons to withdraw the case were not related to the taxpayer's grounds of appeal. Consequently, the delay was not considered to be unreasonable in the circumstances.

Housesimple provides a useful case study for these principles. The company withdrew its appeal relatively late in the process, citing the unexpected pressures on its finance department at the time that the appeal needed particular attention. Although it could have sought a postponement, there was no guarantee that such an application would succeed and it would in any event cause additional costs to be incurred. The tribunal considered that the reasons for withdrawal were reasonable and commercial and therefore dismissed HMRC's application for costs.

Conversely, the tribunal dismissed the company's own application for costs made in respect of what the company considered to be HMRC's unreasonable costs application. The tribunal considered the application to have been reasonably made because, at the time, HMRC knew that the company had withdrawn its appeal at a very late stage but did not know the reasons for the withdrawal.

In *Kellett*, HMRC dropped the case once they received the taxpayer's witness statement which stated nothing more than what the taxpayer (and his adviser) had been repeatedly saying for over two years. Nevertheless, the tribunal considered that, in the absence of that formal evidence, it was reasonable for HMRC to continue to believe in the strength of their case. The author considers that not every judge would be as forgiving towards HMRC and therefore the case emphasises that costs decisions are often a question of discretion where different judges can legitimately reach different views.

In *Marshall Glover*, the taxpayer's representative sent a notice of withdrawal under rule 17 to the tribunal but did not copy this to HMRC. This was held to be inconsiderate and, therefore, unreasonable – particularly as the withdrawal was so close to the hearing date.

In *Quinn*, the tribunal stated that the taxpayer's conduct "whilst reprehensible was not unreasonable". It is the author's view that this statement should be read in the light that the criticism concerned the Appellant's failure to attend a hearing, but where "the hearing would have proceeded even if HMRC had known that the appellant was not going to attend".

In *Wammee*, the tribunal noted that both parties had changed their position at a relatively late stage of the process. However, it continued by remarking that "late developments sometimes happen – they are an inherent risk of the process ... but they are not such that they can generally be characterised as unreasonable conduct so as to sound in costs".

Cases: *Waller v HMRC* [2010] UKFTT 40 (TC); *Executors of David Atkins (deceased) v HMRC* [2011] UKFTT 468 (TC); *Zanaco Investments Ltd v HMRC* [2012] UKFTT 518 (TC); *Tarafdar v HMRC* [2014] UKUT 362 (TCC); *Housesimple Ltd v HMRC* [2017] UKFTT 837 (TC); *Kellett v HMRC* [2018] UKFTT 130 (TC); *Haworth v HMRC* [2019] UKFTT 149 (TC); *Marshall Glover Ltd v HMRC* [2019] UKFTT 271 (TC); *Quinn v HMRC* [2020] UKFTT 51 (TC); *Wammee Holdings Ltd v HMRC* [2020] UKFTT 240 (TC)

When a party presents its winning argument late

A similar approach was taken in *Cheshire*, where HMRC failed to raise its winning argument until late on in the proceedings (in that case, not until the case was before the Upper Tribunal). The Upper Tribunal held that the appropriate considerations were:

- What was the reason for raising the argument late?
- Having regard to that reason, could that party have raised the argument at an earlier stage in the proceedings?
- Was it unreasonable for that party not to have raised the point at an earlier stage?

HMRC argued that they should not be expected to raise an argument that was not expressly in response to the grounds of appeal put forward by the taxpayer. See also **4.7.12**. The Upper Tribunal disagreed saying that, irrespective of what grounds of appeal had been put forward, HMRC should "have stood back and dealt with the appellant's grounds of appeal taking account of the wider context of the appeal in which those grounds arose". Nevertheless, the tribunal considered that the taxpayer's own shortcomings should be a factor when determining how much they could recover in costs from HMRC.

In *Scofield*, the tribunal found HMRC's conduct at a hearing to be unreasonable in the following ways:

- making a very last-minute about-turn in their argument once presented with the *Hansard* extract: the tribunal described this as "a significant error of judgment, which did HMRC no credit". The tribunal emphasised the obligation on the parties to help the tribunal achieve the overriding objective (see **3.3.3**) and "this duty should have overridden considerations (which in the circumstances were manifestly misguided) of narrow partisan advantage"; and
- presenting oral arguments at the hearing which differed significantly from those in the skeleton arguments that had been lodged only four days earlier.

Although, on the facts of the case, the tribunal declined to make a costs award in *Scofield* (see **4.7.10**), in *Rokit*, a last-minute change of tack by HMRC (meaning that previous work undertaken by the taxpayer was wasted) led to a partial costs award. It should, however, be noted that some aspects of HMRC's conduct in *Rokit* did "HMRC little credit" but did not merit any sanction as they were "instances of the cut and thrust of litigation tactics rather than unreasonable conduct".

Cases: *Scofield v HMRC* [2012] UKFTT 673 (TC); *Rokit Ltd v HMRC* [2017] UKFTT 618 (TC); *HMRC v Cheshire Centre For Independent Living* [2020] UKUT 275 (TCC)

Case doomed to failure

In *Ho*, the tribunal held that HMRC's arguments lacked "sufficient evidential foundation": the basis of their case was unsustainable and their cash flow test was flawed. For these reasons, the tribunal held that there had been unreasonable conduct by HMRC.

In *Wallis*, the tribunal suggested the following as examples of conduct that would amount to acting unreasonably in defending proceedings:

- generally persisting with a legal argument which has recently been dismissed by the Supreme Court and where the party has had this fact drawn to his attention; or
- proceeding on a basis of facts which the party accepts (or can only reasonably accept) as incorrect.

This decision was followed in *Roden*. In *Roden*, the tribunal recognised that a party would not be acting unreasonably, when it pursued a case that had no merit, unless the party ought to have known that the case was without merit. When applying the test to HMRC, the tribunal did not focus on the knowledge of an individual officer but was prepared to consider whether HMRC as a whole ought to have realised that the case had no reasonable prospect of success.

In *Perrin*, the Upper Tribunal noted that HMRC were persistently putting forward an argument that had been disproven and criticised on a number of occasions in earlier cases. The Upper Tribunal suggested that this could constitute unreasonable conduct for the purposes of a costs application.

In *Cannon*, the tribunal awarded costs in relation to HMRC's closed-mindedness in a case where they needed to prove deliberate conduct which led to a refusal to enter into any meaningful discussions. HMRC had adopted "an entrenched position ... which was deaf to any kind of explanations ... with a view to a different stance being taken".

Cases: *Ho v HMRC* [2010] UKFTT 387 (TC); *Wallis v HMRC and another* [2013] UKFTT 81 (TC); *Roden v HMRC* [2013] UKFTT 523 (TC); *Cannon v HMRC* [2018] UKFTT 160 (TC); *Perrin v HMRC* [2018] UKUT 156 (TCC)

Late evidence

In *Earthshine (No. 2)*, the tribunal – having permitted HMRC to introduce evidence late on in the proceedings (see rule 15) – considered the costs of dealing with HMRC's application and consequential to it. The tribunal refused to award the company its costs in unsuccessfully contesting HMRC's application; however, it was entitled to the costs it incurred consequentially.

In *Masstech*, a similar case heard by the same judge, it was ordered that the late evidence would be admitted only if HMRC undertook to make good the additional costs incurred by the taxpayer as a result of the evidence being admitted late. The taxpayer's application for costs incurred in the hearing was again refused, as HMRC's application to have it admitted late did not amount to unreasonable conduct.

Cases: *Earthshine Ltd (No. 2) v HMRC* [2010] UKFTT 314 (TC); *Masstech Corporation Ltd (in administration) v HMRC* [2011] UKFTT 649 (TC)

Late engagement with the tribunal process

In *Ward*, the tribunal awarded a taxpayer the additional costs incurred when chasing HMRC's statement of case which was served late, the delay being blamed by HMRC on the "vagaries of the Department's posting procedures".

In *Southwest*, the tribunal criticised HMRC's handling of the case. HMRC withdrew their defence of the assessment on the basis of the contents of the taxpayer's witness statements. However, these witness statements had been received several months earlier but had simply not been considered. The tribunal held that HMRC should have given proper consideration to the evidence much sooner, especially as there were administrative steps that had been taken in relation to the appeal (for example telling the tribunal the estimated duration of the hearing) which presupposed that the evidence had been considered.

In *Ping*, the tribunal recognised that HMRC should be entitled to a reasonable period to consider the evidence provided by the taxpayer. In that case, however, HMRC announced their withdrawal a couple of weeks after what the tribunal considered to be a reasonable period and a modest costs award was given to the taxpayer in relation to the costs incurred in that two-week period.

Cases: *Southwest Communications Group Ltd v HMRC* [2012] UKFTT 701 (TC); *Ping Kong Lam v HMRC* [2014] UKFTT 79 (TC); *Messrs JH & IM Ward (Partnership) v HMRC* [2014] UKFTT 108 (TC)

Unjustified absences from hearings

In *Enviroengineering*, the tribunal held that HMRC's failure to turn up at the tribunal or even to notify the tribunal to explain their absence, when the tribunal was meant to be determining HMRC's own application, amounted to unreasonable conduct and awarded the taxpayer its costs. A similar conclusion was reached in *Ahmed* where the taxpayer should have given HMRC and the tribunal prior notice that he was not pursuing his appeal. Absence *per se*, however, does not amount to unreasonable conduct (see *Bird*).

In a similar vein, in *Walker*, the taxpayer's refusal to answer appropriate requests from HMRC, and her failure to attend the hearing (in which it was held that she had made dishonest claims for input tax), amounted to unreasonable conduct.

In *Wheeler*, the tribunal confirmed that deliberate non-attendance was not in itself unreasonable conduct. However, it was held to be in that case when the taxpayer was expected to know that he could not realistically expect to win in his absence.

Cases: *Bird v HMRC* (2008) Sp C 720; *Enviroengineering Ltd v HMRC* [2011] UKFTT 366 (TC); *Walker v HMRC* [2012] UKFTT 225 (TC); *Wheeler v HMRC* [2019] UKFTT 336 (TC); *Ahmed v HMRC* [2019] UKFTT 701 (TC)

Lying

In *HCA*, the Employment Appeal Tribunal held that a party lying would not, on its own, merit a costs order being made against that party. The tribunal is obliged "to examine the context and to look at the nature, gravity and effect of the lie in determining the unreasonableness of the alleged conduct."

Case: *HCA International Ltd v JL May-Bheemul* (2011) UKEAT/477/10/ZT

4.8 Rule 10 – Orders for costs

Other examples of "unreasonable conduct"

Other matters that have been held to amount to unreasonable conduct include:

- telling the tribunal that the subject matter of the appeal had not been discussed in Parliament when there was in fact a relevant *Hansard* extract. Although the tribunal accepted that the error was innocent, it was considered to be careless and, therefore, unreasonable, given the serious consequences for the taxpayer were the tribunal to have upheld HMRC's decision (*Scofield*);
- unnecessary examination of witnesses (*Wallis*);
- lengthening of an appeal with irrelevant or unnecessary evidence or behaviour (*Wallis*);
- pursuing an appeal merely to defer the inevitable tax liability (*Wilsons*); and
- serving irrelevant evidence (making irrelevant allegations which needed rebutting) (*Wilsons*).

Cases: *Scofield v HMRC* [2012] UKFTT 673 (TC); *Wallis v HMRC and another* [2013] UKFTT 81 (TC); *Wilsons Solicitors LLP v HMRC* [2019] UKFTT 341 (TC).

What costs can be recovered?

Although it will be most common for a costs order to reflect the additional costs that have been incurred by the other party, as a result of the party's unreasonable conduct, TCEA 2007, s. 29 gives the tribunal wider powers to make whatever costs order it considers appropriate. It is suggested that the tribunal can therefore order a party, assuming that there has been *some* unreasonable conduct, to pay some or all of the costs of the case, i.e. even those costs that would inevitably have been incurred had the unreasonable conduct not occurred. This approach seems to have been accepted in a special educational needs case, *HJ*, where the Upper Tribunal held that "an award should cover as a minimum the costs attributable to the unreasonable behaviour".

Although not expressly considered by the tribunal, it is arguable that *Hills* implicitly accepted this approach. In that case, the tribunal had considered the possibility that (on the particular facts of the case)

139

opting out of the costs regime amounted to unreasonable conduct. Although that could not have led to any additional costs, the Upper Tribunal would have made a costs award.

However, tribunals generally prefer to limit cost awards to those additional costs occasioned by the other party's unreasonable conduct. For example, in *Eclipse*, a case where HMRC had failed to comply with a case management direction made by the tribunal, the tribunal commented that that would have been a *prima facie* justification for a costs order against HMRC to compensate the taxpayer for any additional costs that it had incurred as a result of HMRC's failure.

See also **4.7.10**.

In *Liberty*, the taxpayer was awarded its costs. The Director of Border Revenue (DBR) complained that some costs claimed included those incurred trying to persuade DBR to drop the case ("litigation by correspondence"). The tribunal considered that to be no bar to a costs claim:

> "where a dispute can be settled out of court, the parties should be encouraged to do so ... the appellant's approach ultimately succeeded as in the end it appears DBR did decide to check the evidence which it held and withdraw the decision".

In *Gardiner*, the High Court confirmed that there was no bar on a party recovering costs that were paid for by a third party. That concerned a situation where the taxpayers' adviser was prepared to pay for representation by Counsel. However, the decision would be equally relevant for the practice where (typically) avoidance cases are funded by a contribution to the scheme promoters by all of the participants. One should nevertheless be aware of the general distaste within the judiciary towards "champerty", whereby a third party buys into the rights of a court action without proper justification.

See also **4.7.9**.

Cases: *Eclipse Film Partners No. 35 LLP v HMRC (No. 2)* [2010] UKFTT 448 (FT); *HJ v London Borough of Brent (SEN)* [2011] UKUT 191 (AAC); *Hills v HMRC* [2016] UKUT 266 (TCC); *HMRC v Gardiner* [2018] EWHC 1716 (QB); *Liberty Wines Ltd v Director of Border Revenue* [2018] UKFTT 372 (TC)

4.8.6 Complex cases (rule 10(1)(c), (d))

The third scenario is where the case has been allocated to the Complex case category under rule 23 (see **5.6.7** below).

Generally, Complex cases represent the exception to the normal rule in the Tax Chamber that each party bears its own costs. In a Complex case, the default position is that the tribunal can order one party to pay the other party's costs (or some of them).

When costs will be payable

In such cases, it will often be the case that the losing party will be ordered to pay the costs to the winning party. This is the usual position for litigation in the High Court, say, and was the starting point in the Upper Tribunal's thinking in *Colquhoun*.

As shown in *Award*, a success may be identified in the context of individual hearings (for example where there are interim matters that require the tribunal's resolution) rather than only in the light of the overall result of the appeal.

However, it should be noted that in *Capital Air Services*, the then president of the Tax and Chancery Chamber of the Upper Tribunal suggested that a winning party in that tribunal should not assume that a costs order would be made. In particular, the usual position in the High Court is governed by a specific provision in the Civil Procedure Rules (CPR) which provides an assumption that the winner would be entitled to its costs, whereas the tribunal rules have no equivalent provision.

There again, the Upper Tribunal and FTT procedural rules differ in respect of the ability of taxpayers to opt out of the costs regime in the First-tier (see below) and this difference could justify a further distinction between the approaches of the two tribunals. For example, a taxpayer who has not opted out of the costs regime in the First-tier (see below) could be said to have accepted the consequences of losing the appeal and therefore being subject to a costs order.

In *Versteegh*, the FTT proceeded on the assumption (shared by the parties) that the principles applicable under the CPR were the relevant starting point and, therefore, in accordance with the CPR rule 44.2, considered that the general position should be that the loser pays the winner's costs. The tribunal took a similar approach in *BAV*. In the author's respectful opinion, there is a difference between following the principles applicable under the CPR and adopting a rule specifically provided for in the CPR but which does not feature in the tribunal's own set of rules. It is therefore considered that the tribunal erred in this particular regard, although it is not considered that this led to an incorrect decision in that particular case.

Furthermore, in *MacMillan*, the tribunal concluded that there was "no general rule that costs should be borne by the unsuccessful party ... the rule is to seek just and fair exercise of the discretion". On the facts of the case, the tribunal thought that both parties were partly successful, although the taxpayer was the overall winner. Accordingly, HMRC were ordered to pay one half of the taxpayer's costs.

Indeed, in *Spring Capital*, the tribunal noted that (as acknowledged in *Versteegh* itself), identifying the successful party "is only the starting point ... it does not determine the costs order ... it is necessary to take account of all the circumstances".

In *Roger Preston*, however, the tribunal treated it as "necessarily implicit" that, in complex cases, costs should follow the event. The point was made because the tribunal considered that it was unnecessary for the applicant also to argue unreasonable conduct as per rule 10(1)(b). The author considers that the decision should be understood in its proper context. The tribunal should not be taken to have said that a costs award will always be made in cases falling within rule 10(1)(c): instead, the tribunal should be understood as doing no more than confirming that the initial entitlement to a costs award is satisfied in such cases and therefore it is unnecessary to embark upon demonstrating that rule 10(1)(b) is also satisfied.

In summary, the tribunal should consider all of the facts of the case (including the fact that a taxpayer had not opted out of the costs regime). Nevertheless, although a likely outcome, it should not be assumed that a costs order would always be made in favour of the winner of the case.

Cases: *Award Drinks Ltd (in liquidation) v HMRC* [2017] UKFTT 509 (TC); *Capital Air Services Ltd v HMRC* [2010] UKUT 373 (TCC); *Colquhoun v HMRC* [2011] UKUT B10 (TCC); *Versteegh Ltd v HMRC* [2014] UKFTT 397 (TC); *BAV-TMW-Globaler-Immobilien-Spezialfonds v HMRC* [2019] UKFTT 233 (TC); *Spring Capital Ltd v HMRC* [2019] UKFTT 319 (TC); *MacMillan v HMRC* [2019] UKFTT 624 (TC); *Roger Preston Group Ltd v HMRC* [2021] UKFTT 132 (TC)

Opting out of the costs regime

Although many taxpayers will relish the opportunity of recovering costs from HMRC if successful in a Complex case in the Tax Chamber, the risk of HMRC being able to recover costs from the taxpayer can have a deterrent effect on some.

Consequently, rule 10(1)(c)(ii) provides that taxpayers can opt out of the costs regime. If more than one taxpayer is a party to the proceedings, any one taxpayer can elect to take the case out of the costs regime. In *Hills*, it was suggested that a taxpayer may not opt out of the costs regime if to do so would amount to an abuse of process. The author considers the Upper Tribunal to have made an error in making that decision.

In *Brown*, the tribunal considered that, once made, it is not possible to withdraw a notice to opt out of the costs regime. The author considers that the decision to be correct but does not preclude (in appropriate cases) any subsequent costs award reflecting a party's reasons for making and seeking to withdraw a notice to opt out of the costs regime.

If the case is so taken out of the costs regime, costs orders will be made only in respect of wasted costs and/or unreasonable conduct (as per above).

Where a party has been substituted under rule 9, the substitute inherits the predecessor's position so far as any opt-out (or lack of it) is concerned. However, as noted in *Warren*, a substitute may apply for consequential directions and it would be appropriate for any revised views about costs to be dealt with through that process. Otherwise, the substitute could be accused of waiting until the outcome of the appeal with a view to claiming costs if successful but objecting to being liable for HMRC's costs if the appeal turns out to be unsuccessful.

It will be seen that HMRC cannot opt out of the costs regime. That right is exclusive to taxpayers.

For this purpose, rule 10(8) provides that the meaning of taxpayer is extended to any person liable to pay tax, a penalty, a surcharge etc to HMRC.

Cases: *Hills v HMRC* [2016] UKUT 266 (TCC); *N Brown Group plc v HMRC* [2016] UKFTT 445 (TC); *Warren v HMRC* [2017] UKFTT 521 (TC)

Cases becoming "Complex"

A case might not initially be allocated to the Complex case category but can still be reallocated to that category. It was held in *Capital Air Services (Costs)* that costs prior to the reallocation of the case to the Complex category will (retrospectively) come within the tribunal's jurisdiction to award costs. However, it was held that the tribunal ought to take into account this retrospective effect of any reallocation when deciding the terms of any subsequent costs order. This was done in *Hills* where the costs award was limited to those arising from the date of the reallocation.

Cases: *Capital Air Services Ltd v HMRC* (Costs) [2011] UKUT 484 (TCC); *Hills v HMRC* [2016] UKUT 266 (TCC)

Time for opting out of the costs regime

To opt out of the costs regime, the taxpayer must make a written request to the tribunal within 28 days of the taxpayer receiving notice that the case had been allocated as a Complex case. (Strictly, this can work against a taxpayer who is added to proceedings at a later stage. However, rule 5(3)(a) will allow the 28-day period to be extended in appropriate cases.)

It should be noted that, usually, time limits run from dates on which the tribunal did something (as that is a date which the tribunal can keep track of). However, this particular time limit runs from the date that the taxpayer *receives* the relevant notice.

Similarly, as noted in *Rapid Brickwork*, the time limit is (unusually) drafted by reference to the date that an election is *made* to opt out of the costs regime, rather than the date on which the election is *received* by the tribunal. Of course, it is safer to ensure timely receipt wherever possible.

Because of this double level of uncertainty as to whether or not an election to opt out has been made in time, the tribunal in *Rapid Brickwork* considered that any objection to a late election should be made by HMRC as promptly as possible.

In *Clipper*, it was held that including a copy of the reallocation of a case to the complex category in a much larger bundle of documents being used for an interim hearing (when the notice of the reallocation was not pertinent to the hearing itself) did not amount to notice being served on the taxpayer. Therefore, there was no need for the taxpayer to opt out of the costs regime within the subsequent 28 days.

Similarly, in *Albon*, a reference by HMRC to wanting costs (appended to a statement of case) did not constitute sufficient notice so as to start the 28-day period (leaving aside the fact that the statement of case would have been served by HMRC rather than the tribunal).

The tribunal did indicate in *Albon*, however, that notice might be capable of being given orally, rather than necessarily in writing.

Cases: *Clipper Group Holdings Ltd v HMRC* [2016] UKFTT 712 (TC); *Rapid Brickwork Ltd v HMRC* [2017] UKFTT 194 (TC); *Albon Engineering and Manufacturing Ltd v HMRC* [2017] UKFTT 560 (TC)

Notifying HMRC

The rules do not require the opt-out to be copied to HMRC. Thus, a notice sent only to the tribunal would be sufficient to comply with the rule.

This is presumably in recognition of the fact that the details of the litigating team at HMRC will not usually have been communicated to the taxpayer during the 28-day opt-out period. Nevertheless, where the details are known, good practice would be for such notices to be copied to HMRC when being sent to the tribunal.

4.8.7 *Applying for a costs order (rule 10(3), (4))*

Although a tribunal may unilaterally make a costs order (under rule 10(2)), it will be more common for an order to follow an application by a party.

Such an application must be:

- in writing;
- sent or delivered both to the tribunal and to the person against whom the order is sought; and
- accompanied by a schedule of the costs claimed, in sufficient detail to allow the tribunal to assess summarily how much should be paid, should the tribunal choose to do so (see rule 10(6)).

Although not specifically required by the rules, it is advisable for the application to include reasons for it being made, particularly where the application is being made under rule 10(1)(a) or (b) (wasted costs or unreasonable conduct).

Sufficient detail to allow summary assessment

The question of "sufficient detail" was considered in *Distinctive*. In that case, the taxpayer was one of thirty being dealt with together. It was held that the costs application (for £2,500) should have made it clear that it was a straightforward calculation of one thirtieth of the actual costs of £75,000, rather than (as it did) give the impression that the time costs being claimed were in fact only £2,500. This misstatement could have rendered the application invalid. However, the Upper Tribunal considered that the First-tier should have waived the breach given that HMRC themselves were not misled and could have raised the point when making their own representations.

The Upper Tribunal did suggest, however, that the following information should have been included:

- the name of each fee earner;
- the hourly rate for that fee earner;
- a sufficient statement of the level of experience and expertise of that fee earner to enable the FTT to form a view of the appropriateness of the hourly rate claimed and to assess whether it was reasonable for the relevant work to have been done by a fee earner of that standing;
- the fee earner's professional qualification or other status;
- the geographical location of the fee earner;

- the time spent by each fee earner, together with a breakdown showing when the time was spent and giving a brief description of the work done on each occasion;
- any disbursements claimed must also be clearly identified, giving the amount of the cost incurred, what it was incurred on and how that expenditure relates to the proceedings;
- the extent to which any VAT charged is recoverable as input tax by the claiming party; and
- if the figures in the schedule are calculated as some apportioned part of a larger figure, it would always be advisable for details of the apportionment to be included in the application.

Case: *Distinctive Care Ltd v HMRC* [2018] UKUT 155 (TCC)

Timing of the application

The application may be made at any time during the proceedings.

In *Barclays*, the tribunal confirmed that there was no principled reason why a costs order could be made only following the determination of a preliminary issue, or a like "event". In any event, a hotly contested application for a stay of proceedings as had taken place in that case was "an event of the kind which costs can follow".

An application may also be made at any time within 28 days after the tribunal sends out either:

- a decision notice recording the decision which finally disposes of all issues in the proceedings; or
- a notice of a party's withdrawal from proceedings (see rule 17(2)).

See the discussion of the *Rana* case under rule 5(3)(a) as to the effect on a time limit when a document is sent to the wrong address.

Per *Filmlab*, an application for wasted costs should be made only after the full hearing of proceedings, other than in exceptional circumstances. The main reason for this is the difficulty for a tribunal to judge fairly the appropriateness of a representative's conduct without the benefit of hindsight. In addition, as happened in *Filmlab* itself, the application led to the other side's barrister withdrawing from the case: as that could have serious repercussions for the representative's client, the court stated that this was another reason why such applications should very rarely be made other than at the end of the proceedings.

It is suggested that an exception would arise if, for example, one party's financial position were so precarious that the absence of any such award could impact upon its ability to continue to fight the case. Other exceptions were cited by the Family Division of the High Court in *B v B*. In that case, the application related to a discrete issue and not the main issue between the parties; secondly, there had already been a change of legal representatives by the time that the application was considered; thirdly, the main trial was already bound to have been delayed and the court considered that further delaying any consideration of the wasted costs application was inappropriate; finally, the court considered the application one that could have been dealt with summarily.

In *Aozora*, the FTT recognised that the case was likely to be the subject of an appeal. It duly extended the time limit for applying for costs until 28 days after the case became final. That was a case allocated to the Complex case category where it was unlikely that issues relating to a party's conduct would be pertinent. It is considered that a similar extension will not be so readily granted in cases where the costs application is likely to be made under rule 10(1)(a) or (b). Of course, each case will need to be considered on its own merits.

Cases: *Rana v London Borough of Ealing* [2018] EWCA Civ 2074; *Filmlab Systems International Ltd v Pennington* [1995] 1 WLR 673; *B v B (Wasted Costs: abuse of process)* [2001] 1 FLR 843; *Aozora GMAC Investment Ltd v HMRC* [2021] UKFTT 222 (TC); *Barclays Services Ltd v HMRC* [2021] UKFTT 269 (TC)

Timing of the tribunal's consideration of a costs application

Although the rules specify the time limits for an application for costs, they say nothing about the time when such an application should be considered by the tribunal. In *Starmill*, the taxpayer had lost an appeal and, being a VAT case governed by the pre-2009 rules, it was accepted that HMRC were *prima facie* entitled to their costs. However, the taxpayer was seeking permission from the Upper Tribunal to appeal against the First-tier's decision: if permission were granted and the taxpayer subsequently succeeded in the Upper

Tribunal, any previous costs award would clearly have become academic. As a result, the taxpayer argued that the tribunal should defer its decision in relation to the costs issue at least until it was known whether the Upper Tribunal would grant permission to appeal.

The tribunal accepted that a deferral might be appropriate, but only in exceptional circumstances. Those would include cases where a taxpayer could show that it would suffer hardship which would prevent the taxpayer then pursuing its appeal. Alternatively, a deferral might be appropriate if there was a real risk that the party due to pay the costs might be unable to recover the costs from the other party should the appeal prove to be successful. However, the tribunal considered that that was not a risk if the receiving party is HMRC.

Case: *Starmill v HMRC* [2013] UKFTT 681 (TC)

4.8.8 Right to make representations (rule 10(5))

A tribunal may not make any costs order without first giving the paying party the opportunity to make representations. In *Enviroengineering*, the tribunal had initially overlooked this requirement and, so, the original costs order was set aside. However, when HMRC were subsequently given the opportunity to make representations, the tribunal considered that the terms of the original order were still appropriate and remade it in the same terms.

In *Wheeler*, the tribunal considered that, in principle, costs should be recovered by HMRC but it was concerned about the taxpayer's means. The tribunal therefore effectively suspended the costs order, preventing HMRC from enforcing the costs award without the tribunal's express permission.

Cases: *Enviroengineering Ltd v HMRC* [2011] UKFTT 366 (TC); *Wheeler v HMRC* [2019] UKFTT 336 (TC)

4.8.9 Determining the amount of the costs order (rule 10(6), (7), (7A))

The overall approach to be taken

In *Willow Court*, the Upper Tribunal set out a three-stage process (based on the equivalent rules for lands disputes). First, the tribunal should consider whether the objective conditions (above) for a costs award are met. Secondly, the tribunal should then consider whether (applying the overriding objective) the tribunal should then exercise its discretion and make the award. The third stage (if applicable) is to determine how much should be awarded (again, taking into account the overriding objective).

Case: *Willow Court Management Company (1985) Ltd v Alexander* [2016] UKUT (LC)

The three ways of determining how much to award

The tribunal can take one of three routes when determining how much should be paid under a costs order:

- it can summarily assess the amount – this means taking a rough and ready view of how much it would be appropriate to be paid in the circumstances;
- the order can reflect an agreement between the parties as to how much should be paid; or
- the tribunal can refer the matter to be subject to detailed assessment.

Furthermore, since 1 April 2013, the tribunal can direct a party to make a payment on account before the completion of the assessment process. The earlier case of *Curran* suggested that the tribunal had this power in any event, but the 2013 changes put the matter beyond doubt.

Whenever costs are assessed, it should not be assumed that the receiving party will necessarily be awarded every penny that has been incurred in the course of the proceedings. Ultimately, the assessment of costs will be directed at ascertaining how much it would be reasonable to recover. Whilst a taxpayer is undoubtedly free to choose a very expensive firm of advisers, assessment of costs will ensure that only a reasonable part of the fee will be recoverable.

As a result, it would not be advantageous in obtaining the services of a lawyer charging £3,000 per hour in a routine matter on the assumption that the costs could be recovered from the other party. Assessment will consider the appropriateness of the charging rates and the seniority of staff involved in particular aspects of the case.

Costs will usually represent actual expenditure incurred on professional support and will therefore not include indirect costs such as loss of profit whilst attending a tribunal hearing. However, a party with its own in-house legal department will usually be entitled to claim costs in relation to the time spent by that department on the case, even though the expenses of running that legal department are being incurred anyway (*Wiggins Alloys*). Furthermore, such costs are not limited to an estimate of the proportion of the in-house lawyers' respective salaries; other factors will include other overheads etc. In cases involving HMRC's in-house solicitors, HMRC will claim "charge-out" rates equivalent to some commercial firms. Although there is nothing wrong with the principle of claiming such costs, it must remembered that cost orders are intended to be compensatory and not a profit source. Therefore, an hourly rate claimed can be challenged in the course of "assessment" (see below) in just the same way as the number of hours put in. In *Walsh*, the tribunal confirmed that HMRC were also entitled to receive costs in relation to their non-legally qualified staff.

Similarly, the tribunal's practice is to allow taxpayers to claim the costs charged by accountants and tax advisers and not just by lawyers. This deviates from the position set out by the Court of Appeal in *Agassi*. However, such a deviation is entirely reasonable given the clear rules entitling non-lawyers to represent clients in the tribunal. Furthermore, the author maintains the view that the Court of Appeal reached the wrong result in *Agassi* and, given the result of the substantive tax dispute in that case when it made its way to the House of Lords, the question of costs was not revisited.

There is one further exception to the rule that only actually expended costs may be recovered. This is where the recipient is a litigant in person. In *Bogle*, the tribunal applied the civil courts' hourly rate of £19. However, it is not immediately clear whether that rate is applicable in the tribunal. In *Humphries*, the tribunal suggested that this is as a result of s. 48(1) although the author remains unsure.

In *Green*, the tribunal was happy to make an award in favour of a litigant in person which reflected an accurate estimate as to the taxpayer's loss of earnings.

Law: *Litigants in Person (Costs and Expenses) Act* 1975, s. 1(1)(ba), (2)(ba); TCEA 2007, s. 48(1)

Cases: *Wiggins Alloys Ltd v Jenkins* [1981] IRLR 275; *Agassi v Robinson (HM Inspector of Taxes) (Costs)* [2006] 1 WLR 2126; [2006] STC 580; [2006] BTC 3; *Curran v HMRC* [2012] UKFTT 655 (TC); *Bogle v HMRC* [2014] UKFTT 201 (TC); *Green v HMRC* [2018] UKFTT 669 (TC); *Humphries v HMRC* [2019] UKFTT 88 (TC); *Walsh v HMRC* [2019] UKFTT 350 (TC)

Detailed assessment

A detailed assessment is where the individual costs claimed are separately analysed so that it can be ascertained overall how much should be paid. Detailed assessment is likely to be limited to the larger cases.

It will be carried out (usually by costs specialists) within the civil courts system.

From 1 April 2013, the costs incurred by a party in the course of the detailed assessment process can also be taken into account.

"Standard" and "indemnity" bases

When a costs matter is referred for detailed assessment, there are two distinct approaches that can be taken. Costs can be assessed either on the "standard basis" or on what is known as the "indemnity basis".

In both situations, the receiving party cannot recover more than that party has incurred in costs. However, the indemnity basis will usually entitle the receiving party to recover more of the costs. The distinction between the two is where the burden of proof lies in determining which costs are reasonably incurred.

On the standard basis, the receiving party will be able to recover only those costs that can be shown to have been reasonably incurred.

When costs are to be assessed on the indemnity basis, the starting point will be to assume that all costs are recoverable and it is for the paying party to reduce the amount payable by demonstrating that costs have been unreasonably incurred.

Although assessment on the indemnity basis cannot give the receiving party any form of windfall (in that its receipt cannot exceed what it has actually expended), it nevertheless implies disapproval by the tribunal of the paying party's conduct. Although each case must be decided on its own merits (and different judges may legitimately view the same behaviour in different ways), the key principle was set out in *Excelsior*: was there something in the party's conduct of the case or some circumstance which takes the case out of the norm?

In the tax context, costs orders on the indemnity basis were made where the Revenue had advanced a weak case and then withdrew it for reasons previously known to them (*Carvill*). However, as the former Special Commissioners held in that case, the previously high threshold for costs in the Special Commissioners (requiring "wholly unreasonable" conduct) would mean that many cases where costs were payable could have merited costs orders on the indemnity basis. This was implicit in the tribunal's decision in *Thomas Holdings*, where the conduct was described as "unreasonable ... [but not] wholly unreasonable". "Accordingly," concluded the tribunal, "award of costs on an indemnity basis was not appropriate."

An indemnity costs award was made where the Revenue over-relied on business economics exercises (*Farthings Steak House*). Conduct was also considered to be wholly unreasonable where the Revenue continued to maintain a challenge against a set of accounts, when the original basis for the challenge had been satisfactorily explained (*McEwan*).

Pursuing the wrong taxpayer was described as "unreasonable in the extreme" in *Deluca*. It is suggested that, had the matter proceeded to a detailed assessment, the tribunal would have considered directing that costs be assessed on the indemnity basis.

It was mooted in *Vardy* that the indemnity basis might be appropriate in cases involving tax avoidance as a matter of principle. In the author's opinion, however, such an approach would be totally wrong, mainly because of the subjectivity of the term "tax avoidance". However, otherwise than in cases governed by rule 10(1)(c), there would be no direct connection between the underlying scheme and the conduct in the litigation process that gives rise to the costs award.

Cases: *Scott (t/a Farthings Steak House) v McDonald (HM Inspector of Taxes)* (1996) Sp C 91; *Excelsior Commercial and Industrial Holdings Ltd v Salisbury Hammer Aspden and Johnson* [2002] EWCA Civ 879; *Carvill v Frost (HM Inspector of Taxes)* (2004) Sp C 447 and (2005) Sp C 468; *McEwan v HMRC* (2005) Sp C 488; *Deluca v HMRC* [2011] UKFTT 579 (TC); *Thomas Holdings Ltd v HMRC* [2011] UKFTT 656 (TC); *Vardy Properties v HMRC* [2013] UKFTT 96 (TC)

Principles for the application of the indemnity basis

Western Ferries was a transitional case concerning the old "wholly unreasonable" threshold. Although that historical context was particularly relevant to one particular aspect of the company's costs application, the case is nevertheless illustrative of what conduct might be necessary for a costs award to be made on the indemnity basis. The taxpayer's concern was that HMRC were pursuing a legal point which had little chance of success. The tribunal accepted that there must come a point when it is no longer reasonable to pursue a technical point or to establish, as a matter of public policy, what any reasonable tax practitioner would consider the law to be. However, it was considered that that threshold had not been crossed in that particular case. The tribunal's approach was consistent with the statement in HMRC's litigation and settlement strategy, which stated that HMRC would not usually take a point where it was unlikely to succeed unless justified by the particular circumstances (such as a very large amount of tax at stake – either in that particular case or across the taxpaying population as a whole – or a fundamental point of principle or behaviour at issue) (see **2.2.2**).

In *Western Ferries*, the tribunal referred to the former Special Commissioners' refusal to award costs in *Homeowners*. That was a case where the tax officer had himself stated in correspondence that he had little faith in the legal point the Revenue subsequently took to the Commissioners. Whilst not suggesting that the case had been wrongly decided, the tribunal did consider that a tribunal now might reach a different conclusion on the facts.

Cases: *Homeowners Friendly Society Ltd v Barrett (HM Inspector of Taxes)* (1995) Sp C 31; *Western Ferries (Clyde) Ltd v HMRC* [2011] UKFTT 541 (TC)

Guidance: https://www.gov.uk/government/publications/litigation-and-settlement-strategy-lss

Costs of the application

When a costs application is resisted, it will mean that further costs can be incurred simply establishing whether those earlier costs can be recovered.

The author had previously understood the rules to limit the recoverability of those further costs to cases under rule 10(1)(a) because of a potentially anomalous wording of the rules.

However, it is understood that the tribunal and HMRC make no distinction in practice between the different categories and that parties are entitled to seek the costs of costs applications themselves. Of course, those costs will be recoverable only if the application is itself successful and, as always, will be subject to the tribunal's discretion.

In *Mr E*, it was accepted that the costs of the costs application were recoverable.

Case: *Mr E v HMRC* [2018] UKFTT 771 (TC)

4.8.10 Principles for costs awards

It is a fundamental principle that costs awards should reimburse costs actually incurred, and not merely be a way to penalise the other side. Thus, a party that receives its advice free should not be able to get a costs award, irrespective of the conduct of the other party.

Not necessarily limited to additional costs

However, in cases where an award is made in response to unreasonable conduct, that does not necessarily mean that costs awards should be limited to those additional costs incurred as a result of the behaviour complained of (see *HJ* and *Barnsley*).

In *Scofield*, however, the tribunal declined to make a costs award against HMRC for the simple reason that the various incidents of unreasonable conduct (see **4.8.5** above) were dealt with by the taxpayer without any need for additional costs to be incurred.

It is the author's experience that the usual approach of the tribunal is, as per *Scofield*, to limit costs awards to amounts that compensate the additional expenditure caused by the other side's unreasonable conduct. However, as noted by the three-stage process at **4.7.9**, that is a question that should be addressed at the second or third stage of the analysis.

Cases: *HJ v London Borough of Brent (SEN)* [2011] UKUT 191 (AAC); *Barnsley Metropolitan Borough Council v Yerrakalva* [2011] EWCA Civ 1255; *Scofield v HMRC* [2012] UKFTT 673 (TC)

Record keeping

In order to ascertain what costs have been incurred, it was noted in *PSI* that it was unsatisfactory that the schedule of costs had not been based on contemporaneous time records.

Case: *PSI Engineering Ltd v HMRC* [2011] UKUT 765 (TC)

Costs in cases where success is only partial

In many cases, the winning party will not necessarily have won on every single point: there might be "reserve arguments" that fare less well or simply some points that are won whereas others are lost. For example, in *ERF*, the taxpayer was appealing against an assessment and a penalty: it succeeded in part in both, by reducing the amount assessed and the consequential penalty. However, it was held that HMRC had been "substantially the winner" of the case and, being a case subject to a costs regime, HMRC were awarded their costs. This approach was subsequently confirmed by the Upper Tribunal.

In *Bastionpark*, the tribunal noted that there are different permutations available in such circumstances. Each party might be awarded a share of costs from the other to reflect the issues each party won. Or the overall winner might simply receive a proportion of its own costs to reflect its partial success. A further option is that each side will simply bear its own costs. The ultimate decision is at the tribunal's discretion.

4.8 Rule 10 – Orders for costs

In *Talentcore*, the Upper Tribunal was dealing with a case which was won by the taxpayer but where one issue arose during the course of the appeal which required additional work and which was won by HMRC. The judge considered that "in principle HMRC would be entitled to some costs on that account whereas a proportion of the [taxpayer's] costs should be disallowed on that score". However, such a strict approach was considered to be "clearly undesirable" and it was therefore more appropriate to take a broad-brush view with a discount to be taken from the taxpayer's costs award.

Care has to be taken to consider discrete issues separately. In *Western Ferries*, the Revenue made a relatively late application to bring in an additional argument by amendment to their statement of case. The taxpayer unsuccessfully objected to the argument being admitted, but was ultimately successful in defeating the argument at the substantive hearing. The taxpayer sought to recover its costs of objecting to the inclusion of the additional argument. However, the tribunal considered it difficult to see how the taxpayer could have been entitled to recover its costs in objecting to HMRC's application, given that the application itself was actually successful.

Vardy and *Versteegh* were complex cases where HMRC had issued a number of assessments in the alternative, against different taxpayers in the same group. The assessments were to counter tax avoidance schemes which the tribunal concluded were unsuccessful. However, because of the nature of the schemes, the tribunal also had to determine which of the group companies were liable for the additional tax. In *Vardy*, the tribunal took a holistic approach, considering HMRC to be the overall victor and requiring the losing company to pay all of HMRC's costs. This approach was endorsed in *Versteegh* but, because of the additional complexities of the case, the final order was more nuanced.

Cases: *Western Ferries (Clyde) Ltd v HMRC* [2011] UKFTT 541 (TC); *HMRC v Talentcore Ltd (t/a Team Spirits)* [2012] 2 Costs LR 418 [2011] BTC 1941; *ERF Ltd v HMRC* [2012] UKUT 105 (TCC); *Vardy Properties v HMRC* [2013] UKFTT 96 (TC); *Versteegh Ltd v HMRC* [2014] UKFTT 397 (TC); *Bastionpark LLP v HMRC* [2016] UKUT 425 (TCC)

A case study (BSkyB)

In *British Sky Broadcasting*, however, the tribunal considered that the successful taxpayers should not be entitled to their costs. In the case of one of the taxpayers, this decision is readily explained on the basis that it need not have pursued its appeal and could have applied for its case to be stayed behind a lead case. Furthermore, it did not win on all of its arguments.

However, the decision so far as it concerns the other taxpayer initially seems harder to justify. The facts were unusual because the case involved a challenge to the classification of certain goods for the purposes of customs duty which necessitated a reference to the Court of Justice of the European Union. That led to the court agreeing that the goods had been wrongly classified. The tribunal ruled that a costs order should not be made because HMRC had done nothing wrong in applying the incorrect classification (something that they were bound to do until the court corrected it). However, it appears that this was a case where HMRC took more of a neutral stance and effectively facilitated the reference to Europe. For this reason, it seems that it was after all an appropriate exception to the rule that a successful taxpayer in a Complex case should generally be entitled to its reasonable costs.

Case: *British Sky Broadcasting Group plc & Pace plc v HMRC* [2012] UKFTT 386 (TC)

4.8.11 Partial compliance with the rules

It should be obvious that it is usually better to comply with the rules than to fail to adhere to a procedural requirement. However, it must also be acknowledged that the tribunal endeavours to encourage flexibility in proceedings, especially where the costs of rigid adherence to the rules would be disproportionate (see rule 2). Part of this flexibility is reflected in rule 7, which permits procedural oversights to be waived by the tribunal.

Although rule 7 does not specifically allow the tribunal to waive compliance with a rule prospectively, the tribunal has, on occasion, given a direction which has dispensed with a particular requirement. For example, in *Eclipse*, the tribunal noted that a costs application would inevitably be subject to the detailed assessment procedures (see **4.8.9** above) and it would therefore be a pointless duplication of effort for any formal application to the tribunal to include a schedule of costs as required by rule 10(3)(b). Indeed, in *Warren*, the taxpayer's objection to a costs application which omitted any detailed costs information on the (correct) assumption that the matter would proceed to a detailed costs assessment was criticised as "technical".

A similarly flexible approach was mentioned in *Vardy*. The tribunal considered that the case was particularly complicated and that compliance with rule 10(3)(b) would require a considerable amount of detail which would all be in vain if the tribunal were to decide in the end that no costs order would be made. In such a case, the tribunal said that it would have waived the requirement in rule 10(3)(b) so as to allow the tribunal to focus instead on the principle: i.e. whether to allow the party to recover some or all of its costs.

It should be noted that this flexibility is to be welcomed. However, whether it is strictly in compliance with the rules is not so clear. Given that a failure to comply with the requirement of rule 10(3)(b) can always be repaired retrospectively (for example, by waiving the requirement altogether), the issue is unlikely to be formally considered in any appeal. Nevertheless, it means that a tribunal could be well within its rights not to waive a procedural requirement on a prospective basis.

The matter was considered in *First Choice*, where HMRC pointed to an unpublished decision of the Upper Tribunal which refused to waive the requirement to provide a schedule. In the Upper Tribunal, the receiving party was directed to remedy the omission within 21 days. In *First Choice*, however, the tribunal considered that the position differed in the different tribunals and that it was appropriate to waive the requirement to provide a costs schedule.

The approach in *Vardy* was stated to be limited to those complex cases where the preparation of a schedule as required by rule 10(3)(b) would inevitably be a complex task. However, the principle (if it is right) ought to be relevant to many more cases. For example, a case which is allocated to the Basic category might be decided by the tribunal at the hearing itself. Under a strict interpretation of the rules, if a party were to seek costs, it would then have to make a formal application together with a schedule. Although less onerous than in a Complex case, the exercise would still seem like a waste of time if the tribunal subsequently turns around and decides that no costs order should be made. It is suggested that the tribunal ought to be prepared to allow oral applications to be made "in principle" with any formal schedule prepared only if the tribunal agrees that such an order will follow.

On the other hand, if the paying party has no idea of the magnitude of costs being sought, it will have no idea whether it is worth challenging any application in principle for a costs award. The author considers that it would be appropriate, in any case where a party seeks to avoid preparing a schedule upfront, for the party claiming costs to provide a "ballpark" indication as to the level of costs that are likely to be claimed.

In *RP Baker*, a case concerning a written application for costs, the tribunal commented that where a case was likely to be dealt with by summary assessment of the costs, the schedule of costs claimed ought to be included in the application.

Cases: *HMRC v Eclipse Film Partners No. 35 LLP* [2013] UKUT 141 (TCC); *Vardy Properties v HMRC* [2013] UKFTT 96 (TC); *RP Baker (Oxford) Ltd v HMRC* [2014] UKFTT 420 (TC); *Warren v HMRC* [2017] UKFTT 521 (TC); *First Choice Recruitment Ltd v HMRC* [2019] UKFTT 412 (TC)

4.8.12 *Role of the Upper Tribunal*

In the vast majority of cases, when a decision of the First-tier is appealed against to the Upper Tribunal, the Upper Tribunal's decision will consider to a large extent the correctness of the FTT's earlier decision. Thus, in the context of a costs dispute, the Upper Tribunal will usually be required to consider the extent of any liability of one party to pay costs to another party.

However, the Upper Tribunal also has the power to make any decision that the First-tier had the power to make, provided it has already decided to remake the First-tier's decision: that can be done only if the Upper Tribunal finds an error in the First-tier's decision leading to it being set aside. Accordingly, if a case is taken to the Upper Tribunal, it is possible to make a fresh application for costs in relation to the proceedings in the First-tier.

Such an application will rarely be appropriate if a costs application has already been made in the First-tier (as the decision in relation to that application should instead be the subject of its own appeal).

Similarly, the Upper Tribunal is likely to consider whether or not the taxpayer should have made an application to the First-tier, rather than keep its powder dry until the Upper Tribunal proceedings.

The *Cheshire* case is an illustration of where it was considered appropriate for costs to be considered in the first instance by the Upper Tribunal. See **5.8.3** and **4.7.6**.

Law: TCEA 2007, s. 12(2)(b)(ii), (4)(a)
Case: *HMRC v Cheshire Centre For Independent Living* [2020] UKUT 275 (TCC)

4.8.13 Cases arising from before 1 April 2009

Although now of diminishing relevance, there are specific transitional provisions relating to costs where the case was originally notified to a predecessor of the FTT (the General or Special Commissioners or the VAT and Duties Tribunal) and the case was then transferred to the Tax Chamber.

Although the tribunal's powers to award costs are not themselves overridden, an order may be made if and only if (and only to the extent that) an order could have been made before 1 April 2009 by the transferring tribunal. Thus, cases originating in the General Commissioners may not be subject to costs orders and cases originating in the Special Commissioners are subject to the "wholly unreasonable" threshold that formerly applied.

So far as VAT cases are concerned, the general rule that costs orders could be given quite generally was tempered by a practice announced in Parliament, known as the *Sheldon Practice*, whereby HMRC would generally not seek costs from an unsuccessful party at the tribunal (even though a successful taxpayer would generally recover costs from HMRC). The exceptions to the rule were those "exceptional substantial and complex cases where large sums are involved and which are comparable with High Court cases" or where the taxpayer had misused the tribunal procedure.

In *South Herefordshire*, the tribunal judge, when considering an application for costs by HMRC, held that he would not make such an award as it would fall outside HMRC's stated practice.

In 2009, HMRC announced that they would continue to honour the *Sheldon Practice* in cases transferred to the Tax Chamber. In *Innocent*, the tribunal considered that, although the practice was extra-statutory, it would normally give effect to it in the exercise of its discretion to award costs.

Law: SI 2009/56, Sch. 3, para. 7(7)

Cases: *South Herefordshire Golf Club v HMRC* (2006) VDT 19767; *Innocent Ltd v HMRC* [2011] UKFTT 607 (TC)

Guidance: *Sheldon Practice* (as restated by Rt Hon Peter Brooke MP), *Hansard*, Vol 102, 24 July 1986, cols 459-460

4.9 Rule 11 – Representatives

11(1) A party may appoint a representative (whether a legal representative or not) to represent that party in the proceedings.

11(2) If a party appoints a representative, that party (or the representative if the representative is a legal representative) must send or deliver to the Tribunal and to each other party to the proceedings written notice of the representative's name and address.

11(3) Anything permitted or required to be done by a party under these Rules, a practice direction or a direction may be done by the representative of that party, except signing a witness statement.

11(4) A person who receives due notice of the appointment of a representative–

(a) must provide to the representative any document which is required to be provided to the represented party, and need not provide that document to the represented party; and

(b) may assume that the representative is and remains authorised as such until they receive written notification that this is not so from the representative or the represented party.

11(5) At a hearing a party may be accompanied by another person who, with the permission of the Tribunal, may act as a representative or otherwise assist in presenting the party's case at the hearing.

> 11(6) Paragraphs (2) to (4) do not apply to a person (other than an appointed representative) who accompanies a party in accordance with paragraph (5).
>
> 11(7) In this rule "legal representative" means a person who, for the purposes of the Legal Services Act 2007, is an authorised person in relation to an activity which constitutes the exercise of a right of audience or the conduct of litigation within the meaning of that Act, an advocate or solicitor in Scotland, or a barrister or solicitor in Northern Ireland.

4.9.1 Overview

Although the tribunals are supposed to be more informal than courts and should be accessible to taxpayers acting on their own, this rule recognises that many taxpayers will want a representative to act for them in the course of proceedings.

Such a representative will be the person through whom all correspondence relating to the appeal process will pass. If a party is proposing to instruct an individual solely to act as an advocate at the eventual hearing (for example, a barrister) then the barrister is *not* a representative for these purposes. Indeed, most barristers are forbidden by their professional body to "conduct litigation", that is to engage in correspondence with the other parties or the tribunal. See **4.8.4**.

If a representative is appointed, correspondence from the tribunal and the other parties should be sent to the representative rather than direct to the party.

It was confirmed in *Elder* that officers of HMRC are not considered to be representatives for the purposes of rule 11 but automatically have the right to act on behalf of HMRC.

Although undoubtedly each case should be considered on its own facts, the decision in *Browne* makes it clear that a party cannot be shielded by a representative's failings. In that case, the representative had not done anything following the tribunal's dismissal of the taxpayer's appeal – neither sought permission to appeal nor even advised the taxpayer of the decision. The First-tier refused an application for permission to appeal to be considered late.

Cases: *Elder v HMRC* [2014] UKFTT 728 (TC); *Browne v HMRC* [2017] UKFTT 867 (TC)

4.9.2 Appointment of representative (rule 11(1), (3), (7))

Any party may appoint a representative.

The representative need not be a solicitor or barrister ("a legal representative"). Very often, the representative will be an accountant or tax adviser, or even just a friend who is willing to help a taxpayer with the tribunal proceedings.

Effect of appointment

When a representative is appointed, the representative is entitled to do anything required by the tribunal rules to be done by the party. The only exception is the signing of witness statements which must be done by each individual witness personally.

In *Technetix*, it was held that an appointment will ordinarily continue so as to cover matters (such as costs applications and applications for permission to appeal) which are dealt with after the main proceedings are concluded.

However, if the matter is subsequently notified to the Upper Tribunal, any appointment will need to be renewed with the Upper Tribunal.

Case: *Technetix v HMRC* [2015] UKFTT 369 (TC)

4.9.3 Notification of representative (rule 11(2), (4))

When a representative is appointed, written notification of the representative's name and address should be given to the tribunal and to the other parties.

Strictly, this duty falls on the representative only if the representative is a legal representative. It should be carried out by the party itself if the representative is not a legal representative.

In practice in the Tax Chamber, most representatives are accountants and tax advisers and, until late 2012, all representatives would effectively carry out this role for the taxpayer when notifying the tribunal of the appeal. However, the standard appeal form has since been modified so as to make it clear that the tribunal will communicate with non-legal representatives only if the taxpayer formally advises the tribunal that the representative is acting on the taxpayer's behalf. That can be by separate letter or on the appeal form itself. There is now also a standard form.

The tribunal and other parties must from then on communicate with the representative either instead of, or as well as, communicating directly with the party.

If a person ceases to be authorised to be a representative, written notification should be sent to the tribunal and the other parties. Until such notification has been received, the tribunal and other parties may continue to assume that the authorisation of the representative continues to be in force.

Guidance: https://www.gov.uk/government/publications/form-t239-authorise-a-representative

4.9.4 Representation at a hearing (rule 11(5), (6))

At a hearing itself, a party may be represented by either the same or a different representative for the purposes of presenting the party's case.

This rule ensures that barristers (who are not generally permitted under the Bar Council rules to conduct the day-to-day litigation of the case (correspondence between the parties, etc)) can be instructed to present the arguments at the actual hearing.

In *Cresswell*, it was suggested that the flexibility of this rule militated against the taxpayer's application in that case for his advocate to participate in the hearing via a telephone.

In *Porter*, the taxpayer argued that the rule was *ultra vires* and that non-legally qualified individuals were not allowed to represent a party at a hearing. The tribunal rejected the argument.

In *Pickles*, the tribunal ruled that it was impermissible for an individual to act at the hearing both as an advocate and as an expert witness. In the circumstances of the case, the tribunal allowed the individual to act as an advocate but treated his expert report as written submissions rather than as evidence.

Cases: *Cresswell v HMRC* [2017] UKFTT 481 (TC); *Porter & Co v HMRC* [2018] UKFTT 264 (TC); *Pickles v HMRC* [2020] UKFTT 195 (TC)

4.10 Rule 12 – Calculating time

> 12(1) An act required by these Rules, a practice direction or a direction to be done on or by a particular day must be done before 5pm on that day.
>
> 12(2) If the time specified by these Rules, a practice direction or a direction for doing any act ends on a day other than a working day, the act is done in time if it is done on the next working day.
>
> 12(3) In this rule "working day" means any day except a Saturday or Sunday, Christmas Day, Good Friday or a bank holiday under section 1 of the Banking and Financial Dealings Act 1971.

4.10.1 Overview

Very often, rules and directions provide that steps are to be taken by a particular day, sometimes calculated by reference to other events. This rule clarifies how such rules and directions are to be interpreted.

4.10.2 Day ends at 5pm (rule 12(1))

Sometimes a direction will specify that a step should be taken by a particular date. In these cases, rule 12(1) provides that that step should be taken by 5pm on that day.

Sometimes, tribunal judges provide for other types of time limit (e.g. "by 4pm on a particular day"). In those cases, rule 12 will not apply.

4.10.3 Where time limits expire on a non-working day (rule 12(2), (3))

Occasionally, a time limit will expire on a non-working day (Saturday, Sunday, Christmas Day, Good Friday or a bank holiday). In such a case, the time limit is carried forward until the next working day.

The definition of bank holiday is taken from the *Banking and Financial Dealings Act* 1971 which provides for bank holidays across the UK. Strictly, this can mean that a time limit which falls on a Scottish bank holiday (say) will not need to be complied with until the next working day (even in a case in which all the parties are based elsewhere in the UK).

Law: *Banking and Financial Dealings Act* 1971, s. 1

4.11 Rule 13 – Sending and delivery of documents

13(1) Any document to be provided to the Tribunal under these Rules, a practice direction or a direction must be–

(a) sent by pre-paid post or document exchange, or delivered by hand, to the address specified for the proceedings; or

(b) sent or delivered by such other method as the Tribunal may permit or direct.

13(2) Subject to paragraph (3), if a party or representative provides a fax number, email address or other details for the electronic transmission of documents to them, that party or representative must accept delivery of documents by that method.

13(3) If a party informs the Tribunal and all other parties that a particular form of communication (other than pre-paid post or delivery by hand) should not be used to provide documents to that party, that form of communication must not be so used.

13(4) If the Tribunal or a party sends a document to a party or the Tribunal by email or any other electronic means of communication, the recipient may request that the sender provide a hard copy of the document to the recipient. The recipient must make such a request as soon as reasonably practicable after receiving the document electronically.

13(5) The Tribunal and each party may assume that the address provided by a party or its representative is and remains the address to which documents should be sent or delivered until receiving written notification to the contrary.

4.11.1 Overview

This rule provides the framework for the use of written and electronic communications between the parties and the tribunal.

In *Mattu*, a case concerning the similarly worded rule in the Upper Tribunal rules, the taxpayer noted that the rule permits documents to be posted to the tribunal. He proceeded to rely on that rule to argue that a statutory obligation to notify the tribunal of his appeal by a particular day can be met simply by ensuring that the appeal is put in the post by that day. The tribunal disagreed.

Case: *HMRC v Mattu* [2021] UKUT 245 (TCC)

4.11.2 Generally use hard-copy documents for the tribunal

If a document is to be provided to the tribunal, it should ordinarily be sent either by post, through the DX (the Document Exchange, a private postal system used particularly by lawyers) or by hand. Rule 13(1)(b) permits other communication methods to be used, but only as permitted or directed by the tribunal. For instance, fax communications were accepted by the tribunal only until July 2011.

4.11.3 Communications with parties (rule 13(2), (3), (5))

If a party or representative ever provides a fax number, e-mail address or other method of electronic communication then that is generally taken as an acceptance that such methods may be used to receive communications. Similarly, parties and the tribunal may assume that an address provided by one party remains in force until notified in writing to the contrary.

In *Rashidi*, the taxpayer did not monitor the e-mail address he had given to HMRC and the tribunal for correspondence purposes. Not only did this lead to the case being decided against him in his absence but it was also the main reason for the tribunal's refusal to set aside that decision under rule 38.

Case: *Rashidi v HMRC* [2016] UKFTT 357 (TC)

Opting out of particular method of receiving communications

A party can stipulate that it does not wish to accept a particular form of communication. This ensures that a person is not obliged to receive communications by e-mail etc. A party cannot opt out of receiving communications through the post or by hand delivery.

4.11.4 Requesting hard copies (rule 13(4))

Whenever a party receives an electronic communications from either the tribunal or another party, the receiving party may request a hard copy as well. Such a request must be made as soon as is reasonably practicable after the electronic communication is received.

4.12 Rule 14 – Use of documents and information

> 14 The Tribunal may make an order prohibiting the disclosure or publication of–
>
> (a) specified documents or information relating to the proceedings; or
>
> (b) any matter likely to lead members of the public to identify any person whom the Tribunal considers should not be identified.

4.12.1 Overview

This rule recognises that certain documents or information created for the purposes of, or disclosed during, proceedings may be confidential or otherwise sensitive.

In *Aria*, the Upper Tribunal (referring to the equivalent provision in its own rules) considered that the wording of the rule implied that the tribunal had an inherent power to permit the release of documents or information to the public, subject to the risk of any harm that the disclosure could cause. This conclusion was said to be consistent with the principles of open justice which applied to the courts and statutory tribunals alike.

Case: *Aria Technology Ltd v HMRC* [2018] UKUT 111 (TC)

Information and documents

Rule 14(a) enables the tribunal to make an order which prohibits the disclosure or publication of specified documents or information relating to the proceedings.

Identification of persons

Similarly, persons might be mentioned in the course of evidence or legal arguments who are not themselves parties to the proceedings. In some cases, those persons might not be mentioned in the most flattering fashion, where they do not have the opportunity to put forward an alternative explanation.

The tribunal can therefore make an order prohibiting the disclosure or publication of any matter that could lead the public to identify a person that the tribunal considers should not be identified.

See also rule 32 which permits the tribunal to hold a hearing in private.

Physical threats

In *Murray Group* (often referred to as the "*Rangers*" case), the tribunal recognised that football often generates strong feelings. The case concerned tax-planning arrangements entered into by the football team and there was a perceived risk that the tax officers investigating the case and who gave evidence would be subject to physical threats. Although it was subsequently accepted by the tribunal that there was no longer any evidence of any continuing threat, the officers had given evidence anonymously and the tribunal saw "no justification for exposing public servants carrying out their duty to a potential risk without good cause" and continued the direction that their identities remain private.

There were other witnesses in that case who gave evidence on the understanding that their identities would remain concealed. The tribunal noted that some of these witnesses might have given evidence in any event and furthermore that the identity of some of these witnesses might, in fact, be deducible from other information in the public domain concerning the club's finances. However, as a matter of pragmatism, the tribunal considered that it would be wrong in principle for a witness to be offered anonymity only for that protection to be removed at a later stage.

Case: *HMRC v Murray Group Holdings Ltd* (2013) FTC/15/2013

4.13 Rule 15 – Evidence and submissions

15(1) Without restriction on the general powers in rule 5(1) and (2) (case management powers), the Tribunal may give directions as to–

    (a) issues on which it requires evidence or submissions;

    (b) the nature of the evidence or submissions it requires;

    (c) whether the parties are permitted or required to provide expert evidence, and if so whether the parties must jointly appoint a single expert to provide such evidence;

    (d) any limit on the number of witnesses whose evidence a party may put forward, whether in relation to a particular issue or generally;

    (e) the manner in which any evidence or submissions are to be provided, which may include a direction for them to be given–

        (i) orally at a hearing; or

        (ii) by written submissions or witness statement; and

    (f) the time at which any evidence or submissions are to be provided.

15(2) The Tribunal may–

    (a) admit evidence whether or not the evidence would be admissible in a civil trial in the United Kingdom; or

    (b) exclude evidence that would otherwise be admissible where–

        (i) the evidence was not provided within the time allowed by a direction or a practice direction;

        (ii) the evidence was otherwise provided in a manner that did not comply with a direction or a practice direction; or

        (iii) it would otherwise be unfair to admit the evidence.

> 15(3) The Tribunal may consent to a witness giving, or require any witness to give, evidence on oath, and may administer an oath for that purpose.

4.13.1 Overview

This is the key rule concerning the nature of evidence that will be considered by the tribunal. Read with rules 2 and 5, it ensures that the tribunal's proceedings retain flexibility, subject to the overriding need to be fair.

As emphasised by the Upper Tribunal in *Elbrook*, witness statements should be limited to evidence that is relevant and there can be adverse costs implications if this rule is not adhered to.

See also **8.8.3** below for some practical issues in relation to evidence given at a hearing itself.

Case: *Elbrook Cash and Carry Ltd v HMRC (No. 2)* [2019] UKUT 201 (TCC)

The tribunal will decide the facts on the basis of available evidence

However, it is worth emphasising one point here. That is that one cannot overstate the importance of the evidence that a party wishes to rely upon. In virtually all cases, the tribunal will have to decide what the facts of the case are, and such a process will inevitably be based on the evidence available to the tribunal. An assertion at a hearing that "I have proof at home" or "My neighbour can confirm that but I did not know you would need to hear from her" will carry very little weight. If a party wishes to refer to a particular document or the evidence of a neighbour, say, then steps should be taken to ensure that that evidence is made available when evidence is first being presented and that it is not left as an afterthought.

Thus, if evidence is to be provided in advance, then that is the time to present this additional evidence. Similarly, if there are no directions for evidence to be given in advance, then it is essential that all evidence being relied upon is brought to the hearing itself and if that means ensuring that another person is available to give that evidence then that is a point that must be addressed when the hearing dates are arranged.

A tribunal might, in appropriate cases, accept a witness's assertion that corroborative evidence exists elsewhere. However, the persuasive nature of such an assertion is relatively weak and parties should not rely on the tribunal's generosity in this regard.

If a case is decided against a party due to the lack of evidence, the failure to put forward the relevant evidence will generally not be capable of rectification in any further appeal in the Upper Tribunal. Again, there are exceptions (so as to maintain flexibility and to adhere to the overriding objective (see rule 2 above, as considered in *Prospect*)). However, again, the Upper Tribunal's forbearance should be treated as the exception and not the norm and should therefore not be relied upon. Indeed, one aspect of the overriding objective is to promote the finality of litigation and not to encourage ongoing appeals with new facts being introduced at each stage.

Case: *Prospect Origin Ltd v HMRC* [2021] UKUT 511 (TCC)

Some directions that the tribunal may give

Rule 15(1) gives a non-exhaustive list of the types of direction that a tribunal may give concerning evidence. For example, the tribunal may consider that it does not need to hear the same evidence from more than one individual and can therefore place a limit on the number of witnesses put forward.

Similarly, the tribunal may direct that evidence be given orally at a hearing (and therefore might be subject to cross examination from the other side or questions from the tribunal itself). Alternatively, the tribunal might consider it sufficient for it to receive only written witness statements. A further option would be that the tribunal might want evidence to be given orally (so as to permit questions to be put to the witness) but the contents of the evidence to be submitted in advance in the form of a witness statement.

Withdrawing a witness statement

In *Aleena*, the taxpayer attempted to withdraw a witness statement that had been previously given, but HMRC still wanted to rely upon the statement and the tribunal decided that HMRC were entitled to do so.

The author has had experience of a slight variant to this in a case where HMRC had the burden of proof but where their evidence was considered to be deficient. In order to comply with tribunal directions, the taxpayer was required to produce a witness statement ahead of the hearing but made it clear that the statement was produced on a protective basis. The tribunal accepted that the contents of the witness statement were not formally before the tribunal until specifically presented to the tribunal at the hearing.

Case: *Aleena Electronics Ltd v HMRC (No. 2)* [2015] UKFTT 61 (TC)

4.13.2 Expert evidence

Rule 15(1)(c) refers to expert evidence. Generally, the law dislikes witnesses giving opinions, and witnesses should instead restrict their evidence to statements of fact.

However, certain matters are inherently matters of opinion, such as the appropriate accounting treatment of a particular transaction or the value of the shares of a company on a particular date. In those cases, it will be appropriate for evidence to be provided from an expert in the field.

In *Henke*, a case concerning main residence relief, a Special Commissioner (a judge of one of the predecessor tribunals) was required to identify the "permitted area", being "the area required for the reasonable enjoyment of the dwelling-house (or of the part in question) as a residence, having regard to the size and character of the dwelling-house". The taxpayer did not supply an expert witness, whereas HMRC did. As the Special Commissioner held, "In the absence of anything manifestly wrong with [the District Valuer's] expert evidence, I have to take it into account in arriving at my decision." It is considered that the question of permitted area is one that does not actually require expert evidence although a tribunal should clearly not dismiss any such evidence out of hand.

There is one area, however, where an expert should not offer an opinion: that is on the effect of the law. The effect of the law is a matter that is wholly within the jurisdiction of the tribunal itself. Where expert evidence might be appropriate, however, is in respect of the practice of UK law, although in the light of the Tax Chamber being a specialist tribunal, and one where its specialist expertise should be used (see rule 2(2)(d)), it is arguable that the practice of UK tax law is not something that would usually require the evidence of an expert.

Foreign law, however, is something that should generally be the subject of expert evidence.

Within the usual courts system, "foreign" extends to other nations within the Union. For example, an English court will require expert evidence as to the effect of Scots law. However, within the tribunal (which is UK-wide) a judge is deemed to have "judicial notice" of the effect of the law in all parts of the UK and it is therefore both unnecessary and inappropriate for expert evidence to be called (*Spring Capital 2*). In an earlier *Spring Capital* decision, the tribunal considered the rare case where there is conflicting authority between the Scottish Court of Session and the English Court of Appeal; it was noted that the tribunal should follow the guidance of the senior court governing the jurisdiction in which the hearing is taking place.

In *Deloitte*, the tribunal considered expert evidence which contained inadmissible statements concerning the law. It ruled that the witness statements should be admitted but with the inadmissible elements ignored.

In *Madden*, the tribunal admitted the evidence of the taxpayer's accountant including evidence as to the accountant's opinions. However, it emphatically rejected the idea that the accountant could represent an expert witness. It noted that the accountant could not give unbiased evidence, having been representing the taxpayer throughout the investigation. Secondly, the tribunal recognised that its own knowledge (as an expert tribunal with the benefit of an accountant sitting as a member) meant that expert evidence would not be appropriate in the case.

Finally, in *Maitland-Hudson*, a divisional court noted that "no court is ever bound to accept the expert evidence before it, even if that evidence is agreed".

Cases: *Henke v HMRC* (2006) Sp C 550; *Deloitte LLP v HMRC* [2016] UKFTT 479 (TC); *Madden v HMRC* [2018] UKFTT 414 (TC); *Maitland-Hudson v Solicitors Regulation Authority* [2019] EWHC 67 (Admin); *Spring Capital Ltd v HMRC* [2021] UKFTT 147 (TC); *Spring Capital Ltd v HMRC* [2021] UKFTT 345 (TC)

When expert evidence should be admitted

The admissibility of expert evidence was the focus of the procedural hearing in *Eclipse (No. 3)*. The long-running case concerned the viability of what are generally known as "film-schemes", the main argument being whether or not the partnership was carrying on a trade with a view to profit.

Ahead of the main hearing, HMRC produced a witness statement in the form of an expert report from an individual claiming to be an expert in structured finance and banking transactions. The taxpayer partnership applied for the statement to be excluded. Its main objections were that much of the material opined on the effect of UK tax law (and therefore inadmissible); the balance, it was argued, was no more than submissions on behalf of HMRC dressed up as evidence.

Agreeing with the taxpayer, the tribunal held that expert evidence should be restricted to that which is reasonably required to resolve the proceedings. However, the tribunal agreed with HMRC that the evidence should be admitted initially; at the main hearing (and in the light of all the evidence and the submissions there), it would be for the tribunal to decide what is in fact inadmissible and, where evidence is admissible, how much weight it should be given.

In short, it was considered that the tribunal was not, at the directions hearing at least, in a position to conclude whether the evidence would be helpful to it in resolving any issue in the case justly.

In *Deloitte*, the following principles were given:

- Relevant evidence should be admitted unless there are compelling reasons not to. The prejudice to each party of respectively admitting/not admitting the evidence should be weighed.
- An expert's evidence of opinion is admissible because it is the product of a special expertise which the tribunal does not possess, or even if it does, which is not its function to apply.
- Expert reports are not rendered inadmissible simply because they refer to legislation, matters of law or indeed the very issue before the court or tribunal.

- Even if reports contain inadmissible expert evidence of fact they can be admitted and should be admitted without requiring excision particularly if the admissible/inadmissible evidence of fact is intertwined.

Cases: *Eclipse Film Partners No. 35 LLP v HMRC (No. 3)* [2011] UKFTT 401 (TC); *Deloitte LLP v HMRC* [2016] UKFTT 479 (TC)

Independence of expert witnesses

A firmly-established principle is that expert witnesses owe their primary duty to the tribunal and not to the party calling them as a witness.

However, it is not uncommon for HMRC (in particular) to rely upon their own employees as independent experts. This approach was expressly considered to be permissible in *Pickles* although the tribunal noted that the fact that the expert is an employee of a party could affect the weight given to that expert's opinion.

A further example showing the importance of an expert's independence arose in *Wired Orthodontics*. That was a case in which not all the facts were known (because parties are not generally required to disclose correspondence with their solicitors). However, the limited evidence available suggested that HMRC's expert (who was also an HMRC employee) was being unduly influenced by the HMRC solicitor instructing him. The tribunal noted that the dangers highlighted by that case should make HMRC reconsider their usual stance of instructing internal experts.

One approach that the author considers to be worth pursuing in many cases (and which is understood to be favoured by the tribunal) is for parties to appoint a "single joint expert", who prepares a single report for the tribunal, rather than the parties relying on their own experts which then compete for the tribunal's endorsement. Indeed, in *Europcar*, this preference was made clear when dealing with an application by the taxpayers (opposed by HMRC) for the tribunal to direct that a joint expert be appointed, rather than have both parties appoint their own experts. The tribunal approached the case by stating that there should be a single joint expert unless there was good reason not to.

In the author's experience, HMRC would often require that single joint expert to be their own employee. The author recognises that taxpayers will often be reluctant to accept such a stipulation. However, given the concerns raised in *Wired Orthodontics*, it is possible that HMRC will modify their approach.

Cases: *Pickles v HMRC* [2020] UKFTT 195 (TC); *Wired Orthodontics Ltd v HMRC* [2020] UKFTT 290 (TC); *Europcar Group UK Ltd v HMRC* [2021] UKFTT 359 (TC)

Applications to have expert evidence admitted

As noted at **2.4.4**, there is no obligation on the tribunal to adopt aspects of the Civil Procedure Rules ("CPR"). Indeed, it would be an error of law for the tribunal to consider reference to those rules as obligatory.

One particular aspect of the CPR is the rule that expert evidence should not be admitted without a specific direction from the court. It was made clear in *Megantic*, however, that this blanket rule does not apply in the tribunal. However, HMRC often interpret the rule differently in an attempt to exclude expert evidence submitted on behalf of a taxpayer. In such cases, it is possible to ask for the tribunal to admit the evidence already prepared. However, this procedure should not be necessary.

This debate was also considered by the tribunal in *Laurence Supply*. Unfortunately, the tribunal's analysis is not entirely clear. It is nevertheless the author's view that the decision supports the position that rule 15(1)(c) is only permissive (in that it allows the tribunal to control the use of expert evidence but does not require parties to seek permission in advance).

However, in a subsequent case, *Singleton* (which made no reference to the *Laurence Supply* case), the tribunal adopted the view that expert evidence may not be admitted without the tribunal's permission. Interestingly, that was a case in which HMRC had put forward the expert evidence.

In *Leeds*, the tribunal deprecated HMRC's evidence, which was largely a matter of opinion rather than fact and, for the former, "no permission was given or sought [or] required". Those comments might be interpreted as reinforcing the need for any opinion evidence to be preceded or accompanied by an application for its admission. However, the author considers that the tribunal's comments should not be read in such a way but merely as noting that HMRC's evidence in that case was simply inappropriate.

Cases: *Megantic Services Ltd v HMRC* [2013] UKFTT 492 (TC); *Leeds Cricket Football & Athletic Company Ltd v HMRC* [2019] UKFTT 568 (TC); *Laurence Supply Co (Leather Bags) Ltd v HMRC* [2021] UKFTT 264 (TC); *Singleton Birch Ltd v HMRC* [2021] UKFTT 440 (TC)

Additional procedural requirements for expert evidence

Furthermore, expert evidence is subject to considerable discussion in the CPR with an entire practice direction devoted to the topic ("PD35") with the aim of promoting the interests of justice and fairness.

In *Chandanmal*, the tribunal recognised that, while tribunal procedures generally favoured informality, such informality was of no advantage to the parties in that case – in which nearly £5m was at stake and where both parties were fully represented by solicitors and Counsel. The tribunal concluded: "there is every advantage to expert witnesses in the tribunal following CPR Practice Direction 35 and no disadvantage".

Case: *Chandanmal and Others t/a C Narain Bros v HMRC* [2012] UKFTT 188 (TC)

4.13.3 Admissibility of evidence (rule 15(2)(a))

Traditionally, there are rules of law that govern whether or not evidence may be admitted in a case being argued in the courts. These principles have been amended over the years, for example, by statute restricting the common law rule that prevented hearsay evidence (effectively, second-hand evidence i.e. evidence that the witness reports as having been said by someone else) from being admitted.

The Tribunal Rules are not bound by such principles and provide that all evidence may be admissible, whether or not the evidence would ordinarily be admitted in a civil court.

In *Gardiner*, the tribunal expressed a reluctance to admit documentary evidence from HMRC (which was ambiguous) in a penalty case in the absence of an appropriate witness who could be cross-examined on the documentation.

In *McIlroy*, the taxpayer was seeking to rely on evidence in the form of a letter. The provenance of that letter was not clear and this was considered by the tribunal to be unhelpful to the taxpayer's cause.

Hearsay evidence was expressly admitted in *Russell* but the tribunal noted that it has less weight than direct evidence.

In *MHA*, a social security case, it was suggested by the Upper Tribunal that a shortcoming in the available evidence could be compensated for by the tribunal using its own specialist expertise.

In *Omagh* the taxpayer sought the exclusion of expert geological evidence on the basis that the sampling techniques were not in accordance with standard procedures. However, the tribunal concluded that the evidence should be admitted, noting that any shortcomings in the expert's methodology could be raised in cross-examination when seeking to undermine the evidence.

A number of penalty appeals have seen HMRC criticised for not producing evidence of (say) the issue of a notice requiring the submission of a tax return. The tribunal in such cases has considered a mere assertion that a notice has been sent as insufficient. In *Jacks*, the tribunal stated that, notwithstanding the relative informality of tribunal proceedings, facts must be proved by "proper evidence" meaning "reliable documents which are admitted or proved in evidence and/or reliable witness evidence". These words strictly require any documents to be accompanied by a witness statement explaining the provenance of any such document. The author is of the view that a document which is clearly a reliable source of the information it contains (e.g. a bank statement) does not actually need to be formally adduced in a witness statement. Nevertheless, it is a precaution that should be taken to avoid potential difficulties.

As held by the Upper Tribunal in *Perrin*, "a mere assertion of [a fact] in a statement of case is not sufficient".

In *Hyrax*, the tribunal suggested that ordinarily the tribunal is "very likely" to admit any document that was on a party's list of documents unless there had been a clear advance challenge to the document's authenticity or relevance. The judge expressed disagreement with the approach take in *Gardiner* but it seems that the actual facts of *Gardiner* were not fully understood when the criticism was made.

In *Daly*, the taxpayer objected to documentary evidence emanating from an overseas tax authority. The tribunal admitted the evidence, noting that:

> "the information and material is not provided informally, as a casual favour, or by way of inter-governmental courtesy, but is provided pursuant to high-level EU legislation ... it is provided officially, openly, and in response to formal inquiry".

Cases: *MHA v Secretary of State for Work and Pensions* [2009] UKUT 211 (AAC); *Gardiner v HMRC* [2014] UKFTT 421 (TC); *McIlroy v HMRC* [2014] UKFTT 429 (TC); *Omagh Minerals Ltd v HMRC* [2015] UKFTT 681 (TC); *Russell v HMRC* [2016] UKFTT 80 (TC); *Jacks v HMRC* [2017] UKFTT 613 (TC); *Perrin v HMRC* [2018] UKUT 156 (TCC); *HMRC v Hyrax Resourcing Ltd* [2019] UKFTT 175 (TC); *Daly v HMRC* [2020] UKFTT 281 (TC)

Unreliable evidence

On the other hand, it should be borne in mind that some evidence may not be considered as reliable as other evidence (for example, hearsay evidence cannot be considered as reliable as first-hand evidence that has been exposed to cross examination) and the tribunal, when assessing the evidence in a case, must ensure that it gives the evidence the appropriate weight according to its relative importance and reliability.

Inadmissible evidence

Furthermore, it is suggested that any overriding common law principles, such as the protection of legal profession privilege – described by Lord Hoffmann in *Morgan Grenfell* as "a fundamental human right" – is not curtailed by rule 15(2)(a), because the tribunals must act within the framework of the *Human Rights Act*. This was the approach taken by the Upper Tribunal in *LM*.

Where a witness statement contains both admissible and inadmissible material, the tribunal in *Elbrook (No. 2)* confirmed that the usual approach should be to let the statement stand and trust the tribunal to ignore that which is inadmissible (although it would be helpful to the tribunal if the parties could make submissions (if not agreed) as to what is and is not admissible).

Law: *Human Rights Act* 1998

Cases: *R v Special Commissioner, ex parte Morgan Grenfell & Co Ltd* [2002] UKHL 21; *LM v London Borough of Lewisham* [2009] UKUT 204 (AAC); *Elbrook Cash and Carry Ltd v HMRC* [2018] UKFTT 252 (TC)

Adverse inferences

Sometimes, HMRC like to suggest that a tribunal should draw an adverse inference from late evidence or, more commonly, the absence of evidence from a particular source. Such suggestions are often no more than assertions without any legal basis to them.

The general position is that an adverse inference may be drawn in a non-criminal case if a party fails to call a witness who has submitted a witness statement, or if a party fails to adduce any evidence from a witness it could be expected to have called. However, an adverse inference on its own is insufficient to satisfy the burden of proof: the party with the burden of proof must still adduce enough evidence to make out a *prima facie* case and an adverse inference will then allow that *prima facie* case to cross the "balance of probabilities" threshold.

In *Thatthiah*, HMRC tried to draw adverse inferences from the fact that the taxpayer (in that case, it was actually the former Senior Accounting Officer who was facing a penalty) had not provided his evidence prior to the hearing. However, as the tribunal noted, neither the rules of the tribunal nor the directions in that case had made it obligatory to do so. Consequently, the tribunal concluded that to draw adverse inferences was "not appropriate" in that case.

Case: *Thatthiah v HMRC* [2017] UKFTT 601 (TC)

4.13.4 Exclusion of evidence (rule 15(2)(b))

The tribunal is not bound to admit all evidence offered to it. In other words, a witness statement might be produced which the tribunal refuses to admit into the proceedings. (This is different from allowing the evidence to be heard and the tribunal not accepting its veracity: if excluded, the evidence is treated as if it just did not exist.)

4.13 Rule 15 – Evidence and submissions

The tribunal may do so if:

- the evidence was provided late;
- it was provided in a way that was otherwise not in compliance with a direction or practice direction; or
- it would be otherwise unfair to admit the evidence.

When evidence should be excluded

In *Atlantic Electronics*, the Court of Appeal stated that there is a presumption "that all relevant evidence should be admitted unless there is a compelling reason to the contrary". Where there are compelling reasons for the late evidence, the tribunal should be slow to exclude it.

Thus, the first question is to ascertain whether or not the evidence is relevant. In *Randall*, relevance of evidence was judiciously defined as:

> "whether the evidence is capable of increasing or diminishing the probability of the evidence of a fact in issue".

If evidence is held to be relevant, it should then be presumed to be admitted, but this presumption can be rebutted if it can be shown that its inclusion would be unfair.

This approach has been frequently followed in the Tax Chamber. For example, in *Earthshine*, the evidence came to light several days into the actual trial and HMRC wished to have it admitted: it was clearly relevant and the only real question was one of fairness. Given that the evidence mainly concerned e-mails originating from the taxpayer company's director, it was held that it would not be unfair to admit it. (See also **4.8.5** above concerning the costs consequences of HMRC's application.)

On the other hand, in *Xentric*, HMRC's application to have evidence admitted late was refused. In that case, the admission would have required the hearing to be further adjourned so as to allow the taxpayer to obtain new evidence to refute what was being said by HMRC. Furthermore, HMRC had had the opportunity to provide their late evidence at a much earlier stage had they been better organised.

In *Purser*, evidence was introduced three days into the main hearing and contrary to an earlier direction from the tribunal concerning the timing of evidence. HMRC had suggested that the evidence ought to be admitted because it could not reasonably be challenged by the taxpayer. The tribunal accepted that the evidence was "straightforward and easily assimilated" and it was therefore "tempting" to admit it. However, the tribunal accepted that the new evidence contradicted some of the evidence already before the tribunal. In view of the taxpayer's objections and the risk that the taxpayer could be prejudiced by having to accept late evidence with little time to reflect, the tribunal refused to admit the late evidence on grounds of fairness.

Masstech contains some useful guidance in relation to a number of different scenarios:

- Late evidence of important probative value was admitted (subject to an undertaking by HMRC to compensate the taxpayer for additional costs incurred).

- Linked evidence of a lower probative value would not have been admitted as it would probably have led to an adjournment of the scheduled hearing. However, due to its link to the other evidence, it was admitted.

- Late expert evidence would ordinarily have been refused: the tribunal suggested that this was because of HMRC's delay in producing it and its modest probative value. However, the tribunal later concluded that its only bar to admission was the lack of time available to the appellant to deal with it properly. On balance, it would be admitted only if the substantive hearing was otherwise adjourned. (But see *Atlantic* above.)

- The tribunal refused to admit a witness statement that contained no new evidence and in effect amounted to submissions which could be made in the course of legal argument at the substantive hearing.

Although the tribunal in *Masstech* considered that the appellant would probably need an adjournment so as to deal with the additional evidence, the tribunal did not order such an adjournment: instead, it gave the appellant the unilateral option to request one.

It will be seen that the risk of delay would be one reason to exclude evidence produced late. However, in *First Class (No. 2)*, any asserted delay should be considered by comparison with the position that

4.13 Rule 15 – Evidence and submissions

would have existed if the late evidence had originally been served on time. (In that case, HMRC had omitted an allegation from its statement of case and later sought to amend its statement by adding a new allegation. The appellant taxpayer argued that this would lead to a delayed hearing. However, the tribunal noted that the case was not ready for listing in any event and neither would it have been ready even if the new allegation had been made in the original statement of case. As a result, the lateness of the allegation would not have had a significant delaying effect on the proceedings. Although that case did not concern late evidence, the principles it is suggested are the same.)

The principles for late evidence were summarised succinctly as follows:

> "A very late amendment [or evidence] needs a great deal of justification as it is almost bound to lead to procedural prejudice to the other party, such as the loss of a hearing date or an inability to prepare for the new evidence properly.
>
> It is, as so many things are, a question of degree. The longer the delay, the more likely there will be procedural prejudice. The greater the procedural prejudice, the less likely it will be admitted. It is also clear that the importance of the evidence to the person seeking to rely on it must be weighed in the balance. Evidence critical to one party's case is more likely to be admitted than evidence of only peripheral relevance."

The tribunal in that case also noted that parties should give the other parties advance warning wherever possible of late evidence. For example, if the evidence is being prepared, a notification of that fact should be made if possible at that stage.

In *Tasca*, an application by the taxpayer to adduce further evidence was refused. The tribunal noted that:

> "The production of witness statements and exhibits is not, beyond that set out in the Directions, an iterative process whereby additional evidence can be produced as and when a party to proceedings 'gets round to it' ".

However, that was a case in which the actual contents of the late evidence was not yet clear – the application was made prospectively. Subject to questions of fairness to HMRC, the application might have

185

fared better had it been delayed until such time as the evidence was ready (or at least a good overview was available).

It should be noted that, in *Hussain*, the tribunal considered that once it was decided that the putative evidence was relevant, the question of late admission should be considered by reference to the *Martland* criteria (see **2.4.4**).

Cases: *R v Randall* [2004] WLR 56; *Earthshine Ltd v HMRC* [2010] UKFTT 67 (TC); *Xentric Limited v HMRC* [2010] UKFTT 249 (TC); *Masstech Corporation Ltd (in administration) v HMRC* [2011] UKFTT 649 (TC); *HT Purser Ltd v HMRC* [2011] UKFTT 860 (TC); *First Class Communications Ltd v HMRC (No. 2)* [2013] UKFTT 342 (TC); *Atlantic Electronics Ltd v HMRC* [2013] EWCA Civ 651; *Tasca Tankers Ltd v HMRC* [2021] UKFTT 25 (TC); *Hussain v HMRC* [2021] UKFTT 92 (TC)

4.13.5 Evidence on oath (rule 15(3))

The author has heard conflicting indications as to the tribunal's general position concerning the need for witnesses to give their evidence on oath (i.e. with a holy book or by affirmation).

On the one hand, it has been suggested that the tribunal will not generally require evidence to be sworn, as that is an aspect of the formality that the tribunal is moving away from. On the other hand, until the onset of Covid, it remained common practice, particularly in the main tribunal centres. The advent of online hearings, however, saw a more relaxed approach.

On balance, and subject to the practical considerations involved with online hearings, it would appear that the more formal procedures are likely to be used in those cases where there is a genuine factual dispute between the parties, rather than where less contentious facts are being brought to the tribunal's attention. However, witnesses in all cases should be prepared to go on oath (or to affirm), just in case.

In *Tager*, which concerned a particularly serious penal matter, the Court of Appeal considered that there should have been a clear division between oral submissions and evidence and that the evidence should have been sworn.

Case: *Romie Tager v HMRC* [2018] EWCA Civ 1727

4.13.6 Contents of a witness statement

See **6.5.1**.

4.14 Rule 16 – Summoning or citation of witnesses and orders to answer questions or produce documents

16(1) On the application of a party or on its own initiative, the Tribunal may–

(a) by summons (or, in Scotland, citation) require any person to attend as a witness at a hearing at the time and place specified in the summons or citation;

(b) order any person to answer any questions or produce any documents in that person's possession or control which relate to any issue in the proceedings.

16(2) A summons or citation under paragraph (1)(a) must–

(a) give the person required to attend at least 14 days' notice of the hearing, or such shorter period as the Tribunal may direct; and

(b) where the person is not a party, make provision for the person's necessary expenses of attendance to be paid, and state who is to pay them.

16(3) No person may be compelled to give any evidence or produce any document that the person could not be compelled to give or produce on a trial of an action in a court of law in the part of the United Kingdom where the proceedings are due to be determined.

16(4) A person who receives a summons, citation or order may apply to the Tribunal for it to be varied or set aside if they did not have an opportunity to object to it before it was made or issued.

16(5) A person making an application under paragraph (4) must do so as soon as reasonably practicable after receiving notice of the summons, citation or order.

16(6) A summons, citation or order under this rule must–

(a) state that the person on whom the requirement is imposed may apply to the Tribunal to vary or set

> aside the summons, citation or order, if they did not have an opportunity to object to it before it was made or issued; and
>
> (b) state the consequences of failure to comply with the summons, citation or order.

4.14.1 Overview

Rule 16 contains rules that ensure that parties are not disadvantaged by a reluctance of witnesses or other parties to provide information or evidence.

In *Royal Bank*, the tribunal noted (in relation to the provision of information, but equally applicable to a witness summons) that this exercise:

> "is not an end in itself but a means to an end, namely to ensure that the Tribunal has before it all the information which the parties reasonably require the Tribunal to consider in determining the appeal."

Citing Court of Appeal authority, the tribunal continued to note a trend to restrict such requests more than previously so that they are more closely related to the issues in dispute in the proceedings:

> "If a party suffers no litigious disadvantage by not seeing a document, it is immaterial that the party is curious about the contents of a document or would like to know the contents of it."

In *Malek*, the test of "closely related to the issues in dispute in the proceedings" requires the tribunal to identify the legal test that will be applied by the tribunal when determining those proceedings.

The Court of Appeal's decision in *Sarnoff* (concerning similar provisions applicable in the Employment Tribunal) states that the words "any person" should be interpreted as "any person other than the parties themselves". Applying that logic to the present rules would mean that orders to be made against the parties themselves should be made under rule 5(2), (3) above, rather than under rule 16. It should be noted, however, that (unlike the situation in the Employment Tribunal rules where there is a geographical limitation on the equivalent to rule 16) there is unlikely to be any practical consequence of this distinction. (Although it could be said that rule

4.14 Rule 16 – Summoning or citation of witnesses and orders to answer questions or produce documents

16(3) imposes a restriction which is not existent in rule 5, it is the author's view that rule 16(3) operates more widely and not solely to orders made under rule 16.)

Cases: *Royal Bank of Scotland Group plc v HMRC* [2020] UKFTT 321 (TC); *Sarnoff v YZ* [2021] EWCA Civ 26; *Malek v HMRC* [2021] UKFTT 339 (TC)

4.14.2 Witness summons (or citation) (rule 16(1)(a), (2))

The tribunal may issue a summons (in Scotland, a witness citation) that requires a person to attend a hearing as a witness. The summons must specify the time and place for attendance.

The summons may be applied for by a party or the tribunal may issue a summons on its own initiative.

In *Hobbs*, the Upper Tribunal noted that a witness summons would be issued only if the tribunal were satisfied both that the person in question had admissible evidence to give and that that evidence was relevant. In *Abbey*, the tribunal made it clear that "the test is not whether the party making the application hopes that the evidence will assist its case" but "whether there is a real likelihood that [the tribunal's] determination [of the case] will be assisted". As an example of the latter, the tribunal suggested that this might be the case if "the evidence would be reasonably likely, one way or another, to resolve an area of uncertainty".

In *Hobbs*, it was also considered that a witness summons under rule 16 did not go so far as to require an individual to give evidence as an expert (see **4.13.2** above).

In *Clavis Liberty*, the Upper Tribunal held that a witness summons cannot be served on an individual who has no substantial presence in the UK. Thus, generally, the individual would need to be resident or have a business address in the UK: alternatively, if the prospective witness were physically present in the UK then a witness summons may be served by being given to the prospective witness by hand.

In *Clavis Liberty*, the Upper Tribunal also noted that a witness summons can be set aside if the application was made in a misleading way.

Cases: *Hobbs v FSA* (Upper Tribunal, TCC) FS/2010/0024; *Abbey Forwarding Ltd (in liquidation) v HMRC* [2014] UKFTT 998 (TC); *Clavis Liberty Fund LP1 v HMRC* [2015] UKUT 72 (TCC)

Notice

Generally, a person is required to be given 14 days' notice (calendar days) but the tribunal can direct a shorter period.

Payment of expenses

If the witness is not a party to the proceedings, the tribunal may decide that expenses necessarily incurred should be reimbursed and may rule on who is to meet that cost.

In *Abbey Forwarding*, the tribunal held that "necessary expenses of attendance" includes financial loss (e.g. loss of earnings) and not merely monies actually expended.

Case: *Abbey Forwarding Ltd (in liquidation) v HMRC* [2014] UKFTT 1102 (TC)

4.14.3 Order for information (rule 16(1)(b))

The tribunal may order any person to answer questions or to produce any documents which are in that person's possession or control which relate to an issue in the proceedings.

This power is useful if, in the lead-up to a hearing, there is part of one party's argument (or the factual background) that is unclear to another party. Generally, such matters will usually be sorted out in routine correspondence between the parties. However, if a party is reluctant to provide the information, the other party may apply to the tribunal for an order directing that the information be given.

The tribunal may also make an order on its own initiative.

As noted in *Royal Bank*, applications for disclosure under this rule should be the exception. The process under rule 27 is the standard provision in the rules for disclosure (in standard and basic cases) and that regime applies "unless and until and except to the extent that the Tribunal directs otherwise". The tribunal should not make an order under rule 16 unless it is "persuaded that it is appropriate in the circumstances of the particular case to depart from the default regime in rule 27".

Suggesting a departure from earlier cases, the tribunal emphasised that there is no presumption that this principle is displaced in "heavy" cases.

Case: *Royal Bank of Scotland Group plc v HMRC* [2020] UKFTT 321 (TC)

Principles for information requests

In *Addo*, the tribunal referred to the general assumption that a party may request sight of a document referred to in another party's witness statement. Although that is the general position, the tribunal retains overall discretion in exercise of its powers to order disclosure.

Also in *Addo*, the tribunal made it clear that a party may request sight of a document even if it is not expressly referred to by the other party.

It is implicit that an order can be required only for the production of information that is relevant to the appeal. The procedure cannot be deployed by either party for the purposes of a general "fishing expedition". In *Fisher*, the tribunal considered a taxpayer's application for HMRC's records of meetings with other taxpayers. The taxpayer had argued that its belief of a particular fact would be shown to have been more credible if it could be shown that other taxpayers had a similar belief at the time. The tribunal refused the request on the basis that the issue in the appeal was whether the taxpayer believed the fact and that belief could be shaped only by information within the taxpayer's knowledge at the time.

In *Worldpay*, the tribunal directed disclosure of pre-contract correspondence between two contracting parties. It was disputed by the party that those documents were determinative of the appeal (unlike the actual agreement as finally reached). However, the tribunal said that HMRC had put those documents in issue and that they were therefore relevant to the substantive hearing (leaving the taxpayer able to challenge their relevance afresh at the substantive hearing). In contrast, internal memoranda not seen by the other contracting party were not considered to be relevant at all and were not the subject of the direction to disclose.

It is the author's view that there will be some cases (at least) where it will be appropriate to address the actual relevance of the documents at a disclosure hearing (and not leave it until the substantive hearing) so as to avoid a fishing expedition. Each case should be considered on its own merits.

In *B&M*, there was general agreement as to what would be considered relevant: "relevant documents are those which might advance the other party's case or hinder that of the party making the disclosure, and included those documents which might lead to a train of enquiry which might have either of those outcomes".

In *Ingenious*, the Upper Tribunal said that disclosure would ordinarily be ordered if it was known that a party had relevant documents that would be harmful to its case.

In cases where fraud is alleged, the Court of Appeal in *Citibank* made it clear that it would expect the party asserting the fraud to make full disclosure of its documents, including those documents that are adverse to its own case. In other words, a disclosure exercise similar to that seen in High Court litigation should be expected.

Cases: *Fisher v HMRC* [2012] UKFTT 335; *Ingenious Games LLP v HMRC* [2014] UKUT 62 (TCC); *B&M Retail Ltd v HMRC* [2017] UKFTT 789 (TC); *HMRC v Citibank NA* [2017] EWCA Civ 1416; *Addo v HMRC* [2018] UKFTT 530 (TC); *Worldpay (UK) Ltd v HMRC* [2019] UKFTT 235 (TC)

Guidelines as to relevance

The tribunal set out the following guidelines in *Tower Bridge*:

- the test of relevance should not be unduly high;
- the person holding the document can usually self-assess its relevance, with the other party seeking a disclosure order if it considers that there are flaws in the self-certification process;
- self-certification is more likely to be sufficient if the request for disclosure is in general terms concerning a class of documents;
- if a document is referred to specifically in a witness statement, it is more likely to be appropriate for that simply to be disclosed;
- applications should be made in the light of proportionality;

4.14 Rule 16 – Summoning or citation of witnesses and orders to answer questions or produce documents

- any valid objections (e.g. on grounds of privilege) should be considered only after it has been determined that a document should otherwise be disclosed.

In *McCabe*, the FTT noted the following criteria:

- In a high-value case, the starting point should be that HMRC should disclose all relevant material unless there is good reason not to. This was subsequently approved of by the Upper Tribunal. However, as noted in *Royal Bank* in reliance on case law from the Court of Appeal, the fact that a case is a high-value one is not on its own sufficient to lead to disclosure being ordered. In *Hyrax*, the case concerned penalties of over £1m. However, that sum was made up of a large number of daily penalties (capped at £600 and £5,000). The tribunal considered that this took the case outside the scope of a high-value case.

- A document that appears relevant from HMRC's statement of case would ordinarily be considered relevant for disclosure purposes.

- Whether or not such a document should then be considered in accordance with the overriding objective. This is a balancing exercise, weighing up the relevant factors.

- The document's relevance to the issues in dispute will generally be a relevant factor, inasmuch as more would be needed to displace the starting proposition in the case of a document that is seen as highly relevant. Again, this proposition was agreed to by the Upper Tribunal.

The Upper Tribunal also confirmed that the question of relevance is not a binary one. Instead, there is a range of degrees of relevance. This allows a tribunal to reach a more nuanced view when considering the question as to the proportionality of a disclosure request. As noted in *IAC*, relevance must be judged:

> "by reference to the issues in the case. This does not mean the issues in some abstract or generalised sense, but the issues and asserted facts as identified from each party's pleaded case."

Similarly, it confirmed that the fact that a document is confidential is not in itself a bar to disclosure, but a factor that should be taken into account in the balancing exercise to be applied by the tribunal.

On the subject of confidentiality, the tribunal in *Lucky* confirmed that HMRC's statutory duties of taxpayer confidentiality contained an exception for disclosures in the course of carrying out HMRC's functions. Accordingly, HMRC do not require the tribunal's permission before disclosing relevant documents that would otherwise be protected from disclosure.

In *Royal Bank* (a case which carefully analysed the authorities from the higher courts), the tribunal suggested the following:

- If a party has failed to comply with the initial disclosure requirements of rule 27, that may be a ground for making a direction under rule 16.
- If there has been no such failure, the tribunal will have to consider:
    - the necessity of the material to allow the case to be dealt with justly (relevance alone is not sufficient);
    - the likelihood that the material exists and is in the other party's control;
    - whether the material has been previously disclosed to the party requesting it;
    - whether the material is likely to be found and disclosed if a direction for disclosure were given; and
    - the proportionality of the request in the light of the importance and complexity of the case.

However, the tribunal then concluded the above summary (which was clearly expressed in general terms) with the comment that "it is unnecessary to determine ... whether the approach ... is applicable in the generality of cases before the Tribunal" and suggested that the approach set out is in fact specific to that case. The author considers that the summary is in fact capable of wider application.

In *Edwards-Moss*, it was noted that objections can be made on grounds of privacy (under the *Human Rights Act* 1998). However, this is not an absolute right and it must be balanced against other interests. Indeed, measures can be taken (for example a private hearing) to minimise the loss of privacy to sensitive data.

4.14 Rule 16 – Summoning or citation of witnesses and orders to answer questions or produce documents

An application was refused in *Colman*. Reasons for refusal included:

- the disproportionate nature of the request;
- delays occasioned by the taxpayers before conducting their own exercise in trying to source material – they had chosen to await the receipt of HMRC's statement of case, rather than start once they knew that the material might be needed;
- the fact that the taxpayers had already agreed a disclosure exercise with HMRC which they were effectively seeking to resile from; and
- the consequential delays that would be suffered by HMRC being obliged to comply with the additional request.

In *Budheo*, the taxpayer expressed concern that he might be required to answer questions and those answers might then be used in parallel criminal proceedings, potentially breaching his human rights. The argument was made in the context of an application to stay proceedings. The tribunal refused a stay, noting that any risk of a breach of human rights could be averted by the tribunal declining to give a direction under rule 16. The tribunal also added that it would be "extremely unusual for a tribunal to require an appellant to give evidence in his own appeal".

In *Hyrax*, the tribunal refused HMRC's application for disclosure of contemporaneous documentation that would corroborate assertions in the taxpayer's witness statements. As the tribunal noted, that was a case where the taxpayer had the burden of proof and if it chose not to reinforce its own case that was a choice it was entitled to make. The tribunal also noted the risk that failure to disclose contemporaneous documentation might lead the tribunal to drawing adverse inferences (see **4.12.3** above).

See also the commentary on rule 5(3)(d) at **4.2.4** above.

In *Trimax*, the tribunal noted the importance of clarity in any request for further information:

> "it is essential where further and better particulars are pursued that the party seeking an answer be precise about the questions asked."

In *B&M*, the tribunal preferred any request to be drafted in general terms based upon the above definition of "relevant".

Cases: *HMRC v IAC Associates* [2013] EWHC 4382 (Ch); *Trimax Trading International Ltd v HMRC* [2014] UKFTT 733 (TC); *Tower Bridge GP Ltd v HMRC* [2016] UKFTT 54 (TC); *Edwards-Moss v HMRC* [2016] UKFTT 147 (TC); *B&M Retail Ltd v HMRC* [2017] UKFTT 789 (TC); *Colman, Key, Schilling & Walton Partnership v HMRC* [2018] UKFTT 141 (TC); *Budheo v HMRC* [2019] UKFTT 216 (TC); *McCabe v HMRC* [2019] UKFTT 317 (TC); *McCabe v HMRC* [2020] UKUT 266 (TCC); *Royal Bank of Scotland Group plc v HMRC* [2020] UKFTT 321 (TC); *Lucky Technology Ltd v HMRC* [2021] UKFTT 55 (TC); *HMRC v Hyrax Resourcing Ltd* [2021] UKFTT 212 (TC)

Timing of such requests

Early in the life of the tribunal, the author inferred from the judge in one case that requests for clarificatory information ought not to be made until after the parties had exchanged witness evidence. However, in a more recent case (*Igen*), the tribunal made clear that there was no such standard practice and, indeed, each case ought to turn on its own facts.

The author agrees with that more flexible approach and suggests the following rules of thumb (which should be adapted as appropriate in individual cases):

- If there is confusion as to a point of principle or a key fact, then this ought to be resolved at the earliest opportunity.
- However, if a party is seeking disclosure of a particular document which might be expected to be disclosed in the other party's evidence, then it is appropriate to await that evidence and, only if it is not included, then to seek disclosure.

Case: *Igen Distribution Ltd (in liquidation) v HMRC* [2020] UKFTT 328 (TC)

Other practical considerations

In *Masstech*, the tribunal was asked by the taxpayer to order the production of certain information held by HMRC. The tribunal ordered the production of two of the items sought: although the tribunal was not convinced that they were relevant to the hearing, being merely the opinion of HMRC officers, they did contain material related to the contents of witness statements put forward by HMRC

4.14 Rule 16 – Summoning or citation of witnesses and orders to answer questions or produce documents

and, because of the importance of the witnesses' credibility, it was considered that it was right that the taxpayer be given the opportunity to cross examine those witnesses on whether their opinion had changed.

So far as the third item sought was concerned, the tribunal refused to order its production because its contents had no apparent relevance to the hearing.

Case: *Masstech Corporation Ltd (in administration) v HMRC* [2011] UKFTT 649 (TC)

4.14.4 "Fairford" decisions

A special procedure has evolved in cases involving what is sometimes known as carousel or missing trader intra-community fraud. However, there is no reason why it cannot be adopted in other similar evidence-heavy cases, although it should be noted that one peculiarity of carousel fraud cases is that HMRC bear the burden of proof.

The procedure involves the taxpayer being asked, in advance of the hearing, to confirm which aspects of HMRC's evidence it accepts, so as to allow HMRC to know which witnesses would be required to attend and to help the tribunal to make a better estimate of the length of the hearing.

The form of direction has evolved since the original *Fairford* case from where the term is derived, and the standard version is as set out by the Upper Tribunal in *Elbrook*. In that case, the Upper Tribunal noted that the purpose of *Fairford* directions is not to force the taxpayer to reveal in advance its potential lines of cross-examination.

In *Everyday*, the taxpayer sought "reverse-*Fairford* directions" by which it sought a summary of HMRC's evidence so as to ensure that it understood HMRC's evidence. The tribunal noted the distinction between the taxpayer being asked what aspects of HMRC's evidence is accepted and HMRC being asked to confirm that the taxpayer has properly understood HMRC's evidence. It should be noted, however, that if there were genuine ambiguities in one party's evidence, the other party ought to be permitted to request clarification ahead of the hearing.

Cases: *Elbrook Cash and Carry Ltd v HMRC* [2019] UKUT 201 (TCC); *Everyday Wholesale Ltd v HMRC* [2021] UKFTT 28 (TC)

4.14.5   Contents of order or summons (rule 16(6))

Any order or summons under rule 16 must state:

- that the person to whom it is addressed may apply to the tribunal to vary it or set it aside if there was not the opportunity to object to it before it was made or issued (see **4.14.7**); and
- the consequences of any failure to comply with the order or summons.

See rule 7 for referrals to the Upper Tribunal to enforce compliance.

4.14.6   Compulsion of witnesses (rule 16(3))

Under the general law of evidence, there are restrictions on who may be required to give evidence on certain occasions. For example, diplomats and members of their family are protected from being compelled as witnesses (under the Vienna Convention) as is the Monarch.

Rule 16(3) provides that the tribunal is bound by the same restrictions that apply in a court in the part of the UK in which the proceedings are due to be determined.

Law: *Diplomatic Privileges Act* 1964, Sch. 1 (Vienna Convention, art. 31.2, 37)

4.14.7   Application for variation or set aside (rule 16(4), (5))

Whenever a person is issued with an order or summons, that person may apply to the tribunal for it to be varied or set aside. Although rule 5(2) permits all directions to be varied or set aside, this particular application is primarily available in cases where the person did not have the opportunity to object to the order or summons before it was originally made.

Such an application should be made as soon as is reasonably practicable after the order or summons is received.

4.14.8 Tribunal practice statement

The tribunal has set out its usual approach to witness summons in a practice statement:

- The witness should have a presence in the UK (either physical presence, a residential address or place of business). Caution will be exercised by the tribunal before issuing a summons to an individual who is temporarily in the UK.
- Normally, a prior request should have been made for the witness to attend voluntarily. If there is a reason why no prior request has been made, the application should explain that reason.
- The tribunal must be satisfied that the witness's evidence will be relevant (see **4.14.3**).

The practice statement also sets out the procedures that the tribunal expects applicants to follow when making such an application.

Guidance: https://tinyurl.com/2p88ype5 (First-Tier Tribunal (Tax Chamber) Practice Direction – Witness Summonses and Orders to Produce Documents)

4.15 Rule 17 – Withdrawal

> 17(1) Subject to any provision in an enactment relating to withdrawal or settlement of particular proceedings, a party may give notice to the Tribunal of the withdrawal of the case made by it in the Tribunal proceedings, or any part of that case–
>
> (a) by sending or delivering to the Tribunal a written notice of withdrawal; or
>
> (b) orally at a hearing.
>
> 17(2) The Tribunal must notify each party in writing of its receipt of a withdrawal under this rule.
>
> 17(3) A party who has withdrawn their case may apply to the Tribunal for the case to be reinstated.

> 17(4) An application under paragraph (3) must be made in writing and be received by the Tribunal within 28 days after–
>
> (a) the date that the Tribunal received the notice under paragraph (1)(a); or
>
> (b) the date of the hearing at which the case was withdrawn orally under paragraph (1)(b).

4.15.1 Overview

Rule 17 deals with the procedures when one party withdraws part of all of its case. This will often arise when it becomes apparent that part of the case will not succeed (because of evidence that has come to light or a decision by a court or tribunal elsewhere).

If the Appellant (typically the taxpayer) withdraws the whole of its case this will usually lead to the end of the proceedings (because the tribunal's jurisdiction was engaged only because the Appellant brought the proceedings in the first place). However, as was made clear in *CM Utilities*, withdrawal, even if notified to the tribunal, does not necessarily bring an immediate end to the proceedings. It is therefore possible for the other party to continue to pursue the case.

In *CM Utilities*, HMRC had wanted to keep the proceedings alive so that they could *increase* the amount of the assessment. Overturning the previous decision of the First-tier, the Upper Tribunal concluded that HMRC had this right and that the tribunal is obliged to increase an assessment if there is evidence to justify doing so.

Indeed, as noted in *Albert House*:

> "where HMRC have made an in-time objection to withdrawal on the basis that the assessments may be incorrect, the Tribunal has a statutory obligation [under TMA s. 50] to determine the appeal by reducing, increasing or confirming the assessments [under appeal]".

That was a case where the taxpayer had notified HMRC of its decision not to proceed with the appeal. Ordinarily, TMA 1970, s. 54(4) provides that that would bring the appeal to an end as if the parties had reached a formal agreement (even though the taxpayer had acted unilaterally). However, such a deemed agreement does not arise if (as happened in the case) HMRC object to the withdrawal within 30 days.

Interestingly, the Upper Tribunal considered that HMRC had made a valid objection to the withdrawal by writing to the First-tier within the statutory 30-day period, even though the statute is quite clear that the notice of objection should be sent to the taxpayer. The Upper Tribunal emphasised that this result was achieved only because it was clear that the tribunal had forwarded the objection to the taxpayer within the 30-day period.

See also **4.14.6** in relation to the 30-day cooling off period.

See also **4.8.5** concerning the potential costs implications of withdrawing from a case.

Law: TMA 1970, s. 50, 54(4); VATA 1994, s. 85; SI 1999/1027, reg. 10
Cases: *HMRC v CM Utilities* [2017] UKUT 305 (TCC); *Albert House Property Finance PCC Ltd (in liquidation) v HMRC* [2020] UKUT 373 (TCC)

4.15.2 When withdrawal should not take place

On many occasions, it is HMRC who belatedly recognise the flaws in their case and "withdraw" the decision under appeal, inviting the taxpayer then to withdraw the appeal from the tribunal.

The taxpayer should never accede to such a request (or should do so only in exceptional circumstances). Instead, the parties should make a joint application for an order by consent, for example allowing the appeal. See rule 34.

In practice, however, the tribunal usually responds unilaterally to HMRC's withdrawal by allowing the appeal. Nevertheless, it does not always happen and the author therefore recommends that the taxpayer seek HMRC's consent to the appeal being allowed, to ensure that loose ends are completely tied up.

4.15.3 When withdrawal may take place

Rule 17(1) provides that a withdrawal may take place at any time before a hearing or orally at a hearing itself.

The original wording of rule 17(1)(a) implied that a withdrawal could not be made after the hearing but before a decision is finally made by the tribunal. Although it is considered that the tribunal could accept withdrawals in such cases (but was not obliged to do so), the matter was put beyond doubt by changes to the rule with effect from 1 April 2013. A notice of withdrawal may now be made at any time.

4.15.4 Giving notice of withdrawals

If the withdrawal is made at the hearing itself, the party may give oral notice of the withdrawal. Otherwise, it should be sent or delivered in writing to the tribunal.

In either case (i.e. even if notice is given orally at a hearing), the tribunal is required to give written notice of the withdrawal to each of the other parties.

4.15.5 Applications for reinstatement

If a party changes its mind after having withdrawn its case, it may apply to the tribunal to have the case reinstated. Such an application must be in writing and received by the tribunal within 28 days of:

- in the case of written withdrawal, the date on which the notice was received by the tribunal or
- in the case of oral withdrawal, the date of the hearing at which the case was withdrawn.

It was confirmed in *Orchid* that only the party that effected the withdrawal can seek the reinstatement of the case (although this is now subject to the Upper Tribunal's refinement of the position in *CM Utilities* (see **4.15.1**)). It was also confirmed that the rule cannot be circumvented by use of rule 38.

It was acknowledged in *Cavanagh* that a decision to reinstate an appeal should consider at least the merits of the appeal itself. In other words, reinstatement is not automatic. It is suggested that a fuller approach, akin to that followed in cases where an application is made to the tribunal for the admission of a late appeal (see **2.4.5**), should be adopted.

In *Pierhead*, the Upper Tribunal expressly approved the use of the same criteria to be used when considering whether an appeal should be admitted out of time. In the author's opinion, this is appropriate, although the fact that the tribunal then went on to consider the concept of delay seems slightly incongruous in cases where the application to reinstate a withdrawn case is in fact made in time.

Essentially, the Upper Tribunal's approach is for the tribunal to step back and consider overall where the interests of justice lie. See also **2.4.5** and **3.3** above.

This conflict was considered by the tribunal in *Vicolo* which in turn expressly declined to follow *Pierhead* and instead suggested that the tribunal should:

> "identify the factors that tend to point towards the reinstatement ... then identify the factors that tend to point against the reinstatement ... [and] weigh them in the balance in the light of the overriding objective to deal with the case fairly and justly".

In *SRN*, the Upper Tribunal made clear that each case should turn on its own circumstances and therefore it was inappropriate to set out any guiding principles as to when reinstatement might be granted.

So far as merits are concerned, there is an argument that these should always be considered but factored in only when the case is obviously very strong or very weak. That is definitely the approach to be followed in cases concerning late appeals and there seems to be no reason for a different approach in reinstatement applications. In *Vicolo*, the tribunal considered that the merits should be considered only in cases "where they disclose no reasonable prospects". The author respectfully suggests that a symmetrical approach should be adopted and that the merits ought also to be factored in the balance in cases with a very strong likelihood of success.

In *Eurobay*, the tribunal listed the following factors which ought to be considered (making it clear that the list was not necessarily exclusive):

- reasons for the initial withdrawal and why it is now sought to reinstate the matter;
- the effect on legal certainty and good administration of justice for the reinstatement to be permitted;
- prejudice to the appellant if the matter is not reinstated;
- prejudice to HMRC if the matter is reinstated; and
- the merits.

Since the *Eurobay* case, the tribunal's approach to giving parties an opportunity to reopen closed matters has consolidated (see *Martland* as discussed at **2.4.4** above). In *OWD*, the tribunal expressly considered the *Martland* approach to be applicable in cases involving rule 17.

Although a modified approach for reinstatement cases was then suggested in *Chappell* (in which the merits of the case would be considered only if the outcome appears obvious), it should be noted that that was in the context of a reinstatement application following a strike out (see **4.6.7**). Nevertheless, in *Rai*, the tribunal saw no reason to impose a harsher test in a case where the party making the reinstatement application had not previously breached a direction of the tribunal.

Interestingly, however, the tribunal in *Rai* seems to have considered the merits of the case only in the context of an obviously weak case, with the implication that an obviously strong case would not be a relevant factor. As already set out, the author considers that, if merits are to be taken into account, both extremes of the scale ought to be relevant.

Cases: *Cavanagh v HMRC* [2011] UKFTT 676 (TC); *Orchid Properties v HMRC* [2012] UKFTT 651 (TC); *Pierhead Purchasing Ltd v HMRC* [2014] UKUT 321 (TCC); *SRN Horizons Ltd v HMRC* [2017] UKUT 246 (TCC); *Eurobay Homecare Ltd v HMRC* [2017] UKFTT 185 (TC); *Martland v HMRC* [2018] UKUT 178 (TCC); *OWD v HMRC* [2018] UKFTT 497 (TC); *Chappell v Pension Regulator* [2019] UKUT 209 (TCC); *Rai v HMRC* [2019] UKFTT 687 (TC); *Il Vicolo Ltd v HMRC* [2020] UKFTT 55 (TC)

4.15.6 When reinstatement may not take place

There will be situations, however, when primary legislation overrides the tribunal's right to consider the reinstatement of an appeal. The point was confirmed in *OWD*.

This is where the taxpayer has written to HMRC notifying them that the appeal is not to be pursued and the statutory 30-day cooling off period has elapsed. In such situations, the statute deems the appeal to have been dismissed.

Law: TMA 1970, s. 54(4); VATA 1994, s. 85(4)
Case: *OWD v HMRC* [2018] UKFTT 497 (TC)

4.16 Rule 18 – Lead cases

18(1) This rule applies if–
(a) two or more cases have been started before the Tribunal;
(b) in each such case the Tribunal has not made a decision disposing of the proceedings; and
(c) the cases give rise to common or related issues of fact or law.

18(2) The Tribunal may give a direction–
(a) specifying one or more cases falling under paragraph (1) as a lead case or lead cases; and
(b) staying (or, in Scotland, sisting) the other cases falling under paragraph (1) ("the related cases").

18(3) When the Tribunal makes a decision in respect of the common or related issues–
(a) the Tribunal must send a copy of that decision to each party in each of the related cases; and
(b) subject to paragraph (4), that decision shall be binding on each of those parties.

18(4) Within 28 days after the date that the Tribunal sent a copy of the decision to a party under paragraph (3)(a), that party may apply in writing for a direction that the decision does not apply to, and is not binding on the parties to, that case.

18(5) The Tribunal must give directions in respect of cases which are stayed or sisted under paragraph (2)(b), providing for the disposal of or further steps in those cases.

18(6) If the lead case or cases are withdrawn or disposed of before the Tribunal makes a decision in respect of the common or related issues, the Tribunal must give directions as to–
(a) whether another case or other cases are to be heard as a lead case or lead cases; and
(b) whether any direction affecting the related cases should be set aside or amended.

4.16.1 Overview

This rule assists the tribunal in its case management. It deals with the situation where there is more than one case before the tribunal dealing with similar facts or issues and allows the tribunal to select one (or more) as a lead case (or lead cases).

Other similar orders

Rule 18 directions should be distinguished from directions where cases are consolidated or otherwise heard together (see rule 5(3)(b) discussed at **4.2.6**).

Rule 5(3)(b) also permits cases to be treated as a lead case outside the scope of rule 18. This distinction was confirmed in *Sub One*. Where the direction for rule 18 to apply is not given, the following consequences of the direction will not follow (unless and to the extent expressly provided for in the direction).

Case: *Sub One Ltd (t/a Subway) v HMRC* [2009] UKFTT 385 (TC)

4.16.2 Consequences of being a lead case

Where a case is selected as a lead case, it will proceed in the ordinary way, but the other cases (the "follower cases") will be stayed (sisted in Scotland) until resolution of the lead case. This ensures that the tribunal (and the parties involved in the other cases) need not spend time dealing with those other cases and all efforts can be focused on the lead case.

In *Sub One*, a case concerning the VAT treatment of supplies made by different *Subway* franchisees, the tribunal considered that "the prospect of holding nearly 200 appeals involving the same area of law, [the] same disputed issue and essentially the same evidence is not in line with the principles of dealing with cases proportionately and avoiding delay". It also recognised the risk of different appellants obtaining different results merely because of a different analysis by another judge would bring the judicial process into disrepute. For these reasons, the tribunal considered a direction under rule 18 appropriate, leaving the parties to decide which case would proceed as the lead case.

Case: *Sub One Ltd (t/a Subway) v HMRC* [2009] UKFTT 385 (TC)

4.16.3 When a direction may be made

A direction under rule 18 may be made whenever there are two or more cases that have been started before the tribunal (i.e. the tribunal has been notified of the cases) and the tribunal has not yet made a final decision disposing of the proceedings.

Rule 18(1)(c) provides that a lead case direction may be made if the cases give rise to common or related issues of fact or law. In *Sub One*, HMRC argued that this condition was not satisfied because the issue in the appeals was the subjective purpose of each individual taxpayer (as to why food would have been served hot) and, therefore, a lead case direction would not have been appropriate. The tribunal considered that, even if HMRC's argument were correct in suggesting that each case ought to be based on its own facts, the relevant question was whether the various appeals gave rise to "common or related issues of fact or law". The tribunal considered that they did and then proceeded to determine whether or not a direction under rule 18 was appropriate. In doing so, the tribunal noted the possibility of individual cases being re-litigated under rule 18(4) (see below).

In *Kingston Maurward*, the tribunal emphasised the need for the common or related issues to be clearly defined.

In *288*, the tribunal considered that the fact that one of the cases raises an issue not arising in the lead case should not, in itself, be a reason to refuse a rule 18 direction. In such circumstances, the tribunal's conclusion in the lead case would initially bind the parties in the related case, but only so far as there are issues which are common to both cases. The tribunal described the purpose of rule 18 as to allow unnecessary litigation to be avoided, hearings to be shortened and to reduce the risk of different compositions of tribunal reaching conflicting views.

The *288* case also considered the potential difficulties that could arise if the losing party in the lead case chooses to appeal against the decision to the Upper Tribunal because the lead case procedure does not apply in the Upper Tribunal. Further potential difficulties could arise if the losing party in the lead case chooses not to appeal against the decision, but a party in a related case does wish to take the case further. The tribunal, whilst recognising these potential difficulties, considered that they did not amount to sufficient grounds to object to a lead case direction.

Cases: *Sub One Ltd (t/a Subway) v HMRC* [2009] UKFTT 385 (TC); *Kingston Maurward v HMRC* [2017] UKFTT 502 (TC); *288 Group Ltd v HMRC* [2013] UKFTT 659 (TC)

4.16.4 Decision in a lead case (rule 18(3)—(5))

Whenever a decision is reached on a lead case in one of the common or related issues, the tribunal must send a copy of that decision to each of the parties in each of the related cases.

Effect on those other cases (rule 18(3)(b), (4))

The initial consequence of a direction under rule 18 is that the decision in the lead case is binding on each of parties in the other cases.

However, a party can try to unbind itself. To do so, it must apply in writing within 28 days of the tribunal notifying it of the decision in the lead case.

> **Example**
>
> Tom, Dick and Harry each receive £60,000 from their former employer on termination of their employments. HMRC have formed the view that the sums received were taxable in full.
>
> The individuals' contracts were not materially different and the tribunal considers it appropriate to select Tom's case a lead case under rule 18, with Dick and Harry's cases stayed pending the outcome.
>
> When Tom's case is decided, the tribunal must notify Dick and Harry (as well as Tom and HMRC) of the outcome. Within 28 days, either Dick or HMRC can apply for the decision in Tom's case not to be binding on Dick's dispute (and, similarly, Harry or HMRC can apply for the result in Tom's case not to be binding on them in Harry's case).

In *General Healthcare*, the tribunal considered that a party making such an application has no right to be unbound. That is a matter for the tribunal's discretion. In *Tadmarton*, the tribunal refused to unbind a party on the basis that, whilst the taxpayer considered itself able to distinguish its facts from those of the lead case, the tribunal decided that there were in fact no material differences. In such an event, the party must embark upon an appeal to the Upper Tribunal (first seeking permission from the First-tier under rule 39).

In *288*, the tribunal considered the possibility that a taxpayer in the lead case might lose the appeal and take the matter to the Upper Tribunal. In such circumstances, the taxpayers in the related cases would initially be bound by the First-tier's decision (in favour of HMRC) even though the taxpayer in the lead case might succeed in the Upper Tribunal (or beyond). (It will be noted that the lead case procedure does not survive beyond the First-tier.) In practice, taxpayers in such cases should apply to be unbound by the decision in the lead case, but the application is generally stayed pending the final resolution of the lead case.

Cases: *288 Group Ltd v HMRC* [2013] UKFTT 659 (TC); *General Healthcare Group Ltd v HMRC* [2014] UKFTT 353 (TC); *Tadmarton Heath Golf Club Company Ltd v HMRC* [2016] UKFTT 376 (TC)

When is a document "sent" (rule 18(4))?

For a case concerning the impact on a time limit when a document is sent to the wrong address, see the discussion of the *Rana* case in the context of rule 5(3)(a).

Case: *Rana v London Borough of Ealing* [2018] EWCA Civ 2074

Future handling of stayed cases (rule 18(5))

Whether or not a party has applied to be unbound from the decision in the lead case, the tribunal must give directions dealing with the future conduct or the disposal of the cases that were stayed behind the lead case.

In *288*, the tribunal considered the possibility that a taxpayer in the lead case might lose the appeal and choose not to pursue the matter further, whereas the taxpayer in a related case might wish to take the matter to the Upper Tribunal. In such circumstances, the tribunal considered that the tribunal would ordinarily dismiss the appeals in the related case, thereby giving the taxpayer a decision which could then be appealed against to the Upper Tribunal.

In *ABL*, HMRC requested that the tribunal issue a summary decision in all the stayed cases dismissing the appeals, so as to follow the decision of the lead case. Their apparent purpose was to release for collection the tax in dispute in those cases, notwithstanding the fact that the lead case was proceeding on appeal to the Upper Tribunal. The tribunal weighed up the pros and cons of this course of action, deciding that the potential cash flow advantage to HMRC was insufficient to justify removing the stay.

Cases: *288 Group Ltd v HMRC* [2013] UKFTT 659 (TC); *ABL (Holding) Ltd v HMRC* [2017] UKFTT 220 (TC)

4.16.5 Withdrawal or other disposal of lead case (rule 18(6))

The benefits of having a lead case are lost if the lead case is withdrawn or is otherwise disposed of (perhaps by strike out) before a decision can be given in respect of the common or related issues. When that occurs, the tribunal must give directions as to whether any other case should be heard as a lead case and whether any directions affecting the related cases should be set aside or amended.

5. Procedures before a hearing

5.1 Introduction

These rules address:

- first, the procedures that deal with a party's initial contact with the tribunal; and
- next, the allocation of a case to one of four categories.

These processes determine how the case will be handled by the tribunal (and some of the procedural steps expected from the parties) up to the time that the tribunal reaches its final decision in the case.

5.1.1 Initial contact with the tribunal (rules 19 to 22)

A case cannot be said to be before the tribunal until the matter is notified to the tribunal. Different procedures apply depending on whether the matter is:

- one party's (generally, HMRC's) unilateral application to the tribunal (for pre-approval of an inspection or information notice) without the need to give notice of the application to the other party – see rule 19;
- a taxpayer's appeal against an HMRC decision – see rule 20; or
- a taxpayer's application (e.g. for a closure notice) or one by HMRC (e.g. for a declaration about the notifiability of an avoidance scheme) – see rule 21.

Also discussed is rule 22 which concerns hardship applications, relevant to indirect taxes, where the tribunal may suspend the ordinary requirement for the tax in dispute to have been paid because that requirement would cause the appellant to suffer hardship.

5.1.2 Allocation of cases to the categories (rules 23 to 28)

Under the Tribunal Procedure rules, cases are allocated to one of four categories, according to the perceived complexity of the case.

Depending on the category allocated, different procedures will apply to the case.

5.2 Rule 19 – Proceedings without notice to a respondent

> 19 If a case or matter is to be determined without notice to or the involvement of a respondent–
>
> (a) any provision in these Rules requiring a document to be provided by or to a respondent; and
>
> (b) any other provision in these Rules permitting a respondent to participate in the proceedings
>
> does not apply to that case or matter.

5.2.1 Overview

This rule governs cases where a matter is dealt with by the tribunal without notice being given to, or without even the subsequent involvement of, another party. In particular, it will be relevant in those cases where HMRC wish to obtain the tribunal's pre-approval of an inspection notice or an information notice under their powers in FA 2008, Sch. 36 without notice to another party (the taxpayer or a third party recipient of the proposed notice).

Law: FA 2008, Sch. 36, para. 3, 5, 13

5.2.2 When does the rule apply?

The rule applies only where a case or matter may be determined without notice or the involvement of a respondent.

The only instances where the tax legislation permits "without notice" applications to the tribunal to be made are where HMRC wish to:

- issue a taxpayer notice under Sch. 36, para. 1;
- issue a third-party notice under Sch. 36, para. 2;
- issue a financial institution notice under Sch. 36, para. 4A without all of the usual (limited) safeguards governing such notices;
- issue a third-party notice in respect of a taxpayer whose identity is not known under Sch. 36, para. 5;

- inspect a taxpayer's premises under Sch. 36, para. 10, 10A, 11 or 12A;
- issue an information notice under their further data gathering powers under FA 2011, Sch. 23; or
- issue an information notice under the POTAS rules.

Law: FA 2008, Sch. 36, para. 3(2A), 4A(8), 5(3A), 13(1A); FA 2011, Sch. 23, para. 5(3); FA 2014, s. 256(2)

When tribunal approval is necessary

In most of these cases, prior approval from the tribunal is not necessary before HMRC issue the notice because, generally, such notices may be given without the tribunal's prior involvement. However, a notice requires the tribunal's prior approval if HMRC wish:

- to issue a third-party notice and the taxpayer has not agreed to the notice being given;
- to issue a third-party notice in respect of a taxpayer whose identity is not known;
- to inspect premises for the purposes of valuation under Sch. 36, para. 12A and the occupier of the premises (or a person otherwise in control of the premises) has not agreed to the inspection being carried out; or
- to obtain information involving third parties under the POTAS rules.

Law: FA 2008, Sch. 36, para. 3(1), 5(3), 12B(1), (4); FA 2014, s. 256(1)

Tribunal approval in other cases

In other cases, HMRC might still wish to obtain the tribunal's pre-approval. Such a course of action will mean that:

- in the cases of information notices:
  - the recipient of the notice is precluded from appealing against the notice (any challenge being limited to judicial review proceedings commenced in the High Court or the Court of Session), and

- it would be an offence for the recipient to conceal, destroy or dispose of any document sought under the notice; and
- in the case of inspection requests, a penalty of £300 (plus potential daily penalties of up to £60) will be charged for any person who deliberately obstructs an HMRC officer in the course of the inspection.

In *Skelly*, the tribunal recognised that HMRC could not proceed in this way unless they had good reason to (for example, the need for secrecy or urgency). Merely seeking to shut out a taxpayer from any subsequent appeal right would not amount to good reason.

Law: FA 2008, Sch. 36, para. 29, 30, 39, 40, 53; FA 2011, Sch. 23, para. 28, 30, 31; FA 2014, s. 266(3), 278 and Sch. 35, para. 2
Case: *Skelly v HMRC* [2014] UKFTT 478 (TC)

5.2.3 Effect of rule 19

When rule 19 applies, all that happens is that the effect of the other Tribunal Rules is modified so as to disapply:

- any rule which would otherwise require a document to be provided by or to a respondent, and
- any rule permitting a respondent to participate in the proceedings.

In *Skelly*, the tribunal considered that this meant that a party that was excluded from the proceedings could not insist upon receiving a decision notice under rule 35. Nor could that party use the non-attendance as a justification for requesting a set-aside under rule 38.

Subsequent case law (*Jimenez*) has questioned the tribunal's practice of hearing information notice requests without the taxpayer's involvement in the application. However, basing itself on Court of Appeal authority (*Derrin Bros*), the First-tier has maintained its existing practice in *Mr E*. More recently, in *Kandore*, the Court of Appeal has supported the earlier decisions made but, read properly, the author considers that the judgment makes it clear that each case has to be considered on its own merits.

For a fuller discussion of the extent to which the respondent (or an interested third party) may make representations to the tribunal, see the author's book *Schedule 36 Notices: HMRC Information Requests*, from Claritax Books.

Cases: *Skelly v HMRC* [2014] UKFTT 478 (TC); *R (oao Derrin Brothers Properties Ltd) v FTT* [2016] EWCA Civ 15; *R (oao Jimenez) v FTT* [2017] EWHC 2585 (Admin); *Mr E v HMRC* [2018] UKFTT 590 (TC); *Kandore Ltd v HMRC* [2021] EWCA Civ 1082

5.3 Rule 20 – Starting appeal proceedings

20(1) A person making or notifying an appeal to the Tribunal under any enactment must start proceedings by sending or delivering a notice of appeal to the Tribunal.

20(2) The notice of appeal must include–

    (a) the name and address of the appellant;

    (b) the name and address of the appellant's representative (if any);

    (c) an address where documents for the appellant may be sent or delivered;

    (d) details of the decision appealed against;

    (e) the result the appellant is seeking; and

    (f) the grounds for making the appeal.

20(3) The appellant must provide with the notice of appeal a copy of any written record of any decision appealed against, and any statement of reasons for that decision, that the appellant has or can reasonably obtain.

20(4) If the notice of appeal is provided after the end of any period specified in an enactment referred to in paragraph (1) but the enactment provides that an appeal may be made or notified after that period with the permission of the Tribunal–

    (a) the notice of appeal must include a request for such permission and the reason why the notice of appeal was not provided in time; and

> (b) unless the Tribunal gives such permission, the Tribunal must not admit the appeal.
>
> 20(5) When the Tribunal receives the notice of appeal it must give notice of the proceedings to the respondent.

5.3.1 Overview

Rule 20 provides the framework for taxpayers to notify the tribunal of an appeal. In direct tax cases, the appeal will have previously been made to HMRC, but in indirect tax cases, an appeal is made directly to the tribunal (although the taxpayer might have previously engaged with HMRC in the internal review process).

5.3.2 Notice of appeal (rule 20(1)—(3))

At the centre of the rule is the need for the taxpayer to send in a notice of appeal.

Contents of notice of appeal

The notice of appeal must include the information set out in rule 20(2) and be accompanied by a copy of the HMRC decision being appealed against (as noted in rule 20(3)). In indirect tax cases, rule 22 provides additional requirements in connection with the need to have paid (or deposited) all tax in dispute prior to commencing appeal proceedings, except in cases where that requirement would cause hardship.

The reference in rule 20(2)(b) to the appellant's representative refers to the person with whom the tribunal and the other parties will generally correspond before and after the hearing. It does not mean any advocate (if different) who might be appointed to represent the appellant at the hearing itself. See also rule 11.

The tribunal's website has recently been updated to provide a smart appeal process which permits documents to be uploaded to the tribunal's server. However, a more conventional "paper" form is also able to be downloaded – ostensibly for notification by post, but also capable of being e-mailed to the tribunal.

Failure to include all the documents required by this rule will mean that there has not been effective notification of the appeal to the tribunal. If any omissions are not rectified until after the time limit for sending a notice of appeal, permission from the tribunal for a late notice will be necessary (see below). As happened in *Wallace*, that can mean that the appeal will not be permitted to proceed.

Guidance: https://www.gov.uk/tax-tribunal/appeal-to-tribunal
Case: *Wallace v HMRC* [2012] UKFTT 433 (TC)

Grounds of appeal

The grounds of appeal must be sufficiently detailed to enable HMRC to understand the area(s) of dispute so that they can prepare a statement of case. In practice, however, this can usually be done quite concisely and the author has experienced no difficulties with the following very brief grounds of appeal:

- The appellant was not resident in the 2019-20 tax year.
- The conditions for a discovery assessment in section 29(1) and/or (3) are not satisfied.

Occasionally, HMRC will insist upon further information although this can often be interpreted as a tactic to delay matters rather than due to an actual failure to understand the taxpayer's concerns. In particular, the author has seen the tribunal refuse HMRC's request for greater particularisation of the taxpayer's grounds in cases where the matter had already been fully debated in the course of a previous internal review. After all, the statement of case (although limited to the grounds of appeal) is meant to be justifying HMRC's decision now under appeal.

Nevertheless, brevity has its limits. For example, in the following two (hypothetical) examples, it is suggested that the italicised words are necessary in order to identify to HMRC (and to the tribunal) the basis of the taxpayer's case:

- The taxpayer has a reasonable excuse for the late return *because he was caring for his injured wife*.
- The penalties charged are excessive *as further mitigation should have been given*.

The sufficiency of the grounds of appeal should, of course, be considered in the context of the decision being appealed against.

As said in *Ecko*, the taxpayer should describe the evidence that it intends to rely upon. However, it does not need to produce that evidence at this stage in the proceedings.

In *Unicorn*, the tribunal rejected the taxpayer's contention that full grounds of appeal were unnecessary because the taxpayer could not understand HMRC's decision letter. Instead, the fact that the decision letter could not be understood would have constituted a ground of appeal in its own right.

In many cases, a taxpayer will be disputing HMRC's right to ask for more tax as well as the amount of tax charged. In *Ecko*, the tribunal made it clear that both lines of argument must be raised in the notice of appeal (as there can be only one appeal against HMRC's decision). This does not preclude (in appropriate cases – see **4.2.6** above) the tribunal subsequently determining the two issues separately, one as a preliminary matter.

If, as a result of HMRC's subsequent statement of case (particularly in situations where the original decision letter was unclear), the taxpayer wishes to amend the grounds of appeal, *Unicorn* makes it clear that this is an appropriate course of action (assuming it is done reasonably promptly).

In *Daly*, HMRC had sought to strike out a taxpayer's appeal on the basis of the paucity of information within the grounds of appeal. Although the tribunal considered the notice of appeal to be lacking in detail, it declined to strike out the appeal because HMRC's application had been made too late (being a year after the appeal had been made).

Cases: *Unicorn Shipping Ltd v HMRC* [2017] UKFTT 64 (TC); *Ecko Ltd t/a Subway v HMRC* [2019] UKFTT 715 (TC); *Daly v HMRC* [2020] UKFTT 281 (TC)

5.3.3　Late appeals (rule 20(4))

If the notification is made to the tribunal outside the time permitted under the relevant statute, the statute generally provides that late notification may still be made to the tribunal. However, the appeal can proceed only if the tribunal gives permission.

This contrasts with the rules that allow direct tax appeals made to HMRC to be made outside the statutory 30-day time limit (see **2.4.1** and **2.4.5** above).

For the factors that the tribunal should consider, see **2.4.4** above.

Refusal of permission

If the tribunal does not give permission, it may not admit the appeal and the matter will have to rest there, subject to any appeal against the refusal (on a point of law) to the Upper Tribunal.

Law: TMA 1970, s. 49G(3), 49H(3); VATA 1994, s. 83G(6); FA 1994, s. 59G(6); FA 1996, s. 54G(6); FA 2000, Sch. 6, para. 121G(6); FA 2001, s. 40G(6)

5.4 Rule 21 – Starting proceedings by originating application or reference

21(1) Where an enactment provides for a person or persons to make an originating application or reference to the Tribunal, the appellant must start proceedings by providing an application notice or notice of reference to the Tribunal within any time limit imposed by that enactment.

21(2) The application notice or notice of reference must state–

(a) the name and address of the appellant;

(b) the name and address of the appellant's representative (if any);

(c) an address where documents for the appellant may be sent or delivered;

(d) the name and address of each respondent (if any);

(e) the facts relevant to the originating application or reference;

(f) the result the appellant is seeking (if any); and

(g) the grounds for making the originating application or reference.

> 21(3) If the appellant provides the application notice or notice of reference to the Tribunal later than the time required by paragraph (1) or by any extension of time under rule 5(3)(a) (power to extend time)–
>
> > (a) the application notice or notice of reference must include a request for an extension of time and the reason why the application notice or notice of reference was not provided in time; and
> >
> > (b) unless the Tribunal extends time for the application notice or notice of reference under rule 5(3)(a) (power to extend time) the Tribunal must not admit the application notice or notice of reference.
>
> 21(3A) The power of the Tribunal under these Rules to extend time for starting proceedings shall not apply in a CAA case.
>
> 21(4) When the Tribunal receives an application notice or a notice of reference it must send a copy of the notice and any accompanying document to any respondent.

5.4.1 Overview

Rule 21 deals with those situations where a matter can be brought to the tribunal, although it is not based upon an appealable decision.

Examples are applications by taxpayers for closure notices (to bring self-assessment enquiries to an end) or joint applications made by a taxpayer and HMRC for the referral of a technical matter to the tribunal in the middle of an enquiry.

It can also refer to cases which are initiated by HMRC but will proceed with the taxpayer's full involvement. Examples include applications for the declaration as to whether a set of arrangements constitutes a notifiable scheme under the DOTAS rules.

It will be noted that the rule refers to "Appellant" even though there is not actually an appeal. This is because of the extended meaning of the word as given in rule 1(3).

Contents of application notice or notice of reference

The notice commencing proceedings must include the information set out in rule 21(2).

5.4 Rule 21 – Starting proceedings by originating application or reference

The reference in rule 21(2)(b) to the appellant's representative refers to the person with whom the tribunal and the other parties will generally correspond before and after the hearing. It does not mean any advocate (if different) appointed to represent the appellant at the hearing itself. See also rule 11.

Standard application forms for closure notices are available on the tribunal's website, as well as a smart application process. For other applications, it is considered that a letter to the tribunal should suffice (provided that all the required information is included in or with the letter).

Guidance: https://www.gov.uk/government/publications/form-t245-application-to-close-enquiry

5.4.2 Late notices (rule 21(3))

If the notification is made to the tribunal outside the time permitted under the relevant statute (something that is not relevant in the context of closure notice applications), the statute generally provides that late notification may still be made to the tribunal, but the case can proceed only if the tribunal gives permission.

This contrasts with the rules that allow direct tax appeals made to HMRC to be made outside the statutory 30-day time limit (see **2.4.1** and **2.4.5** above).

For the factors that the tribunal should consider, see **2.4.4** above.

Unlike rule 20(4), which deals with late notifications of an appeal, rule 21(3) appears to suggest that any time limits may be extended by the tribunal under rule 5(3)(a) (see **4.2.4**). However, it should be noted that rule 5(3)(a) cannot be applied by the tribunal to extend a time limit beyond that permitted by primary legislation. Until 28 November 2010, rules 20(4) and 21(3) were identically worded, but rule 20(4) was amended as a consequence of the tribunal assuming responsibility for MPs' expenses appeals.

On the other hand, no extension is permitted in cases involving apportionments for capital allowances purposes.

Refusal of permission

If the tribunal does not give permission for a late notice, it may not admit the application or reference and the matter will have to rest

Ch. 5 – Procedures before a hearing

there, subject to any appeal against the refusal (on a point of law) to the Upper Tribunal.

5.5 Rule 22 – Hardship applications

22(1) This rule applies where an enactment provides, in any terms, that an appeal may not proceed if the liability to pay the amount in dispute is outstanding unless HMRC or the Tribunal consent to the appeal proceeding.

22(2) When starting proceedings, the appellant must include or provide the following in or with the notice of appeal–

(a) a statement as to whether the appellant has paid the amount in dispute;

(b) if the appellant has not paid the amount in dispute, a statement as to the status or outcome of any application to HMRC for consent to the appeal proceeding; and

(c) if HMRC have refused such an application, an application to the Tribunal for consent to the appeal proceeding.

22(3) An application under paragraph (2)(c) must include the reasons for the application and a list of any documents the appellant intends to produce or rely upon in support of that application.

22(4) If the appellant requires the consent of HMRC or the Tribunal before the appeal may proceed, the Tribunal must stay the proceedings until any applications to HMRC or the Tribunal in that respect have been determined.

5.5.1 Overview

This rule reflects the fact that VAT (and other indirect tax) appeals may generally proceed only if the tax in dispute has been paid first or deposited. In each case, however, the rule is subject to a provision that permits the appeal to proceed if either:

- the taxpayer has applied to HMRC and HMRC are satisfied that the requirement to pay or deposit the amount determined would cause the appellant to suffer hardship; or

- the taxpayer has so applied, HMRC are not satisfied but, on the taxpayer's further application to the tribunal, the tribunal decides that the requirement to pay or deposit the amount determined would cause the appellant to suffer hardship.

Law: VATA 1994, s. 84(3B); FA 1994, s. 60(4A); FA 1996, s. 55(3A); FA 2000, Sch. 6, para. 122(2A); FA 2001, s. 41(2A)

5.5.2 Application of the rule

The rule applies in all cases where there is such a general requirement to pay or deposit the amount in dispute. The rule applies, therefore, whether or not the amount has been paid and whether or not a hardship application is to be made.

5.5.3 Effect of the rule

The rule ensures that the taxpayer must include on the appeal notice:

- a statement as to whether or not the tax in dispute has been paid;
- if the tax has not been paid, a statement as to the status of any hardship application made to HMRC (i.e. an application for HMRC to waive the requirement for the tax to have been paid); and
- if such an application has been refused by HMRC, the further application to the tribunal for consent for the appeal to proceed.

Rule 22(3) provides that, if a hardship application is made to the tribunal, the appeal notice must also include:

- the reasons for the application; and
- a list of any documents the taxpayer intends to produce or rely upon in support of the application.

These statements are all provided for in the standard notices of appeal on the tribunal's website and also the smart application process.

Guidance: https://www.gov.uk/tax-tribunal/appeal-to-tribunal

5.5.4 Stay of proceedings

If the consent of HMRC or the tribunal is still outstanding, any proceedings are stayed until any hardship applications to HMRC or the tribunal have been determined.

Thus, there is nothing to prevent a taxpayer notifying the tribunal of an appeal before an answer has been received from HMRC concerning any hardship application. Indeed, with time limits for making the appeal to the tribunal, it will generally be necessary to make the appeal to the tribunal before any hardship application is dealt with by HMRC. The appeal will then be held in suspense until consent is given by HMRC or (if HMRC refuse) the tribunal.

5.5.5 Refusal by tribunal

The primary legislation provides that taxpayers may not appeal against any refusal by the tribunal to a hardship application. However, in many instances, the primary legislation was inserted by statutory instrument in a fashion that has since been found to be unlawful. See **9.6.3**.

In cases where an appeal is not permissible (essentially, those provisions enacted after 2009), a challenge to the tribunal's decision can be made only by way of judicial review for which it will have to be shown that the tribunal misdirected itself or otherwise acted irrationally when considering the application. The latter is a high hurdle to overcome.

Law: VATA 1994, s. 84(3C); FA 1994, s. 60(4B); FA 1996, s. 55(3B); FA 2000, Sch. 6, para. 122(2B); FA 2001, s. 41(2B); FA 2017, Sch. 10, para. 11; FA 2021, Sch. 11, para. 11

5.6 Rule 23 – Allocation of cases to categories

> 23(1) When the Tribunal receives a notice of appeal, application notice or notice of reference, the Tribunal must give a direction–
>
> (a) in an MP expenses case, a financial restrictions civil penalty case or a CAA case, allocating the case to one of the categories set out in paragraph (2)(c) or (d); and

5.6 Rule 23 – Allocation of cases to categories

(b) in any other case, allocating the case to one of the categories set out in paragraph (2).

23(2) The categories referred to in paragraph (1) are–

(a) Default Paper cases, which will usually be disposed of without a hearing;

(b) Basic cases, which will usually be disposed of after a hearing, with minimal exchange of documents before the hearing;

(c) Standard cases, which will usually be subject to more detailed case management and be disposed of after a hearing; and

(d) Complex cases, in respect of which see paragraphs (4) and (5) below.

23(3) The Tribunal may give a further direction re-allocating a case to a different category at any time, either on the application of a party or on its own initiative.

23(4) The Tribunal may allocate a case as a Complex case under paragraph (1) or (3) only if the Tribunal considers that the case–

(a) will require lengthy or complex evidence or a lengthy hearing;

(b) involves a complex or important principle or issue; or

(c) involves a large financial sum.

23(5) If a case is allocated as a Complex case–

(a) rule 10(1)(c) (costs in Complex cases) applies to the case; and

(b) rule 28 (transfer of Complex cases to the Upper Tribunal) applies to the case.

5.6.1 *Overview*

As noted at **5.1.2** above, cases are allocated to one of four categories, depending on the perceived complexity of the case. Rule 23 provides the framework for the different categories and some of the consequences of a case being allocated to a particular category.

5.6.2 When allocation takes place

The allocation must take place whenever the tribunal receives a notice of appeal or application notice or notice of reference. In practice, it usually occurs within a few weeks (but sometimes longer) of the complete appeal documents being sent to the tribunal.

Until the tribunal administration processes the notice of appeal or application, there is nothing that must be done in relation to the case (and the other side might not even know that the matter is now before the tribunal). (Of course, it will often be appropriate to use this time to undertake some further preparation for the case.)

On the other hand, many time limits will run from the time that the notice of appeal or application is processed by the tribunal. Delays in the tribunal's handling of the notice of appeal or application can therefore lead to uncertainty: is there a delay because of the tribunal's own level of workloads or has something gone astray? If something has gone astray, a person cannot really be blamed for being unaware of what has happened. Nevertheless, a party expecting to hear from the tribunal is expected not to be completely complacent. There again, the tribunal will not want staff being called every 24 hours for a status update.

The author considers that a reasonable compromise would be for an appellant to contact the tribunal if nothing is heard within six or so weeks of the notice being submitted.

It will be seen that allocation does not occur in cases where there is a without notice application to the tribunal under rule 19. The *Surestone* case confirms that pre-April 2009 cases transferred to the tribunal will also not be allocated to a category.

Rule 23(3) provides that a case can be re-allocated to another category at any time (either by the tribunal acting unilaterally or following an application by a party). However, as held in *Babergh*, **re-**allocation cannot apply to a transferred-in case (i.e. one from before 1 April 2009 which was subsequently transferred to the tribunal on that date) because there had been no allocation in the first place.

Cases: *Surestone v HMRC* [2009] UKFTT 352 (TC); *Babergh District Council v HMRC* [2011] UKFTT 341 (TC)

5.6.3 The four categories

The four categories are:

- Default Paper cases;
- Basic cases;
- Standard cases;
- Complex cases.

With the exception of the Complex cases category, the Rules themselves contained no guidance as to which category a case should be allocated to. This is probably because, leaving aside some procedural differences between those categories, there is generally little significance about which of those categories a case has been allocated to (and, indeed, no real need for cases to be reallocated from one category to another). Since 29 November 2010, however, the rules were modified to deal with MP expenses cases and (from 1 April 2013) financial restrictions civil penalty cases and CAA cases. These types of case must all be allocated to the Standard or Complex case categories.

It will be noted (see **4.1.2** above) that the allocation of cases to categories is a function that is initially delegated to administrative staff. To facilitate this, the tribunal has issued a practice statement that determines when a case should be allocated to the Default Paper or Basic cases (and, where applicable, to which category it should be allocated). The practice statement makes it clear that its terms are not applicable in every case: it should be followed "unless the tribunal considers that there is a reason why it is appropriate to allocate the case to a different category".

The effect of the practice statement is summarised at **Appendix 1**.

In *Capital Air Services*, the Upper Tribunal emphasised the flexibility that should be inherent in the allocation process.

In *Newton*, a case concerning a more complex than usual appeal against an information notice, the tribunal suggested that the taxpayer or HMRC should have flagged up the desirability of the case being allocated to the standard case category.

It was noted in *Capital Air Services* that the names of the categories carry some flavour and could be used as "an indicator of the sort of case which is properly to be allocated to each category" with each category representing "an ascending order of difficulty".

As will be seen below, very few cases merit being allocated to the Complex case category.

Cases: *Capital Air Services Ltd v HMRC* [2010] UKUT 373 (TCC); *Newton v HMRC* [2018] UKFTT 513 (TC)

Guidance: https://www.judiciary.uk/publications/categorisation-of-cases-in-the-tax-chamber

5.6.4 Default Paper cases

As the name suggests, such cases are ones that will usually be disposed of without a formal hearing – they will be judged on the papers. The practice statement identifies appeals against late filing and late payment penalties of up to £2,000.

With the onset of Covid-19 and the difficulties in holding face-to-face hearings, the scope of Default Paper cases was temporarily broadened. However, with the greater use of online hearings, this temporary extension appears to have expired on 1 September 2021.

The special procedures for paper cases are dealt with in rule 26. Broadly, they provide that:

- the appellant may reply in writing to HMRC's statement of case (so that the tribunal has papers from both sides to enable it to determine the case); but
- either party may require the tribunal to hold a hearing before determining the case.

Guidance: https://www.judiciary.uk/publications/categorisation-of-cases-in-the-tax-chamber

5.6.5 Basic cases

The practice statement provides that those appeals against penalties that are not subject to the Default Paper case category will generally be allocated as Basic cases. The category also includes:

- mitigation requests on the basis of reasonable excuse for indirect taxes;
- appeals against information notices; and
- appeals against PAYE codes.

The special procedures for such cases are dealt with in rule 24. Broadly, they provide that such cases should typically progress direct to a hearing without any further paperwork.

In the author's experience, appeals against information notices can sometimes justify being taken outside the Basic case category and, in the more complicated cases, the tribunal should be alerted to the need for directions more usually found in Standard or even Complex cases.

Guidance: https://www.judiciary.uk/publications/categorisation-of-cases-in-the-tax-chamber

5.6.6 Standard cases

Cases not allocated to the Default Paper or Basic case categories will almost invariably be allocated to the Standard case category. The process to be followed in such cases is set out in rules 25 and 27.

In practice, the cases will be subject to a timetable which the parties will agree (or the tribunal will determine) which should ensure that the various paperwork required (e.g. copies of witness statements, documents and a summary of legal arguments (skeleton argument)) is provided to each other party and the tribunal in good time for the hearing.

In some cases, it will prove necessary for the parties to attend a "case management hearing" or "directions hearing" to ensure that a timetable is agreed between the parties. Nevertheless, this should be limited to the most exceptional of cases as the tribunal will generally expect case management matters to be capable of agreement by the parties themselves. And, even when there does remain a difference, the parties can agree for the matter to be determined by the tribunal without a hearing so as to save time and expense.

See also **Chapter 6**.

5.6.7 Complex cases

With the exception of the possibility of the special provision in rule 28 (transfer to the Upper Tribunal) being invoked, the management of Complex cases follows that of Standard cases. Thus, the commentary at **5.6.6** above will apply equally to such cases.

The only other practical consequence of a case being allocated to the Complex case category is that it can expose parties to a costs order under rule 10. If a taxpayer wishes to opt out of the costs rules (orders will still be available in cases of unreasonable conduct and/or wasted costs), the taxpayer should write to the tribunal within 28 days of receiving the allocation notice under rule 10(1)(c)(ii) (see **4.8.5** above). HMRC do not have this right.

When a case should be allocated as a Complex case

Rule 23(4) determines that a case cannot be allocated as Complex case unless the tribunal considers that:

- it will involve lengthy or complex evidence or a lengthy hearing;
- it involves a complex or important principle or issue; or
- it involves a large financial sum.

As noted in *Capital Air Services*, it is only in respect of Complex cases that the Rules provide conditions that have to be met before a tax case can be so categorised. Falling within one of these categories, however, will not necessarily mean that a case should be allocated as a Complex case.

Furthermore, as noted in *Capital Air Services*, the rules do not define what is meant by any of these criteria because they can clearly be understood in different ways depending on the context. It was held that they should be understood in the light of the typical caseload passing through the Tax Chamber generally. The tribunal rejected the possibility, however, that the relative complexity of a case be determined by reference to the subject matter of a particular appeal. Therefore, supposing a VAT case were to be before the tribunal, the categorisation of the case should be based on comparing the case with other cases that go before the tribunal, not merely other VAT cases.

In addition, the Upper Tribunal initially refused to give indications as to where the boundaries might fall except to state that:

- a half-day hearing could never be lengthy whereas a 3-month case was inevitably lengthy; and
- tax of £1,000 could not amount to a large financial sum, whereas £100m inevitably did.

Later in its decision, however, the tribunal suggested that a four-day hearing was "very much on the borderline", noting however that many much longer hearings on more prosaic matters (e.g. "mark-up appeals") ought not to be categorised as Complex. The tribunal refused, however, to be drawn on where the boundary was in relation to "a large financial sum".

The Upper Tribunal also dismissed the suggestion that the allocation of a case should depend on the supposed suitability of a case being subject to the costs regime or the possibility of a transfer to the Upper Tribunal (under rules 10 and 28 respectively). These matters represent the consequences of the allocation of a case to that category, not factors that should determine the prior decision-making process. Indeed, there are many cases allocated as Complex (for example, missing trader fraud cases) that should not be transferred to the Upper Tribunal. On the other hand, the Upper Tribunal recognised that these possibilities should be borne in mind when ascertaining the types of case that might have been intended to be categorised as Complex. Furthermore, the 2013 practice statement does suggest that the implications of these matters will be borne in mind, and this is supported by what the Upper Tribunal said.

The practice statement also provides that cases which meet the individual criteria will generally be allocated to the complex category in the absence of "special factors". In *Dreams*, "special factors" was held to mean "exceptional circumstances".

In *Badzyan*, a case lasting two to three days and worth up to £800,000 was considered to merit allocation to the complex category. The author considers that the thresholds in that case are unlikely to be agreed by many other judges.

Cases: *Capital Air Services Ltd v HMRC* [2010] UKUT 373 (TCC); *Dreams plc v HMRC* [2012] UKFTT 614 (TC); *Badzyan v HMRC* [2017] UKFTT 439 (TC)
Guidance: https://www.judiciary.uk/publications/categorisation-of-cases-in-the-tax-chamber

Each aspect of a case is considered on its own merits

Finnforest concerned a closure notice application. It was common ground that were the matter to proceed to an appeal (against any amendments made by closure notice being sought) such an appeal would satisfy the criteria for allocation to the Complex case category.

However, the closure notice application itself did not warrant allocation to the Complex case category as it did not satisfy any of the criteria in rule 23(4). Therefore, the tribunal refused to reallocate the closure notice application to the Complex case category.

Case: *Finnforest UK Ltd (and others) v HMRC* [2011] UKFTT 342 (TC)

Seeking reallocation between the Standard and Complex case categories

If a case has been allocated to the Standard or Complex case categories, it will rarely be appropriate to seek a reallocation under rule 23(3). This is because the formal case management provisions for both categories are identical and, so, it should make very little difference to the parties to which category the case has been allocated.

This does not mean, however, that the parties should simply accept the consequences of the allocation made by the tribunal. From the tribunal's perspective, the allocation also determines the nature of the case management directions that the tribunal will issue. See **Chapter 6**. (Indeed, within the Standard case category, the tribunal has its own informal sub-categories, which each have their own set of standard case management directions.) If the standard directions issued by the tribunal seem inappropriate, the parties should seek to agree a more appropriate way forward. The tribunal should then be invited to endorse what the parties agree (noting that the tribunal will not necessarily rubber-stamp what the parties have agreed) or, in the absence of any agreement between the parties, impose a timetable on the parties.

However, there can occasionally be instances where a formal application for reallocation might nevertheless be appropriate: in particular, reallocating a case from the Standard to the Complex case category. Such an application would still need to bear in mind the conditions for the case to be allocated as Complex case (see above).

For example, if a taxpayer were to wish to be subject to the costs regime available only in Complex cases, the taxpayer would need to persuade the tribunal that it would be appropriate to reallocate the case. It must be emphasised that merely wanting the right to recover costs will not be a sufficient reason to justify a case being reallocated to the Complex case category.

Arguably, the same would apply if one party were to want the case to be transferred to the Upper Tribunal under rule 28: the first hurdle to overcome would be to ensure that the case had been allocated (or reallocated) as a Complex case. However, given that a transfer requires the consent of all parties, the author suggests that reallocation alone would be pointless unless such consent was likely to be forthcoming.

Similarly, there would be no point in HMRC seeking a Standard case to be reallocated to the Complex case category so as to enable the case to be governed by the costs regime if the taxpayer would simply opt out of it (see **4.8.5**).

Example

This example is based upon one of the author's own cases.

The case had been allocated to the Standard case category (correctly, it is suggested). However, HMRC insisted that it ought to have been allocated to the Complex case category and applied to the tribunal accordingly.

The taxpayer did not wish to run the risk of being liable for HMRC's costs, if its appeal were unsuccessful, and saw no real benefit in or likelihood of the case being transferred to the Upper Tribunal. Thus, from the taxpayer's perspective, there was no benefit in the case being reallocated to the Complex case category as it would, in particular, have opted out of the costs regime.

However, the taxpayer felt that such tactical considerations should not interfere with the tribunal's performance of its duties because they are not strictly relevant when ascertaining the correct category to which a case should be allocated.

The taxpayer, therefore, responded to HMRC's application by saying that:

- it considered the original allocation to be correct; but
- it did not wish to incur unnecessary costs by arguing actively against HMRC's application; and

Ch. 5 – Procedures before a hearing

> - the main consequence of a reallocation would be the case entering the costs regime, but this would prove pointless as the taxpayer would opt out in any event.
>
> HMRC's application was refused.

Note that the reallocation of a case to the Complex case category can potentially have the effect of making the losing party liable for all the costs incurred in the case (including those incurred before the reallocation). In *Capital Air Services (Costs)*, whilst this was accepted to be the correct effect of the rules, it was held that the tribunal ought to take into account the retrospective effect of any reallocation when deciding the terms of any subsequent costs order.

Conversely, however, a reallocation of a case from the Complex case category to the Standard case category is likely to be sought by HMRC if they do not wish to be exposed to the costs regime. (A taxpayer can opt out under rule 10 and therefore should not need to seek reallocation.)

However, in all cases, it is suggested that the categorisation of cases should not be governed by any such tactical matters.

Case: *Capital Air Services Ltd v HMRC (Costs)* [2011] UKUT 484 (TCC)

5.7 Rule 24 – Basic cases

> 24(1) This rule applies to Basic cases.
>
> 24(2) Rule 25 (respondent's statement of case) does not apply and, subject to paragraph (3) and any direction given by the Tribunal, the case will proceed directly to a hearing.
>
> 24(3) If the respondent intends to raise grounds for contesting the proceedings at the hearing which have not previously been communicated to the appellant, the respondent must notify the appellant of such grounds.
>
> 24(4) If the respondent is required to notify the appellant of any grounds under paragraph (3), the respondent must do so–
>
> > (a) as soon as reasonably practicable after becoming aware that such is the case; and

> (b) in sufficient detail to enable the appellant to respond to such grounds at the hearing.

5.7.1 Overview

This rule provides the special rules applicable to cases allocated to the Basic case category.

5.7.2 Minimal paperwork

As indicated by the name of the category, Basic cases are those that should be able to be dealt with minimal paperwork.

Thus, the usual requirement for HMRC to prepare a statement of case (see rule 25) is disapplied. The typical approach is that the parties should simply turn up at the hearing and argue their respective cases at a tribunal hearing.

Raising new points (rule 24(4))

However, to ensure that a taxpayer is not caught unawares, if HMRC wish to raise a new point (i.e. one not previously communicated to the taxpayer), they must notify the taxpayer of those grounds as soon as is reasonably practicable after becoming aware that they wish to do so and in sufficient detail to enable the taxpayer to respond to such grounds at the hearing.

If a taxpayer considers that insufficient notice has been given, then it would be appropriate to ask the tribunal to give a direction under rule 5(1) that submissions on the additional points should not be permitted. Such an application should be made at the beginning of the hearing (and, if possible, prior warning ought to be given to HMRC).

Where paperwork is more than minimal

Even if HMRC are not proposing to raise new points, it might sometimes be appropriate for taxpayers to be given advance notice of the documents and arguments that HMRC intend to raise at the hearing. The principles were clearly expressed by the tribunal in *Preferred Refrigeration*:

> "This appeal was classified as a Basic case. In such a case either party may bring evidence to the tribunal which has not

235

previously been disclosed to the other party. Where that happens the tribunal will consider whether the other party needs time to consider the evidence or to gather evidence in rebuttal. It helps speed the appeal if papers are disclosed beforehand but it is not a prerequisite to the hearing of the appeal. In this case the papers in the bundle produced by [HMRC] did not contain information or documents which would have taken the appellant by surprise. It seemed to us that it was not necessary [in order] to ensure a fair hearing to adjourn the appeal to let the appellant comment on the papers [HMRC] produced."

Case: *Preferred Refrigeration Ltd v HMRC* [2011] UKFTT 466 (TC)

5.7.3 Reallocation and case management

It should be noted that some cases allocated to the Basic case category will turn out to be more involved than initially appears to be the case. For this reason, the tribunal can still give directions (as might be more common in Standard and Complex cases). It would therefore seem unnecessary for a party to seek in addition the reallocation of the case to the Standard case category.

5.8 Rule 25 – Respondent's statement of case

25(1) A respondent must send or deliver a statement of case to the Tribunal, the appellant and any other respondent so that it is received–

(a) in a Default Paper case, within 42 days after the Tribunal sent the notice of appeal or a copy of the application notice or notice of reference;

(b) in an MP expenses case, within 28 days after the Tribunal sent the notice of appeal; or

(c) in a Standard or Complex case other than an MP expenses case, within 60 days after the Tribunal sent the notice of appeal or a copy of the application notice or notice of reference.

25(2) A statement of case must–

(a) in an appeal, state the legislative provision under which the decision under appeal was made; and

5.8 Rule 25 – Respondent's statement of case

> (b) set out the respondent's position in relation to the case.
>
> 25(3) A statement of case may also contain a request that the case be dealt with at a hearing or without a hearing.
>
> 25(4) If a respondent provides a statement of case to the Tribunal later than the time required by paragraph (1) or by any extension allowed under rule 5(3)(a) (power to extend time), the statement of case must include a request for an extension of time and the reason why the statement of case was not provided in time.

5.8.1 Overview

This rule deals with the procedures for statements of case. Although the evidential burden of proof is generally on the appellant, the rules recognise that the appellant often requires an explanation of the HMRC position (what is being asserted and why). That is provided for in a statement of case.

A statement of case will be prepared in all cases other than Basic cases.

5.8.2 When a statement of case is to be provided

Rule 25(1) provides the time limit for the provision of HMRC's statement of case. As noted in rules 20(5) and 21(4), the tribunal is required to provide to HMRC copies of the appeal notice (or application or reference) upon receipt from the taxpayer. The time limit for providing the statement of case runs from the date on which the tribunal sends HMRC the copy of the appeal (or application or reference):

- In Default Paper cases, the time given is 42 days.
- In Standard and Complex cases (other than MP expenses cases), the time given is 60 days.
- In MP expenses cases, the time given is 28 days.

A statement of case should be sent, not only to the tribunal, but also to the appellant (or, if a representative has been appointed, to the appellant's representative (see rule 11(4)(a))) and also to any other respondent.

Extensions of time

In the early years of the tribunal HMRC would sometimes request an extension of these time limits due to staff shortages or volume of work.

Taxpayers should decide whether they wish to accede to such requests or whether they wish to let the tribunal determine whether or not an extension should be granted. Very often, such a decision will turn on the extent to which the taxpayer is happy to let matters drift or is keen to have the matter resolved. The author has heard one suggestion that, given that the appeal is against a decision already made by an HMRC officer, that officer ought to be capable of setting out the required information in the time provided for by the rules. Indeed, if a taxpayer were to oppose such an application by HMRC, it could be possible to cite the judgment given in a case (*Hugh Love*) where a taxpayer was seeking to appeal out of time, adapting the references to appeals as appropriate:

> "Section 49 is a provision that is designed to permit appeals out of time. As such, it should in my opinion be viewed in the same context as other provisions designed to allow legal proceedings to be brought even though a time limit has expired. The central feature of such provisions is that they are exceptional in nature; the normal case is covered by the time limit, and particular reasons must be shown for disregarding that limit. The limit must be regarded as the judgment of the legislature as to the appropriate time within which proceedings must be brought in the normal case, and particular reasons must be shown if a claimant or appellant is to raise proceedings, or institute an appeal, beyond the period chosen by Parliament."

In the author's experience, HMRC have ceased to ask for extra time merely because of resource difficulties and it is inferred that the tribunal did not consider that to be a sufficient reason to delay matters. Nevertheless, as noted at **5.3.2** above, HMRC do sometimes seek additional time if they consider that the grounds of appeal are not adequately clear. Each such case should be considered on its own merits.

Even if a delay is to be granted, it will rarely be right for HMRC to be granted a full 60-day extension. This was noted by the tribunal in *HT* although the author has no reason to believe that that was a case involving any wish by HMRC to delay matters for tactical reasons. In that case, HMRC were granted a further 42-day period to produce a statement of case although the tribunal took into account the intervening Christmas period when calculating that period, suggesting that 28 or 30 days might have been more appropriate normally.

Cases: *Advocate General for Scotland v General Commissioners for Aberdeen City (Hugh Love)* [2005] CSOH 135; *HT & Co (Drinks) Ltd v HMRC* [2015] UKFTT 664 (TC)

Late statements of case

Where an extension is not given and the statement of case is provided late (or the statement of case is submitted beyond the expiry of an extension previously granted), rule 25(4) provides that the statement of case must include a request for the extension (or further extension) and the reason why the statement was not provided in time.

It is suggested that a failure to comply with rule 25(4) makes a statement of case incomplete (as it does not satisfy the statutory criteria for a statement of case), unless and until the tribunal extends the time limit retrospectively (under rule 5(3)(a)) or waives the breach (under rule 7(2)). This will then have an impact on the time limits applicable for the subsequent steps to be taken in the case. However, it is suggested that such a failure on its own would not be enough to justify the HMRC case being struck out.

It appears that this requirement applies only in respect of failures to provide the tribunal with a timely statement of case. There appears to be no such requirement if HMRC fail to send an appellant the statement of case on time, although that would defer the timing for compliance with subsequent steps. Of course, such a failure should not occur.

5.8.3 Contents of a statement of case

The rules provide that the statement of case must set out HMRC's position in relation to the case. When the case concerns an appeal against an HMRC decision, the statement of case must also state the legislative provision under which the decision was made. In *Burns*, the Court of Appeal described the role of a statement of case thus:

"the vital function of informing each party, and the tribunal, of the other party's case, thereby enabling them to direct their evidence and submissions to the issues identified by the statements. In particular, the respondent's statement informs the applicant of the case that he has to meet."

In short, the statement of case must give the reader an opportunity to understand the HMRC viewpoint so that the taxpayer can prepare for the appeal. As stated in *Ronald*, a statement of case must be clear and unequivocal and have sufficient detail or particularity.

In *Cheshire*, the Upper Tribunal criticised HMRC for taking a too narrow approach to the drafting of their statement of case:

"In my judgment, in the circumstances of this case, a party defending and conducting the proceedings reasonably in the circumstances of this case would, in reviewing its position on the case when preparing its Statement of Case, have stood back and dealt with the appellant's grounds of appeal taking account of the wider context of the appeal in which those grounds arose, considering them in accordance with the principles relevant to legislative provision in issue, and applying them to the factual background pertinent to the actual supplies in issue which included the uncontested fundamental fact concerning the employee/employer relationship. If that been done and the lack of clarity on the parties' position regarding the status of the principal supply in the previous correspondence between the parties had been recognised, the missing building block to CCIL's case, and the therefore academic nature of the appeal would have been exposed. A reasonable party would not thus in such circumstances have restricted its case simply to the nuanced argument on the qualitative nature of the supply without also flagging its position on the nature of the principal supply."

As confirmed in *E Buyer*, if fraud or dishonesty is alleged, the statement of case must make this clear (but use of those words is not itself necessary). In *Infinity*, the Court of Appeal explained, however, that HMRC evidence which suggests dishonest conduct may be admitted even if HMRC are not pursuing such an allegation. That evidence must, however, be relevant to the actual case being advanced by HMRC.

If the taxpayer is concerned that the statement of case is unclear, or if it is otherwise impossible for the taxpayer to be sure what case is being advanced by HMRC, then one option would be for the taxpayer to request further information from HMRC under rule 16(1)(b). Alternatively, it will often be appropriate to require HMRC to issue a fuller or clearer statement of case.

It was emphasised in *Procter* that unsupported assertions made in a statement of case do not constitute evidence and cannot be relied upon by HMRC as if they were evidence.

It was made clear in *Allpay* that HMRC's statement of case should outline issues which are disputed and the facts HMRC rely on to support their position. In that case, the statement of case was silent on one aspect of what was previously part of HMRC's assertions. Accordingly, the tribunal considered that the taxpayer could assume that this meant that the point had now been conceded. HMRC's subsequent attempt to amend the statement of case failed because the proposed revisions were not sufficiently detailed by failing to explain HMRC's position.

In *Worldpay*, the tribunal held that it was not appropriate for HMRC to "reserve" issues in their statement of case for clarification at a later date. Until a positive case had been advanced by HMRC, a taxpayer was not required to respond to it.

Cases: *Procter v HMRC* [2012] UKFTT 530 (TC); *E Buyer UK Ltd v HMRC* [2016] UKUT 123 (TCC); *HMRC v Infinity Distribution Ltd (In Administration)* [2016] EWCA Civ 1014; *Ronald Hull Junior Ltd v HMRC* [2016] UKFTT 525 (TC); *Burns v Financial Conduct Authority* [2017] EWCA Civ 2140; *Allpay Ltd v HMRC* [2018] UKFTT 273 (TC); *Worldpay (UK) Ltd v HMRC* [2019] UKFTT 235 (TC); *HMRC v Cheshire Centre For Independent Living* [2020] UKUT 275 (TCC).

Assertions of dishonesty

Citibank confirms that, if HMRC are basing their case on a taxpayer's supposed dishonesty, this assertion must be expressly stated in a statement of case.

Case: *Citibank v NA* [2014] UKFTT 1063 (TC)

Responses by taxpayers

It is sometimes assumed that a statement of case from HMRC should then be responded to with a statement of case from the taxpayer. Indeed, the author has seen cases where taxpayers have believed that they should respond to HMRC's statement of case and do not wish to miss the opportunity to do so. However, a response is generally unnecessary, except in Default Paper cases (see rule 26 below), where a response is both expected and advisable.

In Standard and Complex cases, whilst there are usually steps to be taken by all the parties in the meantime, the taxpayer's formal response to the statement of case will usually not need to be prepared until shortly before the actual hearing, usually several months later, and only then in the form of a skeleton argument.

Requests by HMRC for taxpayers to produce statements of case

The author has also seen instances where HMRC have alleged ignorance of the basis of the taxpayer's case and insisted that the taxpayer also prepare a statement of case. Such a tactic should generally be resisted as inappropriate.

In one unpublished decision, the tribunal noted that HMRC's "ignorance" could have been dealt with by them seeking a brief clarification of the particular issues concerning them; indeed, the tribunal considered that the matter could have been resolved by telephone. HMRC's insistence on the taxpayer producing a statement of case was described as "somewhat extreme" and "excessive" and led to the tribunal awarding the taxpayer the costs incurred as a result of having to resist HMRC's application for a statement of case.

Requests by HMRC to revise their statement of case

If the taxpayer's arguments evolve after the submission of a statement of case, it can be appropriate for HMRC to revise their statement of case to deal with the new issues that have arisen.

However, the author has dealt with a case where HMRC sought an adjournment shortly before a scheduled hearing so that they could revisit their statement of case. It was considered that the request in that case was unreasonable because by that stage in the proceedings, HMRC's original statement of case had served its purpose and the parties were fully aware of each other's position. The real question should have been whether HMRC needed an adjournment to deal with the relatively late change in some of the taxpayer's arguments. However, the tribunal refused an adjournment. This was because the taxpayer had generally dropped a number of arguments (and therefore HMRC did not need any time to deal with those that remained). Although one new argument was being raised for the first time, the tribunal considered that it was relatively self-contained and required no new evidence and, therefore, it would have been possible for HMRC to deal with it in time.

In *JSM*, HMRC were permitted to revise their statement of case as emerging evidence radically altered their view of the case.

In *Moreton*, the tribunal considered that HMRC's failure to deal with a particular issue in their statement of case and refused permission for the statement of case to be amended because of the lateness in doing so. The tribunal then applied rule 7(2)(d) (see **4.5.3** above) so as to prevent HMRC from cross-examining the taxpayer's expert witness on a particular aspect of the appeal.

Cases: *JSM Construction Ltd v HMRC* [2016] UKFTT 163 (TC); *Moreton Alarm Services (MAS) Ltd v HMRC* [2016] UKFTT 192 (TC)

5.8.4 Requests for hearings or a case not to be dealt with at a hearing

In a Default Paper case (in particular), HMRC may use the statement of case as an opportunity to request that the matter be dealt with at a hearing. Under rule 26(7), if such a request is made, the tribunal must hold a hearing before determining the case.

Conversely, in other cases, HMRC may request that the matter be dealt with otherwise than at a hearing. However, the tribunal is not bound to accede to such a request in the circumstances.

5.9 Rule 26 – Further steps in a Default Paper case

26(1) This rule applies to Default Paper cases.

26(2) The appellant may send or deliver a written reply to the Tribunal so that it is received within 30 days after the date on which the respondent sent to the appellant the statement of case to which the reply relates.

26(3) The appellant's reply may–

> (a) set out the appellant's response to the respondent's statement of case;
>
> (b) provide any further information (including, where appropriate, copies of the documents containing such information) which has not yet been provided to the Tribunal and is relevant to the case; and
>
> (c) contain a request that the case be dealt with at a hearing.
>
> 26(4) The appellant must send or deliver a copy of any reply provided under paragraph (2) to each respondent at the same time as it is provided to the Tribunal.
>
> 26(5) If the appellant provides a reply to the Tribunal later than the time required by paragraph (2) or by any extension allowed under rule 5(3)(a) (power to extend time), the reply must include a request for an extension of time and the reason why the reply was not provided in time.
>
> 26(6) Following receipt of the appellant's reply, or the expiry of the time for the receipt of the appellant's reply then, unless it directs otherwise and subject in any event to paragraph (7), the Tribunal must proceed to determine the case without a hearing.
>
> 26(7) If any party has made a written request to the Tribunal for a hearing, the Tribunal must hold a hearing before determining the case.

5.9.1 Overview

This rule provides the additional steps that are taken in a Default Paper case. At its heart is the taxpayer's reply to HMRC's statement of case.

It should be noted that a reply is optional. This is particularly relevant because penalty cases (for example) are ones where the burden of proof lies on HMRC. However, as noted below, a reply will usually be advisable.

5.9.2 The taxpayer's reply to the statement of case (rule 26(2)—(4))

If the taxpayer intends to prepare a reply to the statement of case, it should be sent to the tribunal within 30 days of HMRC sending the taxpayer their statement of case. A copy should be sent or delivered at the same time to each respondent.

Due to the voluntary nature of a reply (and the fact that they will often be prepared by taxpayers with little experience of tribunal procedure), the rules do not lay down prescriptive rules about the contents of any reply.

However, any reply given should:

- respond to HMRC's statement of case; and
- provide any further information (including documentation) which has not previously been provided to the tribunal and which is relevant to the case.

It should be remembered that, unless a request has been made for a hearing, the tribunal will determine the case on the basis of what was provided in HMRC's statement of case and any reply by the taxpayer. Therefore, a taxpayer should endeavour to provide a reply that clearly deals with each point made by HMRC in turn. Where evidence is available to the taxpayer, this is the opportunity to provide it so that the tribunal judge can take it into account when reaching a decision.

Late replies

As with all time limits, a party may apply for an extension under rule 5(3)(a). Where an extension is not given and the reply is provided late (or the reply is submitted beyond the expiry of any extension previously granted), rule 26(5) provides that the reply must include a request for an extension (or further extension) and the reason why the reply was not provided in time.

It is suggested that a failure to comply with rule 26(5) makes a reply incomplete (as it does not satisfy the statutory criteria for a reply), unless and until the tribunal extends the time limit retrospectively (under rule 5(3)(a)) or waives the breach (under rule 7(2)). Thus it might not need to be taken into account by the tribunal when dealing with the case on paper (or any request for the case to be determined at a hearing). Depending on the lateness, however, in many cases the tribunal is likely to waive the breach unilaterally.

It appears that this requirement applies only in respect of failures to provide the tribunal with a timely reply. There appears to be no such requirement if an appellant fails to send HMRC the reply on time. Of course, such a failure should not occur.

5.9.3 Request for a hearing (rule 26(3), (7))

As noted at **5.8.4**, HMRC's statement of case may contain a request that the matter no longer be considered on paper but be dealt with at a hearing. Similarly, rule 26(3)(c) permits taxpayers to make a similar request in any reply.

Where such a request is made, the tribunal must hold a hearing before determining the case. This rule applies equally in cases where the request was contained in a separate document and not part of the statement of case and/or any reply.

If a tribunal is to hold a hearing, the case might then be treated in the same way as a Basic case (i.e. a date will be arranged and the parties will turn up and argue their respective cases). However, as is equally true in Basic cases, the tribunal might issue further directions concerning the handling of the case.

5.9.4 Procedure after reply received (rule 26(6), (7))

Once the appellant has replied (or, once the 30-day period for providing a reply has expired), the case would ordinarily proceed to be determined on the papers.

However, this is of course subject to either party having requested a hearing, in which case the tribunal must hold one.

In addition, the tribunal can on its own initiative determine that the overriding objective requires the matter to be dealt with at a hearing.

5.10 Rule 27 – Further steps in a Standard or Complex case

27(1) This rule applies to Standard and Complex cases.

27(2) Subject to any direction to the contrary, within 42 days after the date the respondent sent the statement of case (or, where there is more than one respondent, the date of

> the final statement of case) each party must send or deliver to the Tribunal and to each other party a list of documents—
>
> (a) of which the party providing the list has possession, the right to possession, or the right to take copies; and
>
> (b) which the party providing the list intends to rely upon or produce in the proceedings.
>
> 27(3) A party which has provided a list of documents under paragraph (2) must allow each other party to inspect or take copies of the documents on the list (except any documents which are privileged).

5.10.1 Overview

What marks out the cases allocated to the Standard and Complex case categories is the fact that the parties are generally expected to provide each other (and the tribunal) with additional documentation in advance of the hearing.

This rule considers the one such step that is found in the rules themselves. Other steps usually taken are considered in **Chapter 6** below.

5.10.2 Disclosure of documents

The purpose of this rule is to give the parties advance notice of which documents are likely to be relied upon by the other parties. As stated in *Viking*:

> "The list of documents is an essential step in the preparation of a case for a hearing and a failure to provide such a list brings that process to a halt. Failure to comply with that direction is clearly a serious matter and significant in that it effectively prevents there being any substantive hearing."

However, it is worth remembering what the Court of Appeal stated in *Smart Price*:

> "Disclosure of documents is not an end in itself but a means to an end, namely to ensure that the tribunal has before it all the information which the parties reasonably require the tribunal to consider in determining the appeal. It is only one step in the overall management of the case which should, as the appeal

progresses towards a substantive hearing, identify and if possible narrow the issues between the parties."

The rule requires only the provision of a list of the documents and is limited to those documents which the person has in his possession (or the right to possession or the right to take copies).

Preparing the list usually represents the first active step to be taken by an appellant after notifying the tribunal of the case. It will be seen that the step applies to all parties simultaneously so that they are all required to provide their lists of documents within 42 days of the respondents sending their statement of case.

It should also be noted that the rules (and the usual directions issued by the tribunal) do not require a party to provide a list of any documents that contain information that is adverse to that party's case. In this regard, the tribunal rules and practice differ from the more onerous rules that apply in the High Court under the CPR. Although the parties are free to agree to be bound by the greater obligations imposed by the CPR, it should be noted that the tribunal is unlikely to accede to a request by one party for the CPR version to apply. As noted in *Ebuyer*, the rules were drafted in clear contrast to the CPR version and, wherever further disclosure might prove necessary, there are always opportunities for a party to make a particular request later on (after the exchange of witness evidence).

On the other hand, in *McCabe*, the Upper Tribunal considered that, in a high-value complex dispute, the starting proposition should be that HMRC ought to disclose any relevant documents to the taxpayer unless there is good reason not to.

Cases: *Ebuyer Ltd v HMRC* [2014] UKFTT 912 (TC); *McCabe v HMRC* [2020] UKUT 266 (TCC); *Smart Price Midlands Ltd v HMRC* [2019] EWCA Civ 841; *Viking Enterprises Ltd v HMRC* [2020] UKFTT 306 (TC)

Disclosing unhelpful material

The tribunal's ruling in *Ebuyer* could be interpreted as suggesting that a document that is damaging to one's case can be withheld. Care should be taken, however, not to be pursuing a case dishonestly. Indeed, as noted by the Upper Tribunal in *Karoulla*, parties are under an obligation in rule 2 to further the overriding objective of dealing with cases fairly and justly.

There, HMRC actually refused to substantiate their reasons to suspect dishonest conduct, despite the taxpayer's requests for them to do so. HMRC referred to a concept known as "duty of candour" which they said applied only in judicial review cases and therefore, being in the tribunal, HMRC argued that they did not need to be so candid. The tribunal rejected that, noting:

> "HMRC will be aware, it is long-established practice that HMRC usually accept that the duty applies to them in normal tax appeals."

Furthermore, the tribunal will sometimes consider it appropriate to require a party to make specific documents available to the tribunal and to the other party having first applied a test of fairness and proportionality.

In *Staysure*, the tribunal ordered HMRC to disclose documents that related to the question as to when HMRC became aware of the taxpayer's potential liability to be VAT registered as that question lay at the heart of the calculation of a late-registration penalty. The author has obtained similar directions when seeking evidence of when HMRC had formed a view about a taxpayer's potential under-assessment for the purposes of arguing that an assessment had been issued too long after HMRC had the requisite knowledge of an alleged under-assessment.

Conversely, a party might choose to refer to a particular document in a witness statement but refuse to disclose it (and might exclude it from the list of documents). In *Addo*, the tribunal noted that this is permissible although it can reduce the weight given to the assertion in the witness statement.

Cases: *Ebuyer Ltd v HMRC* [2014] UKFTT 912 (TC); *Kyriakos Karoulla t/a Brockley's Rock v HMRC* [2018] UKUT 255 (TCC); *Addo v HMRC* [2018] UKFTT 530 (TC); *Staysure.co.uk Ltd v HMRC* [2018] UKFTT 584 (TC)

Where a party has no documents on which reliance is sought

In one case, the author was dealing with a case where the taxpayer had no documents to include on the list and the taxpayer therefore wrote to the tribunal (and HMRC) stating the same. The main issue in the case was whether the taxpayer had been negligent (something which is for HMRC to prove, not the taxpayer to disprove).

HMRC responded with an allegation that this "nil return" did not amount to full compliance with rule 27 and an application for the tribunal to direct that the appeal be struck out unless there was proper compliance with the rule. The tribunal (without even inviting the taxpayer's response) refused HMRC's application stating that a party "is only obliged to produce a list of documents if there are documents on which it relies", confirming that the taxpayer's nil return was sufficient for these purposes.

Rule 27 and subsequent evidence

However, in that case, the tribunal noted that a party should not routinely assume that it could include documentary exhibits when later providing evidence for the case, if those documents could have been produced at the time that rule 27 is required to be complied with.

Providing copies of documents on the list

Rule 27 on its own does not require a party to provide a copy of the documents at the same time that it provides the list. Instead, the rules allow the other parties to request or even take copies of documents found on the list. See **5.10.3**.

However, in practice, the tribunal very often issues directions which require (at the same time as providing the list) a party to provide the other parties with a copy of any documents on the list that will not have been seen by the other parties. Such a direction should be adhered to, and, in those cases, the procedures set out at **5.10.3** below are less likely to be needed.

5.10.3 Request for inspection or copies (rule 27(3))

Very often, the documents listed will be those which all the parties are very familiar (for example, previous correspondence between them).

However, there will be cases where one party wishes to rely upon a document that the other has not seen or of which the other does not in any event possess a copy.

To deal with such cases, rule 27(3) requires parties who have listed a document to allow each other party to inspect the document or to take copies.

In *Chandanmal*, the appellants (based in Liverpool) wished to have sent to them six months of material held by HMRC (at one of their London offices). The tribunal had to weigh up the appellants' concerns (the time and travel costs) against those of HMRC (the requirement to photocopy a considerable amount of confidential information, most of which would be unlikely to be referred to at any subsequent hearing of the substantive dispute between the parties). On the facts of the case, the tribunal directed that the inspection of the documents should take place in London.

As noted above, however, the tribunal now often directs the disclosure of all materials not previously sent to or provided by the other party.

Case: *Chandanmal and Others t/a C Narain Bros v HMRC* [2012] UKFTT 188 (TC)

Privileged documentation

However, a party is not required to let another party inspect or take a copy of privileged documents (such as legal advice). However, if a privileged document is going to be deployed by a party, that will inevitably lead to any privilege being waived.

Certain privileged material (that arising from without-prejudice negotiations) requires both parties to waive privilege. Ordinarily, this will be deemed to have occurred if the material is included in both parties' lists of documents.

As noted in *Taylor*, a party may subsequently withdraw a waiver of privilege, thereby preventing the other party from requesting or referring to the privileged material.

Case: *Taylor v HMRC* [2017] UKFTT 769 (TC)

5.11 Rule 28 – Transfer of Complex cases to the Upper Tribunal

> 28(1) If a case has been allocated as a Complex case the Tribunal may, with the consent of the parties, refer a case or a preliminary issue to the President of the Tax Chamber of the First-tier Tribunal with a request that the case or issue be considered for transfer to the Upper Tribunal.

> 28(2) If a case or issue has been referred by the Tribunal under paragraph (1), the President of the Tax Chamber may, with the concurrence of the President of the Tax and Chancery Chamber of the Upper Tribunal, direct that the case or issue be transferred to and determined by the Upper Tribunal.

5.11.1 Overview

Although the Tax and Chancery Chamber of the Upper Tribunal is generally reserved for appeals from the FTT, some cases can be heard there "at first instance". In other words, the case is first heard (with evidence etc) in the Upper Tribunal.

Assuming that the case progresses further through the courts, it would be heard next by the Court of Appeal (or Court of Session in Scotland) and then by the Supreme Court. Thus the Supreme Court stage will be reached at the third hearing, rather than, as is more usual, the fourth.

There are some matters where the case simply starts in the Upper Tribunal, without any involvement of the First-tier. For example, the most serious penalties in relation to information requests require an application to be made to the Upper Tribunal. Similarly, judicial reviews may (in limited circumstances) be commenced in the Upper Tribunal instead of in the High Court.

However, there are also situations where a case starts life in the First-tier, but is then transferred to the Upper Tribunal.

5.11.2 Procedure for transfer

The transfer requires two procedures. First, the tribunal must refer the case to the President of the Tax Chamber with a request that the case be considered for transfer to the Upper Tribunal (rule 28(1)).

Secondly, if such a referral has been made to the President of the Tax Chamber, the President may then direct that the case be transferred to the Upper Tribunal and determined there. This second stage must be made with the concurrence of the President of the Tax and Chancery Chamber of the Upper Tribunal.

5.11.3 Which cases may be transferred?

The first criterion is that the case must have been allocated to the Complex case category. This is a rigid requirement and the only way that this can be overcome in any other situation is for the case to be first reallocated to the Complex case category. That will not always be appropriate. (See rule 23(3), discussed at **5.6.7** above.)

Secondly, the parties must all consent to the transfer. In other words, even if the Presidents of the two chambers think that the case is suitable for transfer, any one of the parties can veto the transfer.

> **Example**
>
> In *Hankinson*, the High Court was being asked to consider a transfer of judicial review proceedings in the High Court to the Upper Tribunal where the taxpayer was hoping to have the case heard in conjunction with a substantive appeal. (The case concerned a taxpayer's claim to be non-resident and his appeal against an assessment made on the basis that he was resident; the judicial review proceedings concerned the taxpayer's reliance on the former IR20 guidance which determined when HMRC would treat an individual as non-resident.)
>
> In order for the two strands of Mr Hankinson's case to be heard together, the appeal would need to be transferred to the Upper Tribunal. One objection raised by HMRC was that the case had not been allocated to the Complex case category and, as mentioned above, this would have precluded any transfer of the case to the Upper Tribunal. However, the evidence from HMRC in that case noted that they were not minded to give consent.
>
> The judge held that there was no requirement for the refusal of consent to be reasonable although, on the facts of that case, he considered a refusal would not be unreasonable.

In *Reed*, however, a different approach prevailed. There the High Court consented to a transfer of the judicial review proceedings to the Upper Tribunal so that case management could be managed by the unified tribunals service. The case did not make any comments about the suitability of a case being transferred from the First-tier to the Upper Tribunal.

Law: SI 2008/2698, rule 10.

Cases: *R (oao Hankinson) v HMRC* [2009] EWHC 1774 (Admin); *Reed Personnel Services plc v HMRC* [2009] EWHC 2250 (Admin)

Duties of parties

It is respectfully suggested, however, that given the parties' duty to help the tribunal to further the overriding objective, parties ought to have good reasons before refusing to consent to any transfer. Although the tribunal cannot compel them to give consent, it is suggested that an unreasonable refusal is likely to give rise to additional costs (if it means an additional hearing becomes necessary) and this unreasonable conduct could lead to a costs order being made under rule 10(1)(b). The Upper Tribunal's decision in *Hills* would support this: in particular, when the tribunal held:

> "I do not accept the argument that, assuming Mr and Mrs Hills had the right to make the request to opt-out in these circumstances, that it could not be unreasonable for them simply to exercise that right. It is clearly the case that a party may make use of tribunal procedures in a way which renders the conduct of the party unreasonable."

Therefore, it is respectfully suggested that HMRC's arguments in *Hankinson* (even if permitted under the rules) did not represent a good reason to object to the transfer. Whilst it is undoubtedly right that a party should tell the tribunal why it thinks that a transfer is inappropriate, it is submitted that it should not object to a transfer on those grounds alone.

For these reasons, it is suggested that HMRC should generally take a neutral stance to the question of transfer to the Upper Tribunal. The same would generally apply to taxpayers with one exception.

As noted at **4.8.5** and **5.6.7** above, taxpayers in cases allocated to the Complex case category can opt out of the costs regime. If a case is transferred to the Upper Tribunal, the taxpayer loses this right. Therefore, if the taxpayer loses the appeal the taxpayer risks being liable for HMRC's costs (whereas there would have been no such risk had the matter stayed in the FTT). For this reason, the taxpayer may justifiably object to a proposed transfer. However, if in such a case a transfer remains the most appropriate way forward (because, say, the matter needs to be dealt with by a superior court without delay), it might be appropriate for the taxpayer to consent to the transfer with HMRC and/or the tribunal directing that no costs order would be made against the taxpayer should the taxpayer lose.

Case: *Hills v HMRC* [2016] UKUT 266 (TCC)

5.11.4 Other criteria for referral to the Upper Tribunal

In *Capital Air Services*, the Upper Tribunal emphasised that not every case allocated to the Complex case category is suitable for transfer to the Upper Tribunal. One important factor is the availability of the judiciary and court space. This was confirmed in *Reed*.

Thus, for example, a complex missing-trader fraud case, lasting several weeks, would not be suitable for transfer to the Upper Tribunal where it would inevitably be heard by more senior judges than if it remained in the First-tier.

Reed concerned an appeal where there were parallel proceedings for judicial review. In that case, it was considered that the underlying appeal alone would not have been suitable for a transfer; however, the possibility of joining the appeal with a judicial review in the Upper Tribunal made a transfer more appropriate (although, in the circumstances of the case, that was not sufficient).

In *Aozora*, the President of the FTT declined to consent to a transfer (even though both parties were content with the proposal). Although the case concerned principally a question of law, he said that, "that is not by itself a sufficient reason for bypassing the first stage of the tax appeal process". Furthermore, even though that was a question of a specialist area of taxation, that again was not sufficient to justify a transfer on the basis that the FTT judiciary was sufficiently capable of dealing with complex tax disputes.

Although the *Aozora* case also involved a judicial review which (had that been transferred to the Upper Tribunal) could have justified the cases coming together, such applications should be "made at the commencement of the proceedings so that both the appeal and judicial review can proceed together". In *Aozora*, however, the judicial review had already been heard and was on its way to the

Court of Appeal. In the circumstances, the tribunal recognised that the benefit of aligning the cases was no longer realistic.

The implication of *Capital Air Services* is that lengthy cases are not generally suitable for transfer to the Upper Tribunal, the assumption being that judicial resources there are more limited than in the First-tier. However, that is clearly not determinative. In *Cobalt*, the case lasted four weeks but was still transferred. However, that was a case where there was a parallel judicial review claim and where it was considered appropriate for both matters to be heard at the same time (unlike other cases where they have been heard in succession or come together only on an appeal from a decision of the First-tier).

Cases: *Capital Air Services Ltd v HMRC* [2010] UKUT 373 (TCC); *Reed Employment plc v HMRC* [2010] UKFTT 596 (TC) (a joint decision of the First-tier and Upper Tribunals); *Aozora GMAC Investment Ltd v HMRC* [2018] UKFTT 706 (TC); *Cobalt Data Centre 2 LLP v HMRC* [2019] UKUT 342 (TCC)

6. The directions stage

6.1 Introduction

Particularly in Standard and Complex cases (see **5.6.5** and **5.6.6** above), the tribunal will issue a set of directions (effectively, laying down a timetable) that will need to be complied with by the parties in order to ensure that they are prepared for the hearing.

6.2 When directions are given

Usually, the directions will first be made after HMRC have provided their statement of case (see **5.8**) and whilst the parties are preparing lists of documents on which they will want to rely during the hearing (see **5.10**).

In some cases, the tribunal will invite the parties to agree directions: as they often follow a standard (see **6.5**), it will usually be possible for agreement to be reached.

6.3 Directions hearings

However, it will sometimes be the case that particular directions cannot be agreed. For example, one party might want more time to prepare evidence etc., there might be a dispute as to which party provides witness evidence first, or there may be a dispute as to whether or not a case ought to be stayed pending other events either in the tribunal (with another case) or elsewhere.

In such cases, any dispute over the directions will usually be resolved by the tribunal holding a directions hearing. Such a hearing will be a mini-trial focusing solely on the dispute concerning the directions. It will often be possible for a hearing to be avoided if both parties are content for the tribunal to consider the matter on the papers.

6.4 Variability of directions

As is made clear in rule 5(2) (see **4.2.3**), directions given are not set in stone: as circumstances change, it is open to the tribunal to vary them. Similarly, the parties are always at liberty to apply to the tribunal for a variation of directions previously given.

6.4.1 "Liberty to apply"

In the past, it was common for a set of directions to conclude with a direction "liberty to apply". This means simply that either party is free to make an application to the tribunal for a new direction or for an existing direction to be varied or set aside. Nowadays, the tribunal will include a direction saying this more explicitly (rather than using the old-fashioned jargon).

Given the provision in rule 5(2), such a direction is strictly unnecessary. However, it is often useful to include it. This is because it is very likely that a judge at a subsequent directions hearing will be different from the judge who gave the first directions and it gives the later judge the confidence to know that the first directions were not meant to be set in stone any more than usual.

6.5 Typical directions

The directions that are usually given cover:

- when each party ought to provide written witness statements and other evidence (see **6.5.1**);
- when each party ought to provide the tribunal with a list of dates on which it cannot (and/or its representatives cannot) attend a hearing (see **6.5.2**);
- which party ought to produce a bundle of all the documents that the tribunal will need to consider (and when) (see **6.5.3**); and
- when each party ought to provide a summary of its submissions (often called a skeleton argument) outlining the facts and legal arguments it wishes to advance (see **6.5.4**).

The first two of these directions are usually complied with during the weeks after the directions are given – by reference to set dates or a number of weeks after the directions were given.

The latter two directions are usually carried out in the period shortly before the substantive hearing – often by reference to a number of days or weeks prior to the hearing.

The decision in *Eclipse (No. 2)* includes a number of examples of typical directions in a Complex case. In paragraph 7, the decision refers to two very typical directions agreed in Standard and Complex cases. The directions given after a detailed directions hearing are listed within paragraph 1 of the decision.

Case: *Eclipse Film Partners No. 35 LLP v HMRC (No. 2)* [2010] UKFTT 448 (TC)

6.5.1 Provision of evidence

Sometimes, evidence will be exchanged simultaneously; on other occasions, sequentially.

Sequential evidence

In cases of evidence being served sequentially, the taxpayer will usually be required to produce evidence before HMRC. This reflects the fact that the burden of proof usually falls on the taxpayer. However, where the evidential burden is on HMRC, it would be appropriate for HMRC to provide their evidence first.

This direction is often required to be complied with fairly soon (often four to six weeks) after the directions are given, depending on the complexity of the case. It is therefore advisable for parties to start collating their evidence at an early stage and not just wait until the directions have been given. The author considers that the exercise should be begun as soon as HMRC's statement of case has been received (as that is the clear indicator that HMRC are continuing to fight the case).

Evidence in reply

The direction will then give the other party (usually HMRC, but the taxpayer in cases where the burden is on HMRC) a period to provide evidence in reply to that provided by the other side. Again, the timing depends on the complexity of the case, but a four-week period is not unusual.

It is not often provided in a direction that the first party to produce evidence may give further evidence to refute that given in reply. However, such evidence – if given reasonably promptly – is not generally refused. Nevertheless, where a party thinks it likely that such evidence should be necessary, it would be appropriate to ask for a direction to be included giving the party the opportunity to provide it, say four weeks after the evidence reply is received from the other side.

Contents of witness statements

If a witness statement is to be produced, it should set out all the facts that the witness wishes to tell the tribunal. The statement should be prepared as if the witness will not have the opportunity to expand upon the contents at the hearing itself. In other words, all factual matters that the witness wants to be considered by the tribunal should be contained in the witness statement itself and not left "unsaid" in the hope that the opportunity will arise at the hearing to clarify matters.

As emphasised in *Ahmad*, "witness statements should ... be written in the witness's own words". Where this is not done, this can lead the tribunal to take what has been said with caution.

It is not usually appropriate to put legal arguments in the witness statement – the statement should be limited to facts. However, if a particular point is addressing a contention being made by another party, then it might be helpful to explain the context when asserting a particular fact.

If a fact is backed up by documentary evidence, then the document should be attached (or "exhibited") to the witness statement.

See **Appendix 5** for a specimen witness statement.

Case: *Ahmad v HMRC* [2019] UKFTT 682 (TC)

6.5.2   List of dates

This direction is usually required to be complied with fairly soon after all evidence has been exchanged, typically within a matter of two or three weeks. The reason that dates are not selected beforehand is because the length of the hearing is much harder to predict without an idea as to the number of witnesses who will need to be heard and cross-examined.

Usually, the tribunal will provide a block of dates (for example, a three-month period, known as a listing window) during which time it expects the hearing to take place.

It is not unusual for parties or their representatives to provide a long list of dates to avoid: in many cases, the "window" available for a hearing will have so many dates blacked out that it is unlikely that a hearing will be possible at all in that period. In such cases, it would be appropriate for the list of dates to extend outside the window so as to help the tribunal find a mutually convenient date.

In some cases, the parties are asked to liaise and to agree a number of dates which are mutually convenient and to offer those sets of dates to the tribunal.

In *Bates*, the High Court considered that non-availability of Counsel should not automatically be a reason to delay a hearing window as there was no principle that Counsel's availability trumped the court's. However, in *Elbrook*, the tribunal took a different approach noting the following distinctions from the facts in *Bates*:

- the case was long-running (and HMRC had instructed the same Counsel throughout the process);
- the application made by the taxpayer (if granted) would have led to only a relatively brief acceleration of the hearing dates.

Cases: *Bates v Post Office Ltd* [2017] EWHC 2844 (QB); *Elbrook (Cash and Carry) Ltd v HMRC* [2021] UKFTT 442 (TC)

Ensuring that the dates offered are and remain available

When offering any date as available, it is essential that all individuals who are likely to be required to attend the hearing (including witnesses) are asked in advance to confirm their availability. Once a date has been offered, each individual should keep that day clear in his or her diary until such time as it is clear that the tribunal no longer requires attendance on that day. The tribunal will not appreciate fixing a date, only to be told nearer the time that the date is not convenient. See **7.3.3**.

In cases where there are many witnesses, it will be clear that individual witnesses will not be needed on each date of the hearing and it should be unnecessary for witnesses to keep every day free. However, in such cases, the parties should liaise (initially with each other and subsequently with the tribunal) so as to agree a timetable, making clear who should be available on any particular date.

In this regard, it is worth noting that the party with the burden of proof will usually give its evidence first. However, this should not be applied too rigidly if one particular witness's availability is limited. It is also noteworthy that, in cases involving "opposing" expert witnesses, it is usual for the experts to give their evidence in succession.

It is also the case that lists of dates often become out of date by the time that a case is finally listed for a particular date (or dates). It is therefore helpful if the tribunal could be made aware of this likelihood and for the parties to liaise with the tribunal and to maintain an up-to-date list of suitable dates.

6.5.3 Hearing bundles

Hearing bundles are the sets of documents that the parties and the tribunal expect to refer to during the hearing. Traditionally, they are assembled in paginated ring-binders or lever arch files. However, restrictions during the Covid-19 pandemic have led to the widespread use of bundles in electronic form instead.

HMRC will often try to ensure that taxpayers produce these bundles. However, particularly where the taxpayers are not legally represented, HMRC are usually quite helpful and will prepare the bundles themselves.

The bundles should usually contain:

- a copy of the decision(s) appealed against;
- a copy of the appeal(s);
- any directions given by the tribunal;
- documents included in the parties' respective lists of documents (see rule 27);
- subsequent correspondence between the parties and the tribunal;
- witness statements and exhibits to those statements; and
- any other documents that the parties have agreed can be included.

Bundles should also be prepared containing copies of relevant statutory provisions, cases and other authorities that the parties are seeking to rely upon (an "authorities bundle").

6.5.4 Skeleton arguments

The detail into which a skeleton argument will go will depend again on the complexity of the case. However, skeleton arguments are designed to have been read by the tribunal before the beginning of the case and so they allow the tribunal to have an early grasp of what the case is about and the main strands of the argument.

As skeleton arguments often go astray, however, it is useful for parties to bring along spare copies to the hearing.

Contents of skeleton arguments

It is generally helpful for a skeleton argument to contain the following:

- a very brief (a sentence or two) explanation of what the case is about and (if applicable) the nature of the decision being appealed against;
- a summary of the key facts (including, where relevant, a chronology);
- the relevant legal principles; and
- how the principles, when applied to the facts, should give the result being argued for.

Although there are no hard and fast rules, it is generally appreciated by the tribunal if skeleton arguments are typed and prepared with numbered paragraphs.

Wherever possible, it is generally considered helpful for skeleton arguments to contain cross-reference to relevant pages in the hearing bundles.

A specimen skeleton argument can be found at **Appendix 6**.

Timing of skeleton arguments

Generally, it was usual for taxpayers to be required to provide their skeleton arguments 14 days before the start of the hearing and for HMRC to provide theirs seven days before the hearing. However, standard directions issued by the tribunal often expect both parties to provide their skeleton arguments at the same time. This is something that the parties will often be able to agree between themselves, subject to the tribunal's ultimate oversight.

Similarly, it is not uncommon for an extra week to be added to these time limits (so as to vary them to 21 days and 14 days respectively), sometimes with the taxpayer being given the option to provide a written reply seven days ahead of the hearing.

When the burden of proof falls on HMRC, it should be possible to ensure that their skeleton argument is produced first.

6.6 Other case management hearings

As well as dealing with cases where the parties cannot agree on a set of directions, directions hearings will also arise if one party has failed to comply with an existing direction or a requirement of the rules. Either that party might wish to ask for an extension (which might be opposed) or the other party might wish to ensure more timely compliance by requesting that an unless order be given (see **4.6.2** above).

Hearings can take place to decide disputes over all procedural aspects of the case. For example:

- whether or not the parties should be required to agree a statement of facts on which they can agree (thereby dispensing with the need for those facts to be asserted as evidence) (see **Appendix 4**);
- the composition of the tribunal;
- the reallocation of the case to a category (see **5.6.7**);
- the possible impact of transitional regulations applicable to pre-April 2009 cases transferred to the tribunal from the former tribunals (see **Appendix 8**);
- whether a case should be heard online or via telephone;
- if the hearing is to take place in person, where the case should be heard;
- how long a case ought to be listed for;
- how many witnesses ought to be allowed to give evidence (see **4.13.1**);
- whether certain evidence ought to be admitted (for example, if it is late) (see **4.13.4**);
- whether an expert witness ought to be appointed (see **4.13.2**);

- whether a case ought to be appointed a lead case or whether cases ought to be joined or otherwise heard together (see **4.2.6** and **4.16.3**);
- whether documents or other information ought to be provided to another party (see **4.14.2**).

7. Procedures at a hearing

7.1 Rule 29 – Determination with or without a hearing

> 29(1) Subject to rule 26(6) (determination of a Default Paper case without a hearing) and the following paragraphs in this rule, the Tribunal must hold a hearing before making a decision which disposes of proceedings, or a part of proceedings, unless–
>
> (a) each party has consented to the matter being decided without a hearing; and
>
> (b) the Tribunal considers that it is able to decide the matter without a hearing.
>
> 29(2) This rule does not apply to decisions under Part 4 (correcting, setting aside, reviewing and appealing Tribunal decisions).
>
> 29(3) The Tribunal may dispose of proceedings, or a part of proceedings, without a hearing under rule 8 (striking out a party's case).

7.1.1 Overview

The general position is that a case cannot be considered by the tribunal without an actual hearing. However, as has been seen in rule 26 (see **5.9** above), the opposite is generally the position in cases allocated to the Default Paper case category.

Rule 29 provides for the other exceptions to the general position.

7.1.2 Scope of the rule

The general requirement for there to be a hearing applies in respect of any decision by the tribunal that disposes of the whole or part of the case.

Therefore, supposing a taxpayer has appealed against an HMRC decision on three separate grounds, a hearing is generally necessary to deal with each of those three grounds.

Case management decisions, however, do not need to be made after a hearing as they will not generally dispose of the whole or part of the proceedings.

7.1.3 Parties consent to waive hearing (rule 29(1))

The first exception to the general requirement is in cases where each party has consented to the matter being decided without a hearing. However, even the parties' consent is not sufficient. The tribunal has also to consider that it can decide the matter without a hearing.

It was noted in *Kandore* that, in those rare cases with only one party, the first condition requires only that party's consent. However, although the judgment in that case could be read differently, it is implicit from the context that, even in those cases, there is still the additional requirement that the tribunal must also consider that a hearing can be dispensed with.

The wording of rule 29(1)(b) indicates that not only should the tribunal feel that it is able to reach a decision without the benefit of hearing oral argument, but the tribunal should also consider that it is appropriate (for example, would it be fair) for the matter to be so decided.

Case: *Kandore Ltd v HMRC* [2021] EWCA Civ 1082

7.1.4 Correction, setting aside, reviewing and appealing against decisions (rule 29(2))

The second exception relates to the procedures that might take place after a decision is made. These are considered in fuller detail in **Chapter 9** beginning at **9.3**.

7.1.5 Strike outs (rule 29(3))

The final exception arises in the context of strike outs (see rule 8). This is perhaps surprising given the consequences of a strike out. However, because of the protection given to parties under rule 8 itself (see **4.6.6** and **4.6.7** above), there should be no infringement of a party's right to a fair trial.

Nevertheless, as noted in *Jones*, this is permissive only: a hearing should be given in every case where the tribunal is in any doubt as to the correct decision to take. Furthermore, in *SRN*, the Upper Tribunal noted that the draconian effect of a strike-out meant that there should be a presumption in favour of any strike-out application being decided after an oral hearing, rather than being determined only on the papers.

The benefits of being able to dispose of certain cases without a hearing are aptly illustrated by the *Gardner* case. In that case, the taxpayer was applying for permission to appeal late (28 years late, in fact). On most of his proposed grounds of appeal, the tribunal had no jurisdiction and therefore these could not be used to justify the late appeal. On the other grounds, the tribunal considered that the taxpayer had no reasonable prospects of success and, therefore, the application for the appeal to be admitted late was doomed to fail (see **2.4.4**). The tribunal felt able to reach its decision without holding a hearing under rule 29(3) on the basis that "the position on the facts of this particular application are so clearly against the appellant based on his own representations that there is no need to hear HMRC's objections to the application nor to hold a hearing".

The decision notice confirms that Mr Gardner had earlier been given the opportunity to make representations in relation to the then proposed striking out in accordance with rule 8(4) (see **4.6.6** above).

Cases: *Gardner t/a Gardner's Transport Co v HMRC* [2010] UKFTT 133 (TC); *SRN Horizons Ltd v HMRC* [2017] UKUT 246 (TCC); *Jones v HMRC* [2017] UKFTT 567 (TC)

7.2 Rule 30 – Entitlement to attend a hearing

> 30 Subject to rules 19 (proceedings without notice to a respondent) and 32(4) (exclusion from a hearing), each party to proceedings is entitled to attend a hearing.

7.2.1 Overview

Rule 30 provides the rule that any party to the hearing is generally entitled to attend a hearing. When read with rule 2(2)(c), this also entitles any party to participate in the proceedings and therefore make representations. There are just two exceptions.

7.2.2 Without notice applications

The first exception is where an application is proceeding "without notice" under rule 19. For example, where HMRC seek the tribunal's prior approval of an information notice. The wording of the rule would appear to mean that respondents in such cases are not entitled to attend any hearing and may therefore not make representations directly to the tribunal.

Of course, rule 32(1) provides that hearings are to be held in public and so a person excluded from attending the hearing (in the sense of not being able to participate at the hearing – if aware of the date and location (see **7.3.1**)) will generally still have the right to be present at the hearing to observe the proceedings, subject to a direction by the tribunal:

- for a hearing in private under rule 32(2); or
- excluding that person from attendance under rule 32(4).

Such a direction might be justified if an application is going to reveal sensitive third-party information (perhaps the identity of the source of information tipping off HMRC to possible tax irregularities). However, it is suggested that a direction should not be automatic in any such "without notice" applications.

Nevertheless, it should be noted that the tribunal has taken the approach of allowing HMRC's applications for information notices to be heard in private. See **5.2.3** above.

See also **7.4.6** below.

7.2.3 Disruptive individuals etc

A party may also be excluded from attending a hearing if a direction has been given (under rule 32(4)) excluding that person's attendance because of likely disruption or the risk of intimidation of a witness or in the case of individuals aged under 18 years.

Rule 32(4) also allows the tribunal to exclude any person whose attendance would defeat the purpose of the hearing.

7.3 Rule 31 – Notice of hearings

> 31(1) The Tribunal must give each party entitled to attend a hearing reasonable notice of the time and place of any hearing (including any adjourned or postponed hearing) and any changes to the time and place of any hearing.
>
> 31(2) In relation to a hearing to consider the disposal of proceedings, the period of notice under paragraph (1)

> must be at least 14 days except that the Tribunal may give less than 14 days' notice–
>
> (a) with the parties' consent; or
>
> (b) in urgent or exceptional circumstances.

7.3.1 Overview

Rule 31 ensures that parties are generally given reasonable notice of the time and place of any hearing (or changes thereto). The rule extends only to persons entitled to attend a hearing. Therefore, in a case where a party is not entitled to attend (see rule 30), the rule does not apply.

7.3.2 Minimum notice

In respect of hearings that are to consider the disposal of proceedings (i.e. final decisions on particular substantive issues rather than directions hearings), rule 31(2) provides that the minimum notice should be at least two weeks.

However, lesser notice may be given if the parties consent to it or in urgent or other exceptional cases.

7.3.3 If dates provided are inconvenient

In many cases, the tribunal will simply allocate a date and place for a hearing. This is particularly so in Basic cases and for directions hearings in other cases. If the date and/or place are inconvenient to a party, it is incumbent on the party to give prompt notice to the tribunal to see if it can be rearranged.

Generally, the tribunal will try to co-operate. However, the tribunal is less likely to be amenable in cases where a party has been slow to announce their non-availability, the party has regularly sought to rearrange a hearing without good reason or the party has been given the opportunity to provide a list of dates to avoid and the tribunal took any response into account when fixing the time and place for the hearing. See also **6.5.2**.

7.4 Rule 32 – Public and private hearings

> 32(1) Subject to the following paragraphs, all hearings must be held in public.

32(2) The Tribunal may give a direction that a hearing, or part of it, is to be held in private if the Tribunal considers that restricting access to the hearing is justified–

(a) in the interests of public order or national security;

(b) in order to protect a person's right to respect for their private and family life;

(c) in order to maintain the confidentiality of sensitive information;

(d) in order to avoid serious harm to the public interest; or

(e) because not to do so would prejudice the interests of justice.

32(2A) The Tribunal may direct that a hearing, or part of it, is to be held in private if—

(a) the Tribunal directs that the proceedings are to be conducted wholly or partly as video proceedings or audio proceedings;

(b) it is not reasonably practicable for such a hearing, or such part, to be accessed in a court or tribunal venue by persons who are not parties entitled to participate in the hearing;

(c) a media representative is not able to access the proceedings remotely while they are taking place; and

(d) such a direction is necessary to secure the proper administration of justice.

32(3) Where a hearing, or part of it, is to be held in private, the Tribunal may determine who is permitted to attend the hearing or part of it.

32(4) The Tribunal may give a direction excluding from any hearing, or part of it–

(a) any person whose conduct the Tribunal considers is disrupting or is likely to disrupt the hearing;

(b) any person whose presence the Tribunal considers is likely to prevent another person from giving evidence or making submissions freely;

> (c) any person where the purpose of the hearing would be defeated by the attendance of that person; or
> (d) a person under the age of eighteen years.
>
> 32(5) The Tribunal may give a direction excluding a witness from a hearing until that witness gives evidence.
>
> 32(6) If the Tribunal publishes a report of a decision resulting from a hearing which was held wholly or partly in private, the Tribunal must, so far as practicable, ensure that the report does not disclose information which was referred to only in a part of the hearing that was held in private (including such information which enables the identification of any person whose affairs were dealt with in the part of the hearing that was held in private) if to do so would undermine the purpose of holding the hearing in private.

7.4.1 Overview

It is a general rule of law that justice must not only be done but must be seen to be done. As attributed variously to Voltaire and to the jurist Jeremy Bentham, "publicity is the very soul of justice". Rule 32(1) recognises this by stating as a general proposition that all hearings must be held in public.

The rest of the rule contains exceptions to this proposition (including one temporarily introduced as an initial response to the Covid-19 pandemic) and, in rule 32(6), one consequence of a hearing being held (at least in part) in private.

7.4.2 Public access in practice

Public access to hearings is relatively easy to achieve in cases heard in the main tribunal centres where there are regularly hearings taking place and, usually, a list of such hearings on display. However, many Tax Chamber hearings occur at *ad hoc* locations across the country, in hotels, town halls and other places where rooms can be hired on a daily basis and where the public does not generally wander.

Nevertheless, wherever a hearing takes place, a member of the public is entitled to attend, unless a direction under rule 32(2) has been given.

Furthermore, since 2020, the tribunal has listed forthcoming hearings on its website so as to facilitate open justice. This extends to providing (upon request) links to allow individuals to observe remote hearings.

Guidance: https://www.gov.uk/government/publications/first-tier-tribunal-tax-hearing-list

7.4.3 When a hearing may be in private (rule 32(2))

The tribunal may give a direction that a hearing may be held in private (or part of it may be held in private). Such a direction may be given only if the tribunal considers that it would be justified under one of five stated grounds:

- the interests of public order or national security;
- to protect a person's right to respect for private and family life (see below);
- maintaining the confidentiality of sensitive information (see below);
- to avoid serious harm to the public interest; or
- to avoid prejudicing the interests of justice.

It is implicit that the hearing should be in private only to the extent necessary to achieve those aims: it would not be right for the entire hearing to be held in private merely because part of it needs to be held in private. Furthermore, in *JK* (a case where the taxpayer was seeking anonymisation) the tribunal noted that this would be granted only if it was "necessary for justice to be done".

In *LD*, the tribunal ordered anonymity to prevent the potential identification of the taxpayer's children as the evidence concerned their well-being and circumstances at certain times.

The tribunal also noted in *JK* that HMRC were correct to take a neutral stance in the application.

Cases: *JK v HMRC* [2019] UKFTT 411 (TC); *LD v HMRC* [2019] UKFTT 526 (TC)

Right to private and family life

Inevitably, tax cases tend to concern issues that most people would ordinarily keep private: for example, an individual's income or capital gains. However, it has been held that such personal matters are not sufficient for a person's hearing to be held in private. The principles were discussed in the *Banerjee* decision, where Henderson J held that "it will only be in truly exceptional circumstances that a taxpayer's rights to privacy and confidentiality could properly prevail". One issue that was particularly relevant to the judge was the desirability that decisions concerning tax, which are generally of wider significance, can be fully appreciated and understood.

In *Banerjee*, the taxpayer's application actually concerned the anonymisation of the decision in her case. However, the judge based his decision on whether or not he would have acceded to the hearing being held in private. He held that he would not have done. As the case had actually been heard in public, he then turned to the question of anonymising the decision. However, he noted that the proceedings would have been recorded and, even if no-one from the public had been present at the proceedings, the transcript might now be obtainable by a member of the public. Consequently, to anonymise the decision would be pointless. Unlike the High Court (and some Upper Tribunal proceedings), hearings are not usually recorded in the Tax Chamber. Thus, when it is clear that there is no member of the public present at a hearing, the concerns raised in *Banerjee* about a transcript being obtainable are of no consequence.

Conversely, the *Sharifee* case involved former restaurant employees giving evidence about their former employer (who was not a party to the case, nor present at the hearing). In the circumstances of that case, the Special Commissioners concluded that the interests of justice led to that evidence being given in private so as to protect the third parties.

Similarly, a privacy direction was given in *A Divorcee* in the context of a difficult divorce and proceedings under the *Children's Act*. Although, in *JK*, the tribunal considered that the taxpayer's mental illness was not sufficiently severe to justify an anonymisation order, the tribunal made it clear that his contact details should not be disclosed. The tribunal added that they would rarely be published in any event but, as they had no relevance to the case, there was no reason for them to be disclosed.

Cases: *Sharifee, Naser & Siddique t/a Café Flutist (anonymised case) v Wood (HM Inspector of Taxes)* (2004) Sp C 423; *HMRC v Banerjee (No. 2)* [2009] EWHC 1229 (Ch); *A Divorcee v HMRC* [2010] UKFTT 612 (TC); *JK v HMRC* [2019] UKFTT 411 (TC)

Other sensitive information

Similarly, sensitive commercial evidence can justify part of proceedings being given in private. Alternatively, the tribunal might choose not to direct that part of the proceedings to be held in private but merely to redact any decision so as to exclude any potentially sensitive information from the public version of the decision. This happened in *DSG*.

In *Anson*, the Upper Tribunal expressed doubt that commercial data that was several years old could be sufficiently sensitive as to justify a private hearing and/or being redacted in any decision notice.

In *Cuco*, the tribunal heard the proceedings in public but then proceeded to anonymise the decision. The case concerned a company's reasonable excuse for the late payment of tax. The tribunal was prepared to anonymise its decision because there was a real risk that the company's creditors, suppliers and potential customers would treat the company less favourably if its financial position (past and present) became known.

Cases: *DSG Retail Ltd v HMRC* [2009] UKFTT 31 (TC); *HMRC v Anson* [2011] UKUT 318 (TCC); *Cuco v HMRC* [2013] UKFTT 121 (TC)

Adverse publicity

In *Moyles* (a case previously referred to as "Mr A"), the taxpayer sought confirmation in advance from the tribunal that he would be entitled to anonymity before embarking upon his appeal. The taxpayer was described as "a well-known broadcaster" who had participated in a marketed tax avoidance scheme. His application was based upon a fear (probably justified) that the public's subsequent learning of his involvement in such a scheme would generate adverse media comment, leading to possible damage to his career. Although earlier cases had suggested that this might be sufficient to warrant a hearing in private, the tribunal considered that reputational damage was no longer sufficient.

The same conclusion was reached in *Clunes* in a case concerning the deductibility of cosmetic treatment incurred by a well-known actor. It is considered that a different outcome might have been reached, however, had the treatment been prompted by medical reasons or had it been of a particularly sensitive nature.

A similar case (originally known as "Mr D", later released as *Andrea*) concerned a celebrity's wish for anonymity so as to protect his children. He had sued a newspaper for libel and sought a deduction for the legal costs of the process. The tribunal considered that "anonymity can be granted only where it is strictly necessary". This is a high hurdle. It added that confidential information could be adduced as written evidence, to be read only by the judge and the parties. Furthermore, the tribunal can direct that the sensitive information should not be disclosed to the wider public.

In *Moyles*, the tribunal noted, correctly it is submitted, that granting privacy to the rich and famous (on the basis of their fame) could be viewed as contrary to the interests of justice as it would unfairly distinguish such taxpayers from less wealthy litigants. Nevertheless, it is submitted that there are inevitably some cases where an individual's notoriety might be sufficient to merit a hearing in private where the adverse consequences of publicity are particularly extreme.

Cases: *Moyles v HMRC* [2012] UKFTT 541 (TC); *Clunes v HMRC* [2017] UKFTT 204 (TC); *Andrea v HMRC* [2017] UKFTT 850 (TC).

7.4.4 Video or audio hearings in private (rule 32(2A))

A further relaxation was temporarily introduced in response to the Covid-19 pandemic.

It applies only if a hearing, or part of it, is being conducted via video or by telephone. In such a case, the tribunal may direct that the hearing (or part of it) may take place in private. It is implicit that any such direction under this provision should be limited to that part (or those parts) of the hearing that are taking place by telephone or video.

It is clear from the rule that a direction for privacy is not automatic but must follow from the exercise of the tribunal's discretion. Furthermore, such a direction may be made only if:

- it is not reasonably practicable for such a hearing, or such part, to be accessed in a court or tribunal venue by non-parties (or parties who are not actually entitled to participate in the hearing);
- a media representative is not able to access the proceedings remotely while they are taking place; and
- such a direction is necessary to secure the proper administration of justice.

The term "media representative" is not defined but will be given its usual meaning.

Expiry of rule 32(2A)

Rule 32(2A) is the second of three temporary provisions introduced following the onset of the Covid-19 pandemic. It took effect on 10 April 2020 and is due to expire on 24 March 2022.

However, a minister can accelerate the expiry date or (for up to six months at a time) defer the expiry date.

The rule provides a temporary relaxation of the usual position that requires a hearing before any decision is made for the disposal of proceedings.

Law: *Coronavirus Act* 2020, s. 89(1), 90; SI 2020/416, r. 1(2)

7.4.5 Dealing with hearings in private (rule 32(3), (6))

Once a tribunal has decided to hold part of a hearing in private, it may then determine who may attend. The parties themselves are entitled to attend under rule 30, subject to the exceptions referred to at **7.2.2** and **7.2.3**. In most cases, the tribunal will permit the parties' representatives and any close family or friends attending to give moral support, plus perhaps legal students observing the proceedings as part of their studies.

Rule 32(6) recognises that many decisions of the tribunal are formally published and that a privacy direction will be of little benefit if the information kept secret is subsequently made more widely available. Therefore, rule 32(6) provides that any information (including information that could lead to the identification of any person) should not be included if publicity would undermine the purpose of holding hearing in private.

Strictly, the rule does not seem to accommodate two versions of a decision as happened in *DSG* (one containing the sensitive data and the published decision being a redacted version) – that was a case where there was no actual direction as to privacy during the hearing itself. However, the approach adopted in *DSG* would be a practical one to follow in any event.

In *Anson*, the judge stated that any redacted decision notice should make clear where the redactions had been made.

Cases: *DSG Retail Ltd v HMRC* [2009] UKFTT 31 (TC); *HMRC v Anson* [2011] UKUT 318 (TCC); *Cuco v HMRC* [2013] UKFTT 121 (TC)

Anonymisation after public hearing

In *XYZ*, the hearing took place in public. However, the tribunal felt that it was nevertheless appropriate for the decision notice to be anonymised, given the evidence concerning the taxpayer's mental state.

Case: *XYZ v HMRC* [2016] UKFTT 402 (TC)

7.4.6 Delegation to tribunal staff

Under paragraph 2 of a practice direction given by the Senior President of Tribunals, a duly authorised member of the tribunal's staff may carry out any of the tribunal's duties under this rule. See also rule 4 and **4.1.2** and **4.1.3**.

Guidance: https://tinyurl.com/ksfw95ju (Delegation of functions to staff in relation to the FTT and the Finance and Tax Chamber of the Upper Tribunal)

7.4.7 Third-party access to key documents

In *JTI*, the tribunal emphasised that non-parties do not have a general right to disclosure of materials considered in the course of a hearing, even though the hearing took place in public. However, as confirmed in *Hastings*, key documents relating to a decided case may be released to a non-party if the non-party has "a legitimate interest in the documents".

A further condition before any disclosure may be made is that there must have been a public hearing or determination by the tribunal. Therefore, it would not apply if the matter had been settled at an earlier stage. However, as made clear in *JTI*, it is not necessary that the case has been formally determined by the tribunal. An application may be considered as soon as there has been a public hearing (and even if the case is later settled by the parties before the hearing is concluded).

It was considered that "legitimate interest" was to be construed broadly and was not confined to journalistic purposes. For example, it could include an interest in related litigation.

Cases: *Hastings Insurance Services v HMRC* [2018] UKFTT 478 (TC); *JTI Acquisition Company (2011) Ltd v HMRC* [2021] UKFTT 446 (TC)

Factors to take into account

In *JTI*, the tribunal considered that a tribunal should weigh up the following three factors when dealing with a third-party disclosure application:

- the purpose of the open justice principle and the potential value of the information in question in advancing that purpose;
- any risk of harm which the disclosure might cause to the maintenance of an effective judicial process or to the legitimate interests of others; and
- the practicalities and proportionality of granting the request.

JTI objected to the disclosure of the parties' skeleton arguments on the basis that it was the result of legal work it had paid for and that work should not be made available to another for free. However, the tribunal dismissed JTI's argument on the basis that, irrespective of the applicant's motives, the applicant should be able to access documents that were read by the court as part of the decision-making process.

Case: *JTI Acquisition Company (2011) Ltd v HMRC* [2021] UKFTT 446 (TC)

Examples to date

In *Hastings*, the documents sought were the parties' skeleton arguments and HMRC's statement of case.

In *Fastklean*, a barrister (the author, as it happens) obtained a copy of an internal e-mail which was referred to in, and relevant to, the tribunal's earlier decision in the case.

In *JTI*, a firm of accountants was entitled to the parties' skeleton arguments. However, the factor of proportionality, when applied to the facts of the case, meant that the tribunal refused to order disclosure of the parties' written post-hearing submissions.

Cases: *Hastings Insurance Services v HMRC* [2018] UKFTT 478 (TC); *Fastklean Ltd v HMRC* [2020] UKFTT 511 (TC); *JTI Acquisition Company (2011) Ltd v HMRC* [2021] UKFTT 446 (TC)

7.5 Rule 32A – Coronavirus temporary rule (recording of remote hearings)

> 32A(1) In the circumstances set out in paragraph (3), the Tribunal must direct that the hearing be recorded, if practicable.
>
> 32A(2) Where the Tribunal has made a direction under paragraph (1), it may direct the manner in which the hearing must be recorded.
>
> 32A(3) The circumstances referred to in paragraph (1) are that the hearing, or part of it, is—
>
> (a) held in private under rule 32(2A); or
>
> (b) only treated as held in public by virtue of a media representative being able to access the proceedings remotely while they are taking place.
>
> 32A(4) On the application of any person, any recording made pursuant to a direction under paragraph (1) is to be accessed with the consent of the Tribunal in such manner as the Tribunal may direct.

7.5 Rule 32A – Coronavirus temporary rule (recording of remote hearings)

7.5.1 Overview

This rule is the third of three temporary provisions introduced following the onset of the Covid-19 pandemic. It took effect on 10 April 2020 and is due to expire on 24 March 2022.

However, a minister can accelerate the expiry date or (for up to six months at a time) defer the expiry date.

The rule provides a temporary relaxation of the usual position that requires a hearing before any decision is made for the disposal of proceedings.

Law: *Coronavirus Act* 2020, s. 89(1), 90; SI 2020/416, r. 1(2)

7.5.2 Recording of hearings (rule 32A(1), (2))

Ordinarily, hearings in the tribunal are not recorded. However, in certain circumstances, the rules provide that the tribunal should ensure that hearings are recorded if practicable.

When a direction for the recording of a hearing is made, the tribunal may also direct the manner in which the hearing is to be recorded.

7.5.3 When recordings should be made (rule 32A(3))

The rule is engaged in two circumstances where the hearing is not as public as would ordinarily be the case, either:

- the hearing is held in private in accordance with the provisions in rule 32(2A) (see **7.4.4**); or
- the hearing is notionally public but only because a media representative is able to access the proceedings remotely.

7.5.4 Access to recordings (rule 32A(4))

When a hearing is recorded under this rule, any person may apply for access to the recording.

As with the disclosure of documents considered by the tribunal during the hearing, there is no automatic right to access a copy of the recording. The author suggests that considerations similar to those applicable in relation to the disclosure of such documents (see **7.4.7**) will be appropriate.

Furthermore, the tribunal is entitled to direct in what manner the recording may be accessed.

7.6 Rule 33 – Hearings in a party's absence

> 33   If a party fails to attend a hearing the Tribunal may proceed with the hearing if the Tribunal–
>
> (a) is satisfied that the party has been notified of the hearing or that reasonable steps have been taken to notify the party of the hearing; and
>
> (b) considers that it is in the interests of justice to proceed with the hearing.

7.6.1 Overview

It is not uncommon for a hearing to take place without all the parties being present. In published decisions, the absent party is almost invariably the taxpayer.

In many cases, it will be inappropriate for a case to be adjourned merely because a party is absent. Rule 33 provides, however, a procedure to be followed.

As shown in *Marsh*, the tribunal will sometimes invoke the rule even if the taxpayer is represented but not present personally. It is considered that this is necessary only in cases (such as *Marsh* itself) where the representative is seeking an adjournment due to the taxpayer's non-attendance. However, in *Newton* the procedure was followed (part way during the hearing, where both sides were represented by Counsel) once it was realised by the tribunal that neither of the appellants was physically amongst the many people inside the room.

Cases: *Marsh v HMRC* [2017] UKFTT 320 (TC); *Newton & Newton-Young v HMRC* [2019] UKFTT 688 (TC)

7.6.2 Procedure when a party is absent

The tribunal must be satisfied that the absent party had been notified of the hearing or that reasonable steps had been taken to notify the party of the hearing. In many cases, the tribunal will adjourn proceedings for a few minutes to ask a member of the tribunal's administrative staff to try to make contact with the party or the party's representative to ascertain whether or not someone is planning to attend.

Even if good efforts have been made to notify the absent party of the hearing, the tribunal may not proceed with the hearing, unless the tribunal considers that to do so would be in the interests of justice. It is clear, therefore, that the attempts to make contact with the absent party (both before the hearing and during any adjournment) represent only part of the story. There has to be a good reason to proceed there and then and not to adjourn.

In this regard, the tribunal has to be conscious of the time and costs incurred by the other party and the likelihood that the absent party would attend any rearranged hearing. Other relevant issues are the complexity of the matter, the substance of the absent party's arguments: effectively, how necessary is the absent party for justice to be achieved?

In *McFarlane*, where an adjournment had been sought, the tribunal noted that the onus is on the person seeking an adjournment to prove the need for it, although a tribunal is entitled to be satisfied that the reasons given are genuine. The tribunal also noted that fairness considers the impact on both sides of any adjournment and took into account the history of non-compliance by the absent party.

Case: *McFarlane v HMRC* [2018] UKFTT 282 (TC)

7.6.3   Costs consequences when a party is absent

In some cases, the tribunal might consider a party's absence as evidence of a refusal to engage in the tribunal process and that the party had pursued the case merely to defer the inevitable. In such cases, the tribunal may justly consider the absent party's conduct to be unreasonable and make the other party the subject of a costs order under rule 10(1)(b).

On the other hand, absence from a hearing will not necessarily mean that a party has acted unreasonably. In *Bird*, the former Special Commissioner considered that a hearing was inevitable and, so, the fact that the taxpayer did not turn up did not lead to any avoidable costs being incurred by HMRC. Although that case concerned the previous "wholly unreasonable" test, it is suggested that the principle continues to apply.

Case: *Bird v HMRC* (2008) Sp C 720

7.6.4 *Other consequences when a party is absent*

One protection given to parties who do not attend a hearing is that any final decision made by the tribunal in their absence can be set aside (under rule 38) if the tribunal considers that to do so would be in the interests of justice.

That would often be relevant in cases where the absent party had intended to attend but either got lost or delayed. However, as discussed at **9.5.4**, it can apply even if a party had previously announced that it would not attend the hearing.

On the other hand, it should be emphasised that a set aside will not be granted as of right – the interests of justice must dictate that course of action being taken.

8. At the hearing – practical considerations

8.1 Introduction

Despite the detailed rules dealing with the administration of a case both before and after the hearing, there are very few provisions that regulate the hearing itself. The few procedural rules that do exist are discussed in the previous chapter.

The following paragraphs aim to explain what is likely to happen at the hearing and why. However, readers are also recommended to read the tribunal's own booklet "At your hearing" and, in particular, section 2 which recommends which documents ought to be brought to the hearing.

It should also be noted that regional customs can sometimes affect the finer details of tribunal procedure, particularly in Scotland.

Guidance: https://tinyurl.com/yc39hvv7 (tribunal leaflet: *At your hearing*)

8.2 The tribunal regulates its own procedures

The tribunal is given a lot of flexibility to reflect that the way that it handles cases should and will differ enormously from case to case. Ultimately, the tribunal is entitled to regulate itself and its own proceedings. It will endeavour to do so by ensuring that the parties are treated fairly.

For example, in *Elder*, the appellant's hearing difficulties meant that oral witness evidence was dealt with in an unconventional fashion, so as to permit each topic to be subject to cross-examination and re-examination, rather than have this all done in one go.

Only in very rare cases will it be considered that a tribunal has adopted a procedure that is so unfair to one party that an appeal may be allowed to be made against the tribunal's own conduct.

Case: *Elder v HMRC* [2017] UKFTT 269 (TC)

8.2.1 Adherence to the overriding objective

In all cases, the tribunal must conduct the hearing with the overriding objective (rule 2) firmly in mind. Thus, for example, the traditional order of hearing arguments (set out below) can often be deviated from. However, where this appears to have happened, it will usually be appropriate for the tribunal to clarify to the parties what has happened to avoid any uncertainty and subsequent challenges.

8.2.2 Parties should not be too dependent on the tribunal

Whilst a tribunal will be sympathetic to a taxpayer who does not have legal representation and will strive to ensure that such a taxpayer receives a fair hearing, one should not expect the tribunal to provide all the legal arguments for the taxpayer.

More importantly, in cases where the taxpayer's arguments are dependent on documentary evidence, the taxpayer will be expected to have brought that evidence to the hearing (assuming it was already dealt with in a pre-prepared witness statement). In addition, if a taxpayer wishes to rely upon a piece of evidence, the taxpayer should make this clear during the hearing itself.

In *Parmar*, the High Court noted that it could not allow an appeal on the basis that evidence had not been seen by a tribunal because the taxpayer's representative was not prompted to produce it to the tribunal.

The importance of ensuring that evidence, on which the taxpayer wishes to rely, is before the tribunal cannot be over-emphasised. Any appeals from the Tax Chamber will be limited to questions of law (as opposed to questions of fact). Therefore, if some of the taxpayer's evidence was not before the tribunal, the taxpayer has effectively lost the chance to rely upon it, even if the case proceeds to a further appeal in the Upper Tribunal or in the higher courts.

In *Household Estate Agents*, a High Court judge refused to allow a case to be remitted to the General Commissioners (one of the forerunners of the Tax Chamber) for additional evidence, even though the taxpayer and the General Commissioners, themselves, were all under the wrong impression that the burden of proof (see below) on the particular point lay on HMRC.

Cases: *Parmar & Ors (t/a Ace Knitwear) v Woods (HM Inspector of Taxes)* [2002] EWHC 1085 (Ch); *HMRC v Household Estate Agents Ltd* [2007] EWHC 1684 (Ch)

8.3 The lines of argument

A related issue is the lines of argument that a party can raise at a hearing. Clearly, any argument must be relevant to the subject matter of the appeal. Therefore, an appeal about the deductibility of a trader's travel expenses should not include arguments about capital gains.

8.3.1 When the boundaries are first laid down

To some extent, the constraints on any arguments will have been laid down before the hearing begins: in most cases, a taxpayer will have listed the grounds of appeal when challenging a decision by HMRC and also when notifying the tribunal of the appeal (see **5.3**). Furthermore, in cases other than Basic cases, HMRC will have prepared a statement of case outlining their position (see **5.8.3**). Even in Basic cases, rule 24(3) requires HMRC to notify taxpayers of any additional arguments that they wish to make at the hearing (see **5.7.2**).

8.3.2 Flexibility of tribunal procedure

Nevertheless, the tribunal is meant to encourage a flexible approach and this will mean that a party is not necessarily precluded from raising new arguments at the hearing itself. As the Supreme Court noted in *Tower MCashback*, provided that they are relevant to the subject matter of the appeal, a tribunal may allow new arguments to be raised at any stage: this is "subject only to [the judge's] obligation to ensure a fair hearing". In practice, this will usually require the party to notify the other party in advance of the hearing of the new argument(s) being taken. However, in some cases, even this will not be necessary.

In *St Martin's*, the tribunal considered that a point raised by HMRC late on in a dispute (but well ahead of the tribunal hearing itself) should not be considered by them. The facts of the case were complex and involved two separate (but associated) companies. One of the companies had had its appeal allowed (on the basis that HMRC had raised their assessment too late) and it was only after that time when HMRC raised a new defence in respect of the other appeal. On the facts of the case, the tribunal considered that it would have been appropriate for HMRC's point to have been raised before the other appeal had been concluded.

See also **4.5.3** and **5.8.3**.

Cases: *HMRC v Tower MCashback LLP1* [2011] UKSC 19; *St Martin's Medical Services Ltd v HMRC* [2012] UKFTT 485 (TC)

Application in penalty cases

A similarly flexible approach was taken by the tribunal in the penalty case of *Collis*. Mr Collis had omitted his benefits-in-kind from his return and he argued that his 15 per cent penalty was over-penal for what he described as a first offence.

The tribunal noted that appeals against penalty determinations can be made against the imposition of the penalty, the amount of the penalty, a refusal to suspend a penalty or the terms of any such suspension. Even if a taxpayer has ostensibly appealed on only one such ground, "in the interests of fairness and justice the tribunal should be slow to exclude any avenue of appeal available to an appellant".

Case: *Collis v HMRC* [2011] UKFTT 588 (TC)

8.4 The people in the tribunal room

8.4.1 Judges and members

There are two types of individual who might sit on a tribunal at any hearing – judges and members. As a general (but not invariable) rule, judges will be legally qualified, whereas members will generally be individuals appointed to the tribunal because of their particular expertise, particularly in the tax and accounting profession. However, for anyone appearing at a tribunal hearing, the distinction between judges and members is of no consequence whatsoever and this book will refer to both members and judges as judges (or, simply, as the tribunal).

8.4.2 Other tribunal staff

The tribunal will often be assisted by a person known as a clerk, particularly in the main hearing centres. Before the hearing starts, it will usually be the clerk who checks the names of the person who will be presenting the case for each side and, if applicable, who is likely to be giving evidence and, where appropriate, check the nature of any oath that they might wish to swear (see **4.13.5**).

In some cases, where documents have been sent to the tribunal in advance of the hearing, it will usually be useful to check with the clerk that the documents have been received.

In addition, if there is a further "last-minute" document that a party wishes the tribunal to see before the hearing starts (so as to allow proceedings to be more efficient), then it would be appropriate to offer it to the clerk. To ensure that the proceedings are fair, the other parties should be given a copy at the same time. In cases where it is not clear whether the other parties are yet present in the building, it is usual to offer a further copy for the clerk to pass on.

8.4.3 HMRC's representatives

Depending on the complexity of the case, HMRC might instruct a barrister ("Counsel") to represent them. Alternatively, a lawyer from their in-house legal team ("Solicitor's Office") might be their representative. Sometimes, HMRC's arguments will be put forward by a member of their specialist Advocacy Unit, made up of trained tax officers who now specialise in presenting cases to the Tax Chamber, and now incorporated into the Solicitor's Office. It is rare now for the officer at the taxpayer's local office to argue the case for HMRC.

Particularly in cases where HMRC have instructed a lawyer to argue the case, the representative will often be accompanied by a colleague (or even more than one). Those colleagues will usually sit at the back and should not give the taxpayer any particular concern.

8.4.4 Friends or family of the taxpayer

It is very common for the taxpayer, even if professionally represented, to bring along a friend or family member for emotional support at a hearing. In many cases, the author would positively recommend that a taxpayer bring along such a companion.

Even in those rare cases where the tribunal has decided that the hearing should take place in private (see 7.4.3 above), the tribunal should be expected to allow the taxpayer's companion to remain in the room.

8.4.5 Members of the public

Most hearings are officially in public, meaning that in theory individuals with no connection to the parties can turn up and watch proceedings (or part of them). In practice this is extremely rare and any observers tend to be limited to law students and, very occasionally, other tax practitioners with a particular interest in the case.

8.5 Formalities during the hearing

It is generally considered that proceedings before the tribunal are less formal than in a traditional court room. However, particularly in cases heard in the tribunal's permanent hearing centres where the hearing room looks like a small courtroom (and in those other hearing centres elsewhere which are actually courtrooms), the signs of informality are often hard to discern. Indeed, there are some aspects of the hearing which to a lay observer would seem anything but informal.

8.5.1 Layout of the tribunal room

Main tribunal centres and other courts

As noted, the tribunal's permanent hearing rooms are usually decorated like small courtrooms, with a slightly raised platform for the judges.

HMRC's representative and the taxpayer (or, the taxpayer's representative) will usually sit at desks facing the judges. There is usually a second row of desks behind which one would usually find the taxpayer (if a representative is sitting in the first row) and also anyone else attending from HMRC.

The usual seating arrangement is that the taxpayer (and anyone attending with the taxpayer) would sit on the left side of the room (i.e. on the judges' right) with HMRC's representatives on the right side (i.e. on the judges' left). However, this is not strictly adhered to and, particularly, when there are a lot of people in the room, some flexibility should be expected. Furthermore, the custom in Scotland tends to sit taxpayers on the right side of the room, with HMRC on the left.

Any members of the public and other observers will usually be able to sit on chairs at the back or side of the room.

In front of the judges will be an area for witnesses to give their evidence and usually a desk for the clerk to sit at. The clerk will not necessarily remain in the tribunal for the entire hearing.

Other tribunal centres

To prevent taxpayers from having to travel to the main tribunal centres (London, Manchester and Edinburgh) in every case, the tribunal will often sit elsewhere in the UK. This is predominantly the case where hearings are less complex.

Where there is a good reason for a case to be heard away from the normal tribunal centres (perhaps one of the parties or key witnesses is unable to travel or if the tribunal will be required to conduct a site visit) then it will usually be possible for a more local hearing to be arranged.

Sometimes, the tribunal will sit in a local courtroom. However, sometimes a meeting room at a local town hall or other civic building will be used.

A similar *ad hoc* arrangement will often be used for some hearings held in London if accommodation at the main tribunal centre is fully occupied.

In all such cases, the layout of the room will be subject to some adjustments to take into account the temporary use of the space. However, it will generally be based on the normal layout described above.

8.5.2 What is worn

The one clear distinction between a tribunal hearing and a trial in a court is that wigs and gowns are most definitely not worn by any of the individuals at the hearing. The judges would ordinarily wear business suits and it is expected that any professional representative would be similarly attired.

There is of course no rule that anyone else should wear a suit but, as one is often told as a child, dressing smartly does give a good impression and the author would certainly suggest, admittedly ambiguously, that individuals should attend "appropriately dressed".

8.5.3 How to address individuals

Addressing judges

Although it is common for the judges to have name plates in front of them, the custom in the tribunal is for male individuals sitting on the tribunal to be addressed as "Sir" and female individuals as "Madam". In those circumstances when someone wishes to address all the judges or members in one go, the tradition is for the third party phrase "The tribunal" to be used. However, the author would not expect any judge to be particularly concerned if the protocol is not fully observed, as long as proceedings do not become too informal.

Referring to the parties or HMRC's representative

As one might expect in a formal meeting, it would rarely be appropriate for the taxpayer (or the taxpayer's representative) to speak directly to HMRC's representative during the course of the hearing and *vice versa*: all remarks ought to be addressed through the tribunal. Consequently, HMRC and their representative will generally be referred to in the third person. The only exception is where HMRC's representative is also acting as a witness: during cross-examination, it will be certainly be acceptable to speak to the representative directly.

There are all sorts of traditions about the way one should address another party or HMRC's representative. Traditionally, the parties would not be referred to by name but as "the appellant" or "the respondents" (HMRC usually being the respondents in the Tax Chamber) and one party's representative would often refer to the other side's representative as "my friend" or if a barrister "my learned friend".

However, the author suggests that, in the slightly more informal atmosphere that the tribunal is supposed to adopt, the tribunal would not object to HMRC being referred to simply as "HMRC", "the Revenue" or "Customs" and any individual (whether the taxpayer or HMRC's representative) as "Mr", "Mrs", "Miss", "Ms" or "Dr" etc. Similarly, if the taxpayer is a company, it should be appropriate to refer to it simply by name.

8.5.4 Standing or sitting

As the judges enter or leave the room

In many hearings, the judges will enter the room formally. Those present in the tribunal room will be asked to stand as they enter.

The judges will make their way to their seats, face those in the room and give a small bow (effectively a slow nod of the head). Those present in the room should give a similar nod in response. The judges will then invite those present to sit down again.

Similarly, at the end of any hearing (or whenever the judges adjourn (see **8.5.6** below)), all present will be asked to stand up, the judges will give a nod to those present (and those present will respond) before the judges leave the room.

At some hearings, however, particularly those outside the main tribunal centres, the judges will remain seated in the tribunal room throughout and individual cases will be invited to come inside in turn. In such cases, there is no formal standing up and/or nodding to the judges.

During the hearing

Tribunal proceedings are conducted sitting down. So, even when one is speaking, it is the custom to remain seated. However, the tribunal recognises that some people when speaking in public feel more comfortable doing so when standing up. In such cases, the tribunal would prioritise a person's comfort over tradition.

If a witness is swearing an oath (or making an affirmation), the witness will usually do so standing up. However, when actually giving the evidence and/or responding to questions from one or more of the representatives or the judges, that will all be done sitting down.

When an individual leaves or enters the room

Except when a witness is swearing an oath, there is no reason why an individual cannot leave the room partway through a hearing. Nor is there any reason why a latecomer cannot be admitted (subject to any risk of the individual causing a distraction etc or a direction that the hearing be in private). In each case, as the person is at the door of the tribunal room, it would be traditional for a nod to be given to the judges. Such a nod will not normally be acknowledged by them.

8.5.5 Speaking to the tribunal

Any person addressing the tribunal should remember that the tribunal will usually be making notes of what the person is saying. Therefore, one should usually pause between sentences to ensure that the tribunal has kept up.

Even if one has not been asked to provide a summary of arguments in advance, it is often helpful if a written note can be prepared of what one is likely to be saying. This will not only ensure that nerves do not take over on the day but should also give the tribunal considerable help in understanding the nature of the argument.

Where such a note has been prepared, it will be useful to bring some spare copies (one for the HMRC representative and one to retain and use as an *aide-mémoire*). However, it will often be possible for photocopies to be made by the tribunal if necessary.

8.5.6 Adjournments

Although the timing is generally quite flexible, it will be usual for a tribunal to adjourn for lunch at about 1pm and for the evening between 4 and 4.30pm.

However, there will occasionally be instances where it may be necessary to adjourn proceedings at other times. For example, the tribunal might need to make a decision on an interim procedural matter partway through the proceedings or, perhaps, the parties need to wait for a witness to arrive or the judges want to read a detailed document and it is considered better if the proceedings are put on hold for 30 minutes or so.

Mid-session adjournments are also very common in cases being conducted remotely (to give eyes a break from the screen) and in cases where stenographers are present (to give hands a rest). The likely timing of such breaks will usually be discussed in advance, but with the proviso that this is usually subject to some flexibility so as to combine any adjournment with a sensible break in proceedings (e.g. at the end of one witness's evidence).

Whenever there is a short adjournment in the proceedings, the judges will usually advise the parties when the hearing is likely to resume.

8.5.7 Recording proceedings

It is a contempt of court for anyone other than the tribunal itself to record tribunal proceedings without the tribunal's express permission.

Law: *Contempt of Court Act* 1981, s. 9(1)(a), 19

8.6 Standard of proof

A party is required to satisfy the "balance of probabilities". This means that the tribunal must be able to conclude that the particular set of facts being argued for by that party are more likely than not to be right: in other words, "more than 50 per cent likely".

See also the burden of proof (**8.7** below) as to who is required to satisfy this standard of proof.

8.6.1 Cases where the tribunal's role is more restricted

Although the balance of probabilities test applies in all cases, it should be noted that there are a few cases where it is not enough for a taxpayer to persuade a tribunal that it would not have made the same decision as HMRC.

These are typically the cases where the appeal is against the exercise of a discretion granted by statute to HMRC (for example, whether or not to allow a penalty to be suspended, the terms of any such suspension or the applicability of a special reason for reducing a penalty). In such cases, statute provides that a tribunal may allow the appeal only if HMRC's approach is flawed: for example, if HMRC took into account an irrelevant consideration in reaching their decision or failed to take into account a relevant one or if there was some other manifest unfairness in HMRC's approach.

Although this seems harsh to taxpayers, it should be noted that most exercises of HMRC discretion are not amenable to appeal in the first place: a taxpayer's only route of legal challenge in those cases is by way of judicial review. See **2.1.3** above.

There are similar restrictions in VAT cases. For example, HMRC may direct that two or more taxpayers should be treated as carrying on a single business for VAT purposes. In such cases, a tribunal may not allow the taxpayers' appeal unless it concludes that the original decision could not have been reasonably made.

Law: VATA 1994, s. 84(4ZA), (4A), (4C), (4D), (7), (7A), (7B); FA 2007, Sch. 24, para. 17

8.7 Burden of proof

It is often said that it is for the taxpayer to prove his/her/its case in the tribunal, so that if the tribunal is not persuaded by the taxpayer's case (even if the tribunal concludes that the two opposing views were equally likely) then the taxpayer should lose the case.

This is indeed the general rule, but it is subject to so many exceptions that it should be viewed with some caution. Ultimately, it depends on the type of case being heard.

In many cases, there will be more than one question that needs to be addressed by the tribunal, with the burden falling on one party for some of the issues but on the other for the remaining issues.

In short, the maxim to be applied is that the person who asserts a particular set of facts is required to prove that part of the case.

8.7.1 Straightforward cases

In the most straightforward cases, the taxpayer has been assessed for tax but disputes the liability.

In cases where the law is relatively clear but the dispute is on the facts, it will be for the taxpayer to prove (i.e. persuade the tribunal on the balance of probabilities) that the taxpayer's account of the facts is correct and that HMRC have got it wrong. The standard authority for this is *Nicholson*.

Example

Sam runs a takeaway restaurant and has prepared accounts showing a profit of £25,000. HMRC believe that the true figure is closer to £35,000, because of concerns about cash takings that appear to have been omitted, and have assessed Sam accordingly.

Sam will be required to disprove the figures in HMRC's assessment.

Law: TMA 1970, s. 50(6)
Case: *Nicholson v Morris (HM Inspector of Taxes)* (1976) 51 TC 95

8.7.2 Transferring the burden of proof to HMRC

The underlying rationale for the rule is that, in straightforward cases, the taxpayer ought (and is more likely than HMRC) to have the information that will enable the correct figures to be identified. For this reason, the taxpayer is generally required to disprove assessments made.

This exercise can sometimes be very difficult, however, as it can require the taxpayer to prove a negative. In such cases, the taxpayer will simply have to come across to the tribunal as a believable witness and the best approach would be to show the flaw in HMRC's approach.

Example

Suppose Sam (see the example at **8.7.1** above) never banks cash takings at his takeaway yet it is clear that he receives cash receipts of £200 each week. Suppose further, however, that the HMRC investigation was being carried out by an inexperienced officer who reaches the conclusion that these unbanked cash takings must inevitably represent undeclared income and therefore adds £10,000 to the profits figure.

However, suppose Sam is actually meticulous in his accounting and can explain what has happened. For example, the cash takings are used to pay the wages of his part-time cook, such wages having been declared in the accounts.

In such a situation, Sam ought to be able to satisfy the burden of proof and it would then be for HMRC to show why Sam's explanation is inadequate.

A similar situation arose in the *Ho* case. Mr Ho, a taxi-driver, had prepared accounts which showed him making two daily journeys to Heathrow Airport where he waited for fares. The HMRC officer refused to believe that Mr Ho would then make a return trip to the airport without a passenger in the back of his cab and effectively doubled his turnover. The tribunal, however, accepted Mr Ho's evidence that he would usually return to the airport without a passenger (because, if Mr Ho had accepted passengers in Central London, he would not have been able to guarantee picking up a fare that would allow him to return to the airport).

Case: *Ho v HMRC* [2010] UKFTT 387 (TC)

8.7.3 Burden of proof with discovery assessments

Discovery assessments are those assessments that allow HMRC to collect tax that ought to have been paid under the self-assessment rules but where the matter was not picked up in the course of a routine enquiry.

In such cases, the statute imposes additional burdens on HMRC if an assessment is to be upheld.

For example, HMRC have to show that a discovery has been made – this is a relatively low threshold and very few cases will turn on this point. In addition, HMRC will have to show that the under-assessment was caused by a careless or deliberate error by the taxpayer or a person acting on the taxpayer's behalf in the preparation of the return. Alternatively, HMRC will have to show that there was insufficient information provided by the taxpayer (typically in the return) to alert HMRC to the possible under-assessment.

As shown in *Household*, in all such cases, the burden of proof will fall on HMRC to show that these statutory hurdles are satisfied.

However, assuming that HMRC are able to satisfy that burden, it will fall on the taxpayer to disprove the underlying assessment (as per above).

In some discovery cases, the taxpayer will wish to rely upon a defence that, even though the tax return proved to be wrong, it was nevertheless prepared in accordance with the practice then generally prevailing. To the extent that such a defence is being put forward, it is then for the taxpayer to satisfy the burden of proof.

Case: *HMRC v Household Estate Agents Ltd* [2007] EWHC 1684 (Ch)

8.7.4 Cases involving penalties

As with discovery assessments, it will be for HMRC to prove that the culpable conduct that has given rise to the penalty has occurred.

In *Ballysillan*, the tribunal considered that HMRC were required to satisfy the criminal standard of proof ("beyond reasonable doubt"). It is respectfully suggested that this approach was wrong and, as suggested in *Khawaja*, HMRC are required to show that the events occurred only on the balance of probabilities, even in penalty cases.

However, if the case turns on statutory defences (such as reasonable excuse) then it is for the taxpayer to prove the requisite facts.

Cases: *HMRC v Khawaja* [2008] EWHC 1687 (Ch); *Ballysillan Community Forum v HMRC* [2011] UKFTT 257 (TC)

8.7.5 Burden of proof with information notices

It is now becoming increasingly clear that HMRC have the burden of proof in appeals against information notices. They need to show that the information is reasonably required and, where relevant, that any additional conditions for such notices are met.

Case: *Hegarty v HMRC* [2018] UKFTT 774 (TC)

8.7.6 Cases where facts are agreed

In many cases, it is possible for the parties to agree a statement of facts (which might or might not address all the factual issues relevant to the appeal). For a specimen agreement, see **Appendix 4**.

As illustrated in *Donnelly*, a particular fact can also be implicitly agreed by the parties if both parties advance their cases in a way which makes it clear that there is no dispute as to the factual position being taken by each party.

In either case, as the Upper Tribunal held in *Donnelly*:

> "Where the parties to adversarial proceedings agree an issue it is not the function of the tribunal to go behind that agreement and undertake its own investigation or reach its own independent determination about the issue. The FTT should not place an onus on one or other party to prove an agreed fact."

Case: *Donnelly v HMRC* [2021] UKUT 296 (TCC)

8.7.7 Application of law to fact

In some cases, the difficulty lies not with the facts themselves, but with how they should be viewed in the eyes of the law.

Some of these cases involve so-called mixed fact and law; others involve purely legal questions.

Cases involving mixed fact and law

These are cases where a tribunal is required to make a finding of fact, based upon other (primary) facts. For example, as concluded by the House of Lords in *Lysaght*, the question as to whether a person is resident or not in the UK is ultimately a question of fact. However, it is a finding of fact that should be reached in accordance with settled legal principles on the basis of the facts found about the person's connection with various jurisdictions.

In such cases, the burden initially falls on the taxpayer. However, as held in *Wood v Holden*, "where the taxpayer has produced evidence which, as matters stand then, appears to show that the assessment is wrong ... the evidential basis must [then] pass to the Revenue".

Cases: *Lysaght v IRC* (1927) 13 TC 511; *Wood v Holden (HM Inspector of Taxes)* [2006] EWCA Civ 26

Cases involving only questions of law

In cases where the facts are undisputed, the question for the tribunal will be merely a question of law. This will arise if, for example, a will needs to be construed or the question is purely one of how the statutory code should be interpreted in the light of the agreed facts.

In such cases, the issue of the burden of proof should not arise. It is instead simply for the tribunal to decide what the correct legal position is.

8.8 Who speaks when?

Generally, the tribunal will seek to ensure that the taxpayer feels at ease during the proceedings and will try to invite the taxpayer to have the first and last word so that the taxpayer does not feel disadvantaged. However, sometimes a judge will invite HMRC to speak first simply so as to allow an unrepresented taxpayer to observe how things are done before being cast into the deep end.

However, it should be emphasised that the order of speaking is subject to variation by the tribunal and, strictly, can also depend on which party has the burden of proof.

8.8.1 The usual order

In typical cases, the hearing can usually be divided into the following stages:

- Opening submissions – setting the scene and summarising the issues in dispute. This is also the time when additional procedural issues should be raised. This stage is often skipped before Scottish judges, who prefer the case to open with the parties' evidence.
- Evidence.
- Closing submissions – This is usually where the legal arguments are made and the parties try to explain how their respective arguments are supported by their view of the facts.

8.8.2 Opening submissions

The tribunal will usually permit the taxpayer to speak first and "open" the case (the main exception being in cases where HMRC have the burden of proof). This usually means no more than summarising the issues to be raised before the tribunal. In rare cases, it can be appropriate to make detailed legal arguments on the law. In the author's experience this can be appropriate when it is helpful for the tribunal to be aware of those issues *before* hearing the actual evidence.

Although it will be the taxpayer's prerogative to go first, a tribunal might invite the HMRC representative to set the scene if it is thought that it is likely to be more time-efficient. This happened in *Ling*, but the tribunal suggested that HMRC ought, in such cases, to limit their opening comments to factual issues and not make submissions to advance their case.

If one party has made opening submissions, it is only right for the other party to have the opportunity to reply. However, in those cases where the taxpayer has made opening submissions, it is actually quite rare for HMRC to respond at that stage (at least in detail).

As already noted, many Scottish judges prefer not to hear opening submissions and commence the case with the parties' respective evidence. In such cases, one would expect the tribunal to have pre-read enough of the documentation to know the issues that the case involves.

Case: *Ling v HMRC* [2011] UKFTT 793 (TC)

Procedural issues raised during opening submissions

Sometimes there are procedural matters that ought to be considered by the tribunal early on in the proceedings. For example, there could be a dispute as to whether a party has the right to raise a particular argument in the proceedings or whether certain evidence may be admitted. These disputes can arise particularly if the argument or evidence is raised late in the day and that delay could cause unfairness to the other side. Or perhaps it is just a simple question as to running order if, for example, one witness cannot be present for the entire hearing.

It is usually helpful for such matters to be aired at an early stage in the hearing so that they can be resolved before the tribunal turns to the main issues in the case.

8.8.3 Evidence

This is considered in more detail in the context of rule 15 at **4.13**.

However, it is appropriate to mention here some practical points.

The first is a rule of the law of evidence. If a party is seeking to assert a particular fact which is not otherwise supported by the evidence, it will be necessary to "put it" to one of the other party's witnesses in cross examination. This requires, at the very least, the assertion to be stated to the witness so as to allow the witness (if appropriate) to dissent from the assertion being made.

The second is more procedural. Unlike criminal cases, it is generally considered acceptable (albeit not obligatory) for witnesses to be present in the tribunal while other witnesses are giving their evidence (even before the witness in question has given his or her own evidence). However, in cases where one party is concerned that a later witness might adjust his or her evidence to match earlier evidence given, then that party can apply to the tribunal to have the witness excluded from the tribunal room until it is time for that witness to give his or her own evidence. In Scotland, however, the default position is that witnesses are excluded from the tribunal room until called to give their own evidence.

Thirdly, where one party seeks to rely on a statement made in a contemporaneous document (such as a report) to dispute the credibility of another party's witness, the tribunal held in *Zahra* that the contemporaneous document would be given less weight if the person who prepared it is unable to give evidence and be available to be cross-examined on that evidence.

Fourthly, in *White*, the Upper Tribunal made clear that it was not necessary for the subject matter of cross-examination to be flagged up in advance.

Fifthly, it should be noted that once a witness has started to give evidence, the witness may not speak to anyone about the case (except, of course, to answer questions in the course of the hearing itself). This means that the witness may not seek to check an answer with his or her adviser or colleagues before responding. More importantly, if the tribunal takes a break (e.g. for lunch or overnight) before the evidence is concluded, it is still not acceptable to discuss the case privately. To avoid any misunderstandings, it is usually best for a witness in such circumstances to avoid any conversation with colleagues or advisers until the tribunal "releases" the witness when the evidence is over. In exceptional cases, the tribunal can relax this rule – for example where there is going to be a long interval before the evidence is able to continue.

Sixthly, there are some cases (particularly those involving so-called "carousel fraud" or MTIC) where a party may be required to identify in advance which parts of the other party's evidence it does not accept. See **4.14.4**. This approach is taken in order to make case management more efficient. In *Elbrook*, the Upper Tribunal made clear that matters may be in dispute even if the disputing party does not itself put forward a positive case (i.e. advance its own evidence) on a particular point. Consequently, the Upper Tribunal made it clear that a party should not be precluded from cross-examining the other party's witnesses on such matters.

Seventhly, there is a view sometimes expressed that the person presenting the case may not appear as a witness. In the author's view, this rule is more applicable to a professional advocate. There should be no restriction on a taxpayer both putting forward his or her own case and giving evidence. Furthermore, in *LD*, the tribunal required the taxpayer's accountant, who was presenting the case, to give evidence. Where care needs to be taken is for the advocate-witness to compartmentalise the two roles: when facts are being put forward, this should be whilst in the witness box to allow the other side the opportunity to cross-examine on the point.

Cases: *Zahra v The Home Office* [2014] UKFTT 519 (TC); *Jamie White v HMRC* [2018] UKUT 257 (TCC); *Elbrook Cash and Carry Ltd v HMRC (No. 2)* [2019] UKUT 201 (TCC); *LD v HMRC* [2019] UKFTT 526 (TC)

What happens when a witness is called

When a witness is called to give evidence, the witness will usually be directed to a table situated between the representatives and the judges.

If evidence is to be given formally under oath or by affirmation, a judge or a clerk will then ask the witness to read the appropriate statement and, if giving evidence under oath, to hold a holy book – the tribunal will have a set of volumes to cover several (but not all) faiths. Despite the range of holy books, the tribunal also recognises that adherents to some faiths might still prefer to give their evidence by affirmation and not under oath.

Once these formalities are complete, the witness will then be asked to state his or her name and to confirm his or her address. The author was trained not to ask for a private home address to be stated in open court but instead to ask the witness to confirm the address as shown on a witness statement.

If there is a pre-submitted witness statement, the witness will be asked to confirm whether that statement should stand as the evidence before the tribunal and to advise the tribunal of any corrections or updates. If there are further matters that the witness needs to address (because of issues arising since the witness statement was prepared) then this is the time to deal with them.

If a case is being conducted by someone (whether the taxpayer or a representative) other than the witness, the witness will be asked the questions by the person conducting the case. The rule is that when addressing witnesses from one's own side, any questions asked of the witness should not be "leading" in the sense that they should not be seen to guide the witness to the desired answer. For example, one can ask "Where were you on the night of ...?" but not "You were at the pub on the night of ... weren't you?". Where the fact is not going to be controversial then the tribunal is likely to be fairly flexible about this rule.

This part of the process is known as "examination in chief".

It is then followed by cross-examination, by the other side(s). In cross-examination, there is no restriction on the use of leading questions and, typically, most questions will in fact be leading.

In *White*, the Upper Tribunal emphasised that cross-examination should be limited to those issues that arise on the pleadings (statements of case, witness statements and skeleton arguments) and must be conducted relevantly and appropriately.

A further overview was given by the Upper Tribunal in *Mungavin*:

> "... speaking generally, it seems to me that the proper purpose of cross-examining a factual witness is two-fold: first, to seek to undermine or qualify or mitigate the effect of evidence they have given which is adverse to the cross-examining party – for example by challenging the credibility or reliability of the witness, or otherwise testing the completeness or accuracy of their evidence – and second, to elicit further factual testimony helpful to the cross-examining party. It is not the proper function of cross-examination to argue the case, or debate issues of law, or seek to get the witness to agree with factual propositions of which they cannot themselves give relevant evidence. In practice counsel is often allowed considerable latitude to stray into these areas, but strictly speaking evidence in cross-examination is no more admissible if it is not evidence of facts of which the witness can speak of his own knowledge than it is in chief."

After cross-examination, the party calling the witness will be given the opportunity to "re-examine" the witness. The purpose of this is to clarify matters that have arisen during cross-examination and to repair any possible damage to the party's case. Again, the rule is not to ask any leading questions.

Re-examination is not always necessary: if the cross-examination left the witness unscathed, there is no need to prolong matters. Furthermore, a decision not to re-examine a witness can give the subliminal message to the tribunal that the other side's attempts to undermine the witness have come to nothing. Furthermore, it is sometimes ill-advised to re-examine a witness in cases where some damage has been caused because it will highlight the party's concerns about weaknesses in the case. On the other hand, leaving a matter unrepaired has its own dangers.

Re-examination should not be used to introduce new evidence which should have been dealt with "in chief". Where an omission is discovered, permission should be sought from the tribunal to adduce this additional evidence and, if granted, the other side will of course be entitled to cross-examine on it if appropriate.

The tribunal might also ask the witness a few questions. If so, then there will be the further opportunity for the party calling the witness to ask some final questions, clarifying any matters that arise from the tribunal's questions.

After that, the witness is then "released" and is once again free to discuss the case.

Cases: *Jamie White v HMRC* [2018] UKUT 257 (TCC); *Mungavin v HMRC* [2020] UKUT 11 (TCC)

8.8.4 Closing submissions

The closing submissions are the opportunity for the parties to explain their view of the relevant law and their understanding of the facts and to bring these two strands of their case together.

Ordinarily, the taxpayer will go first, followed by HMRC, with the taxpayer then being able to reply. This right of reply given to the taxpayer is to ensure that any arguments raised by HMRC in their closing submissions are able to be challenged (in that the taxpayer is not necessarily required to pre-empt such arguments in the taxpayer's own closing submissions). Those arguments that feature in HMRC's skeleton argument should be dealt with in the course of the taxpayer's main submissions and not left to the reply.

HMRC can rightly object to new arguments being raised at this stage, although a tribunal might deviate from this rule in cases of genuine oversight – but, to ensure a fair trial, the tribunal would then invite HMRC to respond to the additional arguments.

8.8.5 Revised order where burden of proof lies on HMRC

In those cases where the burden of proof falls on HMRC this normal order will be revised to reflect the fact that it is for HMRC to prove their case. So they should present their evidence before the taxpayer.

Arguably, HMRC also ought to make their closing submissions first in such cases, with the taxpayer replying and HMRC then responding to any new points raised by the taxpayer. However, as happened in *Stockler*, the tribunal will often revert to the more conventional order so as to allow the taxpayer the right to the final word.

Case: *Stockler v HMRC* [2012] UKFTT 404 (TC)

8.8.6 Cases where the burden of proof falls on both parties

In many cases, however, the burden of proof will fall on the taxpayer in respect of one part of the case and on HMRC in respect of the other. This will often be the situation in the typical "back-duty" case where the taxpayer will be required to disprove the amount of tax assessed, but HMRC are required to show that the conditions for a discovery assessment and/or a penalty are met.

In *Amis v Colls*, Cross J considered that there were two alternative approaches that HMRC could adopt. Either:

- HMRC could open the entire case and call all their evidence "as though the onus was on [them] to support all the additional assessments"; or
- they could limit their opening to such matters where the burden of proof lies on them and leave any remaining issues to be dealt with in the more conventional way (i.e. by the taxpayer making the initial submissions).

In *Hurley v Taylor*, Park J referred to *Amis v Colls* and concluded that, in such cases, a tribunal was possibly bound to permit HMRC to open proceedings.

In *Charlton*, in the Upper Tribunal, although it was HMRC's appeal, there were matters that were subject of a "cross appeal" by the taxpayer where the taxpayer was challenging certain aspects of the decision of the First-tier. In that case, the Upper Tribunal heard submissions in the following order:

- HMRC's submissions in relation to their appeal (plus pre-emptive reply to arguments raised in the taxpayer's skeleton argument);
- the taxpayer's submissions in relation to HMRC's appeal and the taxpayer's submissions in relation to the cross appeal;
- HMRC's reply in relation to their appeal and HMRC's response to the taxpayer's cross appeal;
- the taxpayer's reply in relation to the cross appeal.

Cases: *Amis v Colls (HM Inspector of Taxes)* (1960) 39 TC 148; *Hurley v Taylor (HM Inspector of Taxes)* (1998) 71 TC 268, [1998] STC 202, [1998] BTC 32; *HMRC v Charlton (and others)* [2012] UKFTT 770 (TCC)

8.8.7 Cases where there is more than one taxpayer

On some occasions, a hearing will involve more than one taxpayer. This will be more common in situations where there is some connection between the taxpayers (for example, employer and employee) where the underlying facts and issues are the same.

On those occasions, the interests of the different taxpayers will usually be aligned (in that the taxpayers will be arguing for the same result). Consequently, it will usually be the case that the hearing will proceed in precisely the same way as if there were a single taxpayer.

It is suggested that this will also be the case where the taxpayers have competing interests. For example, in a CGT valuation case, one party's disposal proceeds would be another's acquisition cost: the party making the disposal will usually want to argue for a lower value, and the party making the acquisition wanting a higher value.

There will be some rare instances where two (or more) unconnected cases will be heard together. This will arise only if the issues raised in those cases are so similar that it is considered by the tribunal to be more efficient for them to be argued at the same hearing. See rules 5 and 18 (at **4.2** and **4.16** respectively).

On such occasions, the tribunal will decide on the appropriate running order but it is most likely to involve the two (or more) taxpayers presenting their cases in succession with HMRC then responding to those two cases etc.

8.8.8 Submissions after the hearing

In some cases, an unexpected issue will arise during the course of a hearing which merits further comment from the parties. Alternatively, the parties or the tribunal will be aware of another case (perhaps in a higher court) whose outcome will have an impact on the case currently before the tribunal. In those cases, the tribunal might ask the parties to make further submissions to deal with the new issues that arise. Usually, those additional submissions will be in written form, but in rare cases it might be appropriate for a further hearing to take place before a final decision is given by the tribunal.

In *Scofield*, for example, the tribunal unilaterally raised a point of law for which the parties at the original hearing were unprepared. In that case, the tribunal issued a preliminary decision in writing, but it is not usually necessary to do so.

Very occasionally, it will occur to one of the parties (after a hearing has taken place but before a decision is given) that additional arguments or facts should have been put before the tribunal. As a general rule, a party ought not to be given a second bite of the cherry and one should not expect the tribunal to admit further comment on the case. However, ultimately, it is a balancing exercise between the competing interests of the parties and the efficient use of the tribunal's resources. The tribunal will not want to (and should not) be seen to be giving parties an indefinite right to put forward new facts and arguments, but it retains the inherent flexibility to do so when justice so dictates. It is considered by the author that the tribunal should be more amenable to a submission concerning a binding authority which would determine the case but which had been previously overlooked, than additional evidence that the parties could have produced (but failed to produce) in time for the original hearing. On the other hand, if late evidence comes to light and it would not have been reasonable to expect that evidence to have been available any earlier, then a tribunal should (if considered just) be more willing to admit it.

Case: *Scofield v HMRC* [2010] UKFTT 377 (TC)

8.9 Reference to earlier cases

It is a major part of the country's legal system that decisions from the higher courts (including the Upper Tribunal) are considered to be binding on lower courts including the FTT. Consequently, it will often be helpful to support one's case by referring the tribunal to relevant case law (or "precedents").

The tribunal's directions will state when such case law (if at all) should be provided to the other parties. Although not binding on the tribunal, other decisions of the tribunal on the same point (or cases with a very similar factual basis) can be helpful and should also be provided. However, as held in *Charles*, this should not usually be done if there is actual binding precedent from a higher court.

As noted in *Griffiths*, notwithstanding the fact that First-tier decisions are not binding, an informal, but well-established, practice known as judicial comity sometimes precludes a judge from taking a different stance from that previously taken by a colleague, unless the judge is persuaded that the colleague was "clearly wrong".

Cases: *Charles t/a Boston Computer Group Europe v HMRC* [2014] UKFTT 481 (TC); *JRO Griffiths Ltd v HMRC* [2021] UKFTT 257

8.10 Decisions

In simpler cases, as well as at most directions hearings, a decision will be announced to the parties at the hearing itself. The procedures are discussed in **Chapter 9**.

In some cases, however, a decision will not be communicated to the parties until several weeks (or, in some cases, several months) after the hearing. For such cases, see **8.10.2**.

8.10.1 Not unanimous decisions

In most cases (assuming there to be more than one judge), the decision of the tribunal is unanimous. However, there are a few occasions when there are two individuals sitting on the tribunal and they cannot agree on a particular issue.

In such instances, the case is determined in accordance with the majority of those sitting on the tribunal. For this purpose, members and judges have equal ranking.

However, the most common number of individuals to sit on a tribunal (if not one judge or member alone) is two. In such cases, it is provided for in the *First-tier Tribunal and Upper Tribunal (Composition of Tribunal) Order* 2008 that the person chairing the actual hearing (usually, the more senior judge) has a casting vote.

Law: SI 2008/2835, art. 8

Effect of the casting vote

When the casting vote relates to a question of law, there will rarely be significant consequences of the wrong exercise of the casting vote, provided that the case proceeds on further appeal to the Upper Tribunal or beyond.

However, where the dispute is one of fact, the casting vote could be critical to the outcome of the case.

Exercise of the casting vote

Historically, there had been a tradition that, where there was a deadlock in the General or Special Commissioners, the taxpayer would be deemed to win in a case where the dispute concerned the assessability of income, but the Revenue would be deemed to win if the dispute concerned the availability of a relief. This was effected by one of the Commissioners opting to step down so as to ensure a majority was achieved. Although this practice can be evidenced from some very old cases, there was no clear statutory authority for it.

In 1994, however, the procedural rules for hearings before the Commissioners were recast. They newly provided that, in the event of a tie, the presiding Commissioner should have a casting vote. This change did not prove to have any practical significance until the *Arctic Systems* case (*Jones v Garnett*). That was the first case to experience a tie since the introduction of the specific rule referring to a casting vote. In that case, the more senior Special Commissioner interpreted the provision as allowing her vote to trump that of the other Special Commissioner.

The taxpayer appealed against the exercise of the casting vote (as well as the substantive decision), arguing that the casting vote had to be exercised judiciously and did not simply give the judge a second vote. Although *Arctic Systems* was argued all the way to the House of Lords (and the exercise of the casting vote was raised both in the High

Court and in the Court of Appeal), no judicial comment was made as to the appropriateness of the Special Commissioner's approach.

However, the same approach was followed in two subsequent cases in the Special Commissioners (*Limitgood* and *Vodafone 2*) and, subsequently, in the joint decision of the Upper and First-tier Tribunals in *Reed*. It should be noted that the exercise of the casting vote in *Limitgood* was consistent with the previous practice (in that the taxpayer was deemed to win) and in *Vodafone 2* and *Reed*, the decisions were more procedural in nature.

In more recent cases, it has become clear that the tribunal's practice is simply to allow the more senior judge to outvote the other. The appropriateness of this has not been considered judicially, even though some of the cases have progressed to the Upper Tribunal and beyond.

Cases: *Jones v Garnett (HM Inspector of Taxes)* (2004) Sp C 432; *Limitgood Ltd v HMRC* (2007) Sp C 612; *Vodafone 2 v HMRC* (2007) Sp C 622; *Reed Employment plc v HMRC* [2010] UKFTT 596 (TC) (a joint decision of the First-tier and Upper Tribunals)

8.10.2 Decision notices issued after the hearing

In many cases (particularly those in which the tribunal needs to consider the arguments before it), a detailed decision notice will be e-mailed or posted to the parties some time after the hearing.

On average, this process will take about six weeks but longer periods are not unheard of.

Such decision notices will usually be published on the tribunal's website and other databases which show the results of decided cases, but there is usually a short interval between the time when a decision is notified to the parties and it being formally published. However, this cannot be relied upon.

Theoretically, this interval permits the parties to request or suggest any corrections of a typographical nature, but not ones that substantively change a finding of fact or a conclusion on the law reached by the tribunal. In addition, this interval could be useful in those cases where a party is concerned that particularly sensitive information is included in the decision notice despite an undertaking by the tribunal to exclude such details (see **7.4.3**).

However, that is not the purpose of the interval (which simply permits decisions to be published in batches). Therefore, in cases of sensitive information, it is recommended that concerns are clearly and unambiguously articulated to the tribunal at the hearing itself.

Although the decision notices are not formally published until some time later, parties who wish to appeal against them (or to seek a review or set aside) (see **Chapter 9** below) should note that the time limits run from the date on which the decision notices were sent to the respective party and not any later date on which the decisions are made publicly available.

9. Procedures after a hearing

9.1 Rule 34 – Consent orders

> 34(1) The Tribunal may, at the request of the parties but only if it considers it appropriate, make a consent order disposing of the proceedings and making such other appropriate provision as the parties have agreed.
>
> 34(2) Notwithstanding any other provision of these Rules, the Tribunal need not hold a hearing before making an order under paragraph (1), or provide reasons for the order.

9.1.1 Overview

Sometimes the parties will reach a settlement before the hearing takes place (or, occasionally, after the hearing but before a decision is given). Rule 34 permits any settlement to be formally recognised by the tribunal in the form of a consent order.

Such an order will have the force of having been given by the tribunal. However, the tribunal need not provide any reasons for the order.

9.1.2 When a consent order will be given

By definition, a consent order will require the consent of each of the parties. However, the tribunal must also consider it appropriate.

Therefore, for example, a tribunal that considers the terms of the proposed consent order to be unfair to one party could well refuse to implement it. However, if the parties have relatively equal bargaining power, the tribunal is unlikely to intervene unless it positively considers the proposed order to be contrary to justice.

It could be that the consent order represents only part of an overall settlement by the parties (perhaps because other aspects of the dispute are not before the tribunal): the tribunal should consider the overall fairness when reaching its decision.

9.1.3 When a consent order should be given

In *Rasam Gayatri*, HMRC applied to the tribunal for the striking out of the taxpayer's appeal because HMRC had by then withdrawn the disputed decision. The tribunal refused HMRC's application. Instead, it held that, despite HMRC's apparent withdrawal of the decision, the matter still lay with the tribunal. In fact, HMRC had not actually withdrawn their opposition to the appeal.

In such a case, the appropriate course of action would be for the parties to settle the proceedings by way of a consent order. Where HMRC had withdrawn the appealable decision then the consent order would ordinarily "allow" the appeal. However, as noted in *Fife*, if the appeal itself is premature, the more appropriate course of action would be for the appeal to be struck out for lack of jurisdiction (see **4.6.3**). (In *Fife*, the terminology used was "dismissed" but that is a consequence of the case being considered under the Scottish Tribunal rules where the wording is slightly different.)

The procedure is particularly relevant if the winning party is entitled to a costs order: a consent order would enable that to happen, whereas a withdrawal would not (or a costs order would be harder to come by).

Similarly, if the ultimate settlement reached between the parties has wider repercussions (for example, the taxation of future transactions), it would be better for that to be recorded as part of a consent order from the tribunal as happened in *GE*.

Cases: *Rasam Gayatri Silks Ltd v HMRC* [2010] UKFTT 50 (TC); *GE International Inc v HMRC* [2010] UKFTT 343 (TC); *Fife Resources Solutions LLP v Revenue Scotland* [2018] FTSTC 1

9.2 Rule 35 – Notice of decisions and reasons

35(1) The Tribunal may give a decision orally at a hearing.

35(2) The Tribunal must provide to each party within 28 days after making a decision (other than a decision under Part 4) which finally disposes of all issues in proceedings or of a preliminary issue dealt with following a direction under rule 5(3)(e) or as soon as practicable thereafter, a decision notice which–

(a) states the Tribunal's decision; and

(b) notifies the party of any right of appeal against the decision and the time within which, and the manner in which, the right of appeal may be exercised.

> 35(3) Unless each party agrees that it is unnecessary, the decision notice must–
>
> > (a) include a summary of the findings of fact and reasons for the decision; or
> >
> > (b) be accompanied by full written findings of fact and reasons for the decision.
>
> 35(4) If the Tribunal provides no findings and reasons, or summary findings and reasons only, in or with the decision notice, a party to the proceedings may apply for full written findings and reasons, and must do so before making an application for permission to appeal under rule 39 (application for permission to appeal).
>
> 35(5) An application under paragraph (4) must be made in writing and be sent or delivered to the Tribunal so that it is received within 28 days after the date that the Tribunal sent or otherwise provided the decision notice under paragraph (2) to the party making the application.
>
> 35(6) The Tribunal must send a full written statement of findings and reasons to each party within 28 days after receiving an application for full written reasons made in accordance with paragraphs (4) and (5), or as soon as practicable thereafter.

9.2.1 Overview

Rule 35 provides that decisions may be given orally at a hearing. However, a written decision notice is also necessary.

The rule continues to discuss the requirements for written decision notices and how full decisions may be obtained.

In *Mavisat*, the tribunal was asked to delay announcing its decision pending the determination of separate proceedings involving another taxpayer. The tribunal considered that any such delay would not be in the interests of justice, but noted that different considerations might apply in cases where the tribunal is dealing with mere procedural matters.

In *Skelly*, the tribunal held that, in cases being dealt with under the provisions in rule 19 (proceedings with only one party), there was no obligation for the tribunal to provide a decision notice to a non-party.

Cases: *Mavisat Ltd v HMRC* [2012] UKFTT 253 (TC); *Skelly v HMRC* [2014] UKFTT 478 (TC)

9.2.2   Minimum requirements for decision notices

Even when a decision is given orally, a written decision notice should still be sent to the parties within 28 days (or as soon as is practicable afterwards).

The absolute minimum requirements

The decision notice must contain:

- the decision itself (e.g. "the appeal is allowed" or "the tax assessed is amended to £1,000"); and
- details of the parties' right to appeal (if any, see **9.6.2** below) and the time limits for exercising those rights.

The additional requirements – findings of facts

It will be seen that the bare minimum for a decision notice will contain no explanation of the tribunal's reasoning. In most cases, more information will be provided by the tribunal and the default position is that more information should be provided. However, the parties can decide that this additional information is unnecessary and the tribunal can then dispense with these additional requirements.

Where there is no such agreement for the additional information to be dispensed with then the tribunal must provide a statement of its findings of facts and its reasons for its decision.

The tribunal can choose whether to give its findings of facts and its reasons in summary form or in full.

9.2.3   Request for full findings of facts and reasons (rule 35(4)—(6))

Any party may request a full statement of the tribunal's findings of facts and the tribunal's reasons for a decision. This might be because of curiosity or if the party is considering an appeal. (A full statement is necessary before the appeal process can commence. See rule 39.)

Clearly, no such request is necessary if the tribunal has already issued a full decision on its own initiative. However, in other cases, a party may request a full statement (even if the parties had previously indicated that a summary statement would suffice (or even that no statement of facts and reasons was necessary)).

So as to ensure that the decision is still relatively fresh in the tribunal's minds, a request should be made within 28 days of the tribunal sending or providing the decision notice to the party.

Late requests for full findings of facts and reasons

If a request is made after the 28-day period, the tribunal has the power to extend the time limit under rule 5(3)(a). Both in *Fraser* and in *A&E*, the tribunal expressly adopted the approach set out at **2.4.4** above when deciding whether to extend time.

Cases: *Fraser v HMRC* [2012] UKFTT 189 (TC); *A&E Services (Midlands) Ltd v HMRC* [2013] UKFTT 644 (TC)

9.2.4 Finality of decisions

In some courts and tribunals, a decision is released to the parties (or, in some cases, the legal representatives only) in draft, usually a few days ahead of the formal publication of the written decision.

The Tax Chamber does not generally adopt this approach. Instead, the usual practice of the Tax Chamber is for decisions to be issued only in their final form. Although the tribunal's practice is to publish its decisions in batches and, accordingly, there is usually a short delay before publication, a decision should be considered as final in the form in which it is first notified to the parties. Indeed, in practice, it is now relatively difficult even for typographical errors to be corrected in the interim.

More importantly, this means that time limits (for example, for asking for permission to appeal) run from the date that the tribunal first sends notice of the decision to the parties.

Minor corrections should be dealt with under the procedures in rule 37.

Where a party considers that a more major error has infected the decision, then the correct approach would be for the party to request permission to appeal under rule 39 (which can lead to a review under rule 41) or, if appropriate, apply for a set aside under rule 38.

The Court of Appeal expressed its stern disapproval of an increasing practice of parties seeking substantive changes to a decision at that late stage in *Egan*. Although the court was particularly concerned with those instances where the decision has been released only in draft form, its comments are relevant to all cases where there is a delay between a decision being issued and its wider publication.

In *OCO*, HMRC were unhappy with a decision made in principle as subsequent case law developments suggested that it was incorrect. They applied to the tribunal for the matter to be reconsidered. However, the tribunal ruled that the procedures by which a party can challenge a decision are as set out in the rules and cannot be supplemented by invoking a freestanding right of the tribunal to revisit its decisions.

Cases: *Egan v Motor Services (Bath) Ltd* [2007] EWCA Civ 1002; *OCO Ltd v HMRC* [2017] UKFTT 603 (TC)

9.2.5 Publication of decisions

It should be noted that the tribunal does not publish all of its decisions. However, the expectation should be that any decision which is not issued at the hearing itself will be a full decision and subsequently published.

It was stated in *Ardmore* that unpublished decisions should not, as a general rule, be cited in later cases. This was to ensure that HMRC (who as party to the vast majority of such decisions would have access to a greater resource of authorities) do not obtain a procedural advantage over taxpayers. It would appear, therefore, that where fairness was not compromised, a party could rely on an unpublished decision.

Case: *Ardmore Construction Ltd v HMRC* [2014] UKFTT 453 (TC)

9.3 Rule 36 – Interpretation

> **36** In this Part–
>
> "appeal" means the exercise of a right of appeal against a decision of the Tribunal; and
>
> "review" means the review of a decision by the Tribunal under section 9 of the 2007 Act.

9.3.1 Overview

This rule simply defines the terms "appeal" and "review" for the purposes of Part 4 of the Tribunal Rules (rules 36 onwards).

9.3.2 Options following a decision

Part 4 deals with the various procedures that are available once a decision has been made by the tribunal. These are:

- correction of accidental errors (see rule 37);
- the setting aside of the decision (see rule 38);
- an appeal against the decision to the Upper Tribunal (see rules 39 and 40);
- a review of the decision (see **9.3.3** and rule 41).

Clearly, a party that has won a case will not be concerned with most of these (except, perhaps, to correct any accidental errors under rule 37). However, that party might not have won on all of its arguments on a particular issue. In such a case, it can of course seek permission to appeal against the aspects on which that party lost.

Matters are a little less straightforward if (as is often the case) the broadly successful party is content to leave things as they are but, when the other side seeks to appeal against the parts of the decision which it lost, the broadly successful party wishes to keep its options open and maintain its challenge on the remaining issues. This is considered in more detail at **9.6.13**.

9.3.3 Appeal

An appeal is the process by which a party challenges a decision of the tribunal; such an appeal would be heard by the Upper Tribunal.

9.3.4 Review

Section 9 of the 2007 Act permits the FTT to review a decision it has made. It effectively gives the tribunal (as opposed to the parties) a second bite of the cherry.

The statutory rules concerning reviews are set out below. However, they should be read in conjunction with rule 41 which deals with their application in the Tax Chamber.

Law: TCEA 2007, s. 9

9.3.5 Who may instigate a review?

The review may be made upon an application by one of the parties. Alternatively, under the Act, the tribunal may undertake a review on its own initiative.

For example, the author is aware of one case where the tribunal appeared to have overlooked a particular statutory provision that would have settled the case in the taxpayer's favour. This was not a case where the taxpayer was professionally represented and it is therefore unlikely that the taxpayer would ever have realised the tribunal's error. It is understood that the tribunal, when becoming aware of the error, undertook a review so as to ensure that the correct outcome was reached without the need for a further appeal.

Under rule 41(1) (see **9.8.2**), however, it is not totally clear that the tribunal had the power to instigate a review without a party first putting in an application for permission to appeal. Nevertheless, even if this requirement was inadvertently overlooked, rule 7(1) (see **4.5.2**) would seem to allow the review to be effective. Furthermore, as suggested in *Couldwell*, the provision in rule 41(1) might be an unlawful restriction on the tribunal's right to review a decision.

In *Rodgers*, the tribunal reviewed its original decision and set it aside after being directed to criticism of the original decision as published in an article in the professional press.

Law: TCEA 2007, s. 9(2)
Cases: *Couldwell Concrete Flooring Ltd v HMRC (No. 2)* [2017] UKFTT 85 (TC); *Rodgers v HMRC* [2018] UKUT 709 (TC)

9.3.6 Consequences of a review

If a review is undertaken by the tribunal, it may as a result decide:

- to do nothing;
- to correct accidental errors in the decision or in a record of the decision;
- to amend reasons given for the decision; or
- to set the decision aside.

The last of these will have the effect of cancelling the original decision. When this occurs the tribunal must either re-decide the matter or refer the case to the Upper Tribunal. In the latter scenario, the case should be re-decided by the Upper Tribunal.

It is suggested that it will be rare for the Upper Tribunal to re-decide a case in this way as this is equivalent to the FTT transferring a Complex case to the Upper Tribunal under rule 28. Of course, there is no requirement that the case be allocated to the Complex case category for the case to be re-decided by the Upper Tribunal and it might be the appropriate course of action where there is an important question of law to be determined. However, the tribunal would need to consider the suitability of the Upper Tribunal hearing the case afresh. See the relevant considerations discussed at **5.11.3** and **5.11.4**.

Law: TCEA 2007, s. 9(4)-(8)

9.3.7 Which decisions may be reviewed?

Virtually any decision made by the tribunal is capable of being reviewed. The exceptions are those decisions known as "excluded decisions" within section 11(5) of the 2007 Act. Those excluded decisions are generally the same as those decisions which may not be subject of an appeal to the Upper Tribunal.

So far as proceedings in the Tax Chamber are concerned, the excluded decisions are:

- any decision made following a review of an earlier decision (but see below);
- a decision not to review an earlier decision;
- any decision that has already been set aside; and

- any decision made under a provision listed in the *Appeals (Excluded Decisions) Order* 2009 including:
  - IHTA 1984, s. 35A(2), 79A(2) (variations of undertakings);
  - TCGA 1992, s. 138(4) (advance clearance for company reconstructions);
  - FA 2000, Sch. 15, para. 91(5) (corporate venturing scheme);
  - FA 2004, s. 306A, 308A, 313B, 314A (disclosure of tax avoidance schemes) (and their equivalents in the *National Insurance Contributions (Application of Part 7 of the Finance Act 2004) Regulations* 2007);
  - ITA 2007, s. 697(4) (transactions in securities: opposed notifications);
  - Venture Capital Trust (Winding up and Mergers) (Tax) Regulations 2004, reg. 10(3) (procedure for approval).

Law: TCEA 2007, s. 9(1), 11(5)(d)-(f); SI 2009/275

9.3.8 When review decisions may be reviewed

As noted in the above list, decisions by the tribunal to review or not to review an earlier decision come within the scope of excluded decisions. Similarly, with any action taken by the tribunal following a review. Therefore, it is not possible for a party to challenge such a decision by way of appeal. In other words, one cannot appeal to the Upper Tribunal any of the following:

- a decision not to review an earlier decision;
- a decision to review an earlier decision;
- a decision to amend an earlier decision following a review;
- a decision not to amend an earlier decision following a review;
- a decision to set aside an earlier decision following a review;
- a decision not to set aside an earlier decision following a review.

Where a party feels that the FTT has acted wrongly in such a way, the only remedy is by way of judicial review: either by showing that the process by which the First-tier reached its second decision was flawed or that no reasonable tribunal could have reached the second decision. Although judicial reviews should ordinarily be commenced at the High Court (or in Scotland, in the Court of Session), a judicial review in relation to a review may actually be commenced in the Upper Tribunal (and, if commenced elsewhere, will be transferred to the Upper Tribunal).

Excluded decisions that may be reviewed

However, although it is generally the case that excluded decisions (i.e. non-appealable) may not be subject of a review, there is actually a very minor exception. If a review has concluded that a decision should be set aside, the decision to set aside the earlier decision may itself be subject to a review. However, that review may lead only to the correction of accidental errors in the later decision: in other words, there cannot be a substantive change.

Law: *Senior Courts Act* 1981, s. 31A; TCEA 2007, s. 9(1), (9), 11(5)(d), 18(6), 20(3); SI 2009/275

Guidance: *Practice Direction (Upper Tribunal: Judicial Review Jurisdiction)*

9.3.9 Reviews after decisions on review

Similarly, a decision may not be reviewed more than once; nor may a decision be reviewed if the tribunal has previously decided not to review it.

However, any new decision reached in a case (i.e. if an earlier decision is set aside and then remade) may be subject to a review as if it were an entirely new decision.

Law: TCEA 2007, s. 9(10), (11)

9.4 Rule 37 – Clerical mistakes and accidental slips or omissions

> 37   The Tribunal may at any time correct any clerical mistake or other accidental slip or omission in a decision, direction or any document produced by it, by–
>
>   (a) sending notification of the amended decision or direction, or a copy of the amended document, to all parties; and

> (b) making any necessary amendment to any information published in relation to the decision, direction or document.

9.4.1 Overview

The rule implements what is often known as the "slip rule". It ensures that minor errors in a decision, direction or other document can be corrected by the tribunal.

In theory, rule 37 allows minor errors to be corrected at any time. However, the practical restriction on corrections is that they will usually be relevant only when an appeal is being contemplated (or is under way) in the Upper Tribunal (or perhaps beyond).

In *Tager*, it was held that the rule was designed to correct the record of what the judge decided, rather than a correction of the judge's actual conclusion.

Case: *Tager v HMRC* [2015] UKUT 663 (TCC)

9.5 Rule 38 – Setting aside a decision which disposes of proceedings

> 38(1) The Tribunal may set aside a decision which disposes of proceedings, or part of such a decision, and re-make the decision, or the relevant part of it, if–
>
> (a) the Tribunal considers that it is in the interests of justice to do so; and
>
> (b) one or more of the conditions in paragraph (2) is satisfied.
>
> 38(2) The conditions are–
>
> (a) a document relating to the proceedings was not sent to, or was not received at an appropriate time by, a party or a party's representative;
>
> (b) a document relating to the proceedings was not sent to the Tribunal at an appropriate time;
>
> (c) there has been some other procedural irregularity in the proceedings; or
>
> (d) a party, or a party's representative, was not present at a hearing related to the proceedings.

> **38(3)** A party applying for a decision, or part of a decision, to be set aside under paragraph (1) must make a written application to the Tribunal so that it is received no later than 28 days after the date on which the Tribunal sent notice of the decision to the party.
>
> **38(4)** If the Tribunal sets aside a decision or part of a decision under this rule, the Tribunal must notify the parties in writing as soon as practicable.

9.5.1 Overview

Rule 38 deals with the first substantive method of challenging a decision by the tribunal: setting the decision aside.

It should be noted that this is a type of application that can be considered by the tribunal without a hearing (see rule 29(2)).

9.5.2 Meaning of "set aside"

If a decision is set aside, it is treated as if it had never been made. It therefore means that a new decision will need to be made in its place (unless the parties manage to reach an agreement in the meantime).

Unlike the position when a decision is set aside following a review (see **9.3.3ff.** and **9.8ff.**), where a new decision may be made by the Upper Tribunal, if a decision is set aside under rule 38, the new decision will have to be made by the FTT.

9.5.3 When a decision may be set aside

There are two conditions for a set aside under rule 38.

The first overriding condition is that the tribunal has to consider a set aside to be in the interests of justice (see **9.5.4**).

The second condition is that one of the following procedural irregularities occurred:

- a document relating to the proceedings was not sent to a party or a party's representative at an appropriate time;
- a document relating to the proceedings was not received by a party or a party's representative at an appropriate time;
- a document relating to the proceedings was not sent to the tribunal at an appropriate time;

- there has been some other procedural irregularity; or
- a party or a party's representative was not present at a hearing relating to the proceedings (including a directions hearing).

This second condition is quite prescriptive: it means that there has to be some kind of procedural error or the absence of a party. This condition provides that the ability to set aside decisions is to be limited to those cases where fairness might dictate that the time and costs of the original hearing should be considered as wasted.

In *Skelly*, the tribunal was considering a case where HMRC had applied for the pre-approval by the tribunal of an information notice under FA 2008, Schedule 36 at a private hearing at which the ultimate recipient of the notice would not be entitled to attend. As a result, rule 19 applied. It was held that, as a result, the provision in rule 38 allowing a decision to be set aside because of the non-attendance of that party was overridden.

There are aspects of that decision, however, that seem to suggest that the entirety of rule 38 is disapplied in cases where rule 19 applies. That would have the effect that no procedural irregularity could be corrected by way of set aside by the tribunal and would have to be challenged by way of judicial review. It is respectfully considered that that would not be correct. In the author's view, the *Skelly* decision is not wrong but should have been justified on a slightly different basis. That is that, notwithstanding the non-attendance at the hearing, it would simply not be in the interests of justice for the earlier decision to be set aside (as required by rule 38(1)(a)).

In *Gulamhussein*, the tribunal considered that, in a default-paper case where no party has sought a hearing, it is not possible to seek a set-aside on the grounds of the party's non-attendance at a hearing.

Cases: *Skelly v HMRC* [2014] UKFTT 478 (TC); *Gulamhussein v HMRC* [2019] UKFTT 261 (TC)

Procedural irregularity

In *Rosenbaum* HMRC failed to present adequate evidence at a hearing which led to a taxpayer's appeal succeeding. They then applied for the decision to be set aside on the grounds that their own failure constituted a procedural irregularity. A similar argument was advanced by the taxpayer in *Girotra* where it was argued that the taxpayer's previous representative had been incompetent. Unsurprisingly, in both cases, the tribunal refused to set aside the decision.

In *Girotra*, it was queried by the tribunal whether the incompetence of party's advocate could actually amount to a procedural irregularity. However, the point was not taken by HMRC and the case proceeded on the basis that it could. On that assumption, the tribunal considered that the incompetence of the representation had to be so extreme that no reasonable representative could have been expected to act that way.

In the author's view, the test for whether a representative's incompetent performance would give rise to a procedural irregularity is whether or not the failures were so extreme that the judge should actually have intervened to ensure compliance with the overriding objective.

In *Gilbert*, the tribunal considered that a failure to deal with specific arguments raised in good time would amount to a procedural irregularity. In contrast, in *Tager*, the tribunal held that an error caused by a judge's failure to understand the evidence or a finding that was not supported by the evidence constituted a judicial error rather than a procedural error and would therefore not fall within the scope of this rule.

Cases: *Executor of the Estate of Teresa Rosenbaum (deceased) v HMRC* [2013] UKFTT 495 (TC); *Girotra v HMRC* [2014] UKFTT 775 (TC); *Tager v HMRC* [2015] UKUT 663 (TCC); *Gilbert v HMRC* [2018] UKFTT 437 (TC)

Non-receipt of a document

In *Fraser* it was made clear that the non-receipt of a document had to amount to a procedural error (i.e. something had gone wrong with the system) and that the failing was therefore something more than one party belatedly deciding to rely on a particular document.

Case: *Fraser v HMRC* [2012] UKFTT 189 (TC)

9.5.4 Interests of justice

A set aside is a more drastic outcome than an appeal because it amounts to going back to "square one" and leads to a fresh new hearing with the evidence being heard again. The interests of justice

9.5 Rule 38 – Setting aside a decision which disposes of proceedings

do not usually allow parties a second bite of the cherry; therefore, the tribunal will have to be persuaded that there are overriding concerns that would make it unjust for the original decision to remain intact.

In other words, even when the second condition above is met (i.e. there is such a procedural error or a party is absent), this does not automatically entitle the decision to be set aside. The tribunal must be persuaded that having a second hearing would be in the interests of justice. This was made clear in *Symbiosis*.

Each case will need to be decided on its own merits. However, the decision in *Wright* is worth noting. In that case, the taxpayer had been successful before the former General Commissioners. On HMRC's appeal to the High Court, it became apparent that an error of law meant that the Commissioners' decision was flawed. There was confusion as to whether this meant a new trial before the Commissioners or merely a reconsideration of their decision in the light of the evidence they had previously heard. Ultimately, the case was listed for a retrial and the General Commissioners transferred jurisdiction of the case to the Special Commissioners. By this time, Mr Wright had raised concerns about how the case was becoming more complicated and, eventually, he intimated that he would not attend the hearing. Perhaps due to his decision not to attend, the Special Commissioners revoked their original decision to have the hearing local to Mr Wright's home and work. In the meantime, HMRC missed some deadlines in providing documents to him; some documents were not sent at all.

Ultimately, the case was reheard in London in Mr Wright's absence and so was decided only with the benefit of evidence from HMRC. It was a case concerning the employment status of casual workers and, as the tribunal held, "the type of case where the inequality of arms is particularly unfortunate". Given the nature and history of the case and, as the tribunal noted, the fact that had HMRC complied more fully and more timeously with the case management directions, Mr Wright might have taken a more active approach to the case, it was held that the interests of justice dictated that the original decision should be set aside and the case retried (effectively for a third time).

In *Mainpay*, the tribunal set aside the decision because it recognised that it had overlooked one ground of appeal. The tribunal noted that the taxpayer's representative at the hearing would not have appreciated the tribunal's oversight and concluded that it was in the interests of justice for the matter to be set aside. The tribunal added that, had Counsel been present instead, the matter would have been different.

The facts of *Rodgers* were unusual. The taxpayer, who could not attend the hearing for personal reasons, was offered to participate by telephone conference facility instead. However, he was not advised of this option in sufficient time. As the tribunal noted:

> "If the Tribunal has decided to offer an opportunity for a party to participate by phone it must be an opportunity of which the party can reasonably avail itself. The fact that the Tribunal might have chosen not to make this facility available, and was under no obligation to do so, is irrelevant. The fact that the Appellant did not attempt to participate by phone after receiving the letter is not to the point."

The original decision in *Rodgers* was accordingly set aside.

Cases: *Wright v HMRC* [2009] UKFTT 227 (TC); *Rodgers v HMRC* [2018] UKUT 709 (TC); *Mainpay Ltd v HMRC* [2018] UKFTT 665 (TC); *Symbiosis Imedia Systems Ltd v HMRC* [2019] UKFTT 124 (TC)

Medical absence not necessarily sufficient

In *Decker*, the High Court gave the following guidance:

> "A court faced with an application to adjourn on medical grounds made for the first time by a litigant in person should be hesitant to refuse the application ... This, however, is subject to a number of qualifications [including the following].
>
> First, the decision is always one for the court to make, and not one that can be forced upon it. Parties who think that they thereby compel the Court not to proceed with the hearing or that their non-attendance somehow strengthens the application for an adjournment are deeply mistaken. The decision whether or not to adjourn remains one for the judge.
>
> Secondly, the court must scrutinise carefully the evidence relied on in support of the application. Such evidence should identify the medical attendant and give details of his familiarity with the party's medical condition (detailing all recent consultations), should identify with particularity what the

9.5 Rule 38 – Setting aside a decision which disposes of proceedings

patient's medical condition is and the features of that condition which (in the medical attendant's opinion) prevent participation in the trial process, should provide a reasoned prognosis and should give the court some confidence that what is being expressed is an independent opinion after a proper examination. It is being tendered as expert evidence. The court can then consider what weight to attach to that opinion, and what arrangements might be made (short of an adjournment) to accommodate a party's difficulties. No judge is bound to accept expert evidence: even a proper medical report falls to be considered simply as part of the material as a whole (including the previous conduct of the case)."

Accordingly, in *Robb*, the tribunal rejected an application for a decision to be set aside in a case where the absence was due to medical reasons. The medical evidence was inadequate: it did not address the question as to whether the appellant's medical condition prevented both his attendance and preparation for the hearing. Furthermore, the appellant had previously accepted that the case might have to proceed in his absence.

Cases: *Decker v Hopcraft* [2015] EWHC 1170 (QB); *Robb v HMRC* [2017] UKFTT 232 (TC)

9.5.5 Time limit for applications

Rule 38(3) requires applications for a set aside to be made within 28 days of the decision notice being sent. However, rule 5(3)(a) allows this time limit to be extended.

If a request is made after the 28-day period, the tribunal has the power to extend the time limit under rule 5(3)(a). In *Fraser*, the tribunal expressly adopted the approach set out at **2.4.4** above when deciding whether to extend time.

Furthermore, rule 42 permits an application for permission to appeal (for which there is a 56-day time limit) to be treated as if it were an application for the decision to be set aside.

However, in *Cummaford*, it was held that once a decision has been made on permission to appeal, the tribunal may not then consider a set aside application.

Cases: *Fraser v HMRC* [2012] UKFTT 189 (TC); *Cummaford v HMRC* [2015] UKFTT 675 (TC)

9.6 Rule 39 – Application for permission to appeal

39(1) A person seeking permission to appeal must make a written application to the Tribunal for permission to appeal.

39(2) An application under paragraph (1) must be sent or delivered to the Tribunal so that it is received no later than 56 days after the latest of the dates that the Tribunal sends to the person making the application–

(za) the relevant decision notice;

(a) where–

   (i) the decision disposes of all issues in the proceedings; or

   (ii) subject to paragraph (2A), the decision disposes of a preliminary issue dealt with following a direction under rule 5(3)(e),

   full written reasons for the decision;

(b) notification of amended reasons for, or correction of, the decision following a review; or

(c) notification that an application for the decision to be set aside has been unsuccessful.

39(2A) The Tribunal may direct that the 56 days within which a party may send or deliver an application for permission to appeal against a decision that disposes of a preliminary issue shall run from the date of the decision that disposes of all issues in the proceedings.

39(3) The date in paragraph (2)(c) applies only if the application for the decision to be set aside was made within the time stipulated in rule 38 (setting aside a decision which disposes of proceedings), or any extension of that time granted by the Tribunal.

> 39(4) If the person seeking permission to appeal sends or delivers the application to the Tribunal later than the time required by paragraph (2) or by any extension of time under rule 5(3)(a) (power to extend time)–
>
> (a) the application must include a request for an extension of time and the reason why the application notice was not provided in time; and
>
> (b) unless the Tribunal extends time for the application under rule 5(3)(a) (power to extend time) the Tribunal must not admit the application.
>
> 39(5) An application under paragraph (1) must–
>
> (a) identify the decision of the Tribunal to which it relates;
>
> (b) identify the alleged error or errors in the decision; and
>
> (c) state the result the party making the application is seeking.

9.6.1 Overview

Unlike the rules applicable before 2009, an unsuccessful party does not have the automatic right to appeal against a decision. Under the Tribunal Rules, permission must be obtained first before an appeal can be heard by the Upper Tribunal. Rule 39 provides the mechanics for applying for permission.

Can a previously excluded party make an application for permission?

The *BPP* case was decided in the absence of HMRC who, earlier on in proceedings, had been barred from any future participation (see **4.6.8** above). The tribunal was then obliged to consider how the rules operated in such circumstances.

The tribunal felt unable to decide whether or not HMRC had the right to seek permission to appeal against the tribunal's decision. It chose to await such time as HMRC actually sought permission before ruling on the point.

Case: *BPP University College of Professional Studies Ltd v HMRC* [2018] UKFTT 454 (TC)

9.6.2 Excluded decisions

Statute has provided that certain types of decision may not be the subject of an appeal. The list of such decisions is very similar (but not identical) to the list of decisions that may not be the subject of a review (see **9.3.7** above).

In the context of Tax Chamber proceedings, the following have been declared as excluded decisions:

- a decision to review an earlier decision;
- a decision not to review an earlier decision;
- a decision not to act (or not to take any particular action) following a review of an earlier decision;
- a decision to set aside an earlier decision;
- a decision to refer a matter to the Upper Tribunal;
- a decision not to refer a matter to the Upper Tribunal;
- a decision that has already been set aside following a review (see **9.3.6** above); and
- any decision made under a provision listed in the *Appeals (Excluded Decisions) Order* 2009 including:
    - IHTA 1984, s. 35A(2), 79A(2) (variations of undertakings);
    - TCGA 1992, s. 138(4) (advance clearance for company reconstructions);
    - FA 2000, Sch. 15, para. 91(5) (corporate venturing scheme);
    - FA 2004, s. 306A, 308A, 313B, 314A (disclosure of tax avoidance schemes) (and their equivalents in the *National Insurance Contributions (Application of Part 7 of the Finance Act 2004) Regulations* 2007);
    - ITA 2007, s. 697(4) (transactions in securities: opposed notifications);
    - Venture Capital Trust (Winding up and Mergers) (Tax) Regulations 2004, reg. 10(3) (procedure for approval).

It was held in *LS* that any other decision in a case (for example, to strike out an appeal under rule 8) would not be an excluded decision and may therefore be challenged on appeal. Challenges to excluded decisions must be made by way of judicial review.

Law: TCEA 2007, s. 11(1), (5)(d)-(f); SI 2009/275
Case: *LS v London Borough of Lambeth (HB)* [2010] UKUT 461 (AAC)

9.6.3 Other unappealable decisions

Furthermore, various other statutory provisions which provide for matters to be heard by the FTT specify that the First-tier's decisions are final (thereby preventing an appeal to be made against the First-tier's decision to the Upper Tribunal). Those provisions are:

- FA 2008, Sch. 36, para. 6(4) (pre-approval by the tribunal of information notices and the tribunal's disapplication of the duty to copy third-party notices to the taxpayer);
- FA 2008, Sch. 36, para. 13(3) (pre-approval by the tribunal of HMRC inspections of premises and property and the tribunal's disapplication of the duty to allow the occupier of premises the reasonable opportunity to make representations);
- FA 2008, Sch. 36, para. 32(5) (although taxpayers may appeal against other information notices to the FTT, the tribunal's decision may not be the subject of a further appeal to the Upper Tribunal);
- TIOPA 2010, Sch. 7A, para. 63 (third-party information notices in relation to the soft corporate interest restriction rules);
- FA 2011, Sch. 23, para. 5(6) and 29(5) (appeals under HMRC's other data-gathering powers);
- FA 2012, Sch. 38, para. 13(3) (tribunal's approval of a file access notice in respect of a tax agent's or another person's records);
- FA 2012, Sch. 38, para. 20(6) (although there is a limited right of a recipient of a file access notice to appeal to the FTT, the tribunal's decision may not be the subject of a further appeal to the Upper Tribunal);
- FA 2014, s. 266(10) (appeals against information notices issued to recipients of Conduct Notices under the Promoters of Tax Avoidance Scheme rules);

- FA 2017, Sch. 10, para. 11 (hardship applications in relation to the soft drinks industry levy);
- FA 2020, Sch. 8, para. 46 (postponement applications in relation to the digital services tax); and
- FA 2021, Sch. 11, para. 11 (hardship applications in relation to the plastic packaging tax).

In *Lee*, appeals against information notices were struck out (rather than simply dismissed) because the information sought constituted a statutory record (and therefore no appeal lay against such an information notice). The tribunal followed *LS* and declared that a right of appeal lay against the striking out of the appeals, even though no right of appeal to the Upper Tribunal would have been available had the taxpayer's appeal to the First-tier simply been dismissed.

In a previous edition of this work, the author's stated opinion was that *Lee* was wrongly decided on this point. Instead it was considered that the statutory provision that deems the tribunal's decision to be final actually precludes any challenge by way of appeal, even if the tribunal's decision amounts to a striking out of the case. The author's view was subsequently confirmed by the Upper Tribunal in *Jordan*. Thus, any challenge to the tribunal's decision must be by way of judicial review.

There are other provisions that purport to ensure that the decision of the FTT is final (subject to judicial review). These were inserted into the statute by regulations that were meant to effect the transfer of functions from the pre-2009 tribunals to the present arrangement. However, it was held in *Totel* that those regulations were *ultra vires* to the extent that they curtailed an existing right of appeal. Decisions of the FTT that will therefore be appealable, notwithstanding the legislation apparently denying any right of further appeal, are as follows:

- TMA 1970, s. 33(4) (error and mistake claims for claims made before 1 April 2010);
- TMA 1970, s. 55(4) (postponement of tax following an appeal);
- VATA 1994, s. 84(3B)(b) (VAT hardship applications);
- FA 1994, s. 60(4A)(b) (insurance premium tax hardship applications);

9.6 Rule 39 – Application for permission to appeal

- FA 1996, s. 55(3A)(b) (landfill tax hardship applications);
- FA 2000, Sch. 6, para. 122(2A)(b) (climate change levy hardship applications);
- FA 2001, s. 41(2A)(b) (aggregates levy hardship applications); and
- SI 2007/1509 (*The Control of Cash (Penalties) Regulations 2007*), reg. 7 (money laundering penalties).

Law: FA 2008, Sch. 36, para. 6(4), 13(3), 32(5); FA 2011, Sch. 23, para. 5(6), 29(5); FA 2012, Sch. 38, para. 13(3), 20(6)

Cases: *Lee v HMRC* [2012] UKFTT 312 (TC); *LS v London Borough of Lambeth (HB)* [2010] UKUT 461 (AAC); *R (oao Totel Ltd) v First-tier Tribunal (Tax Chamber) and HMRC* [2012] EWCA Civ 1401; *Jordan v HMRC* [2015] UKUT 218 (TCC)

9.6.4 Error of law

The rules preserve the one restriction that applied before 2009 to further appeals: an appeal may be made from the tribunal only on an error of law. An error of law is one concerning a legal principle or the interpretation of a statutory provision.

The corollary is that errors of facts cannot form the basis of an appeal.

The distinction can be best demonstrated by way of examples.

Example 1

In *Veltema*, the taxpayer was appealing against a discovery assessment made under TMA 1970, section 29. In order for the assessment to be valid, HMRC needed to show either:

- that the taxpayer's return had contained an error due to negligent or fraudulent conduct; or
- that the information on the return would not have been sufficient to alert the Revenue to the insufficiency of the

At the General Commissioners, the taxpayer won on both points.

The first was a finding of fact which the Revenue did not (and could not) challenge. However, in respect of the second, the Revenue's challenge was that the General Commissioners had misapplied the statutory test. That amounted to a question of law and enabled the appeal to proceed on the second point alone.

Example 2

In *Grace*, the taxpayer was held by the Special Commissioner to have been neither resident nor ordinarily resident during the six years under investigation.

Such a finding is generally a finding of fact which cannot be challenged on appeal. However, it was held by the Court of Appeal that errors of law had been made by the Special Commissioner when making her decision. Consequently, the decision could not stand and the matter was required to be remitted to the tribunal for further consideration.

Law: TMA 1970, s. 29(4), (5)
Cases: *Langham (HM Inspector of Taxes) v Veltema* [2004] EWCA Civ 193; *HMRC v Grace* [2009] EWCA Civ 1082

9.6.5 When an error of fact can be an error of law

There will be instances, however, when an error of fact can be challenged on appeal as if it were an error of law. The leading case on this is *Edwards v Bairstow*. In that case, Viscount Radcliffe held that there would be an error of law if "the true and only reasonable conclusion [on the basis of the evidence before a tribunal] contradicts the determination [made by the tribunal]".

In such a case, it would be possible for an appellate court to substitute its finding of fact for the erroneous one.

Furthermore, the Supreme Court held in *Pendragon* that the tribunals should be more flexible as to what amounts to an appealable error of law, although this invitation has rarely been taken up since.

Where no error of law is detected, then the appellate court is required to dismiss the appeal even if the court would be minded to reach a different conclusion on its own understanding of the facts. This was most clearly demonstrated in the *Lysaght* case, where two of the law lords who allowed the Revenue's appeal stated that they would have found for the taxpayer on the facts.

Cases: *Edwards (HM Inspector of Taxes) v Bairstow & Harrison* (1955) 36 TC 207; *HMRC v Pendragon plc* [2015] UKSC 37; *Lysaght v Commissioners of Inland Revenue* (1927) 13 TC 511

9.6.6 Other procedural errors

In very rare cases, it may also be possible to mount an appeal because of a procedural failing by the tribunal. For example, if a key piece of evidence is unaccountably overlooked by the tribunal, the decision will be flawed and susceptible to appeal. However, in such cases, a set aside application (rule 38) might be worth pursuing in the first instance.

Inadequate statement of reasons

In *Flannery*, the Court of Appeal held that there must be an adequate statement of reasons in a decision:

> "... the parties especially the losing party should be left in no doubt why they have won or lost. This is especially so since without reasons the losing party will not know (as was said in *Ex p Dave*) whether the court has misdirected itself, and thus whether he may have an available appeal on the substance of the case. The second is that a requirement to give reasons concentrates the mind; if it is fulfilled, the resulting decision is much more likely to be soundly based on the evidence than if it is not."

The absence of a sufficient statement of reasons would therefore also be grounds for appeal.

In *Barke*, the Court of Appeal held that the appropriate course of action on any successful appeal on such a ground would ordinarily be to remit the case to a differently-constituted tribunal to avoid the risk of a tribunal supplementing its earlier decision with better reasons.

It is thought that appeals based on inadequacy of reasons and other procedural errors would more likely be dealt with by way of review (which rule 41 provides is something that should be considered prior to the FTT considering whether to give permission for an appeal).

However, at whichever tribunal the inadequacy of the original decision is determined, it is suggested that the procedure for a remittal for a fresh hearing should be the same.

Cases: *Flannery v Halifax Estate Agencies Ltd (t/a Colleys Professional Services)* [2000] 1 WLR 377; *Barke v SEETEC Business Technology Centre Ltd* [2005] EWCA Civ 578

9.6.7 *Application for permission (rule 39(1), (5))*

An application for permission to appeal must be made in writing. Although the 2007 Act provides that permission may be given either by the FTT or by the Upper Tribunal, the *Upper Tribunal Rules* require permission first to have been requested from the First-tier (and the First-tier to have refused the application or (if it was late) to have refused to admit it).

The application for permission must include the following information:

- the decision to which it relates;
- the alleged error or errors in the decision; and
- the result (i.e. a set aside, the correction etc.) that the person making the application is seeking.

A standard application form is included on the tribunal's website. That standard form (at time of writing) suggests that representatives who are not legal representatives (see **4.9.3** above) cannot sign the form without the client's authorisation. However, in many cases, the representative will already have been authorised by the client at an earlier stage in the proceedings. In such cases, it is not strictly necessary for that authorisation to be repeated (and it is understood that the form or accompanying guidance may be revised to reflect that). It should be noted that, if the case is subsequently taken to the Upper Tribunal, the client's permission will once again be required as the Upper Tribunal will not be governed by the previous authorisation given to the First-tier.

9.6   Rule 39 – Application for permission to appeal

In a practice statement issued by the Chamber President in May 2013, it was made clear that an application does not need to be copied to the other party. That will be done by the tribunal itself upon receipt.

Law: TCEA 2007, s. 11(4); SI 2008/2698, rule 21(2)

Guidance: https://tinyurl.com/yhs2u3bz (Form T247: Application for permission to appeal decision of the Tax Tribunal); https://tinyurl.com/3rkr2pay (Practice statement: application for permission to appeal)

9.6.8   Time limit for applying for permission (rule 39(2), (2A), (3))

The basic time limit for applying for permission to appeal is 56 days. (This compares very favourably with the three-week time limit applicable in most civil litigation.)

The 56-day period runs from the day immediately following the latest of the following events:

- the full written reasons for the decision were given (noting that these are a pre-requisite for an appeal; see **9.2.3** above);
- the notification of any amendments or correction of the decision following a review (as opposed to minor corrections under rule 37); and
- provided that the application for a set aside was made within the 28-day period (see **9.5.5** above), the notification that the application was unsuccessful.

In cases where the tribunal has determined a matter as a preliminary issue, it has been expressly provided with effect from 1 April 2013 that the tribunal may direct that the 56-day period can run from the date of the decision that deals with the whole case.

When is a document "sent" (rule 39(2))?

For a case concerning the effect of time limits when a document is sent to the wrong address, see the discussion of the *Rana* case in the context of rule 5(3)(a).

Case: *Rana v London Borough of Ealing* [2018] EWCA Civ 2074

9.6.9 Extending the time limit for applying for permission (rule 39(4))

A party may ask the tribunal to extend the time limit under rule 5(3)(a).

If the application for permission to appeal is made outside the 56-day time limit (or, if an extension was granted, it was still made later than the extended time limit), the application must include an application for a retrospective extension (or further extension) of time and a reason why the application was made late.

Factors to be considered for late applications for permission

It is suggested that the tribunal should consider factors similar to those in **2.4.4** above. However, the question of fading memories and the risk of the loss of evidence will not usually be relevant in respect of an appeal to the Upper Tribunal.

On the other hand, if a case is likely to be remitted back to the tribunal for further evidence, it is possible that this will become a relevant factor.

Consequences of a late application

If the tribunal refuses to admit the late application, the party seeking permission may pursue the appeal only by making a fresh application to the Upper Tribunal.

That fresh application must include the reason why the application to the FTT was made late. The Upper Tribunal must refuse to give permission in such cases unless it considers that it would be in the interests of justice for permission to be given. This is a considerably higher hurdle to overcome than normal in that it can mean that many arguable cases will not be granted permission: this is the risk that a party that is late with its application will need to face.

See also **9.6.10** below for the procedures that apply in all cases where permission is sought from the Upper Tribunal.

Law: SI 2008/2698, rule 21(7)
Guidance: https://www.gov.uk/tax-upper-tribunal/how-to-appeal

9.6.10 Refusal of permission (in all cases)

If the FTT refuses to grant permission (for whatever reason), a fresh application will need to be made to the Upper Tribunal.

The application must be made within one month after the refusal notice was sent to the party by the First-tier. This time limit may be extended by the Upper Tribunal (and late applications may be admitted if they include a request for an extension of time and the reason why the application was made late). For a case concerning the effect of a time limit when a document is sent to the wrong address, see the discussion of the *Rana* case in the context of rule 5(3)(a) above.

The principles to be applied by the Upper Tribunal are similar to those in **2.4.4** above (although, again, the risk of fading memories etc. should not be a relevant consideration unless, perhaps, the case is likely to be remitted to the tribunal for further evidence).

A standard notice of appeal and application is available on the Upper Tribunal's website.

See also **9.6.9** for the additional hurdle that needed to be overcome when the First-tier refused permission because the application for permission was made late.

Law: SI 2008/2698, rule 21(3)(b), (6)
Case: *Rana v London Borough of Ealing* [2018] EWCA Civ 2074
Guidance: https://tinyurl.com/ymjn5wk6 (Form FTC1: Application for permission to appeal and notice of appeal from FTT)

9.6.11 Granting of permission

If the First-tier gives permission to appeal, the party seeking permission to appeal must then pursue the appeal by lodging a notice of appeal with the Upper Tribunal within one month of the date on which the notice giving permission was sent. As HMRC learned to their cost in *McCarthy*, missing this further time limit can preclude an appeal going forward even after permission has been granted.

For a case concerning the effect of a time limit when a document is sent to the wrong address, see the discussion of the *Rana* case in the context of rule 5(3)(a) above.

A standard notice of appeal is available on the Upper Tribunal's website.

Law: SI 2008/2698, rule 23(2)(a)

Cases: *HMRC v McCarthy & Stone Developments Ltd* (2014) ref: PTA/345/2013; *Rana v London Borough of Ealing* [2018] EWCA Civ 2074

Guidance: https://tinyurl.com/ymjn5wk6 (Form FTC1: Application for permission to appeal and notice of appeal from FTT)

9.6.12 Second applications for permission

Spring Capital makes clear that there is no reason why a party cannot seek permission on two occasions (on different points). However, given the time limits and other principles that prevent an abuse of process, this power is likely to be exercised very rarely (if at all).

Case: *Spring Capital Ltd v HMRC* [2018] UKFTT 250 (TC)

9.6.13 Cross-appeals

It is often the case that no side is the outright winner after a decision is issued. For a simple example, the tribunal might conclude that tax is payable, but not as much as originally assessed by HMRC.

If neither side is content with the result then the chances are that both will independently seek permission to appeal. For example, in a case where the tribunal is required to determine the market value of a particular asset on a particular date, it is possible that both parties are unhappy with the outcome. In such cases, it will be open for both parties to appeal against the decision: it will then be a matter for the Upper Tribunal to consolidate the two separate appeals.

However, another common outcome is for one party to be sufficiently content with the outcome so as not to take the matter any further, until it is discovered that the other side is pursuing an appeal. In such cases, the first party might wish to "cross appeal" so as to better the result achieved at the first hearing.

The correct procedure in such cases is difficult to discern and has been the subject of much discussion.

Earlier case law on this point

At one time it was generally accepted that the broadly successful party need not commence the appeal process and can wait to see whether or not the other party appeals against the decision. If so, the Upper Tribunal would give the winning party the opportunity to renew those arguments on the subsequent appeal. This practice was reflected in the Upper Tribunal's decision in *Eynsham*.

However, in *Earlsferry*, the Upper Tribunal had previously suggested that a taxpayer could not pursue a cross appeal without engaging with rule 39, i.e. first obtaining permission (or at least requesting and being refused permission to appeal) from the First-tier (even though the appeal became live only once HMRC had notified the appeal to the Upper Tribunal – after permission had been granted by the First-tier).

Law: SI 2008/2698, rule 24(3)(e)

Cases: *Eynsham Cricket Club v HMRC* [2019] UKUT 47 (TCC); *HMRC v Earlsferry Thistle Golf Club* [2014] UKUT 250 (TCC)

Guidance given by the tribunals themselves

In view of the uncertainty, the correct procedure was raised by the author at a meeting of the Tribunals' Users' Group, presided by the Presidents of the First-tier and Upper Tribunals. Although not binding precedent, it is worth noting that the minutes report as follows:

> "The consensus among the judges present was the respondent could identify the issue they wanted to cross appeal in the Respondent's notice before the UT."

In other words, it seemed that a partially successful party is not obliged to second-guess the intentions of the other side.

Binding guidance from the Court of Appeal

However, the matter has since come to a head in the Court of Appeal case of *SSE*.

The court concluded that if a party is unsuccessful on a particular issue in the First-tier, then permission to appeal must first be sought from the First-tier if that matter is to remain alive on any subsequent appeal.

However, the court noted that, in many cases, a party will advance a number of different arguments to make a particular point. A tribunal might agree with the party on the point being pursued without necessarily accepting each of the arguments put forward to support it. In such a case, the court made clear that it is not necessary to seek permission to appeal in respect of the arguments that were not accepted. If the other party wishes to challenge the overall decision, then the successful party is at liberty to rerun the unsuccessful arguments.

Case: *HMRC v SSE Generation Ltd* [2021] EWCA Civ 105

Practical implications of the decision in SSE

The Court of Appeal in *SSE* was not persuaded by the practical implications of its decision (in particular the likelihood of applications for permission being made outside the ordinary time limits by parties). In particular, the First-tier might have to consider whether or not to extend the time in which permission applications should be made.

Although it is thought that the First-tier will take a pragmatic view to late permission applications in such situations, it does introduce a further element of chance in the litigation process. Accordingly, it might now prove tempting for parties who have lost on specific issues to make a timely application for permission to appeal on a protective basis, and to pursue that application only if the other party proposes to take the case further. This can work if the parties co-operate with each other. However, if one party is minded to keep its cards close to its chest right up to the last minute for seeking permission to appeal or for notifying an appeal to the Upper Tribunal, there is a risk that the other party will incur costs unnecessarily or that an application or appeal will be made late.

The author understands that the tribunal is alive to the issues and it is something that might well be remedied through a change in the Upper Tribunal's rules in due course. The fact that the tribunal is alert to the practical issues suggests that it will take a realistic approach to late permission applications.

This pragmatism has already been borne out by the tribunal's decision in *Euromoney* which made it clear that:

- contrary to HMRC's argument, the taxpayer was not required to seek permission on one point as soon as it

learned that HMRC were seeking permission to appeal against the decision; but instead
- it was "reasonable for [the taxpayer] to determine whether it wants to reverse a point decided against it in the FTT once the final position regarding HMRC's application for permission to appeal is established".

Furthermore, in *Dunsby*, an appeal by the taxpayer at which HMRC wished to argue a point they had lost in the First-tier, the Upper Tribunal preferred not to consider the precise boundary between an argument (for which permission would not have been needed) and an issue (for which permission would apparently have been necessary). Instead, it exercised its discretion to waive any earlier breach of the rules by HMRC so as to ensure that their arguments could be heard.

Cases: *HMRC v SSE Generation Ltd* [2021] EWCA Civ 105; *Euromoney Institutional Investor plc v HMRC* [2021] UKFTT 321 (TC); *Dunsby v HMRC* [2021] UKUT 289 (TCC)

A further possible challenge to the decision in SSE

The author has followed this debate with interest, as can be evidenced by the discussion on the subject in the preceding editions of this book. At present, he is minded to accept the correctness of the principle expressed in *SSE* but not necessarily its application in that case.

As the court made clear in *SSE*, an unsuccessful party in the FTT can challenge the decision in the Upper Tribunal only by pursuing the appeal procedures, which commence with an application for permission. However, what is the meaning of "unsuccessful"? In the author's view, this turns on what was the underlying subject of the original appeal in the First-tier.

In the vast majority of cases, the subject of an appeal in the First-tier is an assessment (or equivalent) or, quite frequently, a number of such assessments. For example, different assessments may cover different years, or the appeal might concern an assessment for tax alongside an assessment for a penalty. In such cases, the different assessments under appeal each represent distinct matters (even though the appeal might well hear them all together), and any person wishing to challenge any such matter on appeal must seek permission to do so.

Example 1

Following an enquiry into Mara's 2019-20 tax return, HMRC issue a closure notice which increases her tax liability by £2,000. In addition, HMRC consider that Mara was careless when completing her return and issue her with a £300 penalty.

Mara appeals against both decisions. She loses her appeal against the closure notice but is successful in her appeal against the penalty.

It might be the case that neither party wishes to take the case any further. Alternatively, both might, in which case permission to appeal should be sought by both Mara and HMRC in respect of the elements of the case that they lost.

Of course, it might be the case that one party (say, Mara) is content to let matters rest but that the other (say, HMRC) still wishes to pursue it. In such a case, HMRC would need to apply for permission to appeal in the normal way.

In that last scenario, assuming permission is given, Mara might then feel motivated to pursue the point she lost. Following *SSE*, she would need to follow the procedures in rule 39 and seek permission from the First-tier (and, as will almost certainly be applicable, explain why her application was made outside the normal 56-day period).

However, if one were to focus on an individual appealable decision, that should not require any analysis as to whether a party has lost on an issue or merely an argument. The underlying question for the First-tier in such appeals is whether the assessment (or amendment) is correct: as to why it might be correct falls within the category of "argument" and not "issue".

Thus to take the *Dunsby* case as an example, the underlying question was whether Mr Dunsby was subject to tax on the receipt of £200,000. In the First-tier, HMRC had put forward three different arguments: it was assessable as a distribution, it was caught by the settlements provisions and it was caught by the transfer of assets abroad provisions. (Each argument operated in the alternative.) HMRC lost on the first, but succeeded on the two other grounds. Mr Dunsby sought to overturn the decision on grounds two and three and obtained permission to do so. HMRC wished to renew the "distribution" argument. In the author's view, HMRC did not need to obtain permission from the First-tier before maintaining such a challenge.

In the event, the Upper Tribunal waived the formality. If one follows *SSE* literally, the Upper Tribunal had no power to do so, although for the preceding reasons, it is considered that the right outcome was reached in any event.

In the author's view, a similar approach should be followed when a single assessment is subject to a combination of procedural and substantive challenges.

Example 2

Midnight Ltd appeals against a discovery assessment. Its challenges concern both a substantive challenge (the assessment is for the wrong amount) and a procedural challenge (the conditions for a discovery assessment are not met).

Midnight Ltd is unsuccessful on the substantive challenge but successful on the procedural part of the appeal.

If HMRC take the case to the Upper Tribunal, it is the author's view that Midnight Ltd would be at liberty to renew the substantive challenge without first requiring permission from the First-tier.

Indeed, this approach would also work in cases where no party is wholly successful on a single issue.

Example 3

Olaf appeals against an assessment seeking an additional £100,000 of tax. Olaf is of the view that no further tax is payable but the First-tier concludes that the correct position is that the assessment should be for £40,000.

Either or both parties have the right to challenge the First-tier's decision, by first seeking permission under rule 39.

Supposing that only HMRC seek and obtain permission, it is the author's view that Olaf would be fully entitled to run arguments in the Upper Tribunal to the effect that the assessment should be set aside in its entirety.

It is respectfully suggested that the above approach fully respects the statutory wording as interpreted by the Court of Appeal in *SSE*. Furthermore, it avoids many of the practical difficulties that could be said to arise on a literal application of the *SSE* approach, as well as the rather esoteric question about whether a party has lost on an issue or merely an argument.

It does not rule out altogether the potential problem of late permission applications being made, as illustrated in the first example above (Mara). However, a pragmatic approach by the First-tier should avoid many difficulties. Indeed, without wishing to pre-empt any further real-life cases, which will all need to be considered on their individual merits, the author can see a distinction between:

- cases such as Mara's (Example 1) where the two distinct strands of the case are closely connected (and, indeed, where the liability for the penalty is, strictly, dependent on the closure notice being correct); and
- cases where two wholly unrelated matters are brought together for convenience and dealt with by a single decision notice.

Cases: *HMRC v SSE Generation Ltd* [2021] EWCA Civ 105; *Dunsby v HMRC* [2021] UKUT 289 (TCC)

9.7 Rule 40 – Tribunal's consideration of application for permission to appeal

40(1) On receiving an application for permission to appeal the Tribunal must first consider, taking into account the overriding objective in rule 2, whether to review the decision in accordance with rule 41 (review of a decision).

40(2) If the Tribunal decides not to review the decision, or reviews the decision and decides to take no action in relation to the decision, or a part of it, the Tribunal must consider whether to give permission to appeal in relation to the decision or that part of it.

40(3) The Tribunal must send a record of its decision to the parties as soon as practicable.

40(4) If the Tribunal refuses permission to appeal it must send with the record of its decision–

9.7 Rule 40 – Tribunal's consideration of application for permission to appeal

> (a) a statement of its reasons for such refusal; and
> (b) notification of the right to make an application to the Upper Tribunal for permission to appeal and the time within which, and the method by which, such application must be made.
>
> 40(5) The Tribunal may give permission to appeal against part only of the decision or on limited grounds, but must comply with paragraph (4) in relation to any part of the decision or grounds on which it has refused permission.

9.7.1 Overview

This rule focuses on the tribunal's procedures when an application for permission to appeal is received.

9.7.2 First consider a review

Although a party has asked for permission to appeal, the tribunal must first consider whether or not to carry out a review of the decision under rule 41 (see also **9.3.4ff**.).

The purpose of this rule is clear. If the FTT can spot an obvious error, a review can avoid the time and costs of an appeal hearing before the Upper Tribunal.

This will be of advantage to the parties as well as to the tribunals system.

There are three possible outcomes to this part of the process. Either:

- the tribunal will decide not to carry out a review;
- the tribunal will decide to carry out a review, but will decide to take no action following the review; or
- the tribunal will decide, in light of the review, to take some form of corrective action.

In each case, the decision with regard to the review cannot be the subject of its own appeal as that is an excluded decision under the 2007 Act. However, as noted at **9.3.8**, the matter could be challenged by way of a judicial review (and one that might be commenced at the Upper Tribunal).

In the first two scenarios, the tribunal must then consider whether or not to give permission for the appeal to proceed to the Upper Tribunal (see **9.7.3**).

In the third scenario, the procedures detailed under rule 41 will take over.

It should be noted that, in practice, it is relatively uncommon for a review to be carried out.

Law: TCEA 2007, s. 11(5)(d)

9.7.3 Considering whether or not to give permission

As noted at **9.6.4** above, appeals may be made only in respect of alleged errors of law.

On one interpretation of the primary legislation, parties can take a case to the Upper Tribunal as of right (provided that there is a question of law for the Upper Tribunal to consider). On that interpretation, the permission stage is a process to ensure that the appeal will indeed focus on a question of law.

However, in practice, the FTT does not necessarily give permission to appeal simply because a party has identified a question of law.

Law: TCEA 2007, s. 11(2), (3)

Test for permission

In practice, permission is generally given only if the question of law is arguable or if the case otherwise merits the attention of the Upper Tribunal.

However, in rare cases, even arguability will not be enough. In *Hurst*, the taxpayer had specifically referred to previous decisions of the tribunal as the basis of his appeal. HMRC did not address those cases in their submissions. The taxpayer won his appeal. When seeking permission to appeal, however, HMRC raised arguments for the first time that took issue with the earlier case law. Even though pure points of law may sometimes be raised in later appeals, the tribunal considered it unfair that, were permission to be granted, HMRC would be effectively forcing the taxpayer to argue the case in a forum where there was a greater risk of costs being awarded against him, whereas (had they engaged with the issues in the First-tier) the taxpayer would have had a chance to have them addressed without the risk of an adverse costs decision For those reasons, the tribunal refused to grant permission.

Following the First-tier's refusal, HMRC would have been able to ask the Upper Tribunal for permission. In response to any such application, assuming it decided to grant permission, the Upper Tribunal would have been able to make a direction so as to protect the taxpayer from the risk of HMRC's costs. Although that would not prevent HMRC from arguing the points that it failed to address in the First-tier, it would protect the taxpayer from the adverse costs consequences. On the other hand, it could be said that the First-tier's decision was not tainted by any error of law because it was decided correctly on the basis of the arguments before it.

Case: *Hurst v HMRC* [2019] UKFTT 452 (TC)

Granting permission on limited grounds

Permission to appeal may be limited in that only some of the grounds of appeal requested (see rule 39(5)(b) and **9.6.7**) may be pursued on the appeal.

9.7.4 Notification of tribunal's decision (rule 40(3), (4))

If one party applies for permission to appeal, that application will not necessarily be made known to the other party until the tribunal has considered how to deal with the application. The tribunal must therefore send the parties notification of its decision on the application as soon as is practicable.

If permission is granted, no statement of reasons is needed.

If permission is refused (or refused in part), however, the tribunal must state its reasons for the refusal. It must also advise the applicant of the rights to seek permission (or fuller permission) from the Upper Tribunal (as discussed at **9.6.10**).

9.8 Rule 41 – Review of a decision

> 41(1) The Tribunal may only undertake a review of a decision–
>
> (a) pursuant to rule 40(1) (review on an application for permission to appeal); and

> (b) if it is satisfied that there was an error of law in the decision.
>
> 41(2) The Tribunal must notify the parties in writing of the outcome of any review, unless the Tribunal decides to take no action following the review.
>
> 41(3) The Tribunal may not take any action in relation to a decision following a review without first giving every party an opportunity to make representations in relation to the proposed action.

9.8.1 Overview

This rule contains the procedures for dealing with reviews. The scope of reviews is discussed at **9.3.4ff** above.

As discussed at **9.7.2** above, on receiving an application for permission to appeal, the tribunal must first consider whether or not to carry out a review.

9.8.2 When a review may be carried out (rule 41(1))

Not only is the tribunal required to consider whether or not to carry out a review as the first step when dealing with an application for permission to appeal, but rule 41(1)(a) provides that a review may not be carried out unless an application for permission to appeal is made.

In other words, the rules provide that the tribunal should not consider a standalone application for a review. However, as noted at **9.9.1**, an application for review may be treated by the tribunal as if it were an application for permission to appeal. Furthermore, as suggested in *Couldwell*, the provision in rule 41(1) might be an unlawful restriction on the tribunal's right to review a decision as the primary legislation does not authorise such a restriction.

When considering whether or not a review should be carried out, rule 41(1)(b) provides that the tribunal is essentially determining whether or not there was an error of law in the decision. This could be an error apparent in the decision itself or in the process underlying the decision.

Law: TCEA 2007, s. 9(2)(a), (3)
Case: *Couldwell Concrete Flooring Ltd v HMRC (No. 2)* [2017] UKFTT 85 (TC)

9.8.3 Action on completion of a review (rule 41(2), (3))

If the tribunal decides that no action is to be taken on completion of the review then the tribunal is not required to notify the parties of the outcome.

In practice, however, the tribunal will inevitably move on to consider whether or not permission to appeal should be granted (see **9.7.2**).

If the tribunal considers that action should be taken as a result of its review (such action being to correct accidental errors, to amend the reasons or even to set aside the decision), it should notify the parties in writing of its decision.

Rule 41(3) provides that the tribunal's decision is only provisional. It may not take any such action without giving the parties the opportunity to make representations in relation to the tribunal's proposed action.

Law: TCEA 2007, s. 9(4)

9.8.4 Considerations during a review

The most drastic consequence of a review is that the tribunal could choose to set aside its earlier decision. In *RB*, the Upper Tribunal held that such an outcome should occur only in clear cases. Where the previously successful party is likely to object then this factor (although not determinative) should be borne in mind. Furthermore, even if the FTT considers that there is clearly an error of law then it may still be right for permission to appeal to the Upper Tribunal to be given rather than to set aside the original decision.

It is suggested that this might be right in cases where it would be beneficial for the Upper Tribunal (being a court which can give binding precedents) to give a ruling on the matter. In addition, a set aside might not be appropriate if the error identified is one of law and which can be readily distinguished from the facts, because setting aside an initial decision from the tribunal would mean it more likely that the facts would need to be reargued.

However, as was suggested in one unreported case in which the author was involved, in a case where "the likely result of any appeal to the Upper Tribunal would be a reference back to the First-tier Tribunal for a re-hearing [it] would in those circumstances be more efficient, and in the interests of justice, for the original decision to be set aside in a review by the First-tier Tribunal, and for the appeal to be re-heard by that Tribunal".

It should be noted that the *RB* case concerned a slightly different version of rule 41 (as it related to proceedings in a different Chamber of the FTT). In that case, the rules permitted the parties to apply to the tribunal for the actual review to be set aside. In the unreported case referred to in the previous paragraph, the tribunal agreed that in the Tax Chamber a party may not object to the fact that a review has been undertaken: parties may make representations only in respect of the action proposed by the tribunal upon the conclusion of the review.

Case: *R (RB) v First-tier Tribunal (Review)* [2010] UKUT 160 (AAC)

9.9 Rule 42 – Power to treat an application as a different type of application

> 42 The Tribunal may treat an application for a decision to be corrected, set aside or reviewed, or for permission to appeal against a decision, as an application for any other one of those things.

9.9.1 Overview

A party's various options following a decision are listed at **9.3.2**. Rule 42 provides that an application for any of the procedures listed may be treated by the tribunal as if it were an application for another such procedure.

9.9.2 Effect of the rule

This ensures that a party that erroneously seeks a correction of a decision under the slip rule (rule 37), where the alleged error is more substantive than that, may be treated as having applied for permission to appeal against the decision.

Similarly, where a party has applied for permission to appeal against a decision and the tribunal considers that the matter complained of is in fact a minor typographical error, the tribunal has the flexibility to correct the decision under the slip rule.

Where possible, however, it is helpful for parties to make clear under which rule a particular application is being made. The rule, nevertheless, ensures that the wrong classification will not necessarily be fatal and common sense can prevail.

10. The Scottish tax tribunal

10.1 Introduction

The Tax Chamber of the First-tier Tribunal for Scotland came into being on 24 April 2017, replacing the previous (but short-lived) First-tier Tax Tribunal for Scotland.

The tribunal has jurisdiction over decisions by Revenue Scotland including those made under the Scottish general anti-avoidance rule and the land and buildings transaction tax.

Law: *Revenue Scotland and Tax Powers Act* 2014, s. 233; SSI 2017/106

10.2 The tribunal's rules

The rules are very similar to those applicable in the UK-wide tribunal and as discussed above. As a result, they are not subject to a detailed commentary, except where there is a material difference.

The rules have not been revised to reflect the Covid-19 pandemic although guidance was issued on 1 May 2020. This guidance is reflected, as appropriate, in the commentary below.

Law: SSI 2017/69

Guidance: https://tinyurl.com/rm5avc7j (update on impact of Covid-19 pandemic)

Part 1 – Introduction

Interpretation

> 1 In these Rules–
>
> "the 2014 Act" means the Tribunals (Scotland) Act 2014;
>
> "RSTPA 2014" means the Revenue Scotland and Tax Powers Act 2014;
>
> "appellant" means–
>
> (a) the person who starts proceedings (whether by notifying an appeal, by making an application, by a reference, or otherwise);

(b) in proceedings started jointly by more than one person, such persons acting jointly or each such person, as the context requires;

(c) in any case, a person substituted as an appellant under rule 9 (addition, substitution and removal of parties);

"Basic case" means a case allocated to the Basic category under rule 24 (allocation of cases to categories);

"chairing member" means the chairing member of the First-tier Tribunal, who is the legal member of that tribunal or, as the case may be, the member chosen by the Chamber President in terms of rule 19(1);

"Chamber President" means the Chamber President of the First-tier Tribunal;

"Complex case" means a case allocated to the Complex category under rule 24;

"Convention Rights" has the meaning given to it in section 1 of the Human Rights Act 1998;

"Default Paper case" means a case allocated to the Default Paper category under rule 24;

"document" means anything in which information is recorded in any form, and an obligation under these Rules to provide or allow access to a document or a copy of a document for any purpose means, unless the First-tier Tribunal directs otherwise, an obligation to provide or allow access to such document or copy in a legible form or in a form which can be readily made into a legible form;

"excluded decision" means a decision falling under section 51 of the 2014 Act;

"First-tier Tribunal" means the First-tier Tribunal for Scotland Tax Chamber;

"hearing" means an oral hearing and includes a hearing conducted in whole or in part by video link, telephone or other means of instantaneous two-way electronic communication;

"interested party" means a person other than the appellant or respondent on whom the First-tier Tribunal has ordered the proceedings before it to be served;

"party" means a person who is (or was at the time that the First-tier Tribunal disposed of the proceedings) an appellant or respondent in proceedings before the First-tier Tribunal;

"practice direction" means a direction given under section 74 of the 2014 Act;

"respondent" means–

(a) Revenue Scotland, where Revenue Scotland is not an appellant;

(b) in proceedings brought by Revenue Scotland alone, a person against whom the proceedings are brought or to whom the proceedings relate;

(c) in any case, a person substituted or added as a respondent under rule 9; and

"Standard case" means a case allocated to the Standard category under rule 24.

Overriding objective and parties' obligation to co-operate with the First-Tier Tribunal

2(1) The overriding objective of these Rules is to enable the First-tier Tribunal to deal with cases fairly and justly.

2(2) Dealing with a case in accordance with the overriding objective includes–

(a) dealing with the case in ways which are proportionate to the importance of the case, the complexity of the issues, the anticipated expenses and the resources of the parties;

(b) avoiding unnecessary formality and seeking flexibility in the proceedings;

(c) ensuring, so far as practicable, that the parties are able to participate fully in the proceedings;

10.2 The tribunal's rules

> (d) using any special expertise of the First-tier Tribunal effectively; and
>
> (e) avoiding delay, so far as compatible with proper consideration of the issues.
>
> 2(3) The First-tier Tribunal must seek to give effect to the overriding objective when it–
>
> (a) exercises any power under these Rules; or;
>
> (b) interprets any rule or practice direction.
>
> 2(4) Parties must, insofar as reasonably possible–
>
> (a) help the First-tier Tribunal to further the overriding objective; and
>
> (b) co-operate with the First-tier Tribunal generally.

Mediation

> 3 The First-tier Tribunal should seek, where appropriate–
>
> (a) to bring to the attention of the parties the availability of mediation for the resolution of the dispute; and
>
> (b) if the parties wish, and provided that it is compatible with the overriding objective, to facilitate the use of mediation.

The key difference is the reference to "mediation" rather than "any appropriate alternative procedure". However, it is suggested that this distinction is of little practical import.

Delegation to staff

> 4(1) Staff of the Scottish Courts and Tribunals Service may, with the approval of the Chamber President, carry out functions of a judicial nature permitted or required to be done by the First-tier Tribunal.
>
> 4(2) The approval referred to at paragraph (1) may apply generally to the carrying out of specified functions by members of staff of a specified description in specified circumstances.

4(3)   Within 14 days after the date that the First-tier Tribunal sends notice of a decision made by a member of staff pursuant to an approval under paragraph (1) to a party, that party may make a written application to the First-tier Tribunal for that decision to be considered afresh by a member of the First-tier Tribunal.

Part 2 – General Powers and Provisions

Case management powers

5(1)   Subject to the provisions of the 2014 Act and these Rules, the First-tier Tribunal may regulate its own procedure.

5(2)   The First-tier Tribunal may give an order in relation to the conduct or disposal of proceedings at any time, including an order amending, suspending or setting aside an earlier order.

5(3)   In particular, and without restricting the general powers in paragraphs (1) and (2), the First-tier Tribunal may–

(a) extend or shorten the time for complying with any rule or order;

(b) conjoin or take concurrently two or more sets of proceedings or parts of proceedings raising common issues;

(c) specify one or more cases as a lead case or lead cases where–

(i) two or more cases are before the First-tier Tribunal;

(ii) in each such case the proceedings have not been finally determined; and

(iii) the cases give rise to common or related issues of fact or law;

and sist the other cases until the common or related issues have been determined;

(d) permit or require a party to amend a document;

(e) permit or require a party or another person to provide documents, information, evidence or submissions to the First-tier Tribunal or a party;

(f) deal with an issue in the proceedings as a preliminary issue;

(g) hold a hearing to consider any matter, including a case management hearing;

(h) decide the form of any hearing;

(i) adjourn or postpone a hearing;

(j) require a party to produce a file of documents for a hearing;

(k) sist proceedings;

(l) transfer proceedings to another court or tribunal if that other court or tribunal has jurisdiction in relation to the proceedings and–

    (i) because of a change of circumstances since the proceedings were started, the First-tier Tribunal no longer has jurisdiction in relation to the proceedings; or

    (ii) the First-tier Tribunal considers that the other court or tribunal is a more appropriate forum for the determination of the case;

(m) suspend the effect of its own decision pending the determination by the First-tier Tribunal or the Upper Tribunal, as the case may be, of an application for permission to appeal or an appeal.

Procedure for applying for and giving orders

6(1) The First-tier Tribunal may give an order on the application of one or more of the parties or on its own initiative.

6(2) An application for an order may be made–

(a) by sending or delivering a written application to the First-tier Tribunal; or

(b) orally during the course of a hearing.

6(3) An application for an order must include the reasons for making that application.

6(4) Before making an order, the First-tier Tribunal must afford parties an opportunity to make representations to it concerning whether the order should be made and the terms of the order.

Failure to comply with rules etc.

7(1) An irregularity resulting from a failure to comply with any requirement in these Rules, a practice direction or an order does not of itself render void the proceedings or any step taken in the proceedings.

7(2) If a party has failed to comply with a requirement in these Rules, a practice direction or an order, the First-tier Tribunal may take such action as it considers just, which may include–

(a) waiving the requirement;

(b) requiring the failure to be remedied; or

(c) exercising its power under rule 8 (dismissal of a party's case).

Dismissal of a party's case

8(1) The First-tier Tribunal must dismiss the whole or a part of the proceedings if the First-tier Tribunal–

(a) does not have jurisdiction in relation to the proceedings or that part of them; and

(b) does not exercise its power under rule 5(3)(l) (transfer to another court or tribunal) in relation to the proceedings or that part of them.

8(2) The First-tier Tribunal may dismiss the whole or a part of the proceedings if–

(a) the appellant has failed to comply with an order which stated that failure by the appellant to comply with the

> order could lead to the dismissal of the proceedings or part of them; or
>
> (b) the appellant has failed to co-operate with the First-tier Tribunal to such an extent that the First-tier Tribunal cannot deal with the proceedings fairly and justly.
>
> 8(3) The First-tier Tribunal may not dismiss the whole or a part of the proceedings under paragraph (1) or (2) without first giving the appellant an opportunity to make representations in relation to the proposed dismissal.

The key difference is the reference to "dismissal" rather than "striking out". However, it is suggested that this distinction is of little practical import.

Addition, substitution and removal of parties

> 9(1) The First-tier Tribunal may make an order adding, substituting or removing a party as an appellant or a respondent including where–
>
> (a) the wrong person has been named as a party; or
>
> (b) the addition, substitution or removal has become necessary because of a change in circumstances since the start of proceedings.
>
> 9(2) If the First-tier Tribunal makes an order under paragraph (1) it may make such consequential orders as it considers appropriate.
>
> 9(3) A person who is not a party may make a written application to the First-tier Tribunal to be added or substituted as a party under this rule.
>
> 9(4) If the First-tier Tribunal refuses an application under paragraph (3) it must consider whether to permit the person who made the application to provide submissions or evidence to the First-tier Tribunal.

Orders for expenses

> **10(1)** The First-tier Tribunal may make an order for expenses as taxed by the Auditor of the Court of Session against a party if that party's act, omission or other conduct has caused any other party to incur expense which it would be unreasonable for that other party to be expected to pay, with the maximum recoverable expenses being the expenses incurred.
>
> **10(2)** The First-tier Tribunal, of its own initiative or on the application of a party or the parties, may in exceptional circumstances fix by order a sum payable by a party in discharge of an award of expenses.

The UK-wide rules already recognise the Scottish term "expenses" for "costs".

However, there are other key differences:

- the situations in which expenses might be payable are limited to what the UK-wide rules consider to be "wasted costs" (see **4.8.3** and **4.8.4** above);
- accordingly, the Complex Case category has no consequences so far as expenses are concerned;
- (as expressly approved by the tribunal in *Wind*) the tribunal will not in general summarily assess any expenses and all such assessment (taxation, to use the Scottish term) is undertaken by the specialist department within the Scottish courts;
- as a result, any application for expenses need not provide any details as to what work was undertaken;
- there is also no time limit for any application under the tribunal rules.

In addition, the rules contain no provision for a payment on account, although the Court of Session might well make similar provision.

However, the tribunal can make its own order directing the payment of expenses but only in "exceptional circumstances". There is no guidance as to what those might be and, ultimately, it is down to the discretion of the tribunal on a case-by-case basis. However, this power is likely to be rarely used. The immediately preceding sentence was expressly approved by the tribunal in *Wind*.

A number of issues on the application of the rule arose in the *Wind* case:

- Revenue Scotland argued that paragraphs (1) and (2) operated in the alternative – so that expenses can be fixed by the tribunal even outside the circumstances identified in paragraph (1). However, the tribunal disagreed, saying instead that paragraph (2) operates only when paragraph (1) (or potentially rule 5(3)(g)) is engaged.
- The tribunal also confirmed that the rule did not preclude expenses being payable by Revenue Scotland, even though it was a public body funded by the taxpayer.
- In the circumstances of the *Wind* case, and based at least partly on the fact that the tribunal is the first of potentially four levels of appeal (as is the Sheriff's Court), and the broader rights of audience in the tribunal and the Sheriff's Court, the tribunal awarded the payment of expenses on the Sheriff's Court scale.
- As Revenue Scotland had not consented to the basis of the expenses award and also lost on the argument concerning the scope of paragraph (2), the tribunal determined that the expenses payable should also include the expenses of the expenses hearing itself.

Case: *Wind Energy Renewables LLP v Revenue Scotland* [2021] FTSTC 2

Representatives

11(1) A party may be represented in any proceedings by a legal representative or lay representative whose details must be communicated to the First-tier Tribunal prior to any hearing.

11(2) A party may show any document or communicate any information about the proceedings to that party's lay representative or legal representative without contravening any prohibition or restriction on disclosure of the document or information.

11(3) Where a document or information is disclosed under paragraph (2), the lay representative or legal representative is subject to any prohibition or restriction on disclosure in the same way that the party is.

11(4) Anything permitted or required to be done by a party under these Rules, a practice direction or an order may be done by a lay representative, except signing of a witness statement.

11(5) The First-tier Tribunal may order that a lay representative is not to represent a party if–

(a) it is of the opinion that the lay representative is an unsuitable person to act as a lay representative (whether generally or in the proceedings concerned); or

(b) it is satisfied that to do so would be in the interests of the efficient administration of justice.

Rule 11(2), (3) makes it clear that disclosure of material to a party's representative (whether a lay or legal representative) is permitted even if it would otherwise breach a legal restriction on disclosure.

Supporters

12(1) A party who is an individual may be accompanied by another person to act as a supporter.

12(2) A supporter may assist the party by–

(a) providing moral support;

(b) helping to manage tribunal documents and other papers;

(c) taking notes of the proceedings;

(d) quietly advising on–

(i) points of law and procedure;

(ii) issues which the party might wish to raise with the tribunal.

12(3) The party may show any document or communicate any information about the proceedings to that party's

12(4) Where a document or information is disclosed under paragraph (3), the supporter is subject to any prohibition or restriction on disclosure in the same way that the party is.

12(5) A supporter may not represent the party.

12(6) The First-tier Tribunal may order that a person is not to act as a supporter of a party if–

(a) it is of the opinion that the supporter is an unsuitable person to act as a supporter (whether generally or in the proceedings concerned); or

(b) it is satisfied that to do so would be in the interests of the efficient administration of justice.

There is no equivalent to this rule in the UK-wide tribunal. It provides an express framework for an individual party in a case to be supported by a person who is not acting as their representative.

That supporter may be shown material even if that would otherwise breach a restriction on disclosure.

Calculating time

13(1) An act required by these Rules, a practice direction or an order to be done on or by a particular day must be done before 5pm on that day.

13(2) If the time specified by these Rules, a practice direction or an order for doing any act ends on a day other than a working day, the act is done in time if it is done on the next working day.

13(3) In this rule "working day" means any day except a Saturday or Sunday or a bank holiday in Scotland under section 1 of the Banking and Financial Dealings Act 1971.

Whereas the UK-wide rules exclude from the definition of working day a day that is a bank holiday in any part of the UK (see **4.10.3** above), the Scottish rules consider only Scottish bank holidays.

14(1) Any document to be provided to the First-tier Tribunal under these Rules, a practice direction or an order must be–

(a) sent by pre-paid post or document exchange, or delivered by hand, to the address of the First-tier Tribunal; or

(b) sent or delivered by such other method as the First-tier Tribunal may permit or direct.

14(2) Subject to paragraph (3), if a party or representative provides a fax number, email address or other details for the electronic transmission of documents to them, that party or representative must accept delivery of documents by that method.

In response to the Covid-19 pandemic and the introduction of remote working, the tribunal has issued guidance to encourage parties to communicate by e-mail.

Guidance: https://tinyurl.com/rm5avc7j (update on impact of Covid-19 pandemic)

14(3) If a party informs the First-tier Tribunal and all other parties that a particular form of communication (other than pre-paid post or delivery by hand) should not be used to provide documents to that party, that form of communication must not be so used.

14(4) If the First-tier Tribunal or a party sends a document to a party or the First-tier Tribunal by email or any other electronic means of communication, the recipient may request that the sender provide a hard copy of the document to the recipient. The recipient must make such a request as soon as reasonably practicable after receiving the document electronically.

14(5) The First-tier Tribunal and each party may assume that the address provided by a party or its representative is and remains the address to which documents should be sent or delivered until receiving notification to the contrary.

Disclosure of documents and information

> 15   The First-tier Tribunal may at any stage of the proceedings, on its own initiative or on application by one or more of the parties, make an order with a view to preventing or restricting the public disclosure of any aspect of those proceedings so far as it considers necessary in the interests of justice or in order to protect the Convention Rights of any person.

Unlike the UK-wide rules, the Scottish rules are more prescriptive as to the situations in which such an order might be given. Nevertheless, it is considered that the difference is more of form than of substance.

Evidence and submissions

> 16(1)   Without restriction on the general powers in rule 5(1) and (2) (case management powers), the First-tier Tribunal may give orders as to–
>
> (a) issues on which it requires evidence or submissions;
>
> (b) the nature of any such evidence;
>
> (c) whether the parties are permitted or required to provide expert evidence, and if so whether the parties must jointly appoint a single expert to provide such evidence;
>
> (d) any limit on the number of witnesses whose evidence a party may put forward, whether in relation to a particular issue or generally;
>
> (e) the manner in which any evidence or submissions are to be provided, which may include an order for them to be given–
>
> (i) orally at a hearing; or
>
> (ii) by written submissions or witness statement; and
>
> (f) the time at which any evidence or submissions are to be provided.
>
> 16(2)   The First-tier Tribunal may exclude evidence that would otherwise be admissible where–

(a) the evidence was not, without reasonable excuse, provided within the time allowed by an order or a practice direction.

(b) the evidence was otherwise, without reasonable excuse, provided in a manner that did not comply with an order or a practice direction; or

(c) it would otherwise be unfair to admit the evidence.

16(3) The First-tier Tribunal may consent to a witness giving, or require any witness to give, evidence on oath, and may administer an oath for that purpose.

Citation of witnesses and orders to answer questions or produce documents

17(1) On the application of a party or on its own initiative, the First-tier Tribunal may–

(a) by citation require any person to attend as a witness at a hearing at the time and place specified in the citation;

(b) order any person to answer any questions or produce any documents in that person's possession or control which relate to any issue in the proceedings.

17(2) A citation under paragraph (1)(a) must–

(a) give the person required to attend at least 14 days' notice of the hearing, or such other period as the First-tier Tribunal may order;

(b) where the person is not a party, make provision for the person's necessary expenses of attendance to be paid, and state who is to pay them;

(c) state that the person on whom the requirement is imposed may apply to the First-tier Tribunal to vary or set aside the citation or order, if the person did not have an opportunity to object to it before it was made or issued; and

(d) state the consequences of failure to comply with the citation or order.

Withdrawal

18(1) A party may give notice to the First-tier Tribunal of the withdrawal of the case made by it in the First-tier Tribunal proceedings, or any part of that case–

(a) by sending or delivering to the First-tier Tribunal a notice of withdrawal; or

(b) orally at a hearing.

18(2) The First-tier Tribunal must notify each party of its receipt of a withdrawal under this rule.

Chairing member and voting

19(1) Where a matter is to be decided by two or more members of the First-tier Tribunal, the Chamber President must determine the chairing member.

19(2) The decision of the First-tier Tribunal on an application must be made by majority with the chairing member having a casting vote.

This rule is the equivalent of one given by statutory instrument for the UK-wide tribunal. See **8.10.1** above.

Venue for hearings

20 The First-tier Tribunal is to be convened at such time and place in Scotland as the President of Tribunals may determine.

It will be noted that the hearing must take place in Scotland. The UK-wide tribunal may hear a case anywhere in the UK even if it relates to a different part of the UK.

Law: TCEA 2007, s. 26

Enforcement of decisions

21 An order for the payment of a sum payable in pursuance of a decision of the First-tier Tribunal, or a copy of such an order certified by the First-tier Tribunal, may be enforced

> as if it were an extract registered decree arbitral bearing a warrant for execution issued by the sheriff court of any sheriffdom in Scotland.

This rule does not have an equivalent in the UK-wide rules but is found in primary legislation.

Law: TCEA 2007, s. 27

Part 3 – Procedure for Cases in the First-tier Tribunal

Proceedings concerning late notice of review

> 22(1) A person may apply to the First-tier Tribunal to be allowed a late notice of review under section 236(2)(b) of RSTPA 2014 (late notice of review) only if–
>
> (a) the person has approached Revenue Scotland for agreement under section 236(2)(a); and
>
> (b) agreement has been refused or has been given only on limited grounds.
>
> 22(2) Where permission to be allowed a late notice of review is sought under paragraph (1), the notice of review must include a request for the permission referred to in section 236(2)(b) of RSTPA 2014 and the reason why the notice of review was not provided in time.

This is the equivalent of the various provisions that are found in primary legislation for the UK-wide tribunal allowing the tribunal to admit appeals made late. However, it is limited to permitting late reviews rather than appeals themselves. See **2.4.4** above.

It imposes an obligation that the taxpayer has first approached Revenue Scotland and that that approach has either been unsuccessful or only partially successful.

Notice of appeal to the First-tier

> 23(1) The notice of appeal referred to in section 242(1) of RSTPA 2014 (notice of appeal) must include–
>
> (a) the name and address of the appellant;

10.2 The tribunal's rules

      (b) the name and address of the appellant's representative (if any);

      (c) an address where documents for the appellant may be sent or delivered;

      (d) details of the decision appealed against;

      (e) the result the appellant is seeking; and

      (f) the grounds for making the appeal.

23(2) The appellant must provide with the notice of appeal a copy of any written record of any decision appealed against, and any statement of reasons for that decision, that the appellant has or can reasonably obtain.

23(3) A person may apply to the First-tier Tribunal for permission to appeal under section 243(2)(b) of RSTPA 2014 (late notice of appeal) only if–

      (a) the person has approached Revenue Scotland for agreement under section 243(2)(a); and

      (b) agreement has been refused or has been given only on limited grounds.

23(4) Where permission to appeal may be sought under paragraph (3)–

      (a) the notice of appeal must include a request for the permission referred to in section 243(2)(b) of RSTPA 2014 and the reason why the notice of appeal was not provided in time; and

      (b) unless the First-tier Tribunal gives such permission, the First-tier Tribunal must not admit the appeal.

23(5) When the First-tier Tribunal receives the notice of appeal, it must give notice of the proceedings to the respondent.

Allocation of cases to categories

24(1) When the First-tier Tribunal receives a notice of appeal, the First-tier Tribunal must give an order allocating the case to one of the categories set out in paragraph (2).

24(2) The categories referred to in paragraph (1) are–

(a) Default Paper cases, which will usually be disposed of without a hearing;

(b) Basic cases, which will usually be disposed of after a hearing, with minimal exchange of documents before the hearing;

(c) Standard cases, which will usually be subject to more detailed case management and be disposed of after a hearing; and

(d) Complex cases, in respect of which see paragraphs (4) and (5) below.

24(3) The First-tier Tribunal may give a further order re-allocating a case to a different category at any time, either on the application of a party or on its own initiative.

24(4) The First-tier Tribunal may allocate a case as a Complex case under paragraph (1) or (3) only if the First-tier Tribunal considers that the case–

(a) will require lengthy or complex evidence or a lengthy hearing;

(b) involves a complex or important principle or issue; or

(c) involves a large financial sum.

24(5) If a case is allocated as a Complex case, rule 29 (transfer of Complex cases to the Upper Tribunal) applies to the case.

Basic cases

25(1) This rule applies to Basic cases.

25(2) Rule 26 (respondent's statement of case) does not apply and, subject to paragraph (3) and any direction given by the First-tier Tribunal, the case will proceed directly to a hearing.

25(3) If the respondent intends to raise grounds for contesting the proceedings at the hearing which have not previously been communicated to the appellant, the respondent must notify the appellant of such grounds.

25(4) If the respondent is required to notify the appellant of any grounds under paragraph (3), the respondent must do so–

(a) as soon as reasonably practicable after becoming aware that such is the case; and

(b) in sufficient detail to enable the appellant to respond to such grounds at the hearing.

Respondent's statement of case

26(1) A respondent must send or deliver a statement of case to the First-tier Tribunal, the appellant and any other respondent so that it is received–

(a) in a Default Paper case, within 42 days after the day the First-tier Tribunal sent the notice of appeal;

(b) in a Standard or Complex case, within 60 days after the day the First-tier Tribunal sent the notice of appeal.

26(2) A statement of case must–

(a) in an appeal, state the legislative provision under which the decision under appeal was made; and

(b) set out the respondent's position in relation to the case.

26(3) A statement of case may also contain a request that the case be dealt with at a hearing or without a hearing.

26(4) If a respondent provides a statement of case to the First-tier Tribunal later than the time required by paragraph (1) or by any extension allowed under rule 5(3)(a) (case management powers), the statement of case must include a request for an extension of time and the reason why the statement of case was not provided in time.

In response to the Covid-19 pandemic and the introduction of remote working by both the tribunal and Revenue Scotland, the tribunal has stated that the time limits will be considered on a case-by-case basis.

Guidance: https://tinyurl.com/rm5avc7j (update on impact of Covid-19 pandemic)

Further steps in a Default Paper case

27(1) This rule applies to Default Paper cases.

27(2) The appellant may send or deliver a written reply to the First-tier Tribunal so that it is received within 30 days after the day on which the respondent sent to the appellant the statement of case to which the reply relates.

27(3) The appellant's reply may—

(a) set out the appellant's response to the respondent's statement of case;

(b) provide any further information (including, where appropriate, copies of the documents containing such information) which has not yet been provided to the First-tier Tribunal and is relevant to the case; and

(c) contain a request that the case be dealt with at a hearing or without a hearing.

27(4) The appellant must send or deliver a copy of any reply provided under paragraph (2) to each respondent at the same time as it is provided to the First-tier Tribunal.

27(5) If the appellant provides a reply to the First-tier Tribunal later than the time required by paragraph (2) or by any extension allowed under rule 5(3)(a) (case management powers), the reply must include a request for an extension of time and the reason why the reply was not provided in time.

27(6) Following receipt of the appellant's reply, or the expiry of the time for the receipt of the appellant's reply then, unless it orders otherwise and subject in any event to paragraph (7), the First-tier Tribunal must proceed to determine the case without a hearing.

27(7) If any party has made a written request to the First-tier Tribunal for a hearing, the First-tier Tribunal must hold a hearing before determining the case.

10.2 The tribunal's rules

Further steps in a Standard or Complex case

28(1) This rule applies to Standard and Complex cases.

28(2) Subject to any direction to the contrary, within 42 days after the day the respondent sent the statement of case (or, where there is more than one respondent, the date of the final statement of case) each party must send or deliver to the First-tier Tribunal and to each other party a list of documents–

    (a) of which the party providing the list has possession, the right to possession, or the right to take copies; and

    (b) which the party providing the list intends to rely upon or produce in the proceedings.

28(3) A party which has provided a list of documents under paragraph (2) must allow each other party to inspect or take copies of the documents on the list.

Transfer of Complex cases to the Upper Tribunal

29(1) If a case has been allocated as a Complex case the First-tier Tribunal may, with the consent of the parties, refer a case or a preliminary issue to the Chamber President with a request that the case or issue be considered for transfer to the Upper Tribunal.

29(2) If a case or issue has been referred by the First-tier Tribunal under paragraph (1), the Chamber President may direct that the case or issue be transferred to and determined by the Upper Tribunal.

Unlike the UK-wide rules, a transfer from the Scottish Tribunal does not require the concurrence of the Upper Tribunal.

Decision with or without a hearing

30(1) Subject to rule 27(6) (determination of a Default Paper case without a hearing) and the following paragraphs in this rule, the First-tier Tribunal must hold a hearing before

> making a decision which disposes of proceedings, or a part of proceedings, unless–
>
> (a) each party has consented to the matter being decided without a hearing; and
>
> (b) the First-tier Tribunal considers that it is able to decide the matter without a hearing.
>
> 30(2) This rule does not apply to decisions under Part 4 of these Rules (correcting, reviewing and appealing decisions of the First-tier Tribunal).
>
> 30(3) The First-tier Tribunal may dispose of proceedings, or a part of proceedings, under rule 8 (dismissal of a party's case) without a hearing.

In response to the Covid-19 pandemic and the introduction of remote working, the tribunal has stated that in cases involving no factual dispute, the tribunal will default to deciding the case on the papers, without a hearing. However, parties will be at liberty to apply for an oral hearing, with such application being considered on its merits.

Where there is a factual dispute, the tribunal will decide on the procedure to be adopted on a case-by-case basis after discussion with parties and their representatives.

Guidance: https://tinyurl.com/rm5avc7j (update on impact of Covid-19 pandemic)

Entitlement to attend a hearing

> 31 Subject to rules 11(5) (representatives), 12(6) (supporters) and 33(4) (public and private hearings and powers to exclude), each party is entitled to attend a hearing together with any legal or lay representative and supporter permitted respectively by rules 11 and 12.

Notice of hearings

> 32(1) The First-tier Tribunal must give each party entitled to attend a hearing reasonable notice of the time and place of any hearing (including any adjourned or postponed

10.2 The tribunal's rules

hearing) and any changes to the time and place of any hearing.

32(2) In relation to a hearing to consider the disposal of proceedings, the period of notice under paragraph (1) must be at least 14 days except that the First-tier Tribunal may give less than 14 days' notice–

(a) with the parties' consent; or

(b) in urgent or exceptional circumstances.

Public and private hearings

33(1) Subject to the following paragraphs, all hearings must be held in public.

33(2) The First-tier Tribunal may give an order that a hearing, or part of it, is to be held in private if the First-tier Tribunal considers that restricting access to the hearing is justified–

(a) in the interests of public order;

(b) in order to protect a person's right to respect for their private and family life;

(c) in order to maintain the confidentiality of sensitive information;

(d) in order to avoid serious harm to the public interest; or

(e) because not to do so would prejudice the interests of justice.

33(3) Where a hearing, or part of it, is to be held in private, the First-tier Tribunal may determine who is permitted to attend the hearing or part of it.

33(4) The First-tier Tribunal may give an order excluding from any hearing, or part of it–

(a) any person whose conduct the First-tier Tribunal considers is disrupting or is likely to disrupt the hearing;

(b) any person whose presence the First-tier Tribunal considers is likely to prevent another person from giving evidence or making submissions freely;

(c) any person where the purpose of the hearing would be defeated by the attendance of that person; or

(d) a person under the age of sixteen years.

33(5) The First-tier Tribunal may give an order excluding a witness from a hearing until that witness gives evidence.

33(6) When publishing a decision notice referred to in rule 35(2) (notice of decisions and reasons) resulting from a hearing which was held wholly or partly in private, the First-tier Tribunal must, so far as practicable, ensure that the report does not disclose information which was referred to only in a part of the hearing that was held in private (including such information which enables the identification of any person whose affairs were dealt with in the part of the hearing that was held in private) if to do so would undermine the purpose of holding the hearing in private.

Hearing in a party's absence

34 If a party fails to attend a hearing the First-tier Tribunal may proceed with the hearing if the First-tier Tribunal–

(a) is satisfied that the party has been notified of the hearing or that reasonable steps have been taken to notify the party of the hearing; and

(b) considers that it is in the interests of justice to proceed with the hearing.

Notice of decisions and reasons

35(1) Subject to the remainder of this rule, the First-tier Tribunal may give a decision orally at a hearing.

35(2) The First-tier Tribunal must provide to each party within 30 days after the day of making a decision (other than a decision under Part 4 of these Rules) which finally disposes of all issues in the proceedings or of a preliminary issue dealt with following an order under rule 5(3)(f) (case management powers), or as soon as practicable thereafter, a decision notice which–

> (a) states the First-tier Tribunal's decision; and
>
> (b) notifies the party of any right of appeal against the decision and the time within which, and the manner in which, the right of appeal may be exercised.
>
> 35(3) If the First-tier Tribunal does not provide written reasons for a decision, a party or an interested party may by application in writing made within 30 days after the day of the decision notice request such reasons.
>
> 35(4) The First-tier Tribunal must send a full written statement of findings and reasons to each party within 30 days after the day of receiving an application for written reasons made in accordance with paragraph (3) or as soon as practicable thereafter.
>
> 35(5) The First-tier Tribunal may publish any of its decisions if it considers it in the public interest so to do, with the manner of publication at the discretion of the First-tier Tribunal.

The procedure differs from the UK-wide tribunal. In particular, the parties may not opt out of receiving a decision notice which contains at least a summary of the tribunal's factual findings and reasons. This then has a consequential impact on the remaining rules.

In addition, the timescales are marginally different: here 30 days, in the UK-wide tribunal, 28 days.

Rule 35(5) has no equivalent in the UK-wide tribunal but reflects the practice there.

Part 4 – *Correcting, Reviewing and Appealing Decisions of the First-Tier Tribunal*

Intrepretation

> 36 In this Part—
>
> "appeal" means the exercise of a right of appeal under section 46(1) of the 2014 Act (appeal from the Tribunal); and
>
> "review" means the internal review provided for by section 43(1) of the 2014 Act (review of decisions).

Correction of clerical mistakes or accidental slips or omissions

> 37 The First-tier Tribunal may at any time correct any clerical mistake or other accidental slip or omission contained in a decision, order or any document produced by it, by–
>
> (a) sending notification of the amended decision or order, or a copy of the amended document to all parties; and
>
> (b) making any necessary amendment to any information published in relation to the decision, order or document.

Application for permission to appeal a decision of the First-tier Tribunal

> 38(1) A person seeking permission to appeal must make a written application to the First-tier Tribunal for permission to appeal.
>
> 38(2) An application under paragraph (1) must–
>
> (a) identify the decision of the First-tier Tribunal to which it relates;
>
> (b) identify the alleged point or points of law on which the person making the application wishes to appeal; and
>
> (c) state the result the party making the application is seeking.

The fundamental distinction from the UK-wide provisions is that the Scottish rules do not include any time limits. However, there is in fact a 30-day time limit.

Law: SSI 2016/231

First-tier Tribunal's consideration of application for permission to appeal

> 39(1) The First-tier Tribunal must decide whether to give permission to appeal on any point of law.

10.2 The tribunal's rules

39(2) The First-tier Tribunal must provide a record of its decision to the parties and any interested party as soon as reasonably practicable.

39(3) If the First-tier Tribunal refuses permission on any point of law it must provide with the record of its decision–

    (a) a statement of its reasons for such a refusal; and

    (b) notification of the right to make an application to the Upper Tribunal for permission to appeal and the time within which, and the method by which, such an application must be made.

Unlike the UK-wide rules, an application for permission to appeal is not subject to an automatic requirement to consider reviewing the decision.

Review of a decision

40(1) The First-tier Tribunal may either at its own instance or at the request of a party review any decision made by it where it is necessary in the interests of justice to do so.

40(2) An application for review under section 43(2)(b) of the 2014 Act must–

    (a) be made in writing (and copied to all other parties);

    (b) be made within 14 days of the date on which the decision was made or within 14 days of the date that the written reasons were sent to the parties (if later); and

    (c) set out why a review of the decision is necessary.

40(3) If the First-tier Tribunal considers that the application is wholly without merit, the First-tier Tribunal shall refuse the application and shall also inform the parties of the reasons for the refusal.

40(4) Except where paragraph (3) applies, the First-tier Tribunal shall send a notice to the parties–

    (a) setting a time limit for any response to the application by the other parties and seeking the views of the

> parties on whether the application can be determined without a hearing; and
>
> (b) at the discretion of the First-tier Tribunal, setting out the First-tier Tribunal's provisional views on the application.
>
> 40(5) Except where paragraph (3) applies, the decision shall be reviewed at a hearing unless the First-tier Tribunal considers, having regard to any response to the notice provided under paragraph (4), that a hearing is not necessary in the interests of justice.
>
> 40(6) Where practicable, the review shall be undertaken by one or more of the members of the First-tier Tribunal who made the decision to which the review relates.
>
> 40(7) Where the First-tier Tribunal proposes to review a decision at its own instance, it shall inform the parties of the reasons why the decision is being reviewed and the decision shall be reviewed in accordance with paragraph (4) (as if an application had been made and not refused).
>
> 40(8) A review by the First-tier Tribunal in terms of paragraph (1) either at its own instance or on an application of a party does not affect the time limit of 30 days in regulation 2(1) of the Scottish Tribunals (Time Limits) Regulations 2016 for making an application for permission to appeal. As noted below, the Scottish Tribunal has no power to set aside a decision. However, the broader powers of review encompass a similar power. Unlike the UK-wide Tribunal, any application for a review must be made within 14 days.

If a review is sought, the tribunal will weed out any unmeritorious applications. Otherwise, it will ask each of the parties for views as to whether the application should be determined without a hearing.

Ordinarily, a review will be undertaken by at least one of the members of the tribunal who made the original decision.

Applying for a review does not suspend the ordinary 30-day time limit for applying for permission to appeal, although it is thought that the tribunal will suspend determination of any such application pending the review.

For completeness, it should be noted that the Scottish rules do not contain an equivalent for the following UK-wide rules:

- rule 18 (lead cases);
- rule 19 (applications without notice)
- rule 21 (starting other applications or references)
- rule 22 (hardship applications)
- rule 34 (consent orders)
- rule 38 (setting aside decisions) (but see the discussion on rule 40 above).

Appendix 1 – Allocation of HMRC decisions to the Chambers of the First-tier Tribunal

The allocation of cases to the different chambers of the First-tier Tribunal is determined by the *First-tier Tribunal and Upper Tribunal (Chambers) Order* 2010.

HMRC decisions appealed to the Tax Chamber

Appeals against most appealable decisions by HMRC and the Welsh Revenue Authority are heard in the Tax Chamber.

These include appeals against the following:

- decisions under s. 8 of the *Social Security Contributions (Transfer of Functions, etc.) Act* 1999 (or decisions varying or superseding such decisions); these cover for example:
    - National Insurance – whether someone was an earner and if so, which category of earner;
    - National Insurance – liability to pay contributions of a particular class;
    - Entitlement to statutory payments (maternity pay, sick pay etc.);
- penalty determinations in respect of employers under the Tax Credits legislation (now superseded);
- decisions by HMRC on an annual tax claim under the *Child Tax Fund Regulations*;
- requirements to account for an amount under the *Child Tax Fund Regulations*.

HMRC decisions appealed to the Social Entitlement Chamber

The Social Entitlement Chamber will hear all other appeals against decisions in relation to:

- social security benefits;
- (from 12 March 2020) provision of free childcare in early years;
- child support;
- vaccine damage payments;

Appendix 1

- health in pregnancy grant;
- tax credits; and
- child trust funds.

Other decisions appealed to the Tax Chamber

Other matters that may be heard in the Tax Chamber are those concerning:

- the exercise by the Serious Organised Crime Agency of general Revenue functions or Revenue inheritance tax functions (as defined in s. 323 of the *Proceeds of Crime Act 2002*);
- the exercise by the Director of Border Revenue of functions under s. 7 of the *Borders, Citizenship and Revenue Act* 2009 [see note below];
- a function of the Compliance Officer for the Independent Parliamentary Standards Authority; and
- a function of the Welsh Revenue Authority.

Law: SI 2010/2655

Editor's note (not part of the Order)

In the middle bullet point immediately above, the Order refers to a non-existent "*Borders Citizenship and Revenue Act 2009*". It appears that the reference should be to the "*Borders Citizenship and Immigration Act 2009*".

Appendix 2 – Allocation of Tax Chamber cases to the different categories

By practice statement given on 29 April 2013 by the President of the Tax Chamber, the following guidance is given on which cases should be allocated to the Default Paper and Basic case categories. The practice statement replaced a practice direction given by the then Senior President of Tribunals.

The guidance is subject to the over-arching proviso that "nothing in it affects the powers or discretion of the Tribunal in relation to case categorisation generally, nor the ability of any party to an appeal to make any application regarding categorisation of that appeal". In addition, the guidance in relation to the Default Paper and Basic case categories includes the further proviso that the guidance should usually be followed "unless the Tribunal considers that there is a reason why it is appropriate to allocate the case to a different category". Thus, the following allocation should not be considered as any more than preliminary guidance.

Allocated to the Default Paper case category

The following appeals are generally allocated to the Default Paper case category:

- appeals against fixed penalties amounting to no more than £2,000 for late filing of returns, statements, accounts or documents and late submissions of notices of chargeability to tax or duty;
- appeals against penalties amounting to no more than £2,000 for late payment of any tax or duty.

Allocated to the Basic case category

The following appeals are generally allocated as Basic cases unless allocated to the Default Paper case category under the above criteria:

- appeals against penalties for late filing of returns and documents and late payment;
- appeals against penalties for inaccurate returns or documents, except appeals against penalties for deliberate

Appendix 2

action and those cases where an appeal is also brought against the assessment of the tax to which the return or document relates;

- appeals seeking the mitigation or reduction of penalties and where reasonable excuse is asserted;
- appeals against information notices and penalties for non-compliance with information notices;
- appeals against PAYE codes.

In addition, the following applications are generally allocated to the Basic case category:

- applications for permission to make a late appeal;
- hardship applications (i.e. in the case of indirect taxes, applications for appeals to be heard without payment of the tax at stake);
- applications for the postponement of tax pending an appeal;
- applications for a closure notice concluding an enquiry.

Allocated to the Standard case category

All appeals not allocated to any other case will be categorised as Standard cases.

Allocated to the Complex case category

The practice statement refers to rule 23(4) which provides the following criteria for a case to be treated as a Complex case:

> The Tribunal may allocate a case as a Complex case under paragraph (1) or (3) only if the Tribunal considers that the case–
> (a) will require lengthy or complex evidence or a lengthy hearing;
> (b) involves a complex or important principle or issue; or
> (c) involves a large financial sum.

The practice statement also suggests that the tribunal will take into account all the circumstances of a particular case including the implications of categorisation as a Complex case (potential costs-shifting under rule 10(1)(c) and the possibility that Complex cases may be transferred to the Upper Tribunal).

Guidance: https://www.judiciary.uk/wp-content/uploads/2014/12/categorisation-of-case-in-the-tax-chamber.pdf

Appendix 3 – Constitution of tribunals in particular cases

Under a practice direction issued by the Senior President of Tribunals on 12 March 2009, the following guidance determines who should make decisions in particular cases:

In all cases

If a decision has been given that disposes of proceedings, the following further decisions should generally be made by a single judge:

- any further decision that suspends the effect of the earlier decision pending an application for permission to appeal, a review application or an appeal itself (see rule 5(3)(l)); and
- any decision upon a review of the decision (see **9.3.4ff** above).

However, the President of the Tax Chamber may, if he considers it appropriate, require the further decision to be made either by:

- the original judges or members who gave the original decision; or
- a panel constituted in accordance with the rules for Basic, Standard and Complex cases set out below.

Default Paper cases

Subject to the above, a decision in a Default Paper case must be made by one judge or other member.

Basic cases

Disposing of proceedings at or following a hearing

Decisions made at or following a hearing that dispose of proceedings or those that determine preliminary issues should generally be made by one or two judges or members, as determined by the Chamber President.

If the Chamber President considers it appropriate, the decision may be made by a panel of three judges or members.

Determination of preliminary issues at or following a hearing

Decisions that determine preliminary issues at or following a hearing should also generally be made by one or two judges or members, as determined by the Chamber President.

Again, if the Chamber President considers it appropriate, the decision may be made by a panel of three judges or members.

Other decisions

Other decisions (including striking out a case (see rule 8), but not at or following a hearing) or giving directions (under rule 5) should be made by a single judge (or a single member if designated by the Chamber President to make such decisions).

Standard and Complex cases

Disposing of proceedings at or following a hearing

Decisions made at or following a hearing that dispose of proceedings or those that determine preliminary issues should generally be made by either:

- a single judge; or
- a single judge together with one or two others (either another judge or a member).

Determination of preliminary issues at or following a hearing

Decisions that determine preliminary issues at or following a hearing should also generally be made by a single judge or a judge alongside one or two judges or members, as determined by the Chamber President.

Other decisions

Other decisions (including striking out a case (see rule 8), but not at or following a hearing) or giving directions (under rule 5) should be made by a single judge.

Guidance: https://tinyurl.com/3uh8m8dc (Practice statement: composition of tribunals)

Appendix 4 – Specimen statement of agreed facts and issues

IN THE FIRST-TIER TRIBUNAL (TAX CHAMBER)

CASE No: 2022/TC/0000

BETWEEN:

TAXPAYER LTD

Appellant

and

**COMMISSIONERS FOR
HM REVENUE & CUSTOMS**

Respondents

**STATEMENT OF AGREED
FACTS AND ISSUES**

1. The case concerns the deduction of £60,000 claimed by the Appellant as a trading expense in its corporation tax return for the year ended 31 December 2020.

2. The Appellant is a web designer with 15 officers or employees (ten full-time and five part time). The Appellant is registered for VAT and all of its supplies are taxable for VAT purposes.

3. The Appellant started to trade in 2013 and, since 2015, has occupied premises in a serviced office building in the centre of Trumpton.

4. In April 2020, the Appellant contracted with a company known as Build-A-Pod Ltd for the provision of 15 work pods to be erected in the gardens of the homes of the Appellant's 15 members of staff. The price per pod was £4,000 plus VAT.

5. The Appellant has treated the total expense as a trading deduction.

6. The issues for the tribunal are:

    a. whether the £60,000 costs are revenue or capital in nature; and

    b. if revenue, whether they were incurred wholly and exclusively for the purposes of the Appellant's trade.

7. The parties are agreed that, if the expenditure is considered to be capital in nature then there are further disputes as to whether the pods qualify for plant and machinery allowances and, if so, whether there needs to be a just and reasonable adjustment. However, the

parties are content for a decision in principle at this stage (i.e. whether the expenditure is capital in nature) and will revert to the tribunal if subsequent agreement cannot be reached.

Appendix 5 – Specimen witness statement

IN THE FIRST-TIER TRIBUNAL (TAX CHAMBER)

CASE No: 2022/TC/0000

BETWEEN:

TAXPAYER LTD

Appellant

and

COMMISSIONERS FOR HM REVENUE & CUSTOMS

Respondents

WITNESS STATEMENT OF A TAXPAYER

I, ALBERT TAXPAYER, of 3 THE SQUARE, TRUMPTON, TRUMPTONSHIRE, TU1 2AA, **WILL SAY AS FOLLOWS**:

1. I make this statement from facts and matters within my own knowledge, from information provided to me by my accountants and from my review of documents relevant to these appeals.

2. This statement supplements the statement of agreed facts and issues submitted to the tribunal on 24 December 2022.

3. I am a director of Taxpayer Ltd, having founded the company in 2013.

4. The company has grown quickly and part of its success is the collaborative working practices I have encouraged. Part of my strategy has been to hire desirable office space in the town centre which is easy to access and is close to other local amenities.

5. Our working model was suddenly and unexpectedly challenged by the onset of the Coronavirus pandemic and the instruction for non-essential workers to remain at home.

6. Although some of our staff had facilities at home to work without distraction, we knew that others lived in smaller spaces. So as not to discriminate between different members of staff, I took the view that the harmonious working environment I have developed would be best served by ensuring that pods are made available to all workers.

7. The last of the pods was erected by the end of April 2020.

8. For the rest of 2020, to the best of my knowledge, all company work (that would ordinarily take place in the office) has been carried out in the pods. With the use of remote conferencing facilities, we have as

	well as we could in the circumstances created a virtual office so that staff are able to interact with each other as much as they would have done before the pandemic.
9.	This working model continued into 2021 although from April of that year, we started to combine it with a limited return to the office, albeit with no more than four members of staff at the premises at any one time.
10.	I accept that it is inevitable that the pods will not be used exclusively for the company's business and indeed the part-time workers have confirmed that they have used the pods for part of their other jobs. However, I understand that this should not affect the company's tax treatment.
11.	I have read the HMRC arguments about the "permanence" of the pods. However, when we incurred the expenditure, we had believed that the pandemic would be resolved long before Christmas 2020 and we therefore believe that the expenditure should be written off in that one year.

The contents of this statement are true to the best of my knowledge.

Signed *Albert Taxpayer*
Date 1 August 2023

Appendix 6 – Specimen skeleton argument

IN THE FIRST-TIER TRIBUNAL (TAX CHAMBER)

CASE No: 2022/TC/0000

BETWEEN:

TAXPAYER LTD

Appellant

and

COMMISSIONERS FOR HM REVENUE & CUSTOMS

Respondents

APPELLANT'S SKELETON ARGUMENT

Introduction

1. The case concerns the deductibility of £60,000 when ascertaining the taxable profits of the taxpayer.

Summary of relevant facts and issues

2. The parties have agreed a statement of facts and issues. This is supplemented by a witness statement from the taxpayer's director.

3. The main dispute is whether the expenditure is capital or revenue in nature. If revenue, there is a further dispute as to whether it was incurred wholly and exclusively for the taxpayer's trade.

Capital or revenue

4. Although there is a fundamental distinction in the tax treatment between capital and revenue expenditure, there is no single definition as to where the boundary lies. In truly borderline cases, the taxpayer submits that the accounting treatment (if not obviously wrong) should be followed.

5. It is acknowledged that the pods have been used for over a year (and indeed, have now been used for over two years). However, at the time of the expenditure, the expectation was that the pods would be of limited use after only a few months. This points towards the expenditure being revenue in nature.

6. Furthermore, the pods have been effectively provided to the taxpayer's staff without any precondition as to their use after installation (although it must be acknowledged that a combination of the need to work effectively and a sense of camaraderie has meant that the staff have used these pods when performing work for the taxpayer – except on those occasions when they have actually been in the office). Accordingly, without prejudice to the suggestion that the pods amount to a taxable benefit-in-kind, the pods are more akin to the provision of a staff bonus rather than the provision of some asset of enduring benefit. Again, this points towards the expenditure being revenue in nature. See *Tucker (HM Inspector of Taxes) v Granada Motorway Services Ltd* (1979) 53 TC 92.

Wholly and exclusively

7. The taxpayer relies upon the arguments in the preceding paragraph to support the view that the expenditure was incurred wholly and exclusively for the purposes of its trade.

8. Furthermore, the taxpayer obtained no benefit (not even subconsciously) other than the morale of its workforce and the effective continuation of its trade. Such purposes fall squarely within the statutory phrase "wholly and exclusively for the purposes of the trade".

Conclusion

9. For all these reasons, it is respectfully submitted that the expenses are allowable and the appeal should be allowed in full.

Appendix 7 – Useful websites

Tax Chamber – guidance:

https://www.gov.uk/courts-tribunals/first-tier-tribunal-tax

Tax Chamber – forms:

https://www.gov.uk/tax-tribunal

Tax Chamber – rules:

https://www.gov.uk/government/publications/tax-chamber-tribunal-procedure-rules

Tax Chamber – published decisions:

www.financeandtaxtribunals.gov.uk/Aspx/default.aspx

Upper Tribunal – forms:

https://www.gov.uk/tax-upper-tribunal/how-to-appeal

Upper Tribunal – decisions:

https://www.gov.uk/tax-and-chancery-tribunal-decisions

British and Irish Legal Information Institute – online database of many recent Court and Tribunal decisions:

www.bailii.org

HMRC litigation and settlement strategy:

https://www.gov.uk/government/publications/litigation-and-settlement-strategy-lss

Appendix 8 – Transitional rules

The *Transfer of Tribunal Functions and Revenue and Customs Appeals Order* 2009 (SI 2009/56) contained a wide range of provisions to ensure that the existing statutory code was modified to deal with the introduction of the tribunals on 1 April 2009, so far as tax cases were concerned.

The *Order* included the various rules for internal reviews which were inserted into various parts of the primary tax code.

Schedule 3 to the *Order* contains a number of transitional provisions for cases known as "current proceedings". These are cases that were transferred into the tribunal on 1 April 2009 from predecessor tribunals. The Schedule also deals with (direct tax) cases where an appeal had been made to HMRC before 1 April 2009, but where no appeal had been by then notified to the tribunal.

A summary of the key provisions applicable to those cases referred to as "current proceedings" can be found in earlier editions of this book.

Appendix 9 – Statutory instruments

The following statutory instruments are referred to in the text.

UK instruments

SI 1986/1711	The Stamp Duty Reserve Tax Regulations 1986
SI 1999/1027	The Social Security Contributions (Decisions and Appeals) Regulations 1999
SI 2003/2837	The Stamp Duty Land Tax (Administration) Regulations 2003
SI 2004/2199	The Venture Capital Trust (Winding up and Mergers) (Tax) Regulations 2004
SI 2007/1509	The Control of Cash (Penalties) Regulations 2007
SI 2008/2685	The Tribunal Procedure (First-tier Tribunal) (Social Entitlement Chamber) Rules 2008
SI 2008/2698	The Tribunal Procedure (Upper Tribunal) Rules 2008
SI 2008/2835	The First-tier Tribunal and Upper Tribunal (Composition of Tribunal) Order 2008
SI 2009/56	The Transfer of Tribunal Functions and Revenue and Customs Appeals Order 2009
SI 2009/273	The Tribunal Procedure (First-tier Tribunal) (Tax Chamber) Rules 2009
SI 2009/275	The Appeals (Excluded Decisions) Order 2009
SI 2010/2655	The First-tier Tribunal and Upper Tribunal (Chambers) Order 2010
SI 2014/1264	The Revenue and Customs (Amendment of Appeal Provisions for Out of Time Reviews) Order 2014

Appendix 9

| SI 2020/416 | The Tribunal Procedure (Coronavirus) (Amendment) Rules 2020 |

Scottish instruments

The following Scottish statutory instruments are referred to in the text.

SSI 2016/231	The Scottish Tribunals (Time Limits) Regulations 2016
SSI 2017/69	The First-tier Tribunal for Scotland Tax Chamber (Procedure) Regulations 2017
SSI 2017/106	The First-tier Tribunal for Scotland (Transfer of Functions of the First-tier Tax Tribunal for Scotland) Regulations 2017

Glossary

The terminology used in the context of tribunal proceedings is often misleading as terms are often used with different meanings in a broadly similar context.

In this book, I have attempted to introduce some consistency and have used the following terms with the meanings specified.

Appeal

Can refer to the notification by or on behalf of a taxpayer of an objection to a decision made by HMRC. In practice, it can also refer to the dispute itself when brought to the tribunal and also to any further challenge made by one of the parties against the tribunal's decision (to be heard in the Upper Tribunal).

Generally, the use of the term has been restricted in these pages to the first meaning unless the context makes it clear that another meaning is intended.

Appellant

The party bringing the appeal to the tribunal. In the Tax Chamber, this will almost invariably be the taxpayer.

Application

A procedural step by which one of the parties requests that the tribunal makes a direction concerning the status or progress of a case.

Case

Any dispute that is before the tribunal.

Chamber

A sub-division of the tribunal. See, for example, **Tax Chamber** below.

Costs (or, in Scotland, expenses)

The legal costs incurred by a party in the preparation of a case and the hearing.

Decision

The tribunal's determination of the matter(s) before it. The decision might be procedural in nature resulting in a direction (or a refusal to give a particular direction). Or the decision might be a substantive decision determining the dispute between the parties (or part of it).

Direction

A decision by the tribunal concerning a procedural aspect of the case. For example, the tribunal might direct one party to provide a witness statement by a particular date. Alternatively, the tribunal might direct that the case be allocated to a particular category of cases (see **5.6** above).

The First-tier Tribunal

The venue where cases are first argued before an independent judiciary in the vast majority of tax cases. The lowest level in the hierarchy of courts and tribunals.

Hearing

The consideration of a dispute by the tribunal. Hearings will often be "oral hearings" in that the tribunal will sit formally and hear arguments put orally to it.

However, the tribunal will also consider disputes without a formal hearing, "paper hearings", in which the tribunal will reach a decision purely on the basis of the documents before it.

Lead case

If a point of principle is relevant to two or more different cases, the tribunal might decide to let only one case (the "lead case") proceed initially in the expectation that the remaining cases can be resolved once the outcome of the lead case is known. See also **4.2.6** and **4.16** above.

Parties

Usually, the two sides to any dispute, the taxpayer and HMRC. Sometimes, third parties can be joined to a case where they have a financial interest in the outcome of the case (for example, a question as to the correct operation of PAYE would often impact the employee as well as the employer).

Respondents

The parties in an appeal who are not the appellant or appellants – or in the case of an application, the parties who are not the Applicant or Applicants.

In appeals before the Tax Chamber, HMRC are almost always the respondents. However, third parties who are brought into the case because of an interest in the outcome are technically referred to as respondents.

Furthermore, there are some tax proceedings in the tribunal which are instigated by HMRC (for example in cases where HMRC seek to obtain information from taxpayers). HMRC would then be the Applicants in such cases and any person challenging those proceedings would be a respondent.

Skeleton argument

A document often prepared by a party in advance of a hearing which summarises the factual and legal propositions to be put forward by that party at the hearing itself. See **6.5.4** above and **Appendix 6**.

Stay (or, in Scotland, sist)

Putting the proceedings "in suspense" for a limited or indefinite period. For example, if the matter at the heart of the dispute is being considered by a higher court, the case might be put on hold until the resolution of the matter by that other court. Alternatively, one party might ask for, say, a six-month stay to give it the opportunity to gather more evidence (assuming that such a delay can be justified) or to see if the parties can resolve the dispute through other means.

Tax Chamber/Tax and Chancery Chamber

As the tribunal covers a wide range of subject matters, the specialist expertise of its judiciary is allocated to different chambers, each dealing with a particular segment of the tribunal's caseload.

In the FTT, tax cases are allocated to the Tax Chamber. (Tax credits cases are treated as social security cases and are allocated to the Social Entitlement Chamber.)

Glossary

In the Upper Tribunal, tax cases are allocated to the Tax and Chancery Chamber (previously, the Finance and Tax Chamber).

Taxpayer

The person who has the right to bring the dispute to the tribunal. Usually, that person will be the recipient of an assessment etc. However, particularly in the context of VAT, some third parties have the right to bring appeals to the tribunal. In all cases, even though the person might not actually be liable for any tax, the term "taxpayer" is used.

The tribunal

The over-arching term covering the FTT and the Upper Tribunal (as appropriate).

The term will also be used to refer to the panel of judges and members hearing a particular case, i.e. "The tribunal concluded …"

Tribunals Service

The part of the Civil Service dealing with the administration (such as paperwork and the location) relating to proceedings in the tribunal.

The Upper Tribunal

Where appeals from decisions of the FTT will be argued. In very rare cases, cases will be argued first in the Upper Tribunal having by-passed the First-tier.

The Upper Tribunal is able to give binding precedents and has the status of the High Court in England and Wales.

Wasted costs

See **4.8.3** above.

Table of primary legislation

Arbitration Act 1996
Part 1 .... 3.4
Banking and Financial Dealings Act 1971
1 .... 4.10, 4.10.3, 10.2
Borders, Citizenship and Immigration Act 2009
7 .... 3.2, App. 1
Capital Allowances Act 2001
204(3) 2.3.3
563 .... 3.2, 5.4, 5.6
Civil Procedure Rules
Rule 24.2(a) 4.6.4
Rule 48.7 .... 4.8.4
Contempt of Court Act 1981
9(1) 8.5.7
19 .... 8.5.7
Coronavirus Act 2020
89(1) 4.3.1, 7.4.4, 7.5.1
90 .... 4.3.1, 7.4.4, 7.5.1
Counter Terrorism Act 2008
Sch. 7, para. 26 .... 3.2
Sch. 7, para. 28 .... 3.2
Courts Act 2003
2(1) 4.1
Diplomatic Privileges Act 1964
Sch. 1 .... 4.14.6
Finance Act 1986
98 .... App. 2
Finance Act 1994
59G(6) 5.3.3
60 (4A) 5.5.1
60 (4B) 5.5.5
Sch. 18, para. 17(2) .... App. 2
Sch. 18, para. 17(3) .... App. 2
Sch. 18, para. 31A 2.1.2
Sch. 18, para. 31A(2) 2.3.3
Sch. 18, para. 33(1) 2.1.2
Finance Act 1996
54G(6) 5.3.3
55(3A) 5.5.1

55(3B) 5.5.5
Finance Act 1998
Sch. 18, para. 30(5) 2.3.2
Sch. 18, para. 31A 2.1.2
Sch. 18, para. 31A(2) 2.3.3
Sch. 18, para. 33(1) 2.1.2
Finance Act 1999
Sch. 17, para. 11A(2) 2.4.1
Sch. 17, para. 11A(3) 2.4.2
Finance Act 2000
Sch. 6, para, 121G(6) 5.3.3
Sch. 6, para, 122(2A) 5.5.1
Sch. 6, para, 122(2B) 5.5.5
Sch. 15, para. 91(5) 9.3.7, 9.6.2
Finance Act 2001
40G(6) 5.3.3
41(2A) 5.5.1
41(2B) 5.5.5
Finance Act 2003
76 ..... App. 2
81 ..... App. 2
81A ..... App. 2
93(3) ..... App. 2
93(4) ..... App. 2
Sch. 10, para. 19(2) 2.1.2, 2.3.3
Sch. 10, para. 24(1) 2.1.2
Sch. 10, para. 35(3) 2.3.2
Sch. 10, para. 44(2) 2.4.1
Sch. 10, para. 44(3) 2.4.2
Sch. 17A, para. 3 ..... App. 2
Sch. 17A, para. 4 ..... App. 2
Sch. 17A, para. 8 ..... App. 2
Finance Act 2004
257(1) ..... App. 2
257(2) ..... App. 2
260(1) ..... App. 2
306A 9.3.7, 9.6.2
308A 9.3.7, 9.6.2
313B 9.3.7, 9.6.2
314A 9.3.7, 9.6.2
Finance Act 2007
Sch. 24, para. 15 ..... App. 2
Sch. 24, para. 17 ..... 8.6.1

Finance Act 2008
Sch. 36 .... 2.1.4, 5.2.1, 5.2.2, 9.5.3, App. 2
Sch. 36, para. 1 .... 5.2.2
Sch. 36, para. 2 .... 5.2.2
Sch. 36, para. 3 .... 2.1.2, 5.2.1
Sch. 36, para. 3(1) 5.2.2
Sch. 36, para. 3(2A) 5.2.2
Sch. 36, para. 4A(8) 5.2.2
Sch. 36, para. 5 .... 2.1.2, 5.2.1, 5.2.2
Sch. 36, para. 5(3) 5.2.2
Sch. 36, para. 5(3A) 5.2.2
Sch. 36, para. 6(4) 9.6.3
Sch. 36, para. 10 .... 5.2.2
Sch. 36, para. 10A 5.2.2
Sch. 36, para. 11 .... 5.2.2
Sch. 36, para. 12A 5.2.2
Sch. 36, para. 12B(1) 5.2.2
Sch. 36, para. 12B(4) 5.2.2
Sch. 36, para. 13 .... 2.1.2, 5.2.1
Sch. 36, para. 13(1A) 5.2.2
Sch. 36, para. 13(3) 9.6.3
Sch. 36, para. 29 .... 2.1.4, 5.2.2
Sch. 36, para. 29(3) 4.6.3
Sch. 36, para. 30 .... 2.1.4, 5.2.2
Sch. 36, para. 32(5) 9.6.3
Sch. 36, para. 39 .... 5.2.2
Sch. 36, para. 40 .... 5.2.2
Sch. 36, para. 53 .... 5.2.2
Sch. 36, para. 29(3) 4.6.3

Finance Act 2011
Sch. 23, para. 5(3) 5.2.2
Sch. 23, para. 5(6) 9.6.3
Sch. 23, para. 28 .... 5.2.2
Sch. 23, para. 30 .... 5.2.2
Sch. 23, para. 31 .... 5.2.2
Sch. 23, para. 29(5) 9.6.3

Finance Act 2012
Sch. 38, para. 13(3) 9.6.3
Sch. 38, para. 20(6) 9.6.3

Finance Act 2013
Sch. 33, para. 35(2) 2.3.2
Sch. 33, para. 37(2) 2.4.1

Finance Act 2014
256(1) 5.2.2

256(2)	5.2.2
266(3)	5.2.2
266(10)	9.6.3
278	5.2.2
Sch. 35, para. 2	5.2.2

Finance Act 2017

Sch. 10, para. 11	5.5.5, 9.6.3

Finance Act 2020

Sch. 8, para. 46	9.6.3

Finance Act 2021

Sch. 11, para. 11	5.5.5, 9.6.3

Human Rights Act 1998 .... 4.13.3, 4.14.3

Income Tax Act 2007

697(4)	9.3.7, 9.6.2

Inheritance Tax Act 1984

35A(2)	9.6.2
79A(2)	9.6.2
223(2)	2.4.1
223(3)	2.4.2
35A(2)	9.3.7
79A(2)	9.3.7

Litigants in Person (Costs and Expenses) Act 1975

1	4.8.9
2	4.8.9

Proceeds of Crime Act 2002

317	3.2
323	App. 1

Revenue Scotland and Tax Powers Act 2014

43(1)	10.2
43(2)	10.2
46(1)	10.2
233	10.1
236(2)	10.2
242	10.2
243(2)	10.2

Senior Courts Act 1981

31A	9.3.8
51(6)	4.8.4

Social Security Contributions & Benefits Act 1992

Sch. 1, para. 7	App. 2

Social Security Contributions (Transfer of Functions, etc.) Act 1999

8	App. 1

Taxation (International and Other Provisions) Act 2010
Sch. 7A, para. 63 .... 9.6.3
Taxation of Chargeable Gains Act 1992
138(4) 9.3.7, 9.6.2
Taxes Management Act 1970
28ZA 2.1.2, 4.2.4
28ZA(2) 2.3.3
28A(4) 2.1.2
29 .... 9.6.4
29(4) 9.6.4
29(5) 9.6.4
31(2) 2.3.2
42(3) 2.3.3
49 .... 2.1.2
49(2) 2.4.1
49A(2) 2.3.1, 4.5.2
49(3) 2.4.2
49B 2.3.2
49C 2.3.2
49D 2.3.2
49E 2.3.2
49G 2.3.1, 2.3.2
49G(3) 5.3.3
49H 2.3.1, 2.3.2, 4.5.2
49H(3) 5.3.3
50 .... 4.15.1
50(6) 8.7.1
54 .... **2.5.2**, 4.15.1
54(4) 4.15.6
59C .... App. 2
93(2) .... App. 2
93(3) .... App. 2
93(4) .... App. 2
98A(2)(a) .... App. 2
102 .... 2.1.5
118 .... 2.4.5
Tribunals Courts and Enforcement Act 2007
.... 4.2, 4.8.3, 9.7.2
4(1)(e) 4.2.7
9 .... 9.3, 9.3.4
9(1) 9.3.7, 9.3.8
9(2) 9.3.5, 9.8.2
9(3) 9.8.2
9(4)-(8) 9.3.6

Value Added Tax Act 1994

9(4)	9.3.6, 9.8.3
9(7)	9.3.8
9(9)	9.3.8
9(10)	9.3.9
9(11)	9.3.9
11(1)	9.6.2
11(2)	9.7.3
11(3)	9.7.3
11(4)	9.3.9, 9.6.7
11(5)(d)	9.3.8, 9.7.2
11(5)(d)-(f)	9.3.7, 9.6.2 11.6.2
12(2)	4.8.12
12(4)	4.8.12
18(6)	9.3.8
20(3)	9.3.8
22	3.1.1
23	3.2, 3.2.1, 7.4.6
24(1)(b)	2.2.2
25	4.5, 4.5.4
26	10.2
27	10.2
29(2)	4.8.5
29(4)	4.8, 4.8.3
29(5)	4.8.3
29(6)	4.8.3
40(1)	4.1
48(1)	4.8.9
Sch. 4, para. 14	4.2.7
Sch. 5, para. 3	4.1

Value Added Tax Act 1994

83	2.1.1
83A	2.3.1, 2.3.2
83B	2.3.2
83C	2.3.1, 2.3.2
83D	2.3.2
83E	2.3.2
83E(2)	2.4.5
83F	2.3.2
83G	2.3.1, 2.3.2
83G(4)	2.3.2
83G(6)	5.3.3
84(3B)	2.1.2, 5.5.1
84(3C)	5.5.5
84(4ZA-4D)	8.6.1

84(7-7B) 8.6.1
85 .... 4.15.1
85(4) 4.15.6

Table of statutory instruments

(See **Appendix 9** for full names of SIs.)

1986/1711, reg. 9(2)	2.4.1
1986/1711, reg. 9(3)	2.4.2
1999/1027, reg. 10	4.15.1
2003/2837, reg. 24	App. 2
2004/2199, reg. 10(3)	9.3.7
2007/1509	9.6.3
2008/2685	2.1.3
2008/2698, rule 10	5.11.3
2008/2835, art. 8	8.10.1
2009/56, Sch. 3	App. 8
2009/56, Sch. 3, para. 7	4.8, App. 1
2009/56, Sch. 3, para. 7(7)	4.8.13
2009/273	2.4.5, 3.1.1
2009/273, rule 20(4)	2.4.5
2009/275	9.3.7, 9.3.8, 9.6.2
2010/2655	2.1.3, App. 1
2010/2655, art. 7	Ch. 1
2014/1264	2.3.2
2016/231(S)	10.2
2017/69(S)	10.2
2017/106(S)	10.1
2020/416	4.3.1, 7.4.4, 7.5.1

Index of First-tier Tribunal rules

The following table provides an index to the *Tribunal Procedure (First-tier Tribunal) (Tax Chamber) Rules* 2009 (SI 2009/273). The main coverage of particular rules is shown in bold, with other references in normal font.

PART 1 Introduction
1. ....**3.2**
2. ....**3.3**, 4.2.1, 4.6.4, 4.8.11, 4.13.1, 7.2.1, 8.2.1
3. ....**3.4**

PART 2 General powers and provisions
4. ....3.2.1, **4.1**
5. ....4.1.2, 4.1.4, **4.2**, 4.6.1, 4.6.2, 4.6.7, 4.8.6, 4.13.1, 4.14.7, 4.16.1, 5.4.2, 5.8.2, 5.9.2, 6.4, 6.4.1, 8.8.7, 9.2, 9.5.5, 9.6.9, 10.2, App. 3
5A. **4.3**
6. ....4.2.3, 4.2.4, **4.4**
7. ....4.2.4, **4.5**, 4.8.11, 4.14.5, 5.8.2, 5.8.3, 5.9.2, 9.3.5
8. ....2.5.1, 4.5.3, **4.6**, 4.8.5, 7.1.5, 9.6.2, App. 3
9. ....4.6.8, **4.7**
10. ....3.3.4, 3.4.2, 4.2.4, **4.8**, 5.6.7, 7.6.3, App. 8
11. ....**4.9**, 5.4.1, 5.8.2
12. ....**4.10**
13. ....**4.11**
14. ....**4.12**
15. ....3.3.3, 4.2.4, 4.8.5, **4.13**, 5.7.2, 8.8.3
16. ....4.5.4, **4.14**
17. ....4.8.5, 4.8.7, **4.15**
18. ....4.2.4, **4.16**, 8.8.7

PART 3 Procedure before the Tribunal
Chapter 1 – Starting proceedings and allocation of cases to categories
19-22 ....5.1.1
19 ....**5.2**, 5.6.2, 7.2.2, 9.2.1, 9.5.3
20 ....**5.3**, 5.4.2, 5.8.2
21 ....**5.4**, 5.8.2
22 ....**5.5**

Index of Tribunal rules

23-28..5.1.2
23...3.2.1, 4.1.2, 4.8.6, **5.6**, 5.11.3

Chapter 2 – Procedure after allocation of cases to categories
24.. 4.3, 5.6.5, **5.7**
25...4.5.3, 5.6.6, 5.7.2, **5.8**
26.. 4.3, 5.6.4, 5.8.3, **5.9**, 7.1.1
27...5.6.6, 5.6.7, **5.10**
28...5.6.7, **5.11**, 9.3.6

Chapter 3 – Hearings
29...4.3.2, **7.1**
30..**7.2**, 7.3.1, 7.4.5
31..**7.3**
32...4.1.2, 4.12.1, 7.2.2, 7.2.3, **7.4**
32A..**7.5**
33..**7.6**

Chapter 4 – Decisions
34..3.1.2, **9.1**
35..3.1.2, **9.2**

PART 4 Correcting, setting aside, reviewing and appealing Tribunal decisions
36..**9.3**
37...9.3.2, **9.4**, 9.9.2
38...4.6.7, 4.15.5, 7.6.4, 9.3.2, **9.5**, 9.6.6
39...9.2.3, 9.3.2, **9.6**, 9.7.3
40..9.3.2, **9.7**
41..9.3.2, 9.3.4, 9.3.5, 9.6.6, 9.7.2, **9.8**
42..9.5.5, **9.9**

Index of Upper Tribunal rules

Rule 10	5.11.3
Rule 21(2)	9.6.7
Rule 21(3)(b)	9.6.10
Rule 21(6)	9.6.10
Rule 21(7)	9.6.9
Rule 23(2)(a)	9.6.11

Index of cases

288 Group Ltd v HMRC [2013] UKFTT 659 (TC) 4.16.3, 4.16.4
A Divorcee v HMRC [2010] UKFTT 612 (TC) 7.4.3
A&E Services (Midlands) Ltd v HMRC [2013] UKFTT 644 (TC) 9.2.3
Aabsolute Bond Ltd v HMRC [2012] UKFTT 603 (TC) 4.2.4
Abbey Forwarding Limited (in liquidation) v HMRC
  [2014] UKFTT 998 (TC) 4.14.2
Abbey Forwarding Limited (in liquidation) v HMRC
  [2014] UKFTT 1102 (TC) 4.14.2
ABL (Holding) Ltd v HMRC [2017] UKFTT 220 (TC) 4.16.4
Acornwood LLP v HMRC [2014] UKFTT 416 (TC) 4.2.4
Ad Hoc Property Management Ltd v HMRC [2019] UKFTT
  315 (TC) 4.8.5
Adair v HMRC [2021] UKFTT 66 (TC) 2.4.4
Addo v HMRC [2018] UKFTT 530 (TC) 4.14.3, 5.10.2
Advocate General for Scotland v General Commissioners
  for Aberdeen City (Hugh Love) [2005] CSOH 135 .... 5.8.2
Agassi v Robinson (HM Inspector of Taxes) (Costs) [2006]
  1 WLR 2126; [2006] STC 580; [2006] BTC 3 .... 4.8.9
Ahmad v HMRC [2019] UKFTT 682 (TC) 6.5.1
Ahmed v HMRC [2019] UKFTT 701 (TC) 4.8.5
Albert House Property Finance PCC Ltd (in liquidation) v HMRC
  [2020] UKUT 373 (TCC) 4.15.1
Albon Engineering and Manufacturing Ltd v HMRC [2017]
  UKFTT 560 (TC) 4.8.6
Aleena Electronics Ltd v HMRC [2011] UKFTT 608 (TC) 3.3.2
Aleena Electronics Ltd v HMRC (No. 2) [2015] UKFTT 61 (TC) 4.13.1
Allpay Ltd v HMRC [2018] UKFTT 273 (TC) 5.8.3
Amis v Colls (HM Inspector of Taxes) (1960) 39 TC 148 .... 8.8.6
Andrea v HMRC [2017] UKFTT 850 (TC) 7.4.3
Aozora GMAC Investment Ltd v HMRC [2018] UKFTT 706 (TC) 5.11.4
Aozora GMAC Investment Ltd v HMRC [2021] UKFTT 222 (TC) 4.8.7
Archer v HMRC [2016] UKFTT 141 (TC) 2.3.2
Ardmore Construction Ltd v HMRC [2014] UKFTT 453 (TC) 9.2.5
Aria Technology Ltd v HMRC [2018] UKUT 111 (TC) 4.12.1
Arunvill Global Equity Trading Ltd v HMRC [2018] UKFTT 378 (TC) 4.2.6
Ashfield v HMRC [2020] UKFTT 110 (TC) 2.4.4
Ashraf v HMRC [2016] UKFTT 453 (TC) 2.4.3
Aston Markland v HMRC [2011] UKFTT 559 (TC) 2.4.5, 3.3.2
Atlantic Electronics Ltd v HMRC [2013] EWCA Civ 651 .... 4.13.4
Award Drinks Ltd (in liquidation) v HMRC [2017]

Index of cases

UKFTT 509 (TC)	4.2.4, 4.8.6
B v B (Wasted Costs: abuse of process) [2001] 1 FLR 843	4.8.7
B&M Retail Ltd v HMRC [2017] UKFTT 789 (TC)	4.14.3
Babergh District Council v HMRC [2011] UKFTT 341 (TC)	5.6.2
Badaloo t/a Church Hill Finance v The Financial Conduct Authority [2017] UKUT 158 (TCC)	2.5.1
Badzyan v HMRC [2017] UKFTT 439 (TC)	4.2.4, 5.6.7
Bailey v HMRC [2019] UKFTT 94 (TC)	4.6.8
Ballysillan Community Forum v HMRC [2011] UKFTT 257 (TC)	8.7.4
Barclays Services Ltd v HMRC [2021] UKFTT 151 (TC)	4.2.4
Barclays Services Ltd v HMRC [2021] UKFTT 269 (TC)	4.8.7
Barke v SEETEC Business Advocate Technology Centre Ltd [2005] EWCA Civ 578	9.6.6
Barnsley Metropolitan Borough Council v Yerrakalva [2011] EWCA Civ 1255	4.8.10
Bastionpark LLP v HMRC [2016] UKUT 425 (TCC)	4.8.10
Bates v Post Office Ltd [2017] EWHC 2844 (QB)	6.5.2
BAV-TMW-Globaler-Immobilien-Spezialfonds v HMRC [2019] UKFTT 233 (TC)	3.3.3, 4.8.6
Beadle v HMRC [2020] EWCA Civ 562	2.1.4
Bhardwaj v FDA & Others (2012) UKEAT/0157/11/ZT	4.2.8
Bird v HMRC (2008) Sp C 720	4.8.5, 7.6.3
Blackburn Bros Cattle Company Ltd v HMRC [2014] UKFTT 47 (TC)	4.6.2
Bloomsbury Verlag BmbH v HMRC [2015] UKFTT 660 (TC)	2.3.2
Bogle v HMRC [2014] UKFTT 201 (TC)	4.8.9
Booth v HMRC [2018] UKFTT 694 (TC)	2.4.4
Border Revenue v Turek [2020] UKUT 167 (TCC)	2.4.4
BPP Holdings Ltd v HMRC [2016] EWCA Civ 121	3.3.1, 4.4.2, 4.6.4
BPP University College of Professional Studies Ltd v HMRC (No. 2) [2014] UKFTT 917 (TC)	4.6.7
BPP University College of Professional Studies Ltd v HMRC [2018] UKFTT 454 (TC)	4.6.8, 9.6.1
Bradonbay Ltd v HMRC [2015] UKFTT 229 (TC)	4.7.3
British Sky Broadcasting Group plc & Pace plc v HMRC [2012] UKFTT 386 (TC)	4.8.10
Browne v HMRC [2017] UKFTT 867 (TC)	3.3.1, 4.9.1
Buckinghamshire Bingo Ltd v HMRC [2018] UKFTT 257 (TC)	2.4.4
Budheo v HMRC [2019] UKFTT 216 (TC)	4.14.3
Burns v Financial Conduct Authority [2017] EWCA Civ 2140	5.8.3
Bussau v HMRC [2020] UKFTT 38 (TC)	4.6.2
Butt v HMRC [2017] UKUT 325 (TCC)	4.2.8
BW Jacques v HMRC (2005) Sp C 513	2.1.4
Cannon v HMRC [2018] UKFTT 160 (TC)	4.8.5

Index of cases

Capital Air Services Ltd v HMRC [2010]
UKUT 373 (TCC) 4.8.6, 5.6.3, 5.6.7, 5.11.4
Capital Air Services Ltd v HMRC (Costs)
[2011] UKUT 484 (TCC) 4.8.6, 5.6.7
Carlton Clubs Ltd v HMRC [2016] UKFTT 562 (TC) 3.3.3
Carvill v Frost (HM Inspector of Taxes) (2004)
Sp C 447 and (2005) Sp C 468 .... 4.8.9
Catanã v HMRC [2012] UKUT 172 (TCC) 4.8.3
Cavanagh v HMRC [2011] UKFTT 676 (TC) 4.15.5
CGI Group (Europe) Ltd v HMRC [2010] UKFTT 224 (TC) 2.1.4
Chandanmal and Others t/a C Narain Bros v HMRC [2012]
UKFTT 188 (TC) 4.13.2, 5.10.3
Chappell v Pension Regulator [2019] UKUT 209 (TCC) 4.6.7, 4.15.5
Charles t/a Boston Computer Group Europe v HMRC [2014]
UKFTT 481 (TC) 8.9
Chartwell Estate Agents v Fergies Properties [2014] EWCA Civ 506 ..... 3.3.3
Chidzoy v BBC (2018) UKEAT/0097/17/BA 4.6.4
Citibank v NA [2014] UKFTT 1063 (TC) 5.8.3
Clark v HMRC [2011] UKFTT 302 (TC) 2.1.4
Clavis Liberty Fund LP1 v HMRC [2015] UKUT 72 (TCC) 4.14.2
Clear plc (in liquidation) v HMRC (2014) PTA/88/2011 .... 4.4.4
Clipper Group Holdings Ltd v HMRC [2016] UKFTT 712 (TC) 4.8.6
Clunes v HMRC [2017] UKFTT 204 (TC) 7.4.3
Coast Telecom Ltd v HMRC [2019] UKFTT 596 (TC) 4.2.6
Cobalt Data Centre 2 LLP v HMRC [2019] UKUT 342 (TCC) 5.11.4
Colaingrove Ltd v HMCE (2001) VDT 16,981 .... 4.6.4
Collis v HMRC [2011] UKFTT 588 (TC) 8.3.2
Colman, Key, Schilling & Walton Partnership v HMRC [2018]
UKFTT 141 (TC) 4.14.3
Colquhoun v HMRC [2011] UKUT B10 (TCC) 4.8.6
Copthorn Holdings Ltd v HMRC [2013] UKFTT 190 (TC) 4.2.4
Couldwell Concrete Flooring Ltd v HMRC (No. 2) [2017]
UKFTT 85 (TC) 4.2.8, 9.3.5, 9.8.2
Cresswell v HMRC [2017] UKFTT 481 (TC) 4.2.4, 4.9.4
Cuco v HMRC [2013] UKFTT 121 (TC) 7.4.3, 7.4.5
Cummaford v HMRC [2015] UKFTT 675 (TC) 9.5.5
Cummine v HMRC [2021] UKFTT 67 (TC) 2.4.4
Curran v HMRC [2012] UKFTT 655 (TC) 4.8.9
Daly v HMRC [2020] UKFTT 281 (TC) 4.13.3, 5.3.2
Daniel v HMRC [2012] EWCA Civ 1741 .... 2.1.6
Daryanani and Others t/a Teletape v HMRC [2012] UKFTT 319 (TC) 4.2.4
Data Select Ltd v HMRC [2012] UKUT 187 (TCC) 3.3.4
DDR Distributions Ltd v HMRC [2011] UKFTT 443 (TC) 4.2.7, 4.4.4
De Silva v HMRC [2021] UKUT 275 (TCC) 2.4.4

Decker v Hopcraft [2015] EWHC 1170 (QB) 9.5.4
DEFRA v Downs [2009] EWCA Civ 257 .... 4.2.4
Degorce v HMRC [2016] UKFTT 429 (TC) 4.2.4
Deloitte LLP v HMRC [2016] UKFTT 479 (TC) 4.13.2
Deluca v HMRC [2011] UKFTT 579 (TC) 4.8.9
Distinctive Care Ltd v HMRC [2018] UKUT 155 (TCC) 4.8.5, 4.8.7
Distinctive Care Ltd v HMRC [2019] EWCA Civ 1010 .... 4.8.2
Dollar Financial UK Ltd v HMRC [2021] UKFTT 218 (TC) 4.2.4
Dollar Financial UK Ltd v HMRC [2021] UKFTT 253 (TC) 4.6.3
Donnelly v HMRC [2021] UKUT 296 (TCC) 8.7.6
Dorset Healthcare NHS Foundation Trust v MH
  [2009] UKUT 4 (AAC) 4.4.2
Dreams plc v HMRC [2012] UKFTT 614 (TC) 5.6.7
DSG Retail Ltd v HMRC [2009] UKFTT 31 (TC) 7.4.3, 7.4.5
Duncombe v HMRC [2020] UKFTT 248 (TC) 2.4.4
Dunsby v HMRC [2021] UKUT 289 (TCC) 9.6.13
E Buyer UK Ltd v HMRC [2016] UKUT 123 (TCC) 5.8.3
Earthshine Ltd (No. 2) v HMRC [2010] UKFTT 314 (TC) 4.8.5
Earthshine Ltd v HMRC [2010] UKFTT 67 (TC) 4.13.4
Ebuyer Ltd v HMRC [2014] UKFTT 912 (TC) 5.10.2
Ecko Ltd t/a Subway v HMRC [2019] UKFTT 715 (TC) 2.2.1, 5.3.2
Eclipse Film Partners No. 35 LLP v HMRC [2014]
  EWCA Civ 184 .... 4.8.1
Eclipse Film Partners No. 35 LLP v HMRC [2016]
  UKSC 24 .... 4.2.2
Eclipse Film Partners No. 35 LLP v HMRC (No. 2) [2010]
  UKFTT 448 (TC) 4.5.3, 4.8.5, 6.5
Eclipse Film Partners No. 35 LLP v HMRC (No. 3) [2011]
  UKFTT 401 (TC) 4.13.2
Edwards (HM Inspector of Taxes) v Bairstow & Harrison (1955)
  36 TC 207 .... 9.6.5
Edwards-Moss v HMRC [2016] UKFTT 147 .... 4.14.3
Egan v Motor Services (Bath) Ltd [2007] EWCA Civ 1002 .... 9.2.4
Elbrook (Cash and Carry) Ltd v HMRC [2017] UKFTT 143 (TC) 4.2.4
Elbrook (Cash and Carry) Ltd v HMRC [2018] UKFTT 252 (TC) 4.13.3
Elbrook (Cash and Carry) Ltd v HMRC [2021] UKFTT 442 (TC) 6.5.2
Elbrook (Cash and Carry) Ltd v HMRC [2019] UKUT
  201 (TCC) 4.13.1, 4.14.4, 8.8.3
Elder v HMRC [2014] UKFTT 728 (TC) 4.9.1
Elder v HMRC [2017] UKFTT 269 (TC) 8.2
Enviroengineering Ltd v HMRC [2011] UKFTT
  366 (TC) 4.6.4, 4.8.5, 4.8.8
Environmental Practical Solutions Ltd v HMRC [2014]
  UKFTT 1118 (TC) 4.8.4

Index of cases

ERF Ltd v HMRC [2012] UKUT 105 (TCC) 4.8.10
Essex v Inland Revenue Commissioners (1980) 53 TC 719 .... 2.1.4
Eurobay Homecare Ltd v HMRC [2017] UKFTT 185 (TC) 4.15.5
Euromoney Institutional Investor plc v HMRC [2021]
  UKFTT 321 (TC) 9.6.132
Europcar Group UK Ltd v HMRC [2021] UKFTT 359 (TC) 4.13.2
European Food Brokers Ltd v HMRC [2017] UKFTT
  196 (TC) 3.3.1, 3.3.4, 4.2.4
Everyday Wholesale Ltd v HMRC [2021] UKFTT 28 (TC) 4.14.4
Excelsior Commercial and Industrial Holdings Ltd v Salisbury
  Hammer Aspden and Johnson [2002] EWCA Civ 879 .... 4.8.9
Executor of the Estate of Teresa Rosenbaum (deceased) v HMRC
  [2013] UKFTT 495 (TC) 9.5.3
Executors of David Atkins (deceased) v HMRC [2011]
  UKFTT 468 (TC) 4.8.5
Eynsham Cricket Club v HMRC [2019] UKUT 47 (TCC) 9.6.13
Fairford Group Limited plc (in liquidation) v HMRC
  [2014] UKFTT 319 (TC) 4.6.4
Fanfield Ltd v HMRC, Thexton Training Ltd v HMRC
  [2011] UKFTT 42 (TC) 4.2.4
Fastklean Ltd v HMRC [2020] UKFTT 511 (TC) 7.4.7
Feltham v HMRC [2011] UKFTT 612 (TC) 3.3.3
Fife Resources Solutions LLP v Revenue Scotland [2018]
  FTSTC 1 .... 4.6.3, 9.1.3
Filmlab Systems International Ltd v Pennington
  [1995] 1 WLR 673 .... 4.8.7
Finnforest UK Ltd (and others) v HMRC [2011] UKFTT 342 (TC) 5.6.7
First Choice Recruitment Ltd v HMRC [2019] UKFTT 412 (TC) 4.8.11
First Class Communications Ltd v HMRC [2013] FTT 90 (TC) 4.6.4
First Class Communications Ltd v HMRC (No. 2) [2013] UKFTT
  342 (TC) 4.13.4
The First De Sales Limited Partnership v HMRC [2018]
  UKUT 396 (TCC) 4.6.4
First Talk Mobile Ltd v HMRC, First Talk Ltd v HMRC
  [2011] UKFTT 423 (TC) 4.2.4
Fisher v HMRC [2012] UKFTT 335 .... 4.14.3
Flannery v Halifax Estate Agencies Ltd
  (t/a Colleys Professional Services) [2000] 1 WLR 377 .... 9.6.6
Foneshops Ltd v HMRC [2013] UKFTT 675 (TC) 4.6.2
Foulser v HMRC [2011] UKFTT 642 (TC) 4.2.2, 4.2.4, 4.6.1
Fraser v HMRC [2012] UKFTT 189 (TC) 9.2.3, 9.5.3, 9.5.5
G Wilson (Glaziers) Ltd v HMRC [2012] UKFTT 387 (TC) 4.8.2
Galldris LLP v HMRC [2021] UKFTT 331 (TC) 4.6.4
Gandalf IT Ltd v HMRC [2012] UKFTT 573 (TC) 4.2.4

Gardiner v HMRC [2014] UKFTT 421 (TC) 4.13.3
Gardner-Shaw UK Ltd v HMRC [2018] UKFTT 313 (TC) 4.2.4
Gardner-Shaw UK Ltd v HMRC [2018] UKFTT 432 (TC) 4.2.3
Gardner-Shaw v HMRC [2018] UKUT 419 (TCC) 2.5.3
Gardner t/a Gardner's Transport Co v HMRC
 [2010] UKFTT 133 (TC) 7.1.5
Garland v HMRC [2016] UKFTT 573 (TC) 4.6.5
Garritt-Critchley v Ronnan [2014] EWHC 1774 (Ch) 2.2.2, 3.4.1
GE International Inc v HMRC [2010] UKFTT 343 (TC) 9.1.3
General Healthcare Group Ltd v HMRC [2014] UKFTT 353 (TC) 4.16.4
General Healthcare Group Ltd v HMRC [2014] UKFTT 1087 (TC) 3.3.1
Gilbert v HMRC [2018] UKFTT 437 (TC) 9.5.3
Girotra v HMRC [2015] UKFTT 775 (TC) 9.5.3
GLL BVK Internazionaler Immobilien Spezialfonds v HMRC
 [2019] UKUT 17 (TCC) 4.2.4
Global Active Holdings (in the appeal of Global Active Technologies
 (dissolved) v HMRC) (2006) VDT 19715 .... 4.2.4
Globalised Corporation Ltd v HMRC [2012] UKFTT 556 (TC) 4.6.7
Gold Nuts Ltd v HMRC [2017] UKFTT 354 (TC) 3.3.3
Golden Harvest Wholesale Ltd v HMRC [2020] UKFTT 369 (TC) 4.8.1
Grace v HMRC [2011] UKFTT 36 (TC) 4.2.3
Green v HMRC [2018] UKFTT 669 (TC) 4.8.9
Gui Hui Dong v NCA [2016] UKFTT 116 (TC) 4.2.4
Gulamhussein v HMRC [2019] UKFTT 261 (TC) 9.5.3
Gulliver v HMRC [2017] UKFTT 222 (TC) 2.5.2
Half Penny Accountants Ltd v HMRC [2016] UKFTT 45 (TC) 2.3.2
Hankinson v HMRC (2008) Sp C 649 .... 4.2.6
Hanover Company Services Ltd v HMRC [2010] UKFTT 256 (TC) 2.1.4
Hare Wines Ltd v HMRC [2019] UKFTT 556 (TC) 4.8.5
Harrison's Executors v HMRC [2021] UKUT 273 (TCC) 2.1.4
Hastings Insurance Services v HMRC [2018] UKFTT 478 (TC) 7.4.7
HCA International Ltd v JL May-Bheemul (2011) UKEAT/477/10/ZT.. 4.8.5
Hegarty v HMRC [2018] UKFTT 774 (TC) 8.7.5
Henke v HMRC (2006) Sp C 550 .... 4.13.2
Hill v HMRC [2017] UKFTT 277 (TC) 4.6.5
Hills v HMRC [2016] UKUT 266 (TCC) 4.8.4, 4.8.5, 4.8.6, 5.11.3
HJ v London Borough of Brent (SEN) [2011] UKUT
 191 (AAC) 4.8.5, 4.8.10
HMRC v Anson [2011] UKUT 318 (TCC) 7.4.3, 7.4.5
HMRC v Banerjee (No. 2) [2009] EWHC 1229 (Ch) 7.4.3
HMRC v Bosher [2013] UKUT 579 (TCC) 2.1.5
HMRC v BPP Holdings Ltd [2014] UKUT 496 (TCC) 4.6.7
HMRC v BPP Holdings Ltd [2017] UKSC 55
 .... 2.4.4, 3.3.1, 3.3.4, 4.4.2, 4.5.3, 4.6.1, 4.6.4, 4.6.8

Index of cases

HMRC v BMW Shipping Agents Ltd [2021] UKUT 91
(TCC) 2.4.4, 4.2.4, 4.6.7
HMRC v Charlton (and others) [2012] UKFTT 770 (TCC) 8.8.6
HMRC v Cheshire Centre For Independent Living [2020] UKUT
275 (TCC) 4.8.5, 4.8.12, 5.8.3
HMRC v Citibank NA [2017] EWCA Civ 1416 .... 4.14.3
HMRC v CM Utilities [2017] UKUT 305 (TCC) 4.15.1
HMRC v Earlsferry Thistle Golf Club [2014] UKUT 250 (TCC) 9.6.13
HMRC v Eclipse Film Partners No. 35 LLP [2013] UKUT 141
(TCC) 4.8.11
HMRC v Gardiner [2018] EWHC 1716 (QB) 4.8.5
HMRC v Grace [2009] EWCA Civ 1082 .... 9.6.4
HMRC v Hill [2018] UKUT 45 (TCC) 3.3.3, 4.6.4
HMRC v Household Estate Agents Ltd [2007] EWHC 1684
(Ch) 8.2.2, 8.7.3
HMRC v IAC Associates [2013] EWHC 4382 (Ch) 4.14.3
HMRC v Hyrax Resourcing Ltd [2019] UKFTT 175 (TC) 4.13.3
HMRC v Hyrax Resourcing Ltd [2021] UKFTT 212 (TC) 4.14.3
HMRC v Infinity Distribution Ltd (In Administration) [2016]
EWCA Civ 1014 .... 5.8.3
HMRC v Jackson Grundy Ltd [2017] UKUT 180 (TCC) 4.8.1
HMRC v JP Whitter (Water Well Engineers) Ltd [2015] UKUT 392
(TCC) 2.1.3
HMRC v Khawaja [2008] EWHC 1687 (Ch) 8.7.4
HMRC v Kishore [2021] EWCA Civ 1565 .... 2.5.3
HMRC v Mattu [2021] UKUT 245 (TCC) 4.2.4, 4.11.1
HMRC v Murray Group Holdings Ltd (2013) FTC/
15/2013 .... 2.1.4, 4.2.6, 4.12.1
HMRC v Noor [2013] UKUT 71 (TCC) 2.1.4
HMRC v Pendragon plc [2015] UKSC 37 .... 9.6.5
HMRC v RBS Deutschland Holdings GmbH [2006] CSIH 10 .... 4.2.4
HMRC v Ritchie [2019] UKUT 71 (TCC) 3.3.3, 4.2.4
HMRC v Rogers [2019] UKUT 406 (TCC) 4.2.4
HMRC v SSE Generation Ltd [2021] EWCA Civ 105 .... 9.6.13
HMRC v Talentcore Ltd (t/a Team Spirits) [2012] 2 Costs LR 418
[2011] BTC 1941 .... 4.8.10
HMRC v Total Technology (Engineering) Ltd [2012] UKUT 418
(TCC) 2.1.5
HMRC v Tower MCashback LLP1 [2011] UKSC 19 .... 8.3.2
HMRC v Websons (8) Ltd [2020] UKUT 154 (TCC) 2.4.4
HMRC v Woodstream Europe Ltd [2018] UKUT 398 (TCC) 4.6.3
Ho v HMRC [2010] UKFTT 387 (TC) 4.8.5, 8.7.2
Hobbs v FSA (Upper Tribunal, TCC) FS/2010/0024 .... 4.14.2
Home Office v Altion Ltd [2014] UKFTT 574 (TC) 4.8.4

Homeowners Friendly Society Ltd v Barrett (HM Inspector of
Taxes) (1995) Sp C 31 .... 4.8.9
Housesimple Ltd v HMRC [2017] UKFTT 837 (TC) 4.8.5
HSBC Electronic Data Processing (Guangdong) Ltd v HMRC
[2021] UKUT 58 (TCC) 4.7.3
HT & Co (Drinks) Ltd v HMRC [2015] UKFTT 664 (TC) 2.1.6, 5.8.3
HT Purser Ltd v HMRC [2011] UKFTT 860 (TC) 4.13.4
Huitson v HMRC [2017] UKUT 715 (TCC) 4.4.2
Humphries v HMRC [2019] UKFTT 88 (TC) 4.8.9
Hurley v Taylor (HM Inspector of Taxes) (1998)
71 TC 268, [1998] STC 202, [1998] BTC 32 .... 8.8.6
Hurst v HMRC [2019] UKFTT 452 (TC) 9.7.3
Hussain v HMRC [2021] UKFTT 92 (TC) 4.13.4
Hussain v Nottingham Healthcare NHS Trust (2016)
UKEAT/0080/16/DM 4.2.8
Igen Distribution Ltd (in liquidation) v HMRC [2020]
UKFTT 328 (TC) 4.2.4, 4.6.5, 4.14.3
Ijomah v Nottinghamshire Healthcare NHS Foundation Trust
(2020) UKEAT/289/19/RN 4.6.2
Il Vicolo Ltd v HMRC [2020] UKFTT 55 (TC) 4.15.5
Impact Contracting Solutions Ltd v HMRC [2019] UKFTT 646 (TC) 4.2.5
Infocom IT (UK) Ltd v HMRC [2016] UKFTT 319 (TC) 4.8.5
Ingenious Games LLP v HMRC [2014] UKUT 62 (TCC) 4.14.3
Innocent Ltd v HMRC [2011] UKFTT 607 (TC) 4.8.13
Jacks v HMRC [2017] UKFTT 613 (TC) 4.13.3
Jafari v HMRC [2019] UKFTT 692 (TC) 3.3.4
Jamie White v HMRC [2018] UKUT 257 (TCC) 8.8.3
Jhuti v Royal Mail Group UKEAT/0061/17/RN 2.3.5
JK v HMRC [2019] UKFTT 411 (TC) 7.4.3
John Mander Pension Trustees Ltd v HMRC [2012] UKFTT 686 (TC) 4.2.4
Johnson v Gore Wood & Co [2002] 2 AC 1 .... 2.5.3
Jones v Garnett (HM Inspector of Taxes) (2004) Sp C 432 .... 8.10.1
Jones v HMRC [2017] UKFTT 567 (TC) 7.1.5
Jordan v HMRC [2015] UKUT 218 (TCC) 9.6.3
JRO Griffiths Ltd v HMRC [2021] UKFTT 257 .... 8.9
JSM Construction Ltd v HMRC [2016] UKFTT 163 (TC) 4.6.4, 5.8.3
JTI Acquisition Company (2011) Ltd v HMRC [2021]
UKFTT 446 (TC) 7.4.7
Jumbogate Ltd v HMRC [2015] UKFTT 64 (TC) 4.6.7
Kandore Ltd v HMRC [2021] EWCA Civ 1082 .... 5.2.3, 7.1.3
Katib v HMRC [2019] UKUT 189 (TCC) 2.4.4
Kellett v HMRC [2018] UKFTT 130 (TC) 4.8.5
Kempton v Special Commissioners [1992] BTC 553 .... 2.1.4
Kersner v HMRC [2019] UKFTT 221 (TCC) 4.2.4

Index of cases

Khan v HMRC [2019] UKFTT 751 (TC) 4.6.2, 4.6.4
Kingston Maurward v HMRC [2017] UKFTT 502 (TC) 4.16.3
Kishore v HMRC [2013] UKFTT 465 (TC) 4.2.4, 4.2.6
KSM Henryk Zeman SP Zoo v HMRC [2021] UKUT 182 (TCC) 2.1.4
Langham (HM Inspector of Taxes) v Veltema [2004] EWCA Civ 193 ......9.6.4
Laurence Supply Co (Leather Bags) Ltd v HMRC [2021]
  UKFTT 264 (TC) 4.13.2
LD v HMRC [2019] UKFTT 526 (TC) 7.4.3, 8.8.3
Le Bistingo Ltd v HMRC [2013] UKFTT 524 (TC) 2.1.5
Lee v HMRC [2012] UKFTT 312 (TC) 9.6.3
Leeds Cricket Football & Athletic Company Ltd v HMRC [2019]
  UKFTT 568 (TC) 4.13.2
Lenity v HMRC [2021] UKFTT 272 (TC) 4.8.4
LH Bishop Electric Company Ltd v HMRC [2013] UKFTT 522 (TC) 2.1.4
Liberty Wines Ltd v Director of Border Revenue [2018]
  UKFTT 372 (TC) 4.8.5
Limitgood Ltd v HMRC (2007) Sp C 612 .... 8.10.1
Ling v HMRC [2011] UKFTT 793 (TC) 8.8.2
LM v London Borough of Lewisham [2009] UKUT 204 (AAC) 4.13.3
London Luton Hotel BPRA Property Fund LLP [2019]
  UKFTT 212 (TC) 4.2.4
LS v London Borough of Lambeth (HB) [2010] UKUT 461
  (AAC) 9.6.2, 9.6.3
Lucky Technology Ltd v HMRC [2021] UKFTT 55 (TC) 4.14.3
Lysaght v IRC (1927) 13 TC 511 .... 8.7.7, 9.6.5
Mace v Ponders End International (2014) UKEAT/491/13/LA 4.6.2
MacMillan v HMRC [2019] UKFTT 624 (TC) 4.8.6
Madden v HMRC [2018] UKFTT 414 (TC) 4.13.2
Maharani Restaurant v HMCE (1999) STC 295 .... 4.2.4
Mainpay Ltd v HMRC [2018] UKFTT 665 (TC) 9.5.4
Maitland-Hudson v Solicitors Regulation Authority [2019]
  EWHC 67 (Admin) 4.13.2
Manhattan Systems Ltd v HMRC [2017] UKFTT 862 (TC) 4.2.4, 4.2.5
Marcan Shipping (London) Ltd v Kefalas [2007] EWCA Civ 463 .... 4.6.2
Marsh v HMRC [2017] UKFTT 320 (TC) 7.6.1
Marshall & Co v HMRC [2016] UKUT 116 (TCC) 4.8.5
Marshall Glover Ltd v HMRC [2019] UKFTT 271 (TC) 4.8.5
Martland v HMRC [2018] UKUT 178 (TCC) 2.4.4, 4.2.4, 4.6.7, 4.15.5
Maryan t/a Hazeldene Catering v HMRC [2012] UKFTT 215 (TC) 4.8.5
Masstech Corporation Ltd (in administration) v HMRC
  [2011] UKFTT 649 (TC) 4.8.5, 4.13.4, 4.14.3
The Master and Fellows of St Mary Magdalene College in the
  University of Cambridge v HMRC [2011] UKFTT 680 (TC) 2.1.4
Mavisat Ltd v HMRC [2012] UKFTT 253 (TC) 9.2.1

433

MCashback Software 6 LLP v HMRC [2013] UKFTT 679 (TC) 4.7.2, 4.7.5
McCabe v HMRC [2019] UKFTT 317 (TC) 4.14.3
McCabe v HMRC [2020] UKUT 266 (TCC) 4.14.3, 5.10.2
McEnroe v HMRC [2021] UKFTT 94 (TC) 4.2.4
McEwan v HMRC (2005) Sp C 488 .... 4.8.9
McFadzean v HMRC [2019] UKUT 349 (TCC) 4.7.2, 4.7.6
McFarlane v HMRC [2018] UKFTT 282 (TC) 7.6.2
McIlroy v HMRC [2014] UKFTT 429 (TC) 4.13.3
McKee v HMRC [2014] UKFTT 806 (TC) 4.6.4
Megantic Services Ltd v HMRC [2013] UKFTT 492 (TC) 4.13.2
Mehrban v HMRC [2019] UKFTT 603 (TC) 4.2.4
Mehrban v HMRC [2021] UKFTT 53 (TC) 4.2.6
Messrs JH & IM Ward (Partnership) v HMRC [2014] UKFTT 108 (TC) .. 4.8.5
MHA v Secretary of State for Work and Pensions
 [2009] UKUT 211 (AAC) 3.3.4, 4.2.4, 4.13.3
Michel van de Wiele NV v Pensions Regulator
 [2011] UKUT B3 (FS) 4.6.5, 4.6.8
Microring Ltd v HMRC [2019] UKFTT 456 (TC) 4.2.4
Milligan v HMRC [2017] UKFTT 552 (TC) 4.2.6
Moreton Alarm Services (MAS) Ltd v HMRC [2016] UKFTT
 192 (TC) 4.5.3, 5.8.3
Moss v HMRC [2019] UKFTT 686 (TC) 2.4.4
Moyles v HMRC [2012] UKFTT 541 (TC) 7.4.3
Mungavin v HMRC [2020] UKUT 11 (TCC) 3.3.5, 8.8.3
Mr E v HMRC [2018] UKFTT 590 (TC) 5.2.3
Mr E v HMRC [2018] UKFTT 771 (TC) 4.8.9
N A Dudley Electrical Contractors Ltd [2011] UKFTT 260 (TC) 2.4.2
N Brown Group plc v HMRC [2016] UKFTT 445 (TC) 4.2.4, 4.8.6
New Miles Ltd v HMRC (oao Hilton-Foster) [2012]
 UKFTT 33 (TC) 4.7.2
Newton & Newton-Young v HMRC [2019] UKFTT 688 (TC) 7.6.1
Newton v HMRC [2018] UKFTT 513 (TC) 5.6.3
Nicholson v Morris (HM Inspector of Taxes) (1976) 51 TC 95 .... 8.7.1
North Weald Golf Club v HMRC [2014] UKFTT 130 (TC) 4.2.4
Nowroozi v HMRC [2019] UKFTT 533 (TC) 4.6.2, 4.6.7
Nutro UK Ltd v HMRC [2014] UKFTT 971 (TC) 4.6.4
O'Brien v Chief Constable of South Wales Police [2005]
 2 AC 534 .... 3.3.3
O'Brien v HMRC [2012] UKFTT 581 (TC) 4.6.4
O'Flaherty v HMRC [2013] UKUT 161 (TCC) 2.4.2
Oats Services Ltd v HMRC [2011] UKFTT 455 (TC) 4.8.2
OCO Ltd v HMRC [2017] UKFTT 603 (TC) 9.2.4
Odhams Leisure Group Ltd v HMCE [1992] BVC 11 .... 2.1.4
Omagh Minearls Ltd v HMRC [2015] UKFTT 681 (TC) 4.13.3

Index of cases

Oni v NHS Leicester City (2012) UKEAT/0144/12/LA 4.2.8, 4.8.1
The Open University v HMRC [2013] UKFTT 326 (TC) 2.5.2
Orchid Properties v HMRC [2012] UKFTT 651 (TC).......................................4.15.5
Outram v HMRC [2021] UKFTT 29 (TC)..3.3.3
OWD v HMRC [2018] UKFTT 497 (TC) 4.15.6
Oxfam v HMRC [2009] EWHC 3078 (Ch) 2.1.4
Parmar & Ors (t/a Ace Knitwear) v Woods
 (HM Inspector of Taxes) [2002] EWHC 1085 (Ch)...8.2.2
Peries v HMRC [2011] UKFTT 674 (TC)..4.2.4
Perrin v HMRC [2018] UKUT 156 (TCC) 2.4.2, 4.8.5, 4.13.3
PGPH Ltd v HMRC [2016] UKFTT 46 (TC)...4.6.4
Pickles v HMRC [2020] UKFTT 195 (TC) 4.9.4, 4.13.2
Pierhead Drinks Ltd v HMRC [2019] UKUT 7 (TCC) 4.7.3
Pierhead Purchasing Ltd v HMRC [2014] UKUT 321 (TCC) 4.15.5
Pinewood Studios Ltd v HMRC [2012] UKFTT 370 (TC) 4.2.3, 4.2.4
Ping Kong Lam v HMRC [2014] UKFTT 79 (TC) 4.8.4, 4.8.5
Porter & Co v HMRC [2018] UKFTT 264 (TC) 4.9.4
Preferred Refrigeration Ltd v HMRC [2011] UKFTT 466 (TC)........ 2.1.5, 5.7.2
Prince and Others v HMRC [2012] UKFTT 157 (TC) 2.1.4
Procter v HMRC [2012] UKFTT 530 (TC) 5.8.3
Prospect Origin Ltd v HMRC [2021] UKUT 511 (TCC) 4.13.1
PSI Engineering Ltd v HMRC [2011] UKUT 765 (TC)....................................4.8.10
Push Energy Ltd v HMRC [2021] UKFTT 97 (TC) 4.2.4
Quinn v HMRC [2020] UKFTT 51 (TC) 4.8.5
R & J Birkett t/a The Orchards Residential Home v HMRC
 [2017] UKUT 89 (TCC) 2.1.4
R (oao Browallia Cal Limited) v General Commissioners of Income
 Tax for the City of London [2003] EWHC 2779 (Admin)...........................2.4.4
R (oao C) v. FTT Procedure Committee, the Lord Chancellor
 [2016] EWHC 707 (Admin)..2.3.5
R (oao Cook) v General Commissioners [2007] EWHC 167 (Admin) 2.4.4
R (oao Davies and another) v HMRC [2011] UKSC 47 .... 2.1.6, 4.2.4
R (oao Derrin Brothers Properties Ltd) v FTT [2016] EWCA Civ 15 ....5.2.3
R (oao Hankinson) v HMRC [2009] EWHC 1774 (Admin)..............2.1.6, 5.11.3
R (oao Jimenez) v FTT [2017] EWHC 2585 (Admin)..5.2.3
R (oao Totel Ltd) v First-tier Tribunal (Tax Chamber) and
 HMRC [2012] EWCA Civ 1401 ....9.6.3
R (RB) v First-tier Tribunal (Review) [2010] UKUT 160 (AAC).................9.8.4
R v Inland Revenue ex p Taylor (No. 2) [1990] BTC 281.................................2.1.4
R v Randall [2004] WLR 56 ....4.13.4
R v Special Commissioner, ex parte Morgan Grenfell
 & Co Ltd [2002] UKHL 21 ....4.13.3
RA Drinks Ltd v HMRC [2014] UKFTT 304 (TC) 4.8.2
Rai v HMRC [2019] UKFTT 687 (TC) 4.15.5

Index of cases

Rana v London Borough of Ealing [2018] EWCA
  Civ 2074 .... 4.1.4, 4.2.4, 4.8.7, 4.16.4, 9.6.8, 9.6.10, 9.6.11
Rapid Brickwork Ltd v HMRC [2017] UKFTT 194 (TC) 4.2.4, 4.8.6
Rasam Gayatri Silks Ltd v HMRC [2010] UKFTT 50 (TC) 9.1.3
Rashidi v HMRC [2016] UKFTT 357 (TC) 3.3.4, 4.11.3
Reed Employment plc v HMRC [2010] UKFTT 596 (TC)
  (a joint decision of the First-tier and Upper Tribunals) 5.11.4, 8.10.1
Reed Personnel Services plc v HMRC [2009] EWHC 2250 (Admin) 5.11.3
Rennie Smith & Co v HMRC [2013] UKFTT 638 (TC) 3.3.3
Reno v HMRC [2019]] UKFT 184 (TC) 4.6.7
Ridehalgh v Horsefield [1994] Ch 205 .... 4.8.4, 4.8.5
Robb v HMRC [2017] UKFTT 232 (TC) 9.5.4
Roden v HMRC [2013] UKFTT 523 (TC) 4.8.5
Rodgers v HMRC [2018] UKUT 709 (TC) 9.3.5, 9.5.4
Roger Preston Group Ltd v HMRC [2021] UKFTT 132 (TC) 4.8.2, 4.8.6
Rokit Ltd v HMRC [2017] UKFTT 618 (TC) 4.8.5
Romie Tager v HMRC [2018] EWCA Civ 1727 .... 4.13.5
Ronald Hull Junior Ltd v HMRC [2016] UKFTT 525 (TC) 5.8.3
Rosen v HMRC [2013] UKFTT 466 (TC) 4.2.4
Royal Bank of Scotland Group plc v HMRC [2020]
  UKFTT 321 (TC) 4.14.1, 4.14.3
RP Baker (Oxford) Ltd v HMRC [2014] UKFTT 420 (TC) 4.2.4, 4.8.11
Rt Hon Baron Wrottesley v HMRC [2015] UKUT 637 (TCC) 4.2.6
Russell v HMRC [2016] UKFTT 80 (TC) 4.13.3
Sarnoff v YZ [2021] EWCA Civ 26 .... 4.14.1
Scanwell Freight Services Ltd v HMRC [2014] UKFTT 106 (TC) 2.3.2
Scofield v HMRC [2010] UKFTT 377 (TC) 8.8.8
Scofield v HMRC [2012] UKFTT 673 (TC) 3.3.4, 4.8.5, 4.8.10
Scott (t/a Farthings Steak House) v McDonald (HM Inspector
  of Taxes) (1996) Sp C 91 .... 4.8.9
Scott v HMRC [2016] UKFTT 171 (TC) 4.2.4
Second Mezzanine Film Fund LLP v HMRC [2019] UKFTT 283 (TC) 4.6.2
Serco Ltd v Wells (2016) UKEAT/0330/15/RN 4.2.3
Shahzad v HMRC [2011] UKFTT 397 (TC) 2.4.5
Sharifee, Naser & Siddique t/a Café Flutist (anonymised case) v
  Wood (HM Inspector of Taxes) (2004) Sp C 423 .... 7.4.3
Sharma v Financial Services Authority [2010] UKUT 25 (FS) 4.6.5
Sheiling Properties Ltd v HMRC [2020] UKUT 175 (TCC) 2.1.4
Sheth v HMRC [2021] UKUT 164 (TCC) 4.2.8
Shiner v HMRC [2018] EWCA Civ 31 .... 2.5.1
Singleton Birch Ltd v HMRC [2021] UKFTT 440 (TC) 4.13.2
Skelly v HMRC [2014] UKFTT 478 (TC) 5.2.2, 5.2.3, 9.2.1, 9.5.3
Skywell (UK) Ltd v HMRC [2012] UKFTT 611 (TC) 4.7.2
Smart Price Midlands Ltd v HMRC [2019] EWCA Civ 841 .... 5.10.2

Index of cases

Sood v HMRC [2019] UKFTT 368 (TC) 2.4.3
South Herefordshire Golf Club v HMRC (2006) VDT 19767 .... 4.8.13
Southwest Communications Group Ltd v HMRC [2012] UKFTT
   701 (TC) 4.8.5
Snapcrest v HMRC [2020] UKFTT 320 (TC) 2.4.4
Space Maker Storage 2 Ltd (in liquidation) v HMRC [2014] UKFTT
   296 (TC) 4.7.4
Spring Capital Ltd v HMRC [2017] UKFTT 465 (TC) 2.5.1, 2.5.3
Spring Capital Ltd v HMRC [2018] UKFTT 250 (TC) 4.2.4, 9.6.12
Spring Capital Ltd v HMRC [2019] UKFTT 319 (TC) 4.8.6
Spring Capital Ltd v HMRC [2021] UKFTT 147 (TC) 4.13.2
Spring Capital Ltd v HMRC [2021] UKFTT 345 (TC) 4.13.2
Spring Salmon and Seafood Ltd v HMRC [2016] UKUT 313 (TCC) 2.1.4
SRN Horizons Ltd v HMRC [2017] UKUT 246 (TCC) 4.6.4, 4.15.5, 7.1.5
St Martin's Medical Services Ltd v HMRC [2012] UKFTT 485 (TC) 8.3.2
Starmill v HMRC [2013] UKFTT 681 (TC) 4.8.7
Staysure.co.uk Ltd v HMRC [2018] UKFTT 584 (TC) 5.10.2
Stockler v HMRC [2012] UKFTT 404 (TC) 3.3.3, 8.8.5
Sub One Ltd (t/a Subway) v HMRC [2009]
   UKFTT 385 (TC) 4.6.4, 4.16.1, 4.16.2, 4.16.3
Sunrise Medical Ltd v HMRC [2021] UKFTT 316 (TC) 2.4.4
Surestone v HMRC [2009] UKFTT 352 (TC) 5.6.2
Sutton v HMRC [2014] UKFTT 44 (TC) 4.6.4
Symbiosis Imedia Systems Ltd v HMRC [2019] UKFTT 124 (TC) 9.5.4
Synergy Child Services Ltd v Ofsted [2009] UKUT 125 (AAC) 4.6.7
Tadmarton Heath Golf Club Ltd v HMRC [2016] UKFTT 376 (TC) 4.16.4
Tager v HMRC [2015] UKUT 663 (TCC) 9.4.1, 9.5.3
Tarafdar v HMRC [2014] UKUT 362 (TCC) 4.8.5
Tasca Tankers Ltd v HMRC [2021] UKFTT 25 (TC) 4.13.4
Taylor v HMRC [2017] UKFTT 769 (TC) 5.10.3
Technetix v HMRC [2015] UKFTT 369 (TC) 4.9.2
Thatthiah v HMRC [2017] UKFTT 601 (TC) 4.13.3
Thomas Holdings Ltd v HMRC [2011] UKFTT 656 (TC) 4.8.9
Three Rivers DC v Bank of England [2001] UKHL 16 .... 4.6.4
Thuishyanthan v HMRC [2016] UKFTT 186 (TC) 2.3.1
Tibbles v SIG plc [2012] EWCA Civ 518 .... 4.2.3
Ticketmaster UK Ltd v The Information Commissioner [2021]
   UKFTT 83 (GRC) 4.2.4
Tower Bridge GP Ltd v HMRC [2016] UKFTT 54 .... 4.14.3
Trans-Int SRL v HMRC [2011] UKFTT 326 (TC) 4.6.7
Trimax Trading International Ltd v HMRC [2014] UKFTT 733 .... 4.14.3
Trustees of the BT Pension Scheme v HMRC [2015] EWCA Civ 713 .... 2.1.4
Tucker v HMRC [2019] UKFTT 569 (TC) 4.2.4
Ulster Metal Refiners Ltd v HMRC [2019] UKFTT 385 (TC) 2.5.4

Unicorn Shipping Ltd v HMRC [2017] UKFTT 64 (TC) 5.3.2
The Vaccine Research Limited Partnership v HMRC [2018]
   UKFTT 597 (TC) 4.2.6
Vardy Properties v HMRC [2013] UKFTT 96 (TC) 4.8.9, 4.8.10, 4.8.11
Versteegh Ltd v HMRC [2014] UKFTT 397 (TC) 4.8.6, 4.8.10
Viking Enterprises Ltd v HMRC [2020] UKFTT 306 (TC) 4.6.7, 5.10.2
Vimaleswaran v HMRC [2019] UKFTT 222 (TC) 4.6.4
Vodafone 2 v HMRC (2007) Sp C 622 .... 8.10.1
Walker v HMRC [2012] UKFTT 225 (TC) 4.8.5
Wallace v HMRC [2012] UKFTT 433 (TC) 5.3.2
Waller v HMRC [2010] UKFTT 40 (TC) 4.8.5
Wallis v HMRC and another [2013] UKFTT 81 (TC) 4.8.5
Walsh v HMRC [2019] UKFTT 350 (TC) 4.8.9
Wammee Holdings Ltd v HMRC [2020] UKFTT 240 (TC) 4.8.5
Warren v HMRC [2017] UKFTT 521 (TC) 4.7.7, 4.8.6, 4.8.11
Watson t/a Kirkwood Coaches v HMRC [2013] UKFTT 553 (TC) 4.2.8
Waverton Property LLP v HMRC [2017] UKFTT 853 (TC) 4.2.4
Western Ferries (Clyde) Ltd v HMRC [2011] UKFTT 541 (TC) 4.8.9
Westminster College of Computing Ltd v HMRC [2014] UKFTT
   132 (TC) 4.6.3
Westminster Trading Ltd v HMRC [2017] UKUT 23 (TCC) 4.2.4
Wheeler v HMRC [2019] UKFTT 336 (TC) 4.8.5, 4.8.8
Whitehill Pelham Ltd v HMRC [2017] UKFTT 781 (TC) 4.6.8
Whittalls Wines Ltd v HMRC [2019] UKUT 260 (TCC) 4.2.4
Wiggins Alloys Ltd v Jenkins [1981] IRLR 275 .... 4.8.9
Willow Court Management Company (1985) Ltd v Alexander
   [2016] UKUT (LC) 4.8.9
Wilsons Solicitors LLP v HMRC [2019] UKFTT 341 (TC) 4.8.5
Wimpole Interiors Ltd v HMRC [2014] UKFTT 424 (TC) 4.6.3
Wind Energy Renewables LLP v Revenue Scotland [2021] FTSTC 2 ...... 10.2
Wired Orthodontics Ltd v HMRC [2020] UKFTT 290 (TC) 4.13.2
Wood Green Animal Shelters v HMRC [2013] UKFTT 566 (TC) 4.8.5
Wood v Holden (HM Inspector of Taxes) [2006] EWCA Civ 26 .... 8.7.7
Woodhouse v Hampshire Hospitals NHS Trust
   (2012) UKEAT/0132/12/DM 3.3.3
Workstation Farnham Ltd v HMRC [2015] UKFTT 37 (TC) 2.4.4
World of Enterprise Ltd v HMRC [2011] UKFTT 719 (TC) 2.4.2
Worldpay (UK) Ltd v HMRC [2019] UKFTT 235 (TC)
   .... 2.4.4, 3.3.3, 4.14.3, 5.8.3
Wright (No. 2) v HMRC [2013] UKUT 481 (TCC) 4.2.4
Wright v HMRC [2009] UKFTT 227 (TC) 9.5.4
Wrottesley – see *Rt Hon Baron Wrottesley v HMRC*
Xentric Limited v HMRC [2010] UKFTT 249 (TC) 3.3.3, 4.13.4
XG Concept Ltd v HMRC [2017] UKFTT 92 (TC) 4.6.4

XYZ v HMRC [2016] UKFTT 402 (TC) 7.4.5
Zahra v The Home Office [2014] UKFTT 519 (TC) 8.8.3
Zanaco Investments Ltd v HMRC [2012] UKFTT 518 (TC) 4.8.5

General index

Abandonment of case
   costs orders 4.8.5
Absent party
   consequences (cost) 7.6.3
   consequences (other) 7.6.4
   procedure 7.6.2
   unjustified absence 4.8.5
Abuse of process
   general principles 2.5.1
   inappropriate behaviour 2.5.3
   issue estoppel 2.5.2
   remitted hearings 2.5.4
   res judicata 2.5.2
Accelerated payment notices
   jurisdiction of Tax Chamber 2.1.4
Accountancy advice
   costs orders 4.8.9
Addition of parties
   generally 4.7.3
   in Scotland 10.2
Adjournments
   generally 8.5.6
   lead cases 4.2.4
   medical grounds 4.2.4
Aggregates levy
   appeals from the FTT 9.6.3
Allocation of cases to categories – *see* **Categories (allocation of cases to)**
Allocation of cases to different Chambers .... App. 1
Alternative direction 4.7.5
Alternative dispute resolution and arbitration
   advantages 2.2.1
   generally 3.4.1
   Litigation and settlement strategy (tension with) 2.2.2
Amendment of documents 4.2.4
Annual tax on enveloped dwellings
   appealable decision 2.1.2
   late appeals 2.4.1
Anonymisation of decision notice
   after public hearing 7.4.5

Appeals from tribunal
  aggregates levy hardship applications ... 9.6.3
  applying for permission ... 9.6.7
  climate change levy hardship applications ... 9.6.3
  cross-appeals ... 9.6.13
  definition (limited) ... 9.3, *Glossary*
  digital services tax ... 9.6.3
  error and mistake claims ... 9.6.3
  errors of fact ... 9.6.5
  error of law ... 9.6.4
  excluded decisions ... 9.6.2
  factors to consider ... 9.7.3
  generally ... 9.6
  granting of permission ... 9.6.11, 9.7.3
  insurance premium tax hardship applications ... 9.6.3
  landfill tax hardship applications ... 9.6.3
  notification of decision re permission to appeal ... 9.7.4
  plastic packaging tax ... 9.6.3
  postponement of tax following appeal ... 9.6.3
  procedural errors ... 9.6.6
  refusal of permission ... 9.6.10
  review to be considered first ... 9.7.2
  second applications for permission ... 9.6.12, 9.7.3
  soft drinks industry levy ... 9.6.3
  time limits ... 9.6.8, 9.6.9
  to Upper Tribunal ... 9.3.3, 9.6.1
  Tribunal's consideration of application ... 9.7
  VAT hardship applications ... 9.6.3

Appeals to tribunal
  academic cases ... 2.4.4
  appealable decisions ... 2.1.1, 2.3, 2.3.1
  bringing a case ... 2.3
  factors to consider ... 2.4.4
  grounds of appeal ... 5.3.2
  HMRC discretion ... 2.4.2
  notice of ... 5.3.2
  out of time ... 2.1.2, 2.3.3, 2.4, 5.3.3
  reasonable excuse ... 2.4.2
  starting proceedings ... 5.3
  tribunal discretion ... 2.4.4

Appellant
  Meaning ... 3.2

Application (meaning of) – *see* **Glossary**

Argument
  constraints 8.3.1
  flexibility 8.3.2
  lines of 8.3
Balance of probabilities 8.6
Bank holidays
  generally 4.10.3
  in Scotland 10.2
Bankrupts (undischarged)
  whether able to pursue a case 2.3.6
Barristers
  role at tribunal 4.9.1
Basic case
  allocation to .... 5.6.3, App. 2
  constitution of tribunal .... App. 3
  generally 5.6.5, 5.7
  in Scotland 10.2
  meaning 3.2
  paperwork 5.7.2
  reallocation 5.7.3
Bias
  challenging for 4.2.8
  connection between judges and parties 4.2.8
Bundles – *see* **Trial bundles**
Burden of proof
  balance between fact and law 8.7.7
  discovery assessments 8.7.3
  falling on both parties 8.8.6
  generally 8.7
  information notices 8.7.5
  more than one taxpayer 8.8.7
  penalty cases 8.7.4
  revised order of submissions 8.8.5
  straightforward cases 8.7.1
  transferring to HMRC 8.7.2
Calculation of time
  generally 4.10
  in Scotland 10.2
  non-working days 4.10.3
Capital allowances
  appealable decisions (apportionments) 2.1.2
  CAA case 3.2, 5.4, 5.6.3
  late notices not allowed 5.4.2

443

Capital gains tax
  late appeals 2.4.1
Case management powers (of tribunal)
  generally 4.2
  in Scotland 10.2
  regulation of 4.2.2
Casting vote 8.10.1
Categories (allocation of cases to)
  challenging allocation 5.6.7
  four categories 5.6.3
  generally .... 5.6, App. 2
  in Scotland 10.2
  rule of thumb 5.6.3
  timing 5.6.2
Champerty 4.8.5
Citation, application and interpretation of tribunal rules 3.2
Civil Procedure Rules
  expert evidence 4.13.2
  generally 2.3.4, 4.8
  no real prospect of success 4.6.4
  wasted cost order 4.8.4
Clerical errors 9.4.1
Climate change levy
  appeals from the FTT 9.6.3
Closure notices
  generally 2.1.2, 2.3.1, 2.3.3
  starting proceedings 5.4.1
Communication with parties 4.11.3
Companies in administration
  whether able to pursue a case 2.3.6
Complex case
  allocation to 5.6.3, 5.6.7
  constitution of tribunal .... App. 3
  costs 4.8
  disclosure of documents 5.10.2
  further steps 5.10
  generally 4.8.6, 5.6.7
  in Scotland 10.2
  meaning 3.2
  reallocation as 4.8.6
  tribunal directions 5.10.2
Compliance officer
  meaning 3.2

Consent orders
  bargaining power of parties 9.1.2
  no equivalent in Scotland 10.2
  settlement reached before hearing 9.1.1
  when appropriate 9.1.3
Consolidation of cases
  factors to consider 4.2.4
  joining (distinguished) 4.2.4
  tribunal direction 4.2.4
Construction industry
  appeals re gross payment status 2.1.3
Coronavirus – *see* **Covid-19**
Corporation tax
  late appeals 2.4.1
Costs
  amount of 4.8.5, 4.8.9
  appeal notices (costs of) 4.8.2
  applying for a costs order 4.8.7
  consolidated cases 4.2.4
  costs application itself (costs of) 4.8.9
  expenses (terminology used in Scotland) 4.8.1
  failure to attend tribunal 4.8.5
  mediation refused 3.4.1, 4.8.9
  MP expenses cases 4.8
  not usually made 4.8.2
  of claiming costs 4.8.1
  opting out of costs regime 4.8.6, 5.6.7, 5.11.3
  orders for 4.8
  partial success in appeal 4.8.10
  payments on account 4.8.9
  principles for 4.8.10
  right to make representations 4.8.8
  standard and indemnity bases 4.8.9
  substituted parties 4.7.7
  Tax Chamber different from other chambers 4.8.1
  time limits 4.2.4
  timing of consideration 4.8.7
  transitional provisions (from pre 4/09) 4.8.13
  unreasonable conduct 3.4.1, 4.8.9
  Upper Tribunal (role of) 4.8.12
  wasted 4.8.3
Covid-19
  decisions without a hearing 4.3
  Default Paper cases 5.6.4

duration of temporary provisions 4.3.1
electronic hearing bundles 6.5.3
exception to rule that hearings are public 7.4.1
recording of remote hearings 7.5
Scottish rules 10.2
video or audio hearings in private 7.4.4
Criminal proceedings
interaction with... 4.2.4
Cross appeals
procedures 9.6.13
Cross examination of expert witness
failures in statement of case 4.5.3, 5.8.3
Dates for hearing
direction giving 6.5.2
Decisions
correction, set-aside and review 9.4.1, 9.9.2
finality of 9.2.4, 9.6.3
given at hearing... 8.10
meaning of – *see* **Glossary**
not unanimous... 8.10.1
notices – *see* **Notice of decisions and reasons**
options following a decision.. 9.3.2
publication of 9.2.5
review by tribunal of own decision... 9.3.4
Default Paper cases
allocation to .... 5.6.3, App. 2
constitution of tribunal.. App. 3
Covid-19 temporary measures 5.6.4
further steps... 5.9, 5.9.4
generally... 5.6.4
in Scotland 10.2
meaning.. 3.2
request for a hearing 5.9.3
statement of case (taxpayer's reply) 5.9.2
without a hearing 4.3.4
Definitions
of key terms .... *Glossary*
Delegation
in Scotland 10.2
judicial oversight... 4.1.3
Practice Direction 10 March 2009.. 4.1.2
to tribunal staff.. 4.1

Determination with or without hearing
generally 7.1
waiver by consent 7.1.3
Digital services tax
appeals from the FTT 9.6.3
Direct tax cases
internal reviews 2.3.2
responding to appealable decisions 2.3.1
Directions
applying for and giving 4.4
dates 6.5.2
evidence 6.5.1
examples 4.2.4, 6.6
freedom of tribunal to make 4.2.3
generally .... Ch. 6
hearing bundles 6.5.3
hearings 6.3
liberty to apply 6.4.1
meaning of – *see* **Glossary**
notice of 4.4.4
skeleton arguments 6.5.4
time limits 4.2.4
typical examples 6.5
variability of 6.4
Director of Border Revenue .... Ch. 1, App. 1
Disclosure of tax avoidance schemes
cases initiated by HMRC 5.4.1
Discovery assessments
burden of proof 8.7.3
Dishonesty
express statement of required 5.8.3
Discretion of tribunal
breadth of 3.3.5
exercise of 2.4.4
Dismissal of a party's case
in Scotland 10.2
Document
copies (requesting of) 4.11.4, 5.10.3
disclosure (in Scotland) 10.2
disclosure in standard or complex cases 5.10.2
held by other party 4.2.4
meaning 3.2, 4.2.4
legitimate interest 7.4.7
privileged 5.10.3

   revocation of... 4.2.4
   sending and delivery of 4.11, 4.16.4, 10.2
   use of 4.12
Dress code for hearings... 8.5.2
Enforcement of decisions
   in Scotland 10.2
Error and mistake claims
   appeals from the FTT 9.6.3
Estoppel
   abuse of process 2.5.2
Evidence and submissions
   admissibility 4.13.3
   cross examination 8.8.3
   determination of facts 4.13.1
   directions re.. 6.5.1
   examination in chief 8.8.3
   exclusion of 4.13.4
   expert 4.13.2
   generally... 4.13
   in Scotland 10.2
   late 4.8.5, 4.13.3
   on oath 4.13.5
   provision of 6.5.1
Examination in chief
   witness examination 8.8.3
Excluded decisions from appeal
   generally.. 9.6.2
Excluded decisions from review
   generally.. 9.3.7
   minor exception... 9.3.8
Expediting a hearing.. 4.2.5
Expenses orders (in Scotland)... 4.8, 10.2
Expert evidence 4.13.2
Extra statutory guidance... 2.1.4
Fact and law
   application of law to fact... 8.7.7
   error of law by tribunal 9.6.4, 9.6.5
Failure to attend tribunal
   wasted costs order... 4.8.4
Failure to comply with rules
   by a party 4.5.3
   by the tribunal 4.5.2
   generally.. 4.5

    in Scotland 10.2
    provision of information..4.5.4
Fairford decisions
    witness selection 4.14.4, 8.8.3
Fairness and justice
    admission of evidence...3.3.1
    duty on parties 3.3.4
    not the same as correctness 3.3.3
    overriding objective...3.3
Finality of decisions... 9.2.4, 9.6.3
Financial institution notices
    "without notice" applications to tribunal 5.2.2
Financial restrictions civil penalty case
    appeal categorisation..5.6.3
    counter-terrorism legislation 3.2
First-tier Tribunal (meaning of) – *see* **Glossary**
Flexibility of tribunal powers...4.2, 4.5.1, 8.3.2
Formalities during hearing... 8.5
Friends and family...8.4.4
Grounds for appeal
    new (conditions for adding)..4.2.4
Hardship applications
    generally 5.5
    matters for consideration of Tax Chamber 2.1.2
    no equivalent in Scotland 10.2
Hearing
    adjournments 8.5.6
    closing submissions 8.8.4
    disruptive individuals...7.2.3
    dress code 8.5.2
    entitlement to attend... 7.2
    layout of room 8.5.1
    meaning...3.2, *Glossary*
    notice of.. 7.3, 10.2
    opening submissions..8.8.2
    order of speaking 8.8
    practicalities.. Ch. 8
    procedures at.. Ch. 7
    procedures before .... Ch. 5
    standing and sitting 8.5.4
    submissions after 8.8.8
    waiver of by consent...7.1.3
    with party absent... 7.6

HMRC
  extended meaning 3.2
HMRC6 .... 2.1.4
Human rights
  strike-out applications 4.6.5
Ill health
  medical evidence 9.5.4
Improper conduct
  costs 4.8.4
Inappropriate behaviour
  abuse of process 2.5.3
Incapacitated taxpayers
  litigation friends 2.3.5
Income tax (late appeals) 2.4.1
Indemnity basis
  costs 3.4.1, 4.8
  principles for application of 4.8.9
Independent Parliamentary Standards Authority (IPSA)
  generally .... Ch. 1, App. 1
  meaning 3.2
Indirect taxes
  internal reviews 2.3.2
  responding to appealable decisions 2.3.1
Information notices
  burden of proof 8.7.5
Inheritance tax
  late appeals 2.4.1
In-house lawyers
  costs orders 4.8.9
Insurance premium tax
  appeals from the FTT 9.6.3
Internal review
  alternative to appeal 2.3.2
  generally 2.3, 2.3.1, 2.4.5
  risk of increased charge 2.3.2
IPSA – *see* Independent Parliamentary Standards Authority
Jeopardy amendments
  internal reviews 2.3.2
Joining of cases
  consolidation (distinguished) 4.2.4
Judges and members
  choice of 4.2.7
  form of address 8.5.3
  generally 8.4.1

Judicial comity
   following earlier FTT decisions 8.9
Judicial oversight
   delegation to tribunal staff 4.1.3
Judicial review
   beyond jurisdiction of tribunal 2.1.3, 2.1.4
   parallel proceedings 2.1.6
Jurisdiction of tribunal
   company struck off 4.6.3
   legitimate expectation 2.1.3
   striking out 4.6
Land and buildings transaction tax
   jurisdiction of Scottish tax tribunal 10.1
Landfill tax
   appeals from the FTT 9.6.3
Language
   addressing individuals 8.5.3
   addressing the tribunal 8.5.5
   referring to parties 8.5.3
Late appeals
   academic cases 2.4.4
   considerations 2.4
   HMRC discretion 2.4.2
   right to late appeal 2.4.1
   tribunal discretion 2.4.4
Lead cases
   adjournments 4.2.4
   appeal to Upper Tribunal 4.16.3, 4.16.4
   common or related issues 4.16.3
   consequences 4.16.2
   consolidation (distinguished) 4.16.1
   decision in 4.16.4
   effect on related cases 4.16.4
   generally 4.16
   no equivalent in Scotland 10.2
   withdrawal or disposal of 4.16.5
Legal representatives
   rules governing 4.9
   signing permissions to appeal 9.6.7
Legitimate expectations
   jurisdiction of tribunal 2.1.4
Legitimate interest
   key documents 7.4.7
Liberty to apply directions 6.4.1

Litigation and settlement strategy
  alternative dispute resolution 2.2.2
Litigation friends
  incapacitated taxpayers 2.3.5
Mediation
  in Scotland 10.2
Minors (attendance at hearing) 2.3.5, 7.2.3
MP expenses cases
  generally .... Ch. 1
  meaning 3.2
National Insurance .... Ch. 1, 2.1.1
Negligent conduct
  costs 4.8.4
Non-legal representatives
  communication with (by tribunal) 4.9.3
Notice of appeal
  changes in 2012 .... 4.9.3, 5.3.2, 5.4.1
  late 5.3.3, 5.4.2
  requirement and contents 5.3.2
Notice of decisions and reasons
  minimum requirements 9.2.2
  notices issues after hearing 8.10.2
  request for full findings of fact and reasons 9.2.3
  written notice required 9.2.1
Notice of hearings
  generally 7.3
  inconvenient dates 7.3.3
  minimum notice 7.3.2
Orders and summons
  contents of 4.14.5
  for information 4.14.3
  to answer questions or produce documents 4.14
  variation or set aside 4.14.7
Overriding objective of tribunal rules
  deviation from other rules 8.2.1
  generally 3.3
  in Scotland 10.2
  late appeals 2.4.5, 3.3.2
  limitation of scope 3.3.2
  list of ways of achieving: not exhaustive 3.3.1
Parallel proceedings
  with judicial review 2.1.4, 2.1.6
Parties (to proceedings)
  addition of 4.7.3, 4.7.7

application to tribunal to be added 4.7.4, 4.7.5
meaning .... 3.2, *Glossary*
substitution of 4.7.2, 4.7.6, 4.7.7
PAYE codes
appealable decision 2.1.1
Penalty cases
allocation to default paper case category .... App. 2
burden of proof on HMRC 8.7.4
flexibility of tribunal 8.3.2
People in attendance
clerk 8.4.2
friends and family 8.4.4
HMRC representatives 8.4.3
judges and members 8.4.1
public 8.4.5
Plastic packaging tax
appeals from the FTT 9.6.3
Postponement of tax following an appeal
appeals from the FTT 9.6.3
Practice directions
delegation to staff 4.1.2, 7.4.6
meaning 3.2.1
privacy hearings 7.4.6
Practice statements
generally 3.2.1
Precedents
relevance for tribunals 8.9
Preliminary matters
separate hearings 4.2.8
Premises inspection
"without notice" applications to tribunal 5.2.2
Privacy
anonymisation of decision notice 7.4.5
generally 4.12.1
information orders 4.14.3
Practice Direction 7.4.6
public access in practice 7.4.2, 8.4.5
public or private hearings 7.4
Procedures
after the hearing 9.1
at the hearing .... Ch. 7
before the hearing .... Ch. 5
irregularities 9.5.3

Proceedings
  formality of 3.3.4
  in Scotland 10.2
  starting of 5.3
  withdrawal of 4.15
  without notice to Respondent 5.2.1
Promoters of tax avoidance schemes (POTAS)
  tribunal approval 5.2.2
  unappealable 9.6.3
  without notice applications 5.2.2
Proof (burden of) – see **Burden of Proof**
Proof (standard of) – see **Standard of Proof**
Proportionality
  arguments re 2.1.5
Public and private hearings – see **Privacy**
Public law
  jurisdiction of FTT 2.1.4
Reasonable excuse
  internal review 2.4.5
  meaning 2.4.2
Recording of hearings
  access to recordings 7.5.4
  contempt of court 8.5.7
  Covid-19 temporary rules 7.5
Regulation of procedures 8.2
Reinstatement applications 4.6.7, 4.15.5
Remitted hearings
  abuse of process 2.5.4
Representatives
  appointment of 4.9.2
  in Scotland 10.2
  incompetent 9.5.3
  legal and other 4.9
  notification of 4.9.3
Res judicata
  abuse of process 2.5.2
Residence 2.1.4
Respondent
  meaning 3.2
  statement of case 5.8
Responding to appealable decisions
  timing 2.3.1

Review of tribunal decision
- action on completion 9.8.3
- appeal cases 9.7.2
- consequences 9.3.6
- considerations during review 9.8.4
- excluded decisions 9.3.7
- general principle 9.3.4
- in Scotland 10.2
- instigation by parties 9.3.5
- procedures 9.8
- review of review 9.3.8, 9.3.9

Rules – *see* **Tribunal Procedure Rules**

Scotland
- alternative dispute resolution 2.2.1
- bank holidays 4.10.3
- expert evidence (re Scots law) 4.13.2
- judicial review 2.1.4, 9.3.8
- layout of tribunal room 8.5.1
- legitimate expectation 2.1.4
- opening submissions (omission of) 8.8.1, 8.8.2
- orders for expenses 4.8
- procedural differences 8.1
- Scottish tax tribunal .... Ch. 10
- sisting .... 4.2.4, *Glossary*
- terminology (costs v expenses) 4.8.1
- Upper Tribunal powers 4.5.4
- witness citation 4.14.2

Scottish tax tribunal
- Covid-19 .... 10.2
- generally .... Ch. 10
- jurisdiction 10.1
- rules 10.2

Senior President of Tribunals 3.2.1
Sequential evidence 6.5.1
Serious Organised Crime Agency
- appeals to Tax Chamber .... 1, App. 1

Setting aside a decision
- conditions 9.5.3
- effect 9.5.2
- interests of justice 9.5.4
- no direct equivalent in Scotland 10.2
- time limits 9.5.5

Sisting – *see* **Stayed cases**
Site visits
  tribunal discretion 4.2.4
Skeleton arguments
  generally 6.5.4
  specimen .... App. 6
Slip rule
  generally 9.4.1
  interaction with appeal or review 9.9.2
Social Entitlement Chamber
  appeals to .... App. 1
Social Security
  appealable decisions 2.1.3
Soft drinks industry levy
  appeals from the FTT 9.6.3
Specimen statements
  skeleton argument .... App. 6
  statement of agreed facts and issues .... App. 4
  witness statement .... App. 5
Stamp duties
  late appeals 2.4.1
Standard case
  allocation to 5.6.3, 5.6.6
  constitution of tribunal .... App. 3
  disclosure of documents 5.10.2
  further steps 5.10
  meaning 3.2
  tribunal directions 5.10.2
Standard of proof
  balance of probabilities 8.6.1
Starting appeal proceedings 5.3
Statement of agreed facts and issues
  specimen .... App. 4
Statements of case
  Complex cases 5.8.2
  content 5.8.3
  cross-examination of witnesses 5.8.3
  Default Paper cases 5.8.2, 5.9
  delay requests 2.4.4, 5.8.3
  generally 5.8.1
  HMRC failure to address issue in 4.5.3, 5.8.3
  MP expenses cases 5.8.2
  request by HMRC for a case 5.8.3
  request for a hearing 5.9.3

Standard cases...5.8.2
taxpayer's reply...5.9.2
timing 5.8.2
Statutory maternity pay...2.1.3
Statutory sick pay... 1, 2.1.3
Stayed cases... 4.2.4, 4.16.4
Striking out
   determination without hearing...7.1.5
   discretionary..4.6.4
   effect on appellants and respondents...4.6.8
   generally.. 4.6
   mandatory...4.6.3
   meaning and effect... 4.6.1, 4.6.5
   no reasonable prospect of success..4.6.4
   requirement to allow representations..4.6.6
   unless orders..4.6.2
Submissions
   after the hearing..8.8.8
   closing...8.8.4
   evidence and..4.13
   opening..8.8.2
Substitution and addition of parties
   generally... 4.7
   in Scotland..10.2
Supporters
   in Scotland..10.2
Tax advisers
   costs orders..4.8.9
Tax Chamber
   meaning (and of Tax and Chancery Chamber) – *see*
      Glossary
   scope of decisions allocated to the Chamber............................. App. 1
Tax credits
   appealable decisions 2.1.3
Taxpayer notices
   "without notice" applications to tribunal......................................5.2.2
Telephone hearing
   whether permissible..4.2.4
Third parties
   access to key documents...7.4.7
   appeals from the FTT (information notices) 9.6.3
   "without notice" applications to tribunal......................................5.2.2
Threats
   physical..4.12.1

Time limits
  flexibility of 4.2.4
  in Scotland 10.2
  need to adhere to.. 2.4.4
  tribunal discretion 4.2.4, 9.2.3
Transfer of complex cases to Upper Tribunal
  costs... 5.11.3
  criteria.. 5.11.4
  generally... 5.11
  procedure 5.11.2
  selection of cases 5.11.3
Transitional rules .... App. 8
Trial bundles
  meaning, and typical content... 6.5.3
Tribunal
  clerk... 8.4.2
  constitution of, generally.. App. 3
  expertise of members 3.3.3
  judges and members... 8.4.1
  meaning.. 3.2, *Glossary*
  method of bringing a case 2.3
  over-reliance on.. 8.2.2
Tribunal Procedure Rules
  allocation to categories.. 5.6
  alternative dispute resolution and arbitration 3.4
  applying for and giving directions... 4.4
  basic cases 5.7
  calculation of time... 4.10
  case management powers 4.2
  citation, application and interpretation 3.2
  clerical errors etc.. 9.4
  consent orders.. 9.1
  consideration of application to appeal 9.7
  consolidation... 4.2.4
  cost 4.8
  default paper cases (further steps) 5.9
  delegation to staff... 4.1
  determination with or without a hearing.. 7.1
  entitlement to attend hearing.. 7.2
  evidence and submissions... 4.13
  failure to comply 4.5, 4.8.11
  flexibility of 4.8.11
  generally.. 3.1.1
  hearings with party absent 7.6

458

interpretation ... 9.3
lead cases ... 4.16
notice of decisions and reasons ... 9.2
notice of hearings ... 7.3
orders of costs ... 4.8
overriding objective ... 3.3
partial compliance with ... 4.8.11
Parts ... 3.1.2
power to treat application as if it were a different
    application ... 9.9
public and private hearings ... 7.4
representatives ... 4.9
respondent's statement of case ... 5.8
review of decision ... 9.8
Scotland ... 10.2
sending and delivery of documents ... 4.11, 4.16.4
setting aside a decision ... 9.5
specific rules – *see separate index*
standard or complex cases (further steps) ... 5.10
starting appeal proceedings ... 5.3, 5.4
striking out ... 4.6
substitution and addition ... 4.7
summoning or citation of witnesses ... 4.14
transfer of complex cases to Upper Tribunal ... 5.11
withdrawal of proceedings ... 4.15

Tribunals Service (meaning of) – *see* **Glossary**

Unbinding
  from lead cases ... 4.16.4

Unless orders
  breaches of ... 4.3.4, 4.6.6
  challenging ... 4.6.2
  generally ... 4.6.2

Unreasonable conduct
  costs ... 3.4.1, 4.8.4
  examples and guidance ... 4.8.5

Upper Tribunal
  appeals to ... 9.3.3
  criteria for referral ... 5.11.4
  meaning of – *see* **Glossary**
  permission ... 9.6.7
  powers ... 4.5.4
  review decisions ... 9.3.8
  role ... 4.2.3, 4.8.12
  transfer of complex cases to ... 5.11

VAT
appealable decisions 2.1.1, 9.6.3
default surcharge cases 2.4.4
effect of rule 5.5.3
generally 2.1.4, 2.3.1
hardship applications 5.5.1, 9.6.3
stay of proceedings 5.5.4
Wales
tribunal knowledge re Welsh law 4.13.2
Wasted costs
generally 4.8.3
in Scotland 10.2
orders 4.8.4
Websites
list of useful sites .... App. 7
Welsh Revenue Authority
appeals to the Tax Chamber .... App. 1
Withdrawal of proceedings
application for reinstatement 4.15.5
generally 4.15
giving notice 4.15.4
immediate effect 4.15.1
in Scotland 10.2
not necessarily conclusive 4.15.1
reinstatement not possible 4.15.6
timing 4.15.2
Without notice applications 7.2.2
Witness statement
adverse inference if author not called as witness 4.13.3
generally 6.5.1
specimen statement .... App. 5
withdrawal of 4.13.1
Witnesses
compulsion of 4.14.6
cross-examination of 4.5.3, 4.6.4, 4.13.3, 8.5.3, 8.8.3
exclusion from tribunal room 8.8.3
HMRC representative acting as 8.5.3
in Scotland 10.2
non-resident in UK 4.14.2
payment of expenses 4.14.2
summoning or citation of 4.14.2
tribunal practice statement 4.14.8
witness statements 6.5.1